KÖNIGTUM, STAAT UND GESELLSCHAFT FRÜHER HOCHKULTUREN

Herausgegeben von
Detlev Kreikenbom

4,6

Beiträge zur altägyptischen Königsideologie

Herausgegeben von Horst Beinlich,
Julia Budka und Andreas H. Pries

2019
Harrassowitz Verlag · Wiesbaden

9. Symposion zur ägyptischen Königsideologie / 9th Symposium on Egyptian Royal Ideology

Egyptian royal ideology and kingship under periods of foreign rulers

Case studies from the first millennium BC

Munich, May 31 – June 2, 2018

Edited by Julia Budka

2019

Harrassowitz Verlag · Wiesbaden

Bibliografische Information der Deutschen Nationalbibliothek
Die Deutsche Nationalbibliothek verzeichnet diese Publikation in der Deutschen Nationalbibliografie; detaillierte bibliografische Daten sind im Internet über http://dnb.dnb.de abrufbar.

Bibliographic information published by the Deutsche Nationalbibliothek
The Deutsche Nationalbibliothek lists this publication in the Deutsche Nationalbibliografie; detailed bibliographic data are available on the internet at http://dnb.dnb.de.

For further information about our publishing program consult our website http://www.harrassowitz-verlag.de

Printed on permanent/durable paper.
Printing and binding: Esser printSolutions GmbH, Bretten
Printed in Germany

ISSN 1613-6950
ISBN 978-3-447-11328-1

Preface

The conference series dedicated to "Egyptian Royal Ideology (Symposium zur ägyptischen Königsideologie)" focused at its ninth instalment on "Egyptian royal ideology and kingship under periods of foreign rulers – case studies from the first millennium BC ". The symposium was held from 31 May to 2 June 2018 at Ludwig-Maximilians-University Munich at the Institute of Egyptology and Coptic Studies. Bringing together case studies focusing on distinct features of kingship of foreigners ruling Egypt during the first millennium BC, the organisers aimed to tackle the subject from a fresh perspective, high lightening common features and stressing specific differences. Of the fifteen lectures given at Munich, thirteen are included in this volume. This selection offers a range of various approaches to the topic, emphasising current perspectives and new foci within Egyptology, including aspects from Nubian studies of the first millennium BC as well as results from fresh fieldwork.

As organiser of the symposium, I would like to express my gratitude to my home institution, the Institute of Egyptology and Coptic Studies of LMU for providing the venue for the meeting. Special thanks are due to the organising team, first of all to my colleague Veronica Hinterhuber, but also to the graduate student Mona Dietrich and the undergraduates Sara Gebhardt, Katharina Rymer and Philipp Seyr who all helped at the event.

The realisation of the present volume is much indebted not only to the efforts of the individual contributors for which we are very thankful, but especially to the meticulous work of Veronica Hinterhuber who is also responsible for the layout.

The meeting in Munich kindly received funding from the Adele Hartman Fond of LMU. For general support I am grateful to my co-organisers of the conference series, Horst Beinlich and Andreas Pries. In the name of the three of us, it is with pleasure that we can announce the upcoming "10. Symposium zur ägyptischen Königsideologie". It will be kindly hosted by Ewa Laskowska-Kusztal and colleagues and will take place in Warsaw in 2021, with a special focus on questions about the royal ideology of Hatshepsut and the Eighteenth Dynasty.

Julia Budka — Munich, August 2019

Contents

Introduction

Julia Budka

Egyptian royal ideology and kingship under periods of foreign rulers

The theme of the 9th Symposium on Egyptian Royal Ideology and Kingship held from 31 May to 2 June 2018 at Ludwig-Maximilians-University Munich at the Institute of Egyptology and Coptic Studies was "Egyptian royal ideology and kingship under periods of foreign rulers – case studies from the first millennium BC".

The first millennium BC is a period of intense international networks throughout the ancient world, especially within the Mediterranean, and it is the era when Egypt was repeatedly under the influence of foreigners.[1]

Much has already been written about specific aspects of royal ideology and authority in Egypt under the rule of the Libyans, the Kushites, the Persians, the Ptolemies and the Romans.[2] The Saites, clearly kings of Libyan descents, but appearing as 100% Egyptian

1 See G. Vittmann, Ägypten und die Fremden im ersten vorchristlichen Jahrtausend, Kulturgeschichte der antiken Welt 97, Mainz am Rhein 2003; C. Jurman, ‚Wenn das Fremde zum Eigenen wird'. Identitätsbilder und Repräsentationsstrategien im multiethnischen Milieu Ägyptens während der Dritten Zwischenzeit, in: A. Pülz/E. Trinkl (eds.), Das Eigene und das Fremde: Akten der 4. Tagung des Zentrums Archäologie und Altertumswissenschaften an der Österreichischen Akademie der Wissenschaften, 26.–27. März 2012, Origines 4, Wien 2015, 33–49; G. Vittmann, Zwischen Integration und Ausgrenzung: zur Akkulturation von Ausländern im spätzeitlichen Ägypten, in: R. Rollinger/B. Truschnegg (eds.), Altertum und Mittelmeerraum: Die antike Welt diesseits und jenseits der Levante. Festschrift für Peter W. Haider zum 60. Geburtstag, Oriens et Occidens 12, Stuttgart 2006, 561–595. For more general archaeological records of foreigners see T. Schneider, Foreigners in Egypt: Archaeological Evidence and Cultural Context, in: W. Wendrich (ed.), Egyptian Archaeology, Blackwell Studies in Global Archaeology, Chichester 2010, 143–163; cf. also M. Bietak, Nahostpolitik: Fremdherrschaft und Expansion, in: S. Petschel/M. von Falck (eds.), Pharao siegt immer: Krieg und Frieden im alten Ägypten. Gustav-Lübcke-Museum Hamm, 21. März – 31. Oktober 2004, Bönen 2004, 140–144. For aspects of methodology and Egyptology-specific challenges see T. Schneider, Foreign Egypt: Egyptology and the Concept of Cultural Appropriation, in: ÄgLev 13, 2003, 155–161.

2 See, *e.g.*, J. Willeitner, Taharqa: Ägypten unter nubischer und assyrischer Fremdherrschaft, in: K. Dornisch (ed.), Sudan: Festschrift für Steffen Wenig zum 65. Geburtstag, Nürnberger Blätter zur Archäologie, Sonderheft, Nürnberg 1999, 89–112; K. Jansen-Winkeln, Die Fremdherrschaften in Ägypten im 1. Jahrtausend v. Chr., in: Or 69, 2000, 1–20; C. J. Chimko, Foreign pharaos: self-legitimization and indigenous reaction in art and literature, in: JSSEA 30, 2003, 15–58; S. Pfeiffer (ed.), Ägypten unter fremden Herrschern: zwischen persischer Satrapie und römischer Provinz, Oikumene: Studien zur antiken Weltgeschichte 3, Frankfurt am Main 2007; H. Sternberg-el Hotabi, Ägypter und Perser. Eine Begegnung zwischen Anpassung und Widerstand. Photographs by Enno Fedderken and Hendrik Fedderken, Archäologie, Inschriften und Denkmäler Altägyptens 4, Rahden, Westfalen, 2016.

rulers, are usually not regarded by scholars as the prime candidates when it comes to foreign kings and are often omitted from such lists.[3]

Bringing together case studies focusing on distinct features of kingship of foreigners ruling Egypt during the first millennium BC, we aimed to tackle the subject within this volume from a fresh perspective, high lightening common features and stressing specific differences. Aspects which were discussed during the meeting and are included in its written output – as new food for thought and not as definite arguments – are among others:

- Patterns of succession
- Divine aspects of kingship and associated building activities
- Royal costume and names
- Function, titles and organisation of the administrative elite

In the last years, much research has focused on the complexity of sources for royal ideology and kingship. Especially within the framework of the study of foreign influences and rulers, questions of acculturation, adaption or cultural entanglement connected with periods of foreign rulers have been addressed recently.[4] The corresponding terminology has been debated and various models to describe these processes were proposed. A very convincing scheme was introduced, for example, by Claus Jurman for the so-called Egyptianisation of the Libyans.[5] This scheme can also be used to describe some aspects of the Kushite 'foreignness'.[6]

There has been a general shift in perspectives, a new awareness of biases in our sources during the last years. Royal and elite references are mostly provided by pictorial and textual sources and are thus influenced by a historical narrative; archaeology offers more direct traces of activities and of believe systems across social strata.[7] In line with this, there are diverse sets of memories from the periods of foreign rule in Egypt, all manipulated to a certain degree

3 See Jansen-Winkeln, Or 69, 2000, 1–20. Cf. also A. Spalinger, The Concept of Monarchy during the Saite Epoch – an Essay of Synthesis, in: Or 47, 1978, 12–36; J. F. Quack, Papyrus CtYBR 2885 rt. Reste einer demotischen Königsliste auf Papyrus, in: Journal of Egyptian History 2, 2009, 107–113.

4 See P. Briant, Inscriptions multilingues d'époque achéménide: le texte et l'image, in: D. Valbelle/ J. Leclant (eds.), Le décret de Memphis. Colloque de la Fondation Singer-Polignac à l'occasion de la célébration du bicentenaire de la découverte de la Pierre de Rosette: Paris, 1er juin 1999, Paris 1999, 91–115. Cf. also S. A. Stephens, Seeing double. Intercultural Poetics in Ptolemaic Alexandria, Hellenistic Culture and Society 37, Berkeley 2003, 181–182. For general aspects of entanglement, one of the buzz words of the last decade within Nubian archaeology, see S. T. Smith, Colonial entanglements. Immigration, acculturation and hybridity in New Kingdom Nubia (Tombos), in: M. Honegger (ed.), Nubian Archaeology in the XXIst Century. Proceedings of the Thirteenth International Conference for Nubian Studies, Neuchâtel, 1st–6th September 2014, OLA 273, Leuven 2018, 71–89. The Hyksos can be named as another case study of mixing in Egypt, see B. Bader, Cultural Mixing in Egyptian Archaeology: The 'Hyksos' as a Case Study, in: Archaeological Review from Cambridge 28.1: Archaeology and Cultural Mixture, 2013, 257–286.

5 Jurman, ‚Wenn das Fremde zum Eigenen wird', 33–49.

6 Cf. J. Budka, Individuen, indigene Gruppe oder integrierter Teil der ägyptischen Gesellschaft? Zur soziologischen Aussagekraft materieller Hinterlassenschaften von Kuschiten im spätzeitlichen Ägypten, in: G. Neunert/K. Gabler/A. Verbovsek, Sozialisationen: Individuum – Gruppe – Gesellschaft, Beiträge des ersten Münchner Arbeitskreises Junge Aegyptologie (MAJA 1), 3. bis 5.12.2010, GOF IV/51, Wiesbaden 2012, 45–60, here: 54–55.

7 See, *e.g.*, W. Wendrich, Egyptian Archaeology: From Text to Context, in: W. Wendrich (ed.), Egyptian Archaeology, Blackwell Studies in Global Archaeology, Chichester, 1–14, especially 12.

by Egyptian ideology. A very illustrative case study can here be given with the example of early Ptolemaic ideology and references to Achaemenid rule. Here, in some texts royal piety is described in direct opposition to foreign impiety.[8] A diverse picture emerges, however, by means of archaeology and material evidence. I would like to follow Henry COLBURN in what he stressed for the Achaemenid Period as a general aspect of foreign dominion: "rule of Egypt was experienced differently by different people, and that modern historical narratives obscure that diversity."[9] We should try to address with all possible means this ancient diversity which is often concealed by the monumental discourse of texts and reliefs. Material remains may provide additional answers, but are very often insufficient for other questions. Keeping this in mind, one also needs to stress that it is sometimes impossible for us to differentiate between the simple display of kingship and proper evidence of royal ideology meaning records of a belief system/mind-set. These *caveats* are also to be considered for several assessments throughout this volume.

Foreign kingship display

The display of kingship by foreign rulers is discussed in several chapters. Egyptian iconography and textual symbolism was used in different ways (for Kushite examples see Shih-Wei HSU in this volume). The question of the 'otherness' or 'Egyptiansiation' of the Libyans – an ongoing debate within Egyptology – was most recently re-addressed by Karl JANSEN-WINKELN, who also pointed out methodological issues in trying to reconstruct patterns of Libyan kingship and especially of "Königsideologie".[10]

Kushite building activities are well attested in Egypt and help to address questions of religion and power, as is highlighted in this publication by the papers of Angelika LOHWASSER and Essam NAGY. Anthony SPALINGER presents new material of war scenes of Pianchy at the Great Amun Temple at Gebel Barkal, trying to reconstruct the archaeological setting of these early Kushite scenes.

The Persians as Egyptian kings are discussed in this volume on the basis of the famous Susa-statue of Darius I (see the contribution by Anke BLÖBAUM).[11] Darius I may also be mentioned as a follow-up on remarks about a temple relief from the time of Amasis (Twenty-sixth Dynasty) at Amheida in Dakhla Oasis discussed by Olaf KAPER in this volume. The relief depicts the god Seth spearing the serpent Apopis and a similar depiction in the temple of Hibis can be named for Darius I as foreign living Horus in exactly the same pose. In both cases, the king is accompanied by a lion – whether this can be viewed as a 'Persian element' in an otherwise 'Egyptian' scene is debated and leaves space for interpretation, especially

8 H. P. COLBURN, Memories of the Second Persian Period in Egypt, in: J. M. SILVERMAN/C. WAERZEGGERS (eds.), Political Memory in and after the Persian Empire, Ancient Near East Monographs 13, Atlanta 2015, 165–202, here: 168.

9 COLBURN, Memories of the Second Persian Period in Egypt, 195. Cf. also BUDKA, Individuen, indigene Gruppe oder integrierter Teil der ägyptischen Gesellschaft?, 45–60.

10 K. JANSEN-WINKELN, „Libyerzeit" oder „postimperiale Periode"? Zur historischen Einordnung der Dritten Zwischenzeit, in: C. JURMAN/B. BADER/D. A. ASTON (eds.), A True Scribe of Abydos. Essays on First Millennium Egypt in Honour of Anthony Leahy, OLA 265, Leuven/Paris/Bristol, CT, 2017, 203–238, here: 208–209.

11 For Persian kingship display in Egypt see M. WASMUTH, Ägypto-persische Herrscher- und Herrschaftspräsentation in der Achämenidenzeit, Oriens et Occidens 27, Stuttgart 2017.

because of its use by Amasis.[12] The scene in the temple of Hibis can, however, be associated with a particular approach to Egyptian kingship and was described by Melanie WASMUTH as follows: "The specific translation of Egyptian kingship and the double role of the ruler as pharaoh and Great King into visual display is dependent on its regional setting in the western oases with its local variant of Seth with falcon head. As with the statue of Darius and especially its base, this display allows a number of interpretations – probably deliberately: apart from the reading as 'living foreign Horus', the scene can be understood on a solely divine level – as an icon for general Egyptian kingship by the slaying of Apophis by Horus/Seth or as an elaborate depiction of Seth of the Oases. Additionally, the merging of Horus and Seth into one may have evoked the integration of the roles as Egyptian pharaoh and his Asiatic royal foe into one ruler."[13] The divine level of kingship, this time in relation to the god Osiris, is also addressed in this book in the paper about ancestor veneration (see the contribution by Julia BUDKA).

Another case study for iconography in relation to foreign kingship is Udjahorresnet with his famous statue Museo Gregoriano Egizio 22690 showing elements of the 'Persian' costume (see Alexander SCHÜTZE in this volume).[14]

Indigenous aspects of foreign rulers: Kushite case studies

The Munich conference developed a certain focus on the Twenty-fifth Dynasty and aspects of Kushite kingship which is also reflected in this volume. This is with full intention, because remains of the Kushite rulers in both Egypt and Sudan have much potential for the above mentioned aspects of royal ideology (see the contributions by HSU, SPALINGER, NAGY and LOHWASSER). It is well known that indigenous aspects of foreign rulers as Egyptian kings are especially evident for the Kushites.[15] Regarding Kushite chronology and the succession of the rulers, we follow throughout this volume the new sequence recently established by JURMAN and others.[16]

---

12 Pro Persian element see M. WASMUTH, Political Memory in the Achaemenid Empire: The Integration of Egyptian Kingship into Persian Royal Display, in: J. M. SILVERMAN/C. WAERZEGGERS (eds.), Political Memory in and after the Persian Empire, Ancient Near East Monographs 13, Atlanta 2015, 203–237, here: 214–215, fig. 3; contra see KAPER, in this volume.

13 WASMUTH, Political Memory in the Achaemenid Empire, 215.

14 Cf. also K. SMOLÁRIKOVÁ, Udjahorresnet: the founder of the Saite-Persian cemetery at Abusir and his engagement as leading political person during the troubled years at the beginning of the Twenty-Seventh Dynasty, in: J. M. SILVERMAN/C. WAERZEGGERS (eds.), Political Memory in and after the Persian Empire, Ancient Near East Monographs 13, Atlanta 2015, 151–164; M. WASMUTH, Persika in der Repräsentation der ägyptischen Elite, in: JEA 103, 2018, 241–250.

15 See, *e.g.*, A. LOHWASSER, Fremde Heimat: Selektive Akkulturation in Kusch, in: E. CZERNY/I. HEIN/H. HUNGER/D. MELMAN/A. SCHWAB (eds.), Timelines. Studies in Honour of Manfred Bietak, OLA 149.3, Leuven 2006, 133–138.

16 C. JURMAN, The Order of the Kushite Kings According to Sources from the Eastern Desert and Thebes. Or: *Shabataka was here first!*, in: Journal of Egyptian History 10(2), 2017, 124–151; see also K. JANSEN-WINKELN, Beiträge zur Geschichte der Dritten Zwischenzeit, in: Journal of Egyptian History 10(1), 2017, 23–42, here: 40. Cf. also E. PISCHIKOVA/J. BUDKA/K. GRIFFIN, Introduction, in: E. PISCHIKOVA/J. BUDKA/K. GRIFFIN (eds.), Thebes in the First Millennium BC: Art and Archaeology of the Kushite Period and Beyond, GHP Egyptology 27, London 2018, 1–6, here: 1–2 with more references.

Texts and titles: Saite rulers and their officials

Texts, titles and other prosopographical data are of interest for reconstructing administrative patterns in first millennium BC Egypt. Therefore a large number of statues, both royal and non-royal, are discussed in this volume. Three contributions are focusing on aspects during the Saite dynasty (see Carola Koch and Alexander Schütze in this volume). Of particular interest was whether "the agency of high officials in the reinterpretation of Egyptian royal ideology under foreign rule" (Schütze in this volume) was traceable. Koch had a close look at vizier's position after the New Kingdom and whether the executive powers of this office changed in times of alternating powers and fluctuating territories.

Double images: Ptolemies and Romans

The latest phase of the first millennium BC, the periods of Ptolemaic and Roman rule in Egypt, is a very special case when it comes to royal ideology. Important aspects are addressed in this volume by Martina Minas-Nerpel, Ewa Laskowska-Kusztal and Filip Coppens. Minas-Nerpel focused on the specific power and role of Ptolemaic queens and discussed whether and to what extent these queens and their cults are connected with the heyday and expansion of the Isis cult beyond the borders of Hellenistic Egypt. Laskowska-Kusztal presented with case studies from the First Cataract region and Deir el-Bahari new ideas about Ptolemaic compilations of religious images holding the prime function to provide protection for the 'foreign' ruler by establishing references to deified mortals. A study of the *sn-tꜣ* ("Kissing the Earth") ritual, executed by the foreign ruler before the deities of Egypt during the Ptolemaic and Roman eras is presented by Coppens. Possible reasons for the discontinuity of the occurrence of this ritual are discussed and contextualised.

Outlook

This book examines Egyptian royal ideology and kingship under periods of foreign rulers with a selection of case studies from the first millennium BC.[17] A variety of sources was presented with a focus on indigenous aspects, but also on cultural mixing and the adaptation of various subjects and religious ideas into the Egyptian system. The main aim was to trace evidence for Egyptian kingship during the rule of foreigners, be it authentic Egyptian or a modified version of royal ideology. Some of the topics which appeared as dominant while preparing this volume, and seem to be worth to follow in future studies, are:

- Creation of new religious concepts/images relating the king/queen to deities
- Osiris and temples and their relation to the ruler
- Tombs and temples and their significance to royal ideology
- Officials and their relation to the court/king

Fresh studies like the papers presenting material from new excavations in Abydos, Karnak, Gebel Barkal and other sites underline a novel awareness within the field to conduct a more concise contextualisation for material relating to foreign rulership. The research collected

17 Other case studies from Egypt could be named in particular from the second millennium BC and here especially the Hyksos, see, *e.g.*, M. Bietak, The enigma of the Hyksos, in: BiOr 75 (3/4), 2018, 227–247; T. Schneider, Hyksos Research in Egyptology and Egypt's Public Imagination: A Brief Assessment of Fifty Years of Assessments, in: Journal of Egyptian History 11(1–2), 2018, 73–86 with further literature.

in this volume brings together diverse approaches to aspects of the Kushite, Saite, Persian, Ptolemaic and Roman kingship.

The future aim should be to put these data into a wider context and to try to enlarge the material evidence for certain interpretations and assessments proposed in this book. First millennium BC scholarship in Egypt and Sudan has already advanced during the last decade to a new level,[18] but needs to be further strengthened in the future. It is my hope that this volume can provide some thought-provoking contributions and will inspire new studies on the ideology, religion and kingship of ancient Egypt during periods of considerable political changes but with strong ideological constants in the royal display.

18 See, *e.g.*, E. Pischikova/J. Budka/K. Griffin (eds.), Thebes in the First Millennium BC, Newcastle upon Tyne 2014, *passim*; E. Pischikova/J. Budka/K. Griffin (eds.), Thebes in the First Millennium BC: Art and Archaeology of the Kushite Period and Beyond, GHP Egyptology 27, London 2018.

The question of ancestor cult in the first millennium BC.

Some thoughts based on archaeological findings

Julia Budka

Abstract

During the first millennium BC, foreign rulers (Libyans, Kushites, Saites and Persians) had a considerable impact on Egyptian royal ideology. The paper will address the question whether besides general developments related to changes in Egyptian kingship and religion during the Late Period, foreign kingship can also be linked to an increase of genealogies and various attestations of ancestor cult. Case studies, in particular from Abydos/Umm el-Qaab, will be discussed and the role of the god Osiris in connection with the worship of earlier kings highlighted.

1 Introduction

Within the general theme of the conference, "Egyptian royal ideology and kingship under periods of foreign rulers", it seems of particular interest to highlight aspects of ancestor cult. Are there common features or specific differences how the Libyans, the Kushites, the Saites and Persians addressed their ancestors as Egyptian kings? Can specific patterns of legitimisation for foreign rulers in connection with predecessors be traced, as was already proposed by Anke Blöbaum?[1]

This paper will present some case studies, with a focus on material from Abydos/Umm el-Qaab, and aims to illustrate the role and function of the god Osiris for ancestor cult in the first millennium BC. Whether the worship of previous generations and earlier kings took on specific features during periods of foreign rulers will be discussed based on archaeological, pictorial and textual evidence. For pure reasons of practicability, Alexander the Great and the Ptolemies are not included here. These later examples could, without doubt, also add up interesting thoughts as "last outcome of royal ancestor cult"[2] in Egypt.[3]

---

1 See A. I. Blöbaum, „Denn ich bin ein König, der die Maat liebt". Herrscherlegitimation im spätzeitlichen Ägypten. Eine vergleichende Untersuchung der Phraseologie in den offiziellen Königsinschriften vom Beginn der 25. Dynastie bis zum Ende der makedonischen Herrschaft, AegMon 4, Aachen 2006, *passim* and 280: "Auffallend ist ebenfalls, daß insbesondere Fremdherrscher sich durch Anknüpfung an einen Amtsvorgänger legitimieren."

2 M. Fitzenreiter, Allerhand Kleinigkeiten, IBAES 20, Berlin/London 2018, 53–75, here: 66.

3 See, *e.g.*, M. Minas, Die hieroglyphischen Ahnenreihen der ptolemäischen Könige: ein Vergleich mit den Titeln der eponymen Priester in den demotischen und griechischen Papyri, AegTrev 9, Mainz am Rhein 2000; F. Herklotz, Der Ahnenkult bei den Ptolemäern, in: M. Fitzenreiter (ed.), Genealogie –

2 Preliminaries about ancestor cult in ancient Egypt

Within Egyptology, there is a still ongoing debate about the existence and role of ancestor cult.[4] Several findings from ancient Egypt suggest, however, that in particular non-royal ancestor cult is well established since earliest times, especially by means of funerary cult and offerings to the dead.[5] Martin FITZENREITER, Nicola HARRINGTON and others have stressed and illustrated the importance of ancestors for the living and established the concept of ancestor cult as part of the funerary beliefs.[6] Ancestor worship and ancestor cult can be regarded as religious practice within Egyptian religion[7] and there are different manifestations traceable throughout time.[8] In the words of Juan Carlos MORENO GARCÍA: "Ancestor worship thus appears as an active, multifaceted social activity, operating at different levels (individual, domestic/family, community, palace), whose distinctive idiosyncrasies depended on the context in which it operated. Tensions but also mutual influences permeated all these spheres, thus making ancestor cults a dynamic manifestation of social values, political practices, and religious beliefs in pharaonic Egypt."[9]

Realität und Fiktion von Identität. Workshop am 04. und 05. Juni 2004, IBAES 5, London 2005, 155–164; see also S. PFEIFFER, Herrscher- und Dynastiekulte im Ptolemäerreich: Systematik und Einordnung der Kultformen, MBP 98, München 2008; M. MINAS-NERPEL, Koregentschaft und Thronfolge: Legitimation ptolemäischer Machtstrukturen in den ägyptischen Tempeln der Ptolemäerzeit, in: F. HOFFMANN/ K. S. SCHMIDT (eds.), Orient und Okzident in hellenistischer Zeit: Beiträge zur Tagung „Orient und Okzident – Antagonismus oder Konstrukt? Machtstrukturen, Ideologien und Kulturtransfer in hellenistischer Zeit", Würzburg 10.–13. April 2008, Vaterstetten 2014, 143–166.

4 See, *e.g.*, D. WILDUNG, Ahnenkult, in: W. HELCK/E. OTTO (eds.), Lexikon der Ägyptologie I, Wiesbaden 1975, 111–112; E. ENDESFELDER, Götter, Herrscher, König: zur Rolle der Ideologie bei der Formierung des ägyptischen Königtums, in: R. GUNDLACH/M. ROCHHOLZ (eds.), Ägyptische Tempel – Struktur, Funktion und Programm (Akten der Ägyptologischen Tempeltagungen in Gosen 1990 und in Mainz 1992), HÄB 37, Hildesheim 1994, 47–54, here: 49; M. FITZENREITER, Zum Ahnenkult in Ägypten, in: GM 143, 1994, 51–72; J. C. MORENO GARCÍA, Ancestral Cults in Ancient Egypt, in: J. BARTON et al. (eds.), Oxford Research Encyclopedia of Religion, Oxford, August 2016, 24 pages, DOI: 10.1093/acrefore/9780199340378.013.242. Accessed on 07.06.2019; FITZENREITER, Allerhand Kleinigkeiten, 53–54.

5 See, *e.g.*, R. J. DEMARÉE, The *ꜣḫ iḳr n rꜥ*-stelae: on ancestor worship in ancient Egypt, EU 3, Leiden 1983; M. FITZENREITER, *ꜣḫ n jtn* als *ꜣḫ jḳr n rꜥ*: Die königlichen Familienstelen und die religiöse Praxis in Amarna, in: SAK 37, 2008, 85–124; M. MÜLLER, Feasts for the Dead and Ancestor Veneration in Egyptian Tradition, in: V. RIMMER HERRMANN/J. D. SCHLOEN (eds.), In Remembrance of Me: Feasting with the Dead in the Ancient Middle East, Oriental Institute Museum Publications 37, Chicago 2014, 85–94; FITZENREITER, Allerhand Kleinigkeiten, 53–75.

6 FITZENREITER, GM 143, 1994, 51–72; N. HARRINGTON, Living with the dead: ancestor worship and mortuary ritual in ancient Egypt, Oxford 2013, in particular 28–64; see also Y. EL SHAZLY, Royal ancestor worship in Deir el-Medina during the New Kingdom, Wallasey 2015; MORENO GARCÍA, Ancestral Cults in Ancient Egypt.

7 See H. HARDACRE, Ancestor: Ancestor worship, in: L. JONES (ed.), Encyclopedia of Religion I, 2nd edition, Detroit 2005, 320–325, here: 321; for a more general discussion of the problematic history of research on the relation of religion and ancestor cult/worship see T. INSOLL, Ancestor Cults, in: T. INSOLL (ed.), The Oxford Handbook of the Archaeology of Ritual and Religion, Oxford 2012, online version, 17 pages, DOI: 10.1093/oxfordhb/9780199232444.013.0066. Accessed on 07.06.2019.

8 FITZENREITER, GM 143, 1994, 55. "A change in the status of ancestors" seems to be traceable in conjunction with the so-called personal piety during the New Kingdom, see HARRINGTON, Living with the dead, 30.

9 MORENO GARCÍA, Ancestral Cults in Ancient Egypt, 1.

A difference must be made between royal and non-royal ancestor cult. Whereas evidence for the latter is clearly attested, the first has been debated and proof is mostly explained as references to royal succession, but not to ancestor cult. King-lists and annals are confirmed from the earliest times onwards,[10] but are very often regarded as unrelated to ancestor cult, but as mirroring simply aspects of the royal succession.[11] From non-royal contexts, genealogies are well-known, showing interesting peaks in the first millennium BC.[12]

For both royal and non-royal contexts, a general division can be made between anonymous and identified ancestors, thus the veneration of anonymous or named ancestors. Throughout this paper, most examples will be addressing ancestors as individuals.[13] Cults for such ancestors have a limited existence, which finds parallels in ancient and modern cultures, depending on the remembrance of the deceased and probably just lasting a few generations.[14]

Without doubts, the royal/divine ancestor par excellence is the god Osiris – the ruling king is an embodiment of the living Horus, his predecessor Osiris granting legitimacy to his son and successor.[15] Originally limited to the royal sphere, this concept was extended beyond this from late Old Kingdom times onwards.[16] Father and son are in Egypt the keys to reach eternity and essential elements of the structure of Egyptian funerary cult.[17] Several Egyptian terms reflect complex semantic concepts of ancestors and different spiritualties of

10 See L. Popko, History-writing in ancient Egypt, in: W. Grajetzki/W. Wendrich (eds.), UCLA Encyclopedia of Egyptology, Los Angeles 2014 (August), 16 pages, here: 4–5 with references. https://escholarship.org/uc/item/73v96940 Accessed on 15.05.2019. For a new non-Manethonian king-list see L. Popko/M. Rücker, P.Lips. Inv. 1228 und 590: Eine neue ägyptische Königsliste in griechischer Sprache, in: ZÄS 138, 2011, 43–62. I am grateful to Lutz Popko for this reference.

11 *E.g.* Wildung, LÄ I, 111–112; Moreno García, Ancestral Cults in Ancient Egypt. For a different opinion about king-lists, see J. Cervelló-Autuori, The thinite "royal lists": typology and meaning, in: B. Midant-Reynes/Y. Tristant (eds.), Egypt at its Origins 2: Proceedings of the International Conference "Origin of the State. Predynastic and Early Dynastic Egypt", Toulouse (France), 5th-8th September 2005, OLA 172, Leuven 2008, 887–899, here: 895.

12 See K. Jansen-Winkeln, Die Entwicklung der genealogischen Informationen nach dem Neuen Reich, in: M. Fitzenreiter (ed.), Genealogie – Realität und Fiktion von Identität. Workshop am 04. und 05. Juni 2004, IBAES 5, London 2005, 137–145; F. Payraudeau, Généalogie et mémoire familiale à la Troisième Période Intermédiaire : le cas de la statue Caire JE 37880, in: RdE 64, 2013, 63–92. Cf. also Fitzenreiter, Allerhand Kleinigkeiten, 67.

13 See Harrington, Living with the dead, 30, fig. 13.

14 Harrington, Living with the dead, 146. See also Fitzenreiter, Allerhand Kleinigkeiten, 67.

15 Cf. U. Effland, Das Grab des Gottes Osiris in Umm el- Qaʿāb/Abydos', in: I. Gerlach/D. Raue (eds.), Forschungscluster 4. Sanktuar und Ritual. Heilige Plätze im archäologischen Befund. Menschen – Kulturen – Traditionen, Studien aus den Forschungsclustern des Deutschen Archäologischen Instituts 10, Berlin 2013, 321–330, here: 323–324; J. Budka, Abydos. Totenstadt der Pharaonen, in: R. Achenbach (ed.), Heilige Orte der Antike. Gesammelte Studien im Anschluss an eine Ringvorlesung des Exzellenzclusters „Religion und Politik in den Kulturen der Vormoderne und der Moderne" an der Universität Münster im Wintersemester 2013/2014, Kasion 1, Münster 2018, 67–93, here: 71–72 with references.

16 See M. Fitzenreiter, Jenseits im Diesseits – Die Konstruktion des Ortes der Toten im pharaonischen Ägypten, in: C. Kümmel/B. Schweitzer/U. Veit (eds.), Körperinszenierung – Objektsammlung – Monumentalisierung: Totenritual und Grabkult in frühen Gesellschaften. Archäologische Quellen in kulturwissenschaftlicher Perspektive, Tübinger Archäologische Taschenbücher 6, Münster/New York/München/Berlin 2008, 75–106, here: 81.

17 For the role of the king as son of the gods during the Early Dynastic Period and thus before the establishment of the cult of Osiris see Endesfelder, Götter, Herrscher, König, 47–54.

the dead (*e.g.* ba, ka and akh; the first two which are attested for kings and gods as well as for humans).[18]

Sources

Aspects of ancestor cult are diverse, but are especially evident in the following group of sources which I divide as primary and secondary evidence.[19] One needs to stress that as a starting point also aspects simply linked to the veneration and/or memory of predecessors are included in this list.

Primary evidence (mostly referring to specific ancestors):

- Archaeological evidence in general (ritual traces, *e.g.* Breaking the Red Pots[20]; votive offerings in general; traces of building activities; installations for ancestor busts and the busts themselves[21] etc.)
- Textual evidence (*e.g.* letters to the dead[22], stelae[23], text on statues[24], *e.g.* connected with statue cult, see the example of Nimlot A below; for some authors: also the king-lists[25] etc.)

Secondary evidence (referring both to anonymous and specific ancestors):

- Art/pictorial evidence (statues and reliefs, depictions of earlier kings/ancestors as well as pictures which are in artistic style and/or iconography relating to earlier depictions, thus revitalising old cultural models and elite representations) as well as 'archaising' pottery vessels (this paper)

A special case are 'archaising' aspects traceable in personal or royal names, thus in re-using names of older and deceased individuals/idealised kings as a conscious act aiming for legitimisation.[26] This seems to be comparable to the re-use of older titularies as common sources of inspiration from the Libyan Period onwards:

18 See FITZENREITER, Allerhand Kleinigkeiten, 58.

19 Cf. the different model by FITZENREITER who divides the sources into: installations, pictures and texts as well as Egyptian terminology, see FITZENREITER, Allerhand Kleinigkeiten, 55–58.

20 See HARRINGTON, Living with the dead, 37–40; J. BUDKA, V. Die Keramik des Osiriskults: Erste Beobachtungen zu Formen, Datierung und Funktion, in: U. EFFLAND/J. BUDKA/A. EFFLAND, Studien zum Osiriskult in Umm el-Qaab/Abydos – Ein Vorbericht, in: MDAIK 66, 2010, 35–64, here: 61–62.

21 HARRINGTON, Living with the dead, 49–59. See also J. TROCHE, The living dead at Deir el-Medina, in: A. DORN/S. POLIS (eds.), Outside the box: Selected papers from the conference "Deir el-Medina and the Theban Necropolis in Contact" Liège, 27–29 October 2014, AegLeod 11, Liège 2018, 465–475.

22 HARRINGTON, Living with the dead, 34–37 with literature.

23 HARRINGTON, Living with the dead, 59–60.

24 See HARRINGTON, Living with the dead, 40–49.

25 *E.g.* CERVELLÓ-AUTUORI, The thinite "royal lists", 895: "The Thinite king-lists are the first recorded stage of the pharaonic ancestor cult." See also FITZENREITER, Allerhand Kleinigkeiten, 66 with further references.

26 Cf. C. JURMAN, Legitimisation through Innovative Tradition – Perspectives on the Use of Old Models in Royal and Private Monuments during the Third Intermediate Period, in: F. COPPENS/J. JANÁK/H. VYMAZALOVÁ (eds.), 7. Symposium zur ägyptischen Königsideologie/7th Symposium on Egyptian Royal Ideology. Royal versus Divine Authority. Acquisition, Legitimization and Renewal of Power, Prague, June 26–28, 2013, Königtum, Staat und Gesellschaft früher Hochkulturen 4,4, Wiesbaden 2015, 177–214: here: 177. See also D. WILDUNG, Die Rolle ägyptischer Könige im Bewusstsein ihrer Nachwelt. Teil I: posthume Quellen über die Könige der ersten vier Dynastien, MÄS 17, Berlin 1969.

- Names and titularies (for studies about 'archaising' aspects of royal names see, among others, Jochem KAHL and Anke BLÖBAUM, highlighting a specific use of references to predecessors for foreign rulers and usurpators).[27]

Especially the sources for secondary evidence are particularly common during the first millennium BC, overlapping, however, with more general references to older rulers/deified individuals. The phenomenon of so-called archaisms is well known in Late Period art, but also in other periods. As Robert MORKOT, Claus JURMAN and others have shown in the last decades, various conscious references to cultural modes of the past are already well attested since the late Libyan Period in Egypt.[28] References to antiquity/earlier times can be located in an inspiring set of cultural repertoire between innovation and tradition. The appearance of various phenomena of 'archaisms' in the late Twenty-second Dynasty is contemporaneous to the attestation of extraordinary long genealogies and thus unlikely to be a coincidence[29], but rather aiming for legitimisation.[30] All in all, we need to consider that different media were used for the communication with ancestors,[31] but also that this communication and respective references had a broad spectrum of varying degrees and diverse foci.

Methodological challenges

Within ancestor cult in Egypt, there exists a very fine and blurred line between ancestor worship and funerary cult (see above). Case studies from outside the funerary sphere can thus help in defining archaeological traces as sources for ancestor cult. I believe that the votives for Osiris at Umm el-Qaab, which will be discussed in the following, represent another context that is suitable in this respect, although certain methodological challenges remain.

Similar to other assessments of archaeological remains like the study of ritual activities, there is the general danger of archaeological sources, which form the majority of the material presented in this paper, that they turn out as a) very vague in interpretation or b) as being interpreted in more detail than what is evident from the archaeological findings themselves. It remains often impossible to determine a specific act or ritual based solely on the archaeological evidence.[32] A contextual interpretation that is also considering all textual and pictorial sources is more purposeful and may lead to some results. For example, for

27 J. KAHL, Zu den Namen spätzeitlicher Usurpatoren, Fremdherrscher, Gegen- und Lokalkönige, in: ZÄS 129, 2002, 31–42; BLÖBAUM, Herrscherlegitimation, 144–151 and *passim*. For titularies and names of Libyan officials referring to older models see JURMAN, Legitimisation through Innovative Tradition, 177–214.

28 R. G. MORKOT, Archaism and Innovation in Art from the New Kingdom to the Twenty-sixth Dynasty, in: J. TAIT (ed.), 'Never Had the Like Occurred': Egypt's view of its past, Encounters with ancient Egypt, London 2003, 79–99; C. JURMAN, The Trappings of Kingship: Remarks about Archaism, Rituals and Cultural Polyglossia in Saite Egypt, Aegyptus et Pannonia 4, 2010, 73–118, here: 74–87; R. G. MORKOT, All in the Detail: Some Further Observations on "Archaism" and Style in Libyan-Kushite-Saite Egypt, in: E. PISCHIKOVA/J. BUDKA/K. GRIFFIN (eds.), Thebes in the First Millennium BC, Newcastle upon Tyne 2014, 379–395; JURMAN, Legitimisation through Innovative Tradition, 177–183 with further references. See also F. PAYRAUDEAU, Les prémices du mouvement archaïsant à Thèbes et la statue Caire JE 37382 du quatrième prophète Djedkhonsouiouefânkh, in: BIFAO 107, 2007, 141–156.

29 JANSEN-WINKELN, Die Entwicklung der genealogischen Informationen, 142.

30 See JURMAN, Legitimisation through Innovative Tradition, 177–214.

31 HARRINGTON, Living with the dead, 63.

32 For general difficulties in interpretation, especially connected with the analyses of archaeological deposits see, *e.g.*, M. K. H. EGGERT, Prähistorische Archäologie. Konzepte und Methoden, Tübingen/

traces of banquets celebrated by the living and the ancestors in ancient Egypt, we rely on addition sources and supporting information for the identification of the specific context and aspects of the ancient performance.[33] Also for the here discussed case studies of votives from Umm el-Qaab possible referring to ancestor cult, the archaeological and ceramicological contexts will be complemented by textual references and secondary sources where suitable.

3 Case studies from Umm el-Qaab/Abydos

My thoughts outlined in this paper are based on work by the Osiris cult project of the German Archaeological Institute Cairo, directed by Ute EFFLAND.[34] This project focusses on the cultic activities at Umm el-Qaab which post-date the Early Dynastic Period and are connected with rituals for the god Osiris. My own task within this project is the assessment of the ceramics from the site.[35] The name of Umm el-Qaab derives from the small votive cups, the so-called qaabs, attested in millions on the site – "mother of pots" is, therefore, an appropriate name.[36] During the last decade it became obvious that the long-lasting tradition of pottery votive offerings at Umm el-Qaab, reaching from the Predynastic Period until late Roman times with a florescence in the Kushite Period, refers to 1) kingship, 2) royal ancestors and 3) the god Osiris.[37] These new results and the close connections between the three spheres will be illustrated in the following.

It is essential to contextualise the votive pots deposited at Umm el-Qaab in a first step. Depositing pots had a very long tradition at Abydos and started already during the Naqada III Period, thus before the re-use of the Early Dynastic cemetery. The Predynastic cemetery Cemetery U yielded early evidence for votive pottery. In the vicinity of the famous tomb U-j[38], offering cult and the deposition of ceramic vessels was observed. The excavator Günter

---

Basel 2001, 78; G. GÖRMER, Bronzezeitliche Depots in Mitteleuropa und ihre Deutung, in: Ethnographisch-Archäologische Zeitschrift 47/3, 2006, 289–298.

33 Cf. V. MÜLLER, Archäologische Relikte kultischer Aktivitäten in Umm el-Qaᶜab/Abydos, in: J. MYLONOPOULOS/H. ROEDER (eds.), Archäologie und Ritual. Auf der Suche nach der rituellen Handlung in den antiken Kulturen Ägyptens und Griechenlands, Vienna 2006, 37–52 for some thoughts on ritual traces at Abydos.

34 See EFFLAND/BUDKA/EFFLAND, MDAIK 66, 2010, 19–91; U. EFFLAND/A. EFFLAND, "Ritual Landscape" und "Sacred Space" – Überlegungen zu Kultausrichtung und Prozessionsachsen in Abydos, in: MOSAIKjournal 1, 2010, 127–158; EFFLAND, Das Grab des Gottes Osiris, 321–330; U. EFFLAND/A. EFFLAND, Abydos. Tor zur ägyptischen Unterwelt, Darmstadt/Mainz am Rhein 2013; U. EFFLAND/A. EFFLAND, „Und dann kam Osiris aus der Unterwelt…" – Kultbild und Naos des Osiris vom „Gottesgrab" in Abydos, in: Sokar 34, 2017, 6–23.

35 See BUDKA, MDAIK 66, 2010, 42–58; J. BUDKA, Votivgaben für Osiris. Neue Forschungen in Umm el-Qaab/Abydos, in: Sokar 29, 2014, 56–65; J. BUDKA, Kushites at Abydos: A View from Umm el-Qaab', in: C. JURMAN/B. BADER/D. A. ASTON (eds.), A True Scribe of Abydos. Essays on First Millennium Egypt in Honour of Anthony Leahy, OLA 265, Leuven/Paris/Bristol, CT, 2017, 53–63; J. BUDKA, Umm el-Qa'ab and the sacred landscape of Abydos: New perspectives based on the votive pottery for Osiris, in: I. REGULSKI (ed.), Abydos: the sacred land at the western horizon, British Museum Publications on Egypt and Sudan 8, Leuven, in press.

36 See F. PUMPENMEIER, Heqareschu-Hügel, in: G. DREYER et al., Umm el-Qaab, Nachuntersuchungen im frühzeitlichen Königsfriedhof, 9./10. Vorbericht, in: MDAIK 54, 1998, 123–137, here: 125–26; MÜLLER, Archäologische Relikte, 38; BUDKA, MDAIK 66, 2010, 35; BUDKA, Sokar 29, 2014, 57.

37 BUDKA, Umm el-Qa'ab and the sacred landscape of Abydos, in press. See also BUDKA, Abydos, 67–93.

38 G. DREYER, Umm el-Qaab I. Das prädynastische Königsgrab U-j und seine frühen Schriftzeugnisse, AV 86, Mainz am Rhein 1998; G. DREYER, Abydos, Umm el-Qa'ab, in: K. A. BARD (ed.), Encyclopedia

DREYER documented an offering place (in German "Opferplatz"): a cultic area with more than 100 votive vessels on the desert surface.[39] Most common are simple dishes and plates, usually deposited upside-down on the ground.[40] One example shows irregular red paint, maybe a reference to blood and to real food offerings. Both the upside-down position of dishes and plates on the ground and red splashes on votive vessels are common features of the later cult associated with Osiris.[41] It is important to note that the cult at tomb U-j lasted until the First Dynasty and was obviously covering several generations of rulers. Can this long-lasting funerary cult at a royal tomb be regarded as the root for ancestor veneration at the site or is it simply an early reference for funerary rites?

The tomb of Osiris

Within the Early Dynastic cemetery of Umm el-Qaab, the tomb of king Djer of the First Dynasty stands out because it is the earliest substantial monumental monument with hundreds of subsidiary tombs.[42] During the Middle Kingdom, the main chamber was re-excavated and equipped with a staircase-building connected with the re-interpretation of the tomb as the burial place of the god Osiris.[43] With reference to ancestor cult, FITZENREITER has stressed here some important points: "To interpret the tomb of one specific king from times immemorial as the burial place of the mythic king Osiris is in some respects also reminiscent of the tendency to worship local heroes as 'saints'."[44]

The most impressive relic of the Middle Kingdom re-modification of the tomb of Djer is the Osirian bed representing a mortuary bed with the recumbent Osiris.[45] The location of this statue discovered by Émile AMÉLINEAU was reconstructed by Ute EFFLAND and Andreas EFFLAND in the central chamber, enclosed in a limestone shrine, newly discovered by the German Archaeological Institute Cairo.[46] The Osirian bed, and especially texts and reliefs from the temple of Seti I at Abydos, illustrate the main themes of the Osirian cult[47]: the regeneration of the god; his awakening from a passive mode and the impregnation of Isis, which are all essential for the cosmic cycle, and for both the royal and the funerary cult.[48] These aspects also include the treatment of ancestors as the creative power of the deceased Osiris as well as the guarding carried out by Isis. The power of creation and the protective factor are made available for the living, here represented by the god Horus.[49]

---

of the Archaeology of Ancient Egypt, London 1999, 109–114.

39 DREYER, Umm el-Qaab I, 15–16.

40 DREYER, Umm el-Qaab I, 15–16, figs. 8–9.

41 See BUDKA, Umm el-Qa'ab and the sacred landscape of Abydos, in press.

42 G. DREYER, Nebengräber ohne Ende. Der Grabkomplex des Djer in Abydos, in: Sokar 24, 2012, 6–11.

43 W. M. F. PETRIE, The royal tombs of the earliest dynasties II, EEF 21, London 1901, 9; MÜLLER, Archäologische Relikte, 44; D. O'CONNOR, Abydos. Egypt's First Pharaohs and the Cult of Osiris, Cairo 2009, 89–90.

44 FITZENREITER, Allerhand Kleinigkeiten, 61.

45 A. EFFLAND/U. EFFLAND, IV. Der Schrein des Osiris, in: EFFLAND/BUDKA/EFFLAND, MDAIK 66, 2010, 30–35, here: 33–35 with references.

46 EFFLAND/EFFLAND, Abydos, 17–20.

47 See R. DAVID, A Guide to Religious Ritual at Abydos, Warminster 1981; R. DAVID, Temple Ritual at Abydos, London 2016.

48 Cf. O'CONNOR, Abydos, 31–41.

49 See FITZENREITER, Allerhand Kleinigkeiten, 62.

References to royal ancestors' cult and especially to royal succession are specific for Abydos and can be illustrated, for example, with the complex of Ahmose and the pyramid for Tetisheri,[50] but also the famous king-list from the Seti I temple where royal ancestors are named for political reasons and questions of legitimacy.[51] Reflections of ancestors' cult may go back as early as to the First Dynasty,[52] although this has been questioned by some scholars.[53] From my point of view, the most likely interpretation of the necropolis seals from the tomb of Qaa[54] and the tomb of Dewen[55] is the one originally proposed by DREYER[56]: Horus Qaa appears here as first of the westerners (Khentamentiu) in front of his predecessors on the royal throne, illustrating the awareness of the importance of lists with royal names in a chronological order already at the very beginning of Egyptian kingship. Is this to be regarded as simple information on the royal succession, or rather as reflecting administrative units responsible for the funerary cult at the tombs of the named kings?[57] And if the latter, which seems much more likely[58], can it possible be regarded as indication of the actual veneration of the earliest kings buried at Umm el-Qaab? This is what Josep CERVELLÓ-AUTUORI proposed with the following words: "The seals from Abydos show us the precise terms of the royal ancestral cult in this early time. Two gods are mentioned: Horus, the mythical living royal ancestor which every ruler embodies, and Khentamentiu, who, in my opinion, must be regarded here as the mythical royal dead ancestor, that is to say, the personification of every dead king as well as of the collectivity of the royal ancestors as a whole. I think the Abydos seals already show the dichotomy 'living ancestor / dead ancestor' (later 'Horus/ Osiris') that defines the pharaonic kingship."[59] In line with this, even if certain aspects

50 O'CONNOR, Abydos, 105–110; see also S. P. HARVEY, The Cults of King Ahmose at Abydos, University of Pennsylvania, unpublished PhD thesis, 1998.

51 See B. J. KEMP, Ancient Egypt – Anatomy of a civilization, London/New York 1989, 21–22; A. EFFLAND, Abydos. Von der Frühzeit bis zur Zeitenwende, in: Archäologie in Ägypten. Magazin des Deutschen Archäologischen Instituts Kairo 2, 2014, 22–27, here: 27; BUDKA, Umm el-Qa'ab and the sacred landscape of Abydos, in press. For the king-list in the Seti I temple see also M. EL-NOUBI MANSOUR, Die Königsliste von Abydos, in: S. DEICHER/E. MAROKO (eds.), Die Liste: Ordnungen von Dingen und Menschen in Ägypten, Ancient Egyptian Design, Contemporary Design History and Anthropology of Design 1, Berlin 2015, 233–242. For its role within royal ancestor cult see FITZENREITER, Allerhand Kleinigkeiten, 66.

52 L. MORENZ, Bild-Buchstaben und symbolische Zeichen. Die Herausbildung der Schrift in der hohen Kultur Altägyptens, OBO 205, Freiburg/Göttingen 2004, 108, n. 458, G. DREYER, IV. Grabkomplex des Qa'a, 3. Kleinfunde, in: G. DREYER et al., Umm el-Qaab, Nachuntersuchungen im frühzeitlichen Königsfriedhof, 7./8. Vorbericht, in: MDAIK 52, 1996, 71–76, here: 72–73, fig. 26.

53 DREYER, MDAIK 52, 1996, 73; D. WENGROW, The Archaeology of Early Egypt. Social Transformations in North East-Africa, 10,000 to 2650 BC, Cambridge World Archaeology, Cambridge 2006, 131; T. C. HEAGY, Who was Menes?, in: Archéo-Nil 24, 2014, 59–92, here: 80–81.

54 See E.-M. ENGEL, Umm el-Qaab VI: Das Grab des Qa'a, Architektur und Inventar. Mit einem Beitrag von Thomas Hikade, AV 100, Wiesbaden 2017, 283–288, fig. 189.

55 G. DREYER, Ein Siegel der frühzeitlichen Königsnekropole von Abydos, in: MDAIK 43, 1987, 33–43; ENGEL, Umm el-Qaab VI, 283 with note 424.

56 DREYER, MDAIK 43, 1987, 33–43.

57 DREYER, MDAIK 43, 1987, 33–43; ENGEL, Umm el-Qaab VI, 283.

58 See HEAGY, Archéo-Nil 24, 2014, 80: "The seal is not a king list but an administrative document for the funerary cult, but whatever its purpose, it is a list of kings and can be utilized as such." For the identification of the seals as royal lists see also CERVELLÓ-AUTUORI, The thinite "royal lists", 887–888.

59 CERVELLÓ-AUTUORI, The thinite "royal lists", 895.

remain debatable, one can follow Ute EFFLAND who proposed that ancestors' cult might be viewed as the most important impact for the cult at the site of Umm el-Qaab over several millennia.[60] For example, this seems evident for the Kushite rulers and their references to royal ancestors.[61] It remains, however, debateable whether these references aim to legitimise the succession only, following the mythic example by Osiris and Horus, or whether royal predecessors are addressed as ancestors. The model proposed by CERVELLÓ-AUTUORI would allow a combination of both and a focus on the ideological sphere.

3.1 Cult for Osiris or cult for ancestors?

In the following, I will try to highlight some aspects of cult at Umm el-Qaab in the period of key interest throughout this volume, in the first millennium BC. Besides Thebes, Abydos is the best documented site during this period in Upper Egypt. It will be discussed whether the ritual remains attest to a cult for Osiris or rather to a cult for ancestors or both. To start with, as cult for a god, the activities at Umm el-Qaab are not cult of the dead in a regular sense. Since, as was already highlighted, the deceased kings of the Proto- and Early Dynastic Periods were commemorated at the site from the very beginning onwards, it seems more likely that the real focus of the ritual activities around the tomb of Osiris are actually the living. Following FITZENREITER, this is one aspect which speaks for the cult at Umm el-Qaab as ancestor worship, normally defined as "directed much more to the living than to the dead."[62]

Libyan Period

During the late Twenty-first and the first half of the Twenty-second Dynasty burials and monuments of high-ranking individuals are attested, sons of the Theban high priests, *e.g.* Psusennes and also royal sons, *e.g.* Iuput, son of Sheshonq I.[63] Andreas EFFLAND has undertaken the meticulous documentation of the attested kings and high priests from the Twenty-first and Twenty-second Dynasties.[64] More than 150 sherds of votive vessels from Smendes, Sheshonq I, Osorkon I and others were found by the Osiris project. This decorated votive pottery is so far unique and clearly illustrates that the cult at Umm el-Qaab was during the Libyan Period executed as official royal cult.[65] The sherds also stand for a new peak of activity at Umm el-Qaab, which is comparable to the New Kingdom, especially to Ramesside times, when similar votive vessels were used.[66]

One particular important monument for ancestor cult in the Libyan Period at Abydos is the stela Cairo JE 66285. It was found re-used in the temple of Osiris by Auguste MARIETTE and the text represents a very interesting oracular decree of Psusennes II.[67] The Libyan chief and

60 EFFLAND, Das Grab des Gottes Osiris, 324–326; see also BUDKA, Abydos, 81.

61 Cf. J. REVEZ, Looking at History through the Prism of Mythology: Can the Osirian Myth Shed any Light on Egyptian Royal Succession Patterns?, in: Journal of Egyptian History 3, 2010, 47–71 for an adaption of the Osirian myth for the Kushite royal succession under Taharqa.

62 FITZENREITER, Allerhand Kleinigkeiten, 54.

63 See A. LEAHY, Abydos in the Libyan Period, in: A. LEAHY (ed.), Libya and Egypt, c1300-750 BC, London 1990, 155–200; EFFLAND/EFFLAND, Abydos, 56–77; cf. also O'CONNOR, Abydos, 126.

64 EFFLAND/EFFLAND, Abydos, 72, fig. 24.

65 See EFFLAND/EFFLAND, Abydos, 74.

66 EFFLAND/EFFLAND, Abydos, 46–55. See also BUDKA, MDAIK 66, 2010, 57 and 59.

67 For this stela see S. BIRCH, Inscription of Prince Nimrod, in: Records of the Past: Being English Translations of the Assyrian and Egyptian Monuments, Volume XII: Egyptian Texts, London 1881,

later king Sheshonq I asks Amun of Karnak via the ruling king Psusennes II for permission to transport and erect a statue of his father Nimlot A at Abydos, establishing an offering for this statue in the temple respectively the installation of a funerary cult for Nimlot A.[68] Andreas Effland has proposed that the text of the stela and this cult for a statue of Sheshonq's father is one important aspect of the creation of the testimony of a peaceful usurpation – the reference to Osiris seems to guarantee the identification of Sheshonq as living Horus and legitimate successor who is also accepted by Psusennes.[69] Following Effland, the relics by Psusennes II, Sheshonq I and his successors at Umm el-Qaab highlight a new focus on a local cult for ancestors in direct connection to the cult for Osiris and thus of relevance for the royal ideology and legitimacy.[70]

In this respect, the so-called cenotaph of Iuput at Abydos is of particular importance.[71] This monument is the only new building erected during the Libyan Period in the sacred landscape of Abydos. It has a very peculiar architecture and was excavated by Amélineau in winter 1895/6.[72] The so-called cenotaph is a long corridor, with inscribed and decorated granite blocks, including Amduat scenes.[73] According to Amélineau's documentation, no finds were made and the structure was found empty. Since no burial was found, but the names of Sheshonq and Iuput, a cenotaph for the later (who might have been buried in the Ramesseum) was suggested.

It would require a new archaeological investigation of this unique monument to verify its function, but for now one has to stress its very prominent location and that its orientation points directly to Umm el-Qaab.[74] Andreas Effland has proposed that this could have marked the location of the royal stela found in the temple of Osiris with the oracular decree, illustrating the established statue cult of the Libyan Dynasty. According to Effland, this so-called cenotaph could actually represent a gallery for the ancestors – a "House of Ancestors" connected with the Libyan father Nimlot A of Sheshonq I.[75]

As mentioned above, there is much cult activity at Umm el-Qaab during the Libyan Period. Several sherds are of particular interest within the framework of foreign rulers – they belong to Iuwelot, high priest of Amun and son of Osorkon I.[76] On these votive vessels for Osiris his name was classified with a person with a feather on his head, thus with an 'ethnical' classifier, stressing the Libyan identity of the official.[77]

93–99; A. M. Blackman, The stela of Shoshenḳ, great chief of the Meshwesh, in: JEA 27, 1941, 83–95; B. Menu, La fondation cultuelle accordée à Sheshonq, in: CRIPEL 5, 1979, 183–189.

68 O'Connor, Abydos, 126–128; R. Meffre, D'Héracléopolis à Hermopolis: la Moyenne Égypte durant la Troisième Période intermédiaire (XXIe-XXIVe dynasties), Paris 2015, 265. For details of the text see also K. Jansen-Winkeln, Beiträge zur Geschichte der Dritten Zwischenzeit, in: Journal of Egyptian History 10(1), 2017, 23–42, here: 30–33.

69 Effland/Effland, Abydos, 73–74.

70 Effland/Effland, Abydos, 74.

71 Effland/Effland, Abydos, 75–77.

72 Effland/Effland, Abydos, 75.a

73 Effland/Effland, Abydos, figs. 27–30 for the architectural layout and position of the cenotaph.

74 Effland/Effland, Abydos, 75.

75 Effland/Effland, Abydos, 75–76.

76 Effland/Effland, Abydos, 68–69.

77 A. Effland, Iuwelot der Libyer – Zwei neue Belege für den thebanischen Hohepriester des Amun aus der 22. Dynastie und ein ungewöhnliches Personendeterminativ, in: E.-M. Engel/V. Müller/

The sudden end of cult activities at Umm el-Qaab might be explained with political changes and a new ruling family in the later Twenty-second Dynasty. It is noteworthy to stress that the latest evidence for votives for Osiris at Umm el-Qaab can be attributed to direct descendants of Sheshonq I, illustrating the importance of the site for the House of Sheshonq.[78] For almost 100 years, the cult for Osiris and royal investment at Abydos seems to fade, before it was reinstalled during the Twenty-fifth Dynasty.

Kushite Period

Following the Libyan interest in Abydos, also the next foreign rulers of Egypt, the kings of the Twenty-fifth Dynasty, were very active at the site. After a lack of activity of approximately 100 years, Umm el-Qaab encounters one of its heydays, comparable to the New Kingdom. There is some textual evidence, for example of Taharqa and Amenirdis I, and especially millions of votive vessels for Osiris found at Umm el-Qaab.[79] Together with burials of royal women and high officials in Cemetery D, the Kushite remains at Abydos are extensive.[80]

Within the Kushite investment at Abydos, it is particularly interesting that the New Kingdom sacred landscape is re-evocated. The latter is best illustrated by the famous Seti I complex. Within its main east–west axis there is a so-called desert pylon in the western part of the precinct, opening towards Umm el-Qaab. Remarkably, in front of this desert pylon, a large deposit of votive pottery is noticeable.[81] Based on a surface check, this pottery mainly dates to the Late Period, especially to the Kushite Period. Thus, the area behind the Osireion was clearly of importance during this era. This nicely corresponds to the choice of substructure of king Taharqa for his pyramid in Nuri: as several authors have stressed, he copied the Abydene Osireion with his royal tomb.[82]

U. Hartung (eds.), Zeichen aus dem Sand: Streiflichter aus Ägyptens Geschichte zu Ehren von Günter Dreyer, Wiesbaden 2008, 59–69.

78 Effland/Effland, Abydos, 75.

79 See Effland/Effland, Abydos, 78–81; Budka, MDAIK 66, 2010, 53–54, 60.

80 See A. Leahy, Kushite Monuments at Abydos, in: C. Eyre/A. Leahy/L. M. Leahy (eds.), The Unbroken Reed. Studies in the Culture and Heritage of Ancient Egypt in Honour of A. F. Shore, EES Occasional Publications 11, London 1994, 171–192; J. Budka, Kuschiten in Abydos: Einige Überlegungen zur Nutzung von *Cemetery D* (Mace) während der 25. Dynastie, in: GM 232, 2012, 29–51; A. Leahy, Kushites at Abydos: The Royal Family and Beyond, in: E. Pischikova/J. Budka/K. Griffin (eds.), Thebes in the First Millennium BC, Newcastle upon Tyne 2014, 61–95.

81 Effland/Effland, MOSAIKjournal 1, 2010, 142.

82 See T. Kendall, Why did Taharqa Build his Tomb at Nuri?, in: W. Godlewski/A. Łajtar/I. Zych (eds.), Between the Cataracts. Proceedings of the 11th Conference of Nubian Studies, Warsaw University, 27 August – 2 September 2006. Part One: Main Papers, PAM, Supplement Series 2,1 Warsaw 2008, 117–147; Budka, Kushites at Abydos, 54–63. It is noteworthy that the pyramid of Taharqa is not the only monument of the Twenty-fifth Dynasty recalling the Osireion: certain influences are also traceable in Theban monumental temple tombs, see D. Eigner, Die monumentalen Grabbauten der Spätzeit in der Thebanischen Nekropole, UZK 6, Vienna 1984, 163–183; J. Budka, Bestattungsbrauchtum und Friedhofsstruktur im Asasif. Eine Untersuchung der spätzeitlichen Befunde anhand der Ergebnisse der österreichischen Ausgrabungen in den Jahren 1969–1977, UZK 34, Vienna 2010, 71 and 78. Cf. most recently C. Traunecker, Abydenian Pilgrimage, Immortal stars and Theban Liturgies in the Tomb of Padiamenope (TT 33), in: E. Pischikova/J. Budka/K. Griffin (eds.), Thebes in the First Millennium BC: Art and Archaeology of the Kushite Period and Beyond, GHP Egyptology 27, London 2018, 126–151. See also the contribution by Angelika Lohwasser in this volume.

The investigations of Ute and Andreas EFFLAND have shown that there were several important connections between North Abydos, Umm el-Qaab, the Seti I complex and South Abydos. A significant landmark at Umm el-Qaab was the so-called Southern Hill (Fig. 1).[83] It is striking that the main cultic axes constructing the sacred landscape of Abydos and representing the processional ways during the festival for Osiris were marked by votive

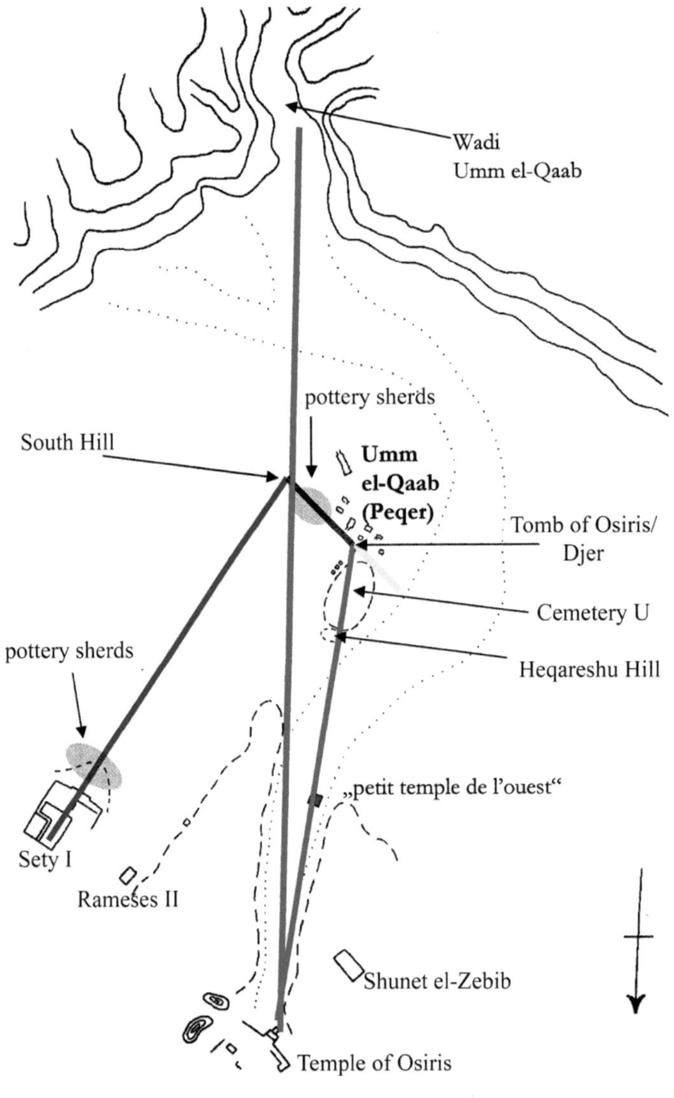

Fig. 1: Processional ways at Abydos with Kushite pottery deposits along the main cult axis (map: U. and A. EFFLAND)

83 A. EFFLAND/U. EFFLAND, VII. Kult- und Prozessionsachsen, in: EFFLAND/BUDKA/EFFLAND, MDAIK 66, 2010, 78–85, here: 82–83, fig. 52; EFFLAND/EFFLAND, MOSAIKjournal 1, 2010, 137–139.

deposits, predominately dating to the Kushite Period. Thus, the Twenty-fifth Dynasty obviously reused already-existing structures and revived processional features set up during the New Kingdom.

At Umm el-Qaab itself, millions of qaabs datable to the Kushite Dynasty were found. An *in situ* deposit of qaabs in the surroundings of the tomb of Khasekhemwy was investigated by Ute EFFLAND.[84] She was able to demonstrate that this deposit is not a random assemblage, but was carefully laid out, reflecting organised votive activities embedded in the yearly festival of Osiris. Organic remains strongly point to Osiris as god of vegetation, but especially to the aspects of regeneration and fertility.[85]

The discovery of a very large new ceramic deposit at the tomb of Djer/Osiris allowed an updated assessment of Kushite Period votive activity at Umm el-Qaab (Fig. 2).[86] Already in 2011, the first vessels were unearthed along the eastern edge of the subsidiary tombs of Djer, soon identified as belonging to the row of well-preserved vessels leading towards the south[87] found in the area in front of the tomb of Den by Eduard NAVILLE and by Vera MÜLLER.[88] In 2012 and 2013, more vessels of this deposit labelled O-NNO were unearthed. It became obvious that the deposit excavated in 1985 above B40[89] was probably once part of O-NNO in its south-eastern area. All in all, the pottery assemblage comprising O-NNO and the rows of vessels discovered by NAVILLE and MÜLLER once formed an alley from the subsidiary tombs of the tomb of Djer to the tomb of Den and farther towards the so-called Southern Hill.[90]

The votive deposit O-NNO, completely excavated in 2013, was documented and studied in 2014.[91] A total of 2,686 vessels could be reconstructed from 3,806 sherds – the actual number of deposited vessels was probably even larger, as parts of the deposit were disturbed in antiquity. The most important vessel types fall into the two categories of closed and open forms. Of these, 24% are storage vessels of types already well attested at Umm el-Qaab: the so-called Late Period bottles.[92] These large bottles are a very special type of vessel, clearly locally produced in very large numbers (Fig. 3). At Umm el-Qaab, they were arranged to form rows respectively to mark pathways.[93] Prior to the discovery of deposit O-NNO, no traces of any content were found within the bottles, suggesting that they were deposited empty. The majority of vessels from O-NNO are open dishes. More than 2,000 pieces are small qaabs.[94] In addition, a few other dishes and incense burners are present.

84 U. EFFLAND, III. Funde und Befunde, in: EFFLAND/BUDKA/EFFLAND, MDAIK 66, 2010, 24–30.
85 EFFLAND, MDAIK 66, 2010, 30.
86 See BUDKA, Umm el-Qaʿab and the sacred landscape of Abydos, in press.
87 EFFLAND/EFFLAND, MOSAIKjournal 1, 2010, 138.
88 E. NAVILLE, The cemeteries of Abydos I, EEF 33, London 1914, 38, pl. XVIII.4 and pl. XIX.1; MÜLLER, Archäologische Relikte, 39–48.
89 D. A. ASTON, A Group of Twenty-Fifth Dynasty Pots from Abydos, in: MDAIK 52, 1996, 1–10.
90 EFFLAND/EFFLAND, MOSAIKjournal 1, 2010, 138.
91 BUDKA, Sokar 29, 2014, 56–65.
92 J. BUDKA, The use of pottery in funerary contexts during the Libyan and Late Period: A view from Thebes and Abydos, in: L. BAREŠ/F. COPPENS/K. SMOLÁRIKOVÁ (eds.), Egypt in Transition. Social and Religious Development of Egypt in the First Millenium BCE. Proceedings of an International Conference, Prague, September 1–4, 2009, Prague 2010, 22–72, here: fig. 16.
93 BUDKA, The use of pottery in funerary contexts, 56–57.
94 See BUDKA, MDAIK 66, 2010, fig. 23; BUDKA, Sokar 29, 2014, fig. 5.

Interestingly, as observed in other votive deposits, there are several references to rituals in O-NNO.[95] First of all, a large number of killing holes was observed. Secondly, several traces of irregular red paint, possibly also with an apotropaic character, were documented on various types of vessels – on qaabs as well as Late Period bottles. Most important, however, is that for the first time there are traces of contents inside the Late Period bottles, which were previously assumed to have been deposited empty. Complete examples and fragments of qaab-dishes, and remains of their filling (botanical remains and sand) were discovered. Thus, for the first time, the deposition of the large Late Period bottles can be directly associated with the ritual deposition of qaabs. Because the contents of the qaabs are identical with what was documented by Ute EFFLAND in the *in situ* deposits, a similar ritual framework embedded into the calendar of the Osiris cult seems likely.

Fig. 2: Votive pottery deposit O-NNO at Umm el-Qaab – the large vessels form an alley leading towards the south (photo: U. EFFLAND)

Another interesting detail is that the bottles of O-NNO frequently have a hole in the base. In a number of cases, muddy remains closing this perforation (well attested for beer jars) were still found within the vessel. It remains unclear whether this indicates an original filling of these vessels with Nile water (strongly associated with the cult of Osiris) or with Nile mud, as is attested from other periods.

95 BUDKA, Sokar 29, 2014, 57.

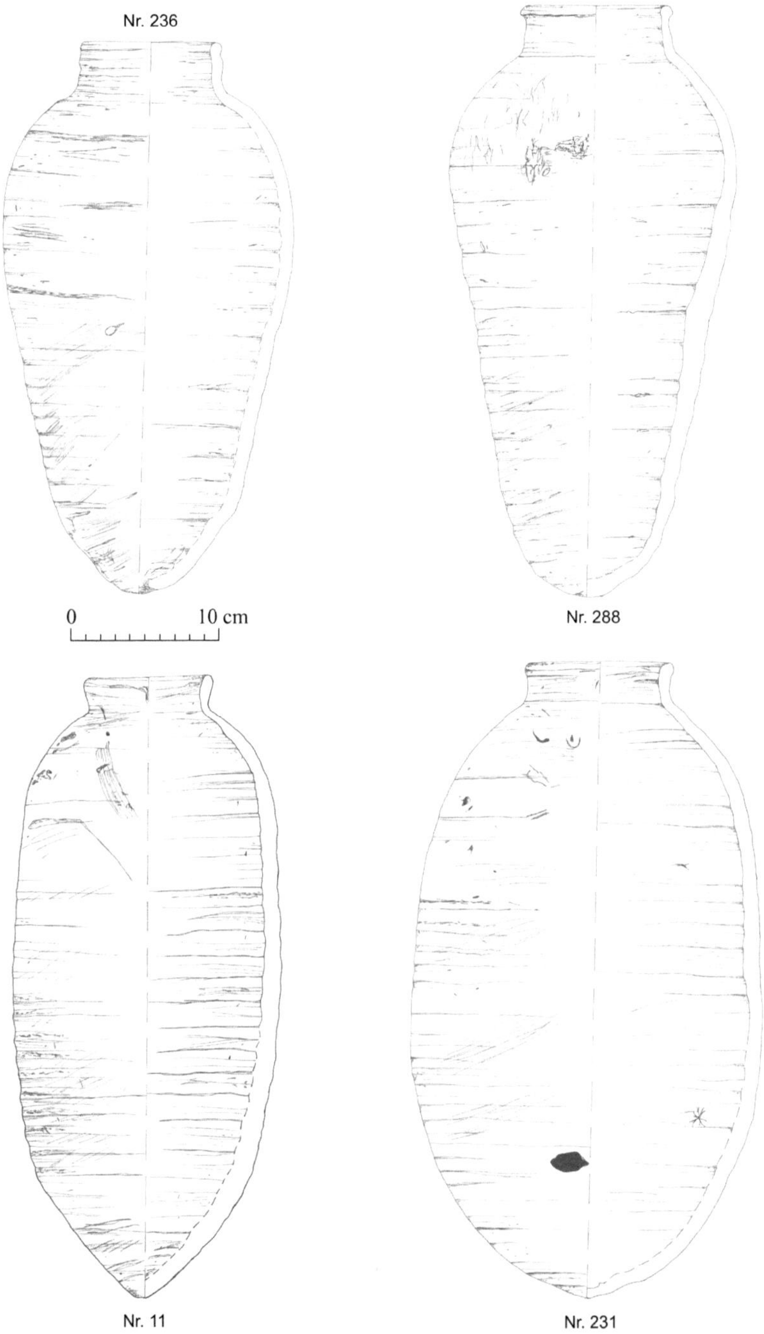

Fig. 3: Types of Late Period bottles from O-NNO (drawings: J. BUDKA)

All in all, the association of the qaabs with the Late Period bottles is of great importance to our understanding of the process of depositing the vessels. In some cases, the votive dishes were obviously positioned in already-laid-out storage vessels. In other cases, small groups of qaabs were put next to the Late Period bottles. This is well illustrated by a small assemblage of sixteen votive dishes found still *in situ* (Fig. 4).

Fig. 4: Qaab-deposit within O-NNO, including an Early Dynastic lid (photo: U. EFFLAND)

All of the vessels of this assemblage were deposited with the opening to the ground – a position already attested for offering dishes during the Naqada III Period at Cemetery U (see above) and also for Late Period dishes found *in situ* in front of the tomb of Dewen.[96] An unusual feature of the assemblage within O-NNO, however, is that from the sixteen vessels, one is not of Late Period date, but is actually an Early Dynastic lid.[97] Therefore, old and new vessels were used side by side within a pottery votive deposit of the eight century BC. The Early Dynastic lid is probably a piece from the original burial of Djer and obviously became ritually important for the votive offerings to Osiris more than 2,000 years later.

This seems unlikely to be an accidental finding and single case – rather, I would propose that 'archaism' and references to the original tomb contents seem to be important aspects in understanding the complex composition of the Late Period votive pottery at Umm el-Qaab.

96 MÜLLER, Archäologische Relikte, 40.
97 BUDKA, Sokar 29, 2014, 63, fig. 17.

In an earlier paper, I have proposed that the so-called Late Period bottles recall ovoid jars from the Pre- and Early Dynastic tombs.[98] There was obviously a clear intention to connect to, and to physically continue, the original inventory for Osiris Djer.[99] Given the Kushites' preferences for 'archaism' in relief and sculpture, it is no coincidence to find this in pottery deposited at Abydos.[100]

Change and continuity seem to have acted as key drives for the votive activities at Umm el-Qaab; the qaabs are nothing other than a continuation of a very specific shape from the Sesostris III complex,[101] but with a slightly modified shape, manufactured in Late Period clay fabrics. Red paint splashes on Late Period dishes find their predecessors in Naqada III dishes from the offering place at Cemetery U (see above). Osiris as king and as god forms a unity, being the essential part within the general dichotomy "living ancestor/dead ancestor" or "Horus/Osiris" (see above), and by this specific way of composing votive offerings making a connection between the original inventory and later activities, an everlasting cycle was evoked in the necropolis of Umm el-Qaab.

Saite Period

The next dynasty, again with foreign descent, the Saites, was also active at Abydos. Besides royal building activity by Psametik I and II in the temple of Osiris, votive vessels are present at Umm el-Qaab. These are less numerous than in Kushite times, but there are still some problems dating ceramics from the period of the late Twenty-fifth and the early Twenty-sixth Dynasty. All in all, the so-called Late Period bottles seem to continue. This would correspond to fragments of a shrine of Apries which were found by William M. Flinders Petrie at Umm el-Qaab.[102] We have to imagine a similar situation as in the tomb of Djer with the shrine and the Osirian bed – and it seems unlikely to be a coincidence that the titularies of the Saite kings recall names of the Thirteenth Dynasty[103] and the main Osirian cult statue at Umm el-Qaab also derives from the Thirteenth Dynasty.[104] This is further emphasised by the autobiographical text on a statue of Paftuemauineith referring to building activities and cultic installations under king Apries.[105]

Similar to Libyan and Kushite times, also burial activities continue at Abydos. A typical Saite tomb monument is the family burial close to the Early Dynastic enclosures of Redi-Anhur. It represents a family monument including the coffins of a large number of family members, presumably his brothers and sisters. A large limestone stela was erected above the tomb and shows the deceased worshiped by his sons and daughters, probably recalling social structures like the famous Middle Kingdom Abydos stelae which were set-up close by to this

98 Budka, The use of pottery in funerary contexts, 60.

99 Budka, Sokar 29, 2014, 56–65.

100 Budka, The use of pottery in funerary contexts, 60 with further literature; see also Budka, Umm el-Qa'ab and the sacred landscape of Abydos, in press.

101 Budka, MDAIK 66, 2010, 58.

102 A. Dodson, The so-called Tomb of Osiris at Abydos, in: KMT 8(4), 1997–1998, 37–47, here: 46; Effland/Effland, Abydos, 84. See also O'Connor, Abydos, 133 for some other royal inscribed fragments from Umm el-Qaab datable to the Twenty-sixth Dynasty.

103 See Blöbaum, Herrscherlegitimation, 146.

104 A. Leahy, The Osiris "Bed" Reconsidered', in: Or 46, 1977, 424–434; Effland/Effland, Abydos, 17–20.

105 O'Connor, Abydos, 128; Effland/Effland, Abydos, 83–84.

new Twenty-sixth Dynasty tomb.[106] Similar like for the Middle Kingdom stelae and funerary chapels, the emphasis of this Saite tomb is on family relations and ancestor worship.[107]

Persian Period
The question of Persians at Abydos is a bit complicated – textual references speak about destructions at the site which were re-established in the Thirtieth Dynasty.[108] Although a number of pottery vessels seem to be of Twenty-seventh Dynasty in date, no clear attestation of Persian kings is notable at Umm el-Qaab.[109] This might be still due to the general bias of the archaeological record for this period. In general, the Persian kings continued throughout Egypt with Saite building activity[110] and made interesting references to earlier kings, in particular to the legendary 'unifier of the two lands' Mentuhotep Nebhepetre by means of adopting his Horus names.[111]

4 Conclusion
Except for the difficult Twenty-seventh Dynasty, all periods with foreign rulers mentioned in this paper revived older structures and the cult of Osiris at Abydos. One can add here major activities at Thebes, since in the Libyan Period the Osirian precinct within Karnak was created, getting extended in Kushite and Saite times.[112] Common features of a particularly strong investment in Abydos and the cult of Osiris are especially notable for the Libyan and the Kushite Periods when rulers appeared also as non-Egyptian and were in need of legitimacy.

Despite these common features, some individual aspects are also present: The proposed "House of Ancestors" for the Libyan family of Sheshonq and the use of the Osiris myth for the legitimation of the succession (see above). The focus of Kushite royal females at Abydos is striking and is mirrored also by the importance of females at Kush. Abydene features like the Osireion and the shape of the qaab-vessels were transferred to Kush, in particular during the reign of Taharqa.[113] The Saites who appear completely Egyptian despite of their Libyan descent maybe referred to Thirteenth Dynasty installations at Abydos. The Persians are a special case as they are presently not attested by means of royal votives at Umm el-Qaab.

The long-lasting tradition of offerings at Umm el-Qaab, reaching from the Predynastic Period until Ptolemaic times with a heyday in the Kushite Period, refers to kingship, royal ancestors and the god Osiris.[114] Concepts of the Egyptian Netherworld were projected on the

106 O'Connor, Abydos, 127, fig. 69, 131, fig. 71.
107 Cf. Harrington, Living with the dead, 63.
108 Effland/Effland, Abydos, 90.
109 See Budka, MDAIK 66, 2010, 54.
110 Cf. J. von Beckerath, Nochmals die Eroberung Ägyptens durch Kambyses, in: ZÄS 129, 2002, 1–5, here: 1 with references.
111 See Kahl, ZÄS 129, 2002, 34 and 38.
112 L. Coulon/A. Hallmann/F. Payraudeau, Historical and Art Historical Overview Based on Recent Fieldwork and Studies, in: E. Pischikova/J. Budka/K. Griffin (eds.), Thebes in the First Millennium BC: Art and Archaeology of the Kushite Period and Beyond, GHP Egyptology 27, London 2018, 271–293 with further references. See also the contribution by Essam Nagy in this volume.
113 See Budka, Kushites at Abydos, 54–63. Cf. also Lohwasser in this volume.
114 See also Effland, Das Grab des Gottes Osiris, 326: "Ahnenkult und Osiris-Kult laufen durch die Zeit hindurch immer wieder parallel und stehen auch nicht im Widerspruch zueinander."

landscape of Abydos which in turn became a sacred place.[115] I would like to propose that the concept of FITZENREITER, connecting "second burials" with ancestor cult (whereas the "first burial" is connected with cult of the dead)[116] works perfectly for the cult at Abydos: the cultic activities at Umm el-Qaab can be regarded as ancestor veneration because the re-interpretation of the royal tombs as tombs of the god Osiris represent "second burials". The prime recipients of this kind of cult are therefore the living, first of all the living rulers. With this focal point, the cult for Osiris at Abydos is mostly directed towards the royal succession and royal ideology.

To sum up, I would strongly agree with Timothy INSOLL that archaeological approaches to ancestor cult should not think of it as isolated aspect of ancient cultures, but rather "as part of a multiple 'package' of phenomena, practices, and beliefs whose configuration and importance can change over time."[117] For the Egyptian context, I believe that ancestor cult was an integral part of royal ideology, especially for foreign rulers. As KAHL, BLÖBAUM and others have shown, the foreign rulers are in a stronger need of legitimacy.[118] This seems to be mirrored with the very specific investments of the Libyans, Kushites and Saites at Abydos. Royal ancestor cult and its main concepts of legitimacy and regularity aim for social and political legitimation.[119] This becomes especially visible with the 'best practice example' set by Sheshonq I with the installation of a cult for his father Nimlot at Abydos, presumably connected with the increase of ceramic votives at Umm el-Qaab. I would furthermore propose that since Ramesside times, one general aspect of the Egyptian *Zeitgeist* was to refer to gods as legitimation. This becomes also obvious from the increase of importance of the Osirian cult during the first millennium BC.

In conclusion, the significance of Abydos throughout the ages seems to be first of all connected with royal ancestor cult at the site which goes back to Early Dynastic times of which all later generations were very well aware of and took advantage for questions for legitimacy. The understanding of ancestorship as a basis of fertility allows stressing the closeness of ancestors in Egypt with Abydos/Umm el-Qaab since this aspect relates to the site's main god and to the "Osirian concept of recreation out of the death."[120]

115 See EFFLAND/EFFLAND, Abydos, 11; EFFLAND, Magazin des Deutschen Archäologischen Instituts Kairo 2, 2014, 27.

116 FITZENREITER, Allerhand Kleinigkeiten, 54.

117 INSOLL, Ancestor Cults, 13.

118 KAHL, ZÄS 129, 2002, 31–42; BLÖBAUM, Herrscherlegitimation, 139–142.

119 FITZENREITER, Allerhand Kleinigkeiten, 67.

120 FITZENREITER, Allerhand Kleinigkeiten, 68.

The Egyptian royal costume in the Late Period

Olaf E. Kaper

Abstract
The depictions of the royal costume from the Late Period are highly standardised. In order to study the royal costume of the Late Period, it is useful to include the representations of gods. A recent find in Dakhla Oasis has highlighted how the Egyptian gods acquire royal traits at this time. An elaborate image of Seth of Dakhla from the reign of Amasis displays the god in royal dress, which allows comparison with the royal costume of the New Kingdom on the one hand and with Roman images of the emperor-pharaoh on the other. It remains a matter for discussion in what way this costume resembled items actually worn by the king.

Introduction

In images from the Late Period, the pharaoh was represented in accordance with age-old traditions. The standard representations show him bare-chested and wearing the *shendyt* or the royal kilt with triangular apron combined with a wig, a head cloth or a basic type of crown and always with an uraeus and only the simplest items of jewellery.[1] Yet, it will be discussed below that certain images of the New Kingdom and notably the costume items found in the tomb of Tutankhamun (KV 62) demonstrate that the actual garments and jewellery worn by the king could be far more elaborate than that. The rules of tradition and decorum determined the depiction of the sovereign even when this was contrary to his actual appearance.[2] In the Greco-Roman Period there are again indications that a more elaborate costume was worn, to be outlined below, but the Late Period is noticeable for the lack of opulence in the appearance of the king. In this paper I will argue that there was nevertheless a continuation of the tradition of royal garments as known from the New Kingdom, in which unusual techniques and elaborate decorations were applied.

---

1 A repertory of royal images, albeit without much attention to the costume, is found in K. Myśliwiec, Royal Portraiture of the Dynasties XXI–XXX, Mainz am Rhein 1988. In the Twenty-fifth Dynasty, the jewellery could be more complicated than in other periods, as on Myśliwiec, Royal Portraiture, pls. 30, 34 and 35b; E. R. Russmann, The Representation of the King in the XXVth Dynasty, MRE 3, Brussels/Brooklyn 1974, 25–27.

2 On religiously motivated decorum in the temple reliefs, cf. J. Baines, Restricted Knowledge, Hierarchy, and Decorum: Modern Perceptions and Ancient Institutions, in: JARCE 27, 1990, 1–23, here: 20–21; J. Baines, Visual and written culture in ancient Egypt, Oxford/New York 2007, 14–30, especially 23, 25–26.

The royal costume in the New Kingdom

The study of the Egyptian royal costume has never received much serious attention, in spite of the overwhelming amount of pictorial evidence and the obvious importance of the costume as an expression of royal ideology.[3] By contrast, the textiles worn by private citizens have been the subject of multiple studies.[4] The royal costume has been described for some specific groups of reliefs and/or statues,[5] but a synthesis is still lacking. The textiles of Tutankhamun's tomb have not been published *in extenso* yet, and only a selection of pieces has been studied in detail.[6] A new publication of the textiles from KV62 by Gillian VOGELSANG-EASTWOOD and the present author is in preparation.[7] Separate studies already exist of the royal footwear of Tutankhamun,[8] and of individual items of royal jewellery.[9]

There is a strikingly large difference between the costume in the representations of kings and the actual garments found in KV62. The representations usually depict the king wearing traditional clothes that were first conceived in early dynastic or Old Kingdom times. The

---

3 Note the brevity of the discussions of this topic in popularising works, such as P. J. WATSON, Costume of Ancient Egypt, London 1987, 24–36; E. ZOFFILI, Kleidung und Schmuck im alten Ägypten, Frankfurt am Main/Berlin 1992, 24, 40–43; G. J. SHAW, The Pharaoh: Life at Court and on Campaign, London/Cairo 2012, 75–78; L. PEDRINI, L'arte dell'apparire nell'Egitto faraonico. Una moda per l'eternità, Genoa 2016, 65.

4 H. BONNET, Die ägyptische Tracht bis zum Ende des Neuen Reiches, UGÄA VII,2, Leipzig 1917, which includes remarks on the royal kilt; R. HALL, Egyptian Textiles, Shire Egyptology 4, Princes Risborough 1986; G. M. VOGELSANG-EASTWOOD, Pharaonic Egyptian Clothing, Leiden/New York/Cologne 1993; R. M. H. JANSSEN, Costume in New Kingdom Egypt, in: J. M. SASSON/J. BAINES/G. BECKMAN/K. S. RUBINSON (eds.), Civilizations of the ancient Near East, Vol. I, New York 1995, 383–394; B. J. KEMP/G. M. VOGELSANG-EASTWOOD, The Ancient Textile Industry at Amarna, EM 68, London 2001.

5 For the Old Kingdom, the classic study remains E. STAEHELIN, Untersuchungen zur ägyptischen Tracht im Alten Reich, MÄS 8, Berlin 1966. For the Middle Kingdom, this is H. G. EVERS, Staat aus dem Stein: Denkmäler, Geschichte und Bedeutung der ägyptischen Plastik während des Mittleren Reichs, 2 Vols., München 1929. For Ramesses III there is A. CALVERT, Quantifying Regalia: A Contextual Study into the Variations and Significance of Egyptian Royal Costume Using Relational Databases and Advanced Statistical Analyses, in: P. BRAND/L. COOPER (eds.), Causing His Name to Live: Studies in Egyptian Epigraphy and History in Memory of William J. Murnane, Culture and History of the Ancient Near East 37, Leiden/Boston 2009, 49–64. For the Kushite Period: RUSSMANN, The Representation of the King in the XXVth Dynasty, 25–44.

6 R. PFISTER, Les textiles du tombeau de Toutankhamon, Revue des arts asiatiques 11.4, 1937, 207–218; G. M. CROWFOOT/N. DE GARIS DAVIES, The tunic of Tut'ankhamūn, in: JEA 27, 1941, 113–130; D. CRAIG PATCH, Tutankhamun's Corselet: a Reconsideration of its Function, in: BES 11, 1991, 57–77; G. M. VOGELSANG-EASTWOOD, De kleren van de farao, Amsterdam 1994; G. M. VOGELSANG-EASTWOOD, Tutankhamun's wardrobe: garments from the tomb of Tutankhamun, Rotterdam 1999; S. IBRAHIM, An Amarna Sash of Tutankhamun, in: M. ELDAMATY/M. TRAD (eds.), Egyptian Museum collections around the world. Festschrift Cairo Museum, Studies for the Centennial of the Egyptian Museum, Cairo, Cairo 2002, 557–561; N. A. HOSKINS, Woven patterns on Tutankhamun textiles, in: JARCE 47, 2011, 199–215.

7 G. M. VOGELSANG-EASTWOOD/O. E. KAPER, Tutankhamun's Textiles, Cairo, forthcoming.

8 A. J. VELDMEIJER, Tutankhamun's Footwear: Studies of Ancient Egyptian Footwear, Leiden 2012.

9 E. FEUCHT-PUTZ, Die königlichen Pektorale: Motive, Sinngehalt und Zweck, Bamberg 1967. The general works on Egyptian jewellery are mainly concerned with royal pieces; M. VILÍMKOVÁ, Egyptian Jewellery, London 1969; C. ALDRED, Jewels of the Pharaohs: Egyptian Jewellery of the Dynastic Period, London/New York 1971; A. WILKINSON, Ancient Egyptian Jewellery, London 1971; C. ANDREWS, Ancient Egyptian Jewellery, London 1990.

images are primarily ideological and are not intended to render the king as he (or she) actually dressed at a particular moment. As in Egyptian art in general, the depiction of the king was conceptual rather than perceptual.[10] The images were intended to reflect and maintain the divine order, in which the king was perceived as both superhuman and timeless.

The *shendyt* kilt and the kilt with triangular apron are conventional garments, of which it is hard to imagine that the king wore them in the New Kingdom in the manner of the Old Kingdom Period. In the New Kingdom, Egyptian men generally wore a tunic and a bare chest was only seen on soldiers, farmhands and servants.[11] Egyptology still tends to give credence to the images of the king in official representations, while admitting that the reality may well have been different.[12]

The garments from Tutankhamun's tomb show much more use of colour and elaborate techniques than those of his subjects. Items from his tomb display, for instance, the use of embroidery, tapestry weave, textile appliqué and gold bracteates, all of which lend a character of opulence to the royal appearance, which is not known from private garments. Various items in the tomb were decorated with panels of applied cloth (appliqué), such as a panel from the front of a tunic (Carter 101p [a]), and two sets of protective falcon or vulture wings apparently to be worn on the shoulders (Carter 21m, 21x, 21cc and 44r).[13] This technique involved a basis of undyed linen, upon which decoration was applied with a pattern "created out of folded and rolled strips of red and blue cloth that were fastened to the ground cloth using a small stab stitch".[14] Thus far, appliqué is only rarely attested in Egyptian archaeological finds and only a single other possible piece is known, albeit of a course nature and preserved only as a fragment of the original garment, found in the workmen's village at Amarna.[15]

There are a handful of other surviving items of royal textiles from the New Kingdom, and these also show some extraordinary technical features. A pillow cover with images of the Nine Bows in a multi-coloured tapestry weave was found in the Valley of the Kings,[16] and four other fragments in the same technique come from the tomb of Thutmose IV.[17] An unprovenanced 5.2m sash or girdle bearing the name of Ramesses III survives, made in a warp-patterned weaving technique.[18]

10 On this distinction, cf. D. Laboury, Function et signification de l'image égyptienne, in: Bulletin de la Classe des Beaux-Arts, Académie Royale de Belgique, 6e série, Tome IX, 1998, 131–148; especially 138.

11 R. E. Freed, Costume, in: Egypt's Golden Age: The Art of Living in the New Kingdom 1558–1085 B.C., Boston 1982, 171–72.

12 *E.g.* Shaw, Pharaoh, 78: "Overall then, it would seem that the depictions of the king in art are a faithful representation of what he may have worn on certain occasions. However, the more unusual clothing in Tutankhamun's tomb suggests that in reality the king could wear a much wider variety of styles, some quite plain and practical, others more decorative."

13 Vogelsang-Eastwood, Tutankhamun's wardrobe, 28–29; 103–104.

14 G. Vogelsang-Eastwood, in: Vogelsang-Eastwood/Kaper, forthcoming.

15 Kemp/Vogelsang-Eastwood, The Ancient Textile Industry at Amarna, 215–216, no. 1711.

16 Cairo Museum no. CG 24987; CG 24001–24990, 302–303, pl. LVII.

17 H. Carter/P. E. Newberry, The Tomb of Thoutmôsis IV, Theodore M. Davis' Excavations: Bibân el Molûk, Westminster 1904, 143–44, pls. 10, 28; R. M. Janssen, The "ceremonial garments" of Tuthmosis IV reconsidered, in: SAK 19, 1992, 217–224; M. Abas Mohammed Selem/S. Abd Al-Khalek, Egyptian Textiles Museum, [Cairo 2009], 53.

18 T. E. Peet, The so-called Ramesses girdle, in: JEA 19, 1933, 143–149; P. Bienkowski/A. Tooley, Gifts of the Nile: Ancient Egyptian Arts and Crafts in Liverpool Museum, London 1995, 46.

Some representations from the New Kingdom confirm the use of exceptional textiles in the royal wardrobe, because they show the king wearing more colourful garments than his subjects. A depiction of king Ay in his tomb (WV23) shows the king wearing the common royal kilt with a triangular apron, but this item is exceptionally combined with a brightly coloured and patterned cloth appearing underneath, and covering his knees.[19] The tombs of the sons of Ramesses III in the Valley of the Queens also show the king with much colour and detail in his garments.[20]

The royal costume in the Greco-Roman Period

Thus, I agree with Rosalind HALL's (1986) observation: "The use of patterned textiles, seldom represented before the Late New Kingdom, may have been confined to the royal household throughout the Pharaonic Period".[21] Yet, our only information in this regard stems from the New Kingdom. In the Third Intermediate Period and Late Period the images of kings never show such details, and they are generally more uniform. Already during the Libyan Dynasties, the costume represented is archaising and refers back to Old Kingdom models.[22] The temple of Hibis is one of the richest sources for the royal iconography of the Late Period, but all its representations of Darius I show him wearing conventional royal costumes.[23]

The royal costume is only again represented with more colours in the Ptolemaic Period and especially in the Roman Period. In recent years, conservation and cleaning work undertaken in several temples of the Roman Period has revealed much colour and iconographic details in the royal imagery. Most noticeable in this regard are the newly cleaned pronaos reliefs of the temple of Hathor at Dendera,[24] and the sanctuary reliefs of the temple of Isis at Deir el-

19 A colour photo appears in S. CAUVILLE/M. IBRAHIM ALI, La Vallée des rois: Itinéraire du visiteur, Leuven/Paris/Walpole, MA, 2014, 407.

20 F. HASSANEIN/M. NELSON, La tombe du prince Amon-(Her)-Khepchef, CEDAE, Collection scientifique: Vallée des reines 55, Cairo 1976, 21–23, 26–30; F. HASSANEIN/M. NELSON/G. LECUYOT, La tombe du prince Khaemouaset, CEDAE, Collection scientifique 72: Vallée des reines 44, Cairo 1997, 32–37, figs. 1–4; 50–56, 68–80, pls. 23–25, 28–31, 57–58, 60–64, 70–74; CALVERT, Quantifying Regalia, 52–53. F. ABITZ, Ramses III. in den Gräbern seiner Söhne, OBO 72, Freiburg (Schweiz)/Göttingen 1986, does not comment on the costume of the king.

21 HALL, Egyptian Textiles, 23.

22 O. PERDU, Plaquette ornementale représentant Ioupout II, in: O. PERDU (ed.), Le crépuscule des pharaons: Chefs-d'oeuvre des dernières dynasties égyptiennes, Paris 2012, 174–175. In general on the archaism of the Libyan Period, cf. C. JURMAN, Legitimisation through Innovative Tradition – Perspectives on the Use of Old Models in Royal and Private Monuments during the Third Intermediate Period, in: F. COPPENS/J. JANÁK/H. VYMAZALOVÁ (eds.), 7. Symposium zur ägyptischen Königsideologie/ 7th Symposium on Egyptian Royal Ideology. Royal versus Divine Authority. Acquisition, Legitimization and Renewal of Power, Prague, June 26–28, 2013, Königtum, Staat und Gesellschaft früher Hochkulturen 4,4, Wiesbaden 2015, 177–214.

23 *E.g.* N. DE GARIS DAVIES, The Temple of Hibis in el Khargeh Oasis, Part III: The Decoration, PMMA 17, New York 1953, pl. 60, has a coloured reconstruction by Ch. Wilkinson of an offering scene in which Darius wears an elaborately coloured royal costume, but this is not different from earlier versions of the same.

24 Excellent photographs of details of the ceiling (but without royal figures) appear in S. VANNINI/M. MEGAHED, King Tut: The Journey through the Underworld, Cologne 2018, 200, 238–239, 245, 246, 280–291, 358–365. A more general discussion of these reliefs, including colour photographs of kings, appears in S. CAUVILLE/M. IBRAHIM ALI, Dendara. Itinéraire du visiteur, Leuven/Paris/Bristol, CT, 2015, 10–48.

Shelwit.[25] They depict the king with garments full of brightly coloured details, such as lotus flowers, falcon feathers and other protective imagery.

Some of this could already have been suspected because of the temple reliefs at Dendera, of Ptolemy Caesar on the outside rear wall,[26] of Nero on the outer walls of the pronaos,[27] and the screen walls with depictions of Trajan on the Roman Period mammisi.[28] These reliefs have lost their colour but they contain a wealth of iconographic detail in relief added to the garments. Most notable are the kilts with triangular apron, which are covered in imagery in raised relief, added as an extra layer on top of the usual stripes that radiate from the corners of the apron. Some aprons depict the king vanquishing his enemies and others show the king in the form of a griffin or a trampling sphinx.[29] François DAUMAS imagined that these garments would have been made in embroidery: "Ils forment de véritables tableaux qui devaient être brodés, j'imagine, sur le tissu même, à la manière de certaines étoffes coptes qui nous sont parvenues".[30] However, appliqué seems to correspond better to the raised relief of the representations. DAUMAS could not have known about the appliqué technique in ancient Egypt, which was identified only in recent years.

The colourful Greco-Roman Period images present us with a problem. Whereas the Tutankhamun garments provide proof that the kings wore colourful and elaborate outfits in the New Kingdom, it is unknown what costume was worn by the Ptolemies. These kings are often represented wearing a standard pharaonic costume in the Egyptian reliefs and in some statues, but these images are largely conventional. In theory, the Ptolemaic kings would have dressed as pharaohs when engaging in activities required by the Egyptian religion.[31] It is known that the Ptolemies would occasionally visit temples or attend the installation of a sacred animal,[32] but unfortunately their outfit on these occasions is never described.

---

25 N. ABD EL-TAWAB BADER/A. M. ASHRY, The Cleaning of the Isis Temple's Mural Paintings in Upper Egypt Using Zinc Oxide Nanoparticles and Non-ionic Detergent, International Journal of Conservation Science 7.2 (April–June 2016), 443–458.

26 Identified as the earliest such depiction in J. QUAEGEBEUR, Une statue égyptienne représentant Héraclès-Melqart?, in: E. LIPINSKI (ed.), Studia Phoenicia V. Phoenicia and the East Mediterranean in the First Millennium B.C. Proceedings of the Conference held in Leuven from the 14th to the 16th of November 1985, OLA 22, Leuven 1987, 157–166, here: 163.

27 S. CAUVILLE, Dendara XV. Traduction. Le pronaos du temple d'Hathor: Plafond et parois extérieures, OLA 213, Leuven 2012, pls. 50–103.

28 F. DAUMAS, Les mammisis de Dendara, Cairo 1959, pls. 50–53, 93, 96, 96bis.

29 As depicted in CAUVILLE/IBRAHIM ALI, Dendara. Itinéraire, 218. A similar decoration in raised relief is found on the kilt of a statue of a Roman emperor in Heidelberg; E. FEUCHT, Vom Nil zum Neckar. Kunstschätze Ägyptens aus pharaonischer und koptischer Zeit an der Universität Heidelberg, Berlin/Heidelberg 1986, 118–119 [268].

30 F. DAUMAS, Dendara et le temple d'Hathor. Notice sommaire, Cairo 1969, 74.

31 Plutarch describes Cleopatra VII wearing "the sacred garment of Isis" during a state occasion; S. A. ASHTON, Cleopatra and Egypt, Malden/Oxford/Carlton 2008, 139.

32 *E.g.* Ptolemy III may have attended the foundation of the new temple at Edfu; S. PFEIFFER, Die Ptolemäer. Im Reich der Kleopatra, Stuttgart 2017, 91; and Ptolemy VIII was purportedly present at the inauguration of the Edfu pronaos; S. CAUVILLE, Edfou, BiGen 6, Cairo 1984, 63. Cleopatra VII was present at the installation of a new Bukhis bull in Hermonthis; W. SCHULLER, Kleopatra, Königin in drei Kulturen: Eine Biographie, Reinbek bei Hamburg 2006, 41–42.

It is debated in the case of the royal crowns whether such items as are seen in the images could actually have existed as physical objects,[33] or that they should be seen only as symbolical items.[34] A strong argument for the latter view is the absence of crowns among the burial equipment of Tutankhamun.[35]

It is clear that the Roman emperors never wore traditional pharaonic clothing, even though they were still considered pharaohs within the temples of Egypt and were frequently depicted as such. Günther Hölbl has argued that this role of the pharaoh in Roman times amounted to no more than a "virtual" or "hieroglyphic" status, as the outcome of a lengthy period of decline in the divinity of the reigning king.[36]

It is, therefore, remarkable that the most elaborate renderings of the pharaonic costume date to the Roman Period. The images give the impression that the royal costume still existed, and that this stood in the tradition of the kings of the New Kingdom. Especially the elaborate nature of the depictions at Dendera suggests that the spectator would be able to recognise the emperor's clothes because similar items were still in existence. Perhaps the highest level of the priesthood could wear items of a royal costume, but we lack any evidence of this. The only evidence for the occasional opulence of the priestly costume in Roman times is provided by the golden crown of Dush and by the few depictions of priests that wear similar crowns.[37]

The royal costume in the Late Period

Given the general lack of elaborate or multi-coloured images of pharaohs from the Late Period, we should investigate whether the royal costume had indeed sobered up after the New Kingdom, or whether the representations are misleading because they are determined by archaism and decorum rather than reality. We should consider whether the royal costume had been replaced by a more contemporary costume, or whether the former traditions of elaborate and costly costumes were in fact continued. After the New Kingdom, the kings were mostly foreign by birth, even when their culture could be Egyptian, but we see that the Egyptian traditions were not neglected, and that they even became increasingly important at this time. Claus Jurman has described the tension between tradition and changing circumstances in

33 *E.g.* A. J. Abubakr, Untersuchungen über die ägyptischen Kronen, Glückstadt/Hamburg/New York 1937, still the only monograph on the subject, assumes the crowns' existence as realia and speculates on their possible materials; P. Dils, La couronne d'Arsinoe II Philadelphe, in: W. Clarysse/A. Schoors/H. Willems (eds.), Egyptian Religion. The Last Thousand Years. Part II. Studies dedicated to the memory of Jan Quaegebeur, OLA 85, Leuven 1998, 1299–1330, also accepts a possible physical reality behind the crowns.

34 K. Goebs, Crown (Egypt), in: Iconography of Deities and Demons: Electronic Prepublication 2015, at http://www.religionswissenschaft.uzh.ch/idd/. Accessed on 14.04.2015, sees the crowns as largely symbolic, the reality of which may well have been much different.

35 H. Carter/A. C. Mace, The Tomb of Tut-Ankh-Amen discovered by the late Earl of Carnarvon and Howard Carter, Volume 1, London 1923, 187 still wrote expectantly: "With the mummy ... there should certainly lie the crowns and other regalia of a king of Egypt." Goebs, Crown (Egypt), in: Iconography of Deities and Demons: Electronic Prepublication 2015, 25/30, refers to the virtual absence of surviving royal headdresses as "one of the great puzzles of Egyptology today".

36 G. Hölbl, Altägypten im Römischen Reich. Der römische Pharao und seine Tempel I: Römische Politik und altägyptische Ideologie von Augustus bis Diocletian, Tempelbau in Oberägypten, Mainz am Rhein 2000, 23–24, 116–117.

37 M. Reddé, Douch IV, Le trésor. Inventaire des objets et essai d'interprétation, DFIFAO 28, Cairo 1992, 38–52, especially fig. 92.

relation to images of king Apries as follows: "One might ponder whether a pharaoh reigning during the 6th century BC did indeed occasionally clad himself in archaic ceremonial garments and participated in ritual performances that had been conceived millennia ago while figuring at the same time as the leader of a major power in the Eastern Mediterranean world. (...) Had pharaonic identity become nothing but a stage role that was propped upon the man on the throne in order to meet the demands of preformed religious texts and imagery?"[38] It is noticeable that we have no images of the Late Period kings, notably the Saite kings, dressed in a more contemporary fashion, but neither do they show continuation of the use of elaborate and colourful textiles for the king. This does of course not mean that such garments did not exist.

I would like to take another approach to this problem. In the Late Period, kingship is subject to changes that relate to changes in the religion as a whole. Since the New Kingdom the gods acquire aspects of kingship, which are more than metaphorical.[39] Amun-Re took over the kingship at Thebes and even ruled by means of his oracles, and in his wake also other gods were increasingly portrayed with royal attributes. At the same time, the gods who were most intimately connected to the mythology of kingship, Osiris, Isis and Horus, became the most important gods of Egypt. Many other gods could be depicted with royal attributes, while conversely, the royal sphinx became the manifestation of a new popular deity: Tutu.[40]

As a consequence, items of the royal costume, attributes, and even mythology can be seen to appear in images of the gods of the Late Period. Examples are a kilt decorated with rosettes worn by a male divinity in the Kawa temple,[41] the divine name written in a cartouche, the royal throne flanked by lions that becomes used by several deities, and the emergence of the mammisi in which the old mythology of the royal birth came to be applied to several child gods.[42]

A particularly instructive example in the context we are concerned with here was excavated at Amheida in Dakhla Oasis a few years ago. It is a temple relief from the time of Amasis (Twenty-sixth Dynasty), depicting the god Seth spearing the serpent Apopis (Figs. 1–2).[43]

---

38 C. Jurman, The Trappings of Kingship: Remarks about Archaism, Rituals and Cultural Polyglossia in Saite Egypt, Aegyptus et Pannonia 4, 2010, 73–118; especially 88–89.

39 M. Römer, Gottes- und Priesterherrschaft in Ägypten am Ende des Neuen Reiches: Ein religionsgeschichtliches Phänomen und seine sozialen Grundlagen, ÄUAT 21, Wiesbaden 1994, 81–82; R. Gundlach, Das Königtum des Herihor: Zum Umbruch in der ägyptische Königsideologie am Beginn der 3. Zwischenzeit, in: M. Minas/J. Zeidler (eds.), Aspekte spätägyptischer Kultur. Festschrift für Erich Winter zum 65. Geburtstag, AegTrev 7, Mainz 1994, 133–138.

40 O. E. Kaper, The Egyptian God Tutu: A Study of the Sphinx-God and Master of Demons with a Corpus of Monuments, OLA 119, Leuven 2003, 59–60.

41 M. F. L. Macadam, The Temples of Kawa II: History and Archaeology of the Site, Part II: Plates, Oxford University Excavations in Nubia, London 1955, pl. XII(a); a different interpretation in T. Fahim/H. Bassir, Royal Clothing of the Twenty-Fifth Dynasty: Adaptations and Innovations, Cahiers Caribéens d'Egyptologie 23, 2018, 67–97, here: 93, fig. 25.

42 I can only refer to these aspects briefly here; a full discussion is to be presented elsewhere. Some items are never adopted into the divine iconography, such as the blue crown and the mekes sceptre.

43 R. S. Bagnall/N. Aravecchia/R. Cribiore/P. Davoli/O. E. Kaper/S. McFadden, An Oasis City, New York 2015, 49–50. The image resembles the slightly later image of Seth in the temple of Hibis, albeit without the *shendyt* kilt.

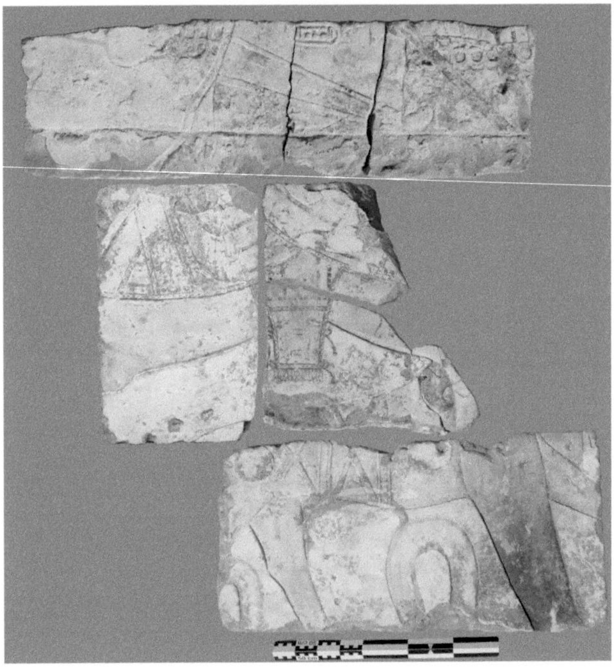

Fig. 1: Photographic reconstruction of the kilt of Seth
from the temple of Amasis at Amheida
(© NYU Excavations at Amheida, O. E. Kaper)

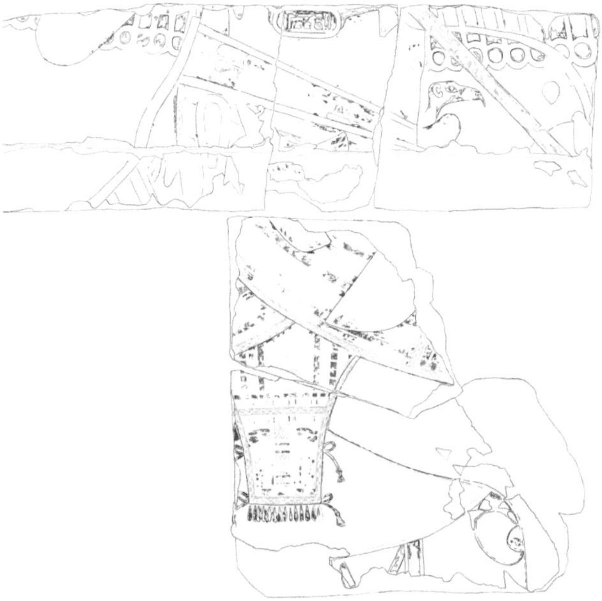

Fig. 2: Preliminary recording of the kilt of Seth in Fig. 1
(© NYU Excavations)

In this relief the god is completely dressed as a pharaoh, with two falcons spread across his torso, the so-called falcon vest; he wears the Double Crown on his head and a *shendyt* kilt. Next to him is a lion, just like the pharaoh would be assisted by a lion in his attack of foreign enemies.[44]

On the kilt, in raised relief, the wings and head of the vulture goddess Nekhbet are added as well as the winged cobra of Wadjet. At the same time, the central tapering panel of the *shendyt*, with its edges narrowing towards the bottom hem, is decorated with a row of drop shaped beads at the bottom and two sets of tasselled cords, which are attached on either side. Especially those additions show that the garment is not an abstraction or an imaginary costume of a deity, but rather the representation of an actual garment that bears a relation to reality. The two goddesses upon the kilt resemble the decorations on the Roman Period reliefs at Dendera, except for the head of Nekhbet, which appears to have been modelled in three dimensions and emerges from the top of the kilt in the Amasis relief.

Conclusions

By looking at the costume of male gods in the Late Period, which sometimes appear with royal attributes, it is possible to observe how the elaborate costume of the king during the New Kingdom developed further. The pharaohs had the privilege of wearing colourful and sophisticated clothing different from those of their subjects, made in a variety of techniques such as appliqué and embroidery. After the New Kingdom, these traditions disappear from view, because the images of the king were increasingly determined by decorum and archaism. Only in late Ptolemaic and Roman Period depictions in temples a continuity of this royal vestment tradition becomes visible again, with a new elaboration of kilt decorations with figurative elements in raised relief.

This paper has shown that there are arguments for a continuation of the royal costume tradition over the first millennium BC. The image of Seth from Amheida from the time of Amasis is dressed in an elaborate type of royal kilt, decorated with images of the goddesses Nekhbet and Wadjet in raised relief. This image provides an indication for an uninterrupted tradition between the New Kingdom and the Roman Period, even though the evidence is indirect because it is based on the adoption of royal attributes by the gods during the Late Period. It remains a matter for future discussion in what way this costume resembled items actually worn by the king in the Late Period.

44 C. De Wit, Le rôle et le sens du lion dans l'Égypte ancienne, Leiden 1951, 34–36.

Pianchy's Great Temple and his early war

Anthony Spalinger

Abstract
A re-investigation of the military scenes in the Great Temple of Pianchy at Gebel Barkal (B 500) has allowed us to reconstruct one, or more than one, early campaigns of his against Nubian locals. These pictorial representations in no way reflect his later great campaign of regnal year twenty. Yet they allow us to see his early warfare from a strategic Kushite-oriented perspective, one separate from Egypt.

1 Introduction

At the time of Pianchy's Great Stela (JE 48862), now standing in the Great Amun Temple B 500 at Gebel Barkal and dated to regnal year 21, the Kushite state was already ensconced in southern Egypt and had extended its control downstream.[1] Although it is impossible to define the precise degree of Kushite influence that was already in place under Kashta, his successor's lengthy narrative indicates that Pianchy's kingdom included a series of political satellites in Middle Egypt up to, but apparently not including – at least at the moment the narrative opens, Hermopolis. The earlier two decades of his rule are very difficult to analyse, especially now that the previously scholarly consensus in assigning the Sandstone Stela (the so-called Coronation Stela, Khartoum SNM 1851) to him has been decisively rejected (I prefer Kashta to be the original "owner" of this important written monument, but there is

1 St. Wenig, Pabatma – Pekereslo – Pekar-tror. Ein Beitrag zur Frühgeschichte der Kuschiten, in: D. Apelt/E. Endesfelder/St. Wenig (eds.), Studia in honorem Fritz Hintze, Meroitica 12, Berlin 1990, 333–352, especially 350. Yet how well developed was the Kushite army c. 750 BC? It was seasoned by many years of fighting north and south along the Nile for dominion over Nubia. But was the cavalry now more central to its operations? This was argued with some reservations by L. Török, Meroe. Six Studies on the Cultural Identity of an Ancient African State, StudAeg Budapest, Budapest 1995, 195–200.
See now the study by M. Buzon/S. T. Smith/A. Simonetti, Entanglement and the Formation of the Ancient Nubian Napatan State, in: AmAnthr 118, 2016, 284–300; L. Török, The Periods of Kushite History from the Tenth Century BC to the AD Fourth Century, StudAeg Budapest, supplements 1, Budapest 2015, 22–24, and with his recent study: L. Török, Nubians move from the margins to the center of their history, in: P. Steiner/A. Tsakos/E. H. Seland (eds.), From the Fjords to the Nile. Essays in honor of Richard Holton Pierce on his 80th birthday, Oxford 2018, 1–18. See also K. Howley, Sudanic Statecraft? Political Organization in the Early Napatan Period, in: Journal of Ancient Egyptian Interconnections 7, 2015, 30–41 – she differs with Török.

no final proof for this assertion).[2] Earlier, as Stuart Tyson SMITH has shown, the expansion of Kushite power northwards to Tombos had been dependent upon military power.[3] That interpretation also has been opined by Steffen WENIG, who placed great emphasis upon the *Machtpolitik* of the earlier rulers of the small Upper Nubian state with its capital at Napata.[4]

We possess a series of military reliefs from the Great Temple at Gebel Barkal, all of which contains pictorial accounts of Pianchy's early activities upstream from Egypt.[5] These depictions were first brought to the attention of scholars in the late 1970s and have, predictably, led to varying interpretations.

I originally felt that a good argument could be made for dating them to an unknown Egyptian-Neo-Assyrian conflict. That early assumption was based upon the enemy's Assyrian style conical helmets, most definitely made of leather or some other soft material and not of metal. Moreover, the placement of these scenes on the inner walls of Hall B 501 was parallel in location to the others in Hall 502, constructed later by Pianchy. Hence, it seems reasonable to date the war scenes in B 501 to his twentieth year or later, the time of the great campaign. This is what Donald REDFORD maintained, following my original hypothesis. Only Lázló TÖRÖK demurred without, however, offering a different historical reconstruction.[6]

At that time I had set aside a difficulty with this interpretation. The evidence from Neo-Assyria did not support an early conflict between Egypt/Kush and Neo-Assyrian *c.* 730 BC. The chronologies of Tiglath-Pileser III and his short-reigned successor Shalmaneser V did not dovetail with Pianchy's, notwithstanding the absence of any written evidence of such warfare. My recent re-evaluations of temple B 500, now in press, go decidedly against the possibility of an encounter.[7]

2 All of our previous suppositions on this matter have been revised by a presentation on 9 September 2016 in Prague by A. LOHWASSER, Deconstructing early Kushite ideology: On the unknown king of the so-called coronation stela of Pi(ankh)y, in: P. ONDERKA (ed.), Proceedings of the 12th International Conference for Meroitic Studies 2016, Prague, forthcoming. For our purposes the significant conclusion is that the Sandstone Stela of Pianchy has nothing to do with an early war of the king against the Libyans or Egyptians in Egypt, as K.-H. PRIESE, Der Beginn der kuschitischen Herrschaft in Ägypten, in: ZÄS 98, 1972, 16–32, among others, had thought.

3 See M. BUZON/S. T. SMITH/A. SIMONETTI, Entanglement; but add S. T. SMITH, Death at Tombos: Pyramids, Iron and the Rise of the Napatan Dynasty, in: Sudan & Nubia 11, 2007, 2–14. Most recently there is the significant overview of S. A. SCHRADER/S. T. SMITH /S. OLSEN/M. BUZON, Symbolic equids and Kushite state formation: a horse burial at Tombos, in: Antiquity 92, 2018, 383–397.

4 WENIG, Pabatma – Pekereslo – Pekar-tror, 350.

5 These scenes are discussed in A. SPALINGER, The Persistence of Memory in Kush: Pianchy and his Temple, in: P. ONDERKA (ed.), Proceedings of the 12th International Conference for Meroitic Studies 2016, Prague, forthcoming, and in my earlier study, A. SPALINGER, Notes on the Military in Egypt During the XXVth Dynasty, JSSEA 11, 1981, 37–58. I have revised some of my historical considerations in the recent full-length volume.

6 D. REDFORD, From Slave to Pharaoh: The Black Experience of Ancient Egypt, Baltimore/London 2004, 190, note 2, and D. REDFORD, Egypt, Canaan, and Israel in Ancient Times, Princeton 1992, 348. See as well L. TÖRÖK, The Image of the Ordered World in Ancient Nubian Art. The Construction of the Kushite Mind (800 BC–300 AD), PÄ 18, Leiden/Boston/Cologne 2002, 55–65. Pages 55–69 cover Halls B 501, B 502, and B 503. Elaboration to L. TÖRÖK's excellent study has been supplied by the detailed archaeological analysis of H. WILSON, Construction Sequences of B 502 Gebel Barkal, unpublished manuscript, University of Auckland. I shall cover her research in Part 2 of this study.

7 SPALINGER, The Persistence of Memory in Kush. Chapters 1 ("Introduction") and 2 ("Enemies in the Reliefs"), in press.

Before proceeding, let me summarise the up-to-date, still unpublished, research of Heather WILSON, who, as part of her PhD Thesis and her work with Timothy KENDALL at Gebel Barkal, established a "construction sequence for Halls B 501 and 502."[8] She recorded the archaeological setting for Pianchy's war reliefs. I should note, as well, that the submission scenes in B 501 relate to his great campaign and cannot be combined with earlier military depictions. The latter ignore his battles in favour of a triumphal reception of the kneeling leaders of Middle Egypt and the Delta.[9] Thus B 501, or at least a portion of the narrative decoration, must be placed later than regnal year twenty. In no way can the carved accounts of B 501 be linked historically to any in B 502. The latter was constructed earlier and then it was adorned. Subsequently, its outer facing pylon was converted into the two rear walls of the next hall, B 501.

2 Construction Sequence of B 503 and 502[10]

B 502 was added to an existing temple at Gebel Barkal later date than the original (the earlier Egyptian temple was constructed of talatat whereas the new addition was not. Its dating is not discussed here). One can divide the hall into left, centre, and right portions, or, following WILSON and others, into corridors: west, central, and east. All of my directions will simply refer to an individual facing the first doorway of B 500. George Andrew REISNER's excavations reports introduced confusion along local, geographic, magnetic, and his personal north, south, east, and west.[11] After him, even the column locations needed re-editing, as WILSON has done, assigning them to her sequence 2. I prefer to follow the easiest solution. All of my direction will be as simple as they are clear one that avoids REISNER's "east" and east (and so forth: local, geographic), as well as the magnetic east, etc.[12] Even the column locations need re-editing, as WILSON has done, assigning them to her sequence 2. TÖRÖK's

8 Reference to WILSON's work is made in the acknowledgments. She also wrote a brief study of two stone features that are still surviving within B 500. Here as well I am dependent upon the work of WILSON. The two stone features are from both the Napatan and the Meroitic periods of the temple. One can add the overview of T. KENDALL/E. H. A. MOHAMED, A Visitor's Guide to The Jebel Barkal Temples, Khartoum 2016, 53–63.

9 I provided a study of Pianchy's northern (Egyptian) war in A. SPALINGER, Pianchy/Piye. Between Two Worlds, in: C. KARLSHAUSEN/C. OBSOMER (eds.), De la Nubia à Qadesh. La guerre dans l'ancienne Égypte/From Nubia to Kadesh. War in Ancient Egypt, Brussels 2016, 235–274. For an earlier detailed analysis, see TÖRÖK, Image of the Ordered World, 376–395. J. POPE, The Double Kingdom under Taharqo. Studies in the History of Kush and Egypt, c. 690–664 BC, Culture and History of the Ancient Near East 69, Leiden/Boston 2014, 258–261, ably covers early Kushite moves into Egypt.

10 The material presented is dependent solely upon WILSON's unpublished work.

11 See D. DUNHAM, The Barkal Temples. Excavated by George Andrew Reisner, Boston 1970, xix. On pages 3–4 he expressed himself clearly, and with a slight degree of frustration, concerning REISNER's designations.

12 Here are my comments from SPALINGER, The Persistence of Memory in Kush, Chapter 1 ("Introduction"), in press. "To be more specific: Local South (LS) is at the rear of the Great Temple whereas, logically, Local North (LN) is situated at the first gateway or entrance. Local West (LW) is therefore in the direction of the river while Local East (LE) faces the Gebel. Magnetic North (MN) is situated to the left, roughly halfway from the perpendicular; *i.e.*, at an obtuse angle. Magnetic South (MS) is thus easy to find. Magnetic East (ME) is thereby situated to the right, again approximately halfway between LS and LW. Magnetic West (MW) is similarly found by carrying down the vector to the left. In fine, the rear of the temple is upstream (U) and its entrance downstream (D) with the left and right directions indicated respectively by G for Gebel and R for River."

remarkable discussion of these pillars has thereby been improved and updated.[13]

There were four construction phases of B 502 (1–4), the lowest being sequence 1. In summary, WILSON provided this analysis:[14]

1. The early talatat path/floor.
2. Fifty-four large columns with their bases associated with the new floor.
3. Second alignment of columns, of which eighteen were retained from sequence 2. The floor of sequence 2 was not modified.
4. Kiosk and refurbished floor, attributed to Tanwetamani.

All the drums of the white sandstone columns of sequence 2 were of the same dimensions. Any present differences are minimal and can be attributed, if not to the reconfiguration of the hall, then to later damage and erosion. The talatat floor blocks of sequence 1 were laid "almost directly" upon the sub-soil with only a shallow cushion of broken stones underneath to establish regularity and firmness.

For the first time there is a C14 date for Hall 502 (see Figs. 1 and 3).[15] The sample, taken from the right (eastern) edge of the talatat floor, consisted of a damaged, reused block, on the underside of which were traces of plaster, as well as pock marks that would have held plaster. The date obtained was 740 +/- 25 BC (2690 BP), late in the reign of Kashta or early in that of Pianchy. The stratigraphic layer was secure, with no underlining fill which could have been contaminated by charcoal of a later period. Accordingly, the earlier temple, with its latest addition of B 503, was definitely Ramesside. Thereafter must have come decay that would eventually have been addressed by the local rulers, the kings of Kush.

The outer (exterior) wall of Pylon III became the inner rear wall of Hall B 502. The inner construction of Pylon II was formed from loosely packed rubble with a neat and regular outer casing. The east wall of Hall B 503 had a ledge at the bottom underneath a regular (vertical) course of blocks, all placed in a horizontal manner. The west side of B 502 had an identical bottom edge.

In his diary REISNER more than once surmised that Hall B 503 was constructed with mud brick walls and a talatat floor.[16] Then the building was renovated with large block walls and the sequence 2 columns and their bases. This hypothesis must be discarded:

---

13 TÖRÖK, Image of the Ordered World, 58–65. He was partly dependent upon DUNHAM, The Barkal Temples, 55. I revised their analysis in SPALINGER, The Persistence of Memory in Kush, Chapter 1 ("Introduction"), in press. But WILSON, Construction Sequences of B 502 Gebel Barkal, 51–93, and especially pages 84–93 for "Sequence 2," has progressed considerably beyond my textual and architectural analysis.
I observed that DUNHAM placed column A in row VIII whereas TÖRÖK places it in row VII. Similarly, column H was in DUNHAM's row X whereas it is in TÖRÖK's row IX. See DUNHAM, The Barkal Temples, 55 and TÖRÖK, Image of the Ordered World, Plate II. There are errors in TÖRÖK's setup, however. DUNHAM's original location of column D, "fourth from north row II," is not the third from the north, row II.

14 WILSON, Construction Sequences of B 502 Gebel Barkal, 6.

15 WILSON, Construction Sequences of B 502 Gebel Barkal, 22–26. I must thank the Research Committee, Faculty of Arts, University of Auckland, for providing me the financial support for the calibration of this sample.

16 Also in this respect, I am still dependent upon WILSON's own research. She covered all the material in Reisner's diary at the Boston Museum of Fine Arts.

1. The mud brick evidence examined by Reisner was in an area that had been heavily disturbed during sequence 2 construction.
2. The 2012–2013 excavation encountered some of this mud brick (and mortar) belonging to deliberately placed fill sur-rounding the column bases of the same sequence.
3. The secure C14 date under the talatat floor post-dates the Ramesside construction.

Sequence 1 employed reused talatat blocks, none of which can be directly related to the Amarna Period. They appear to have been composed of local sandstone, but they may have been reused. Wilson argued that this floor or path was not designed specifically for B 503. They form the first (sub-)feature of Hall B 502. There was no evidence of the walls being sheathed, the inscriptions being recurved and overlaying an earlier king's reliefs. The floor itself seems to have used blocks already fashioned, and they were probably brought from elsewhere.

Sequence 2 refers to the initial building of Hall B 502.[17] The original temple at Gebel Barkal was composed of small talatat blocks which are self-evident in the original exterior wall of Pylon I. B 502 was first dominated by its large columns. They were arranged in groups of nine on either side of the central corridor, with a further two rows flanking the right and left sides of the hall. Reisner's discovery of four "old" sequence 2 column bases, helped with our reconstruction. He set up a configuration encompassing seventy-two columns. Present research delineates a combination of features: a peristyle court, an open courtyard, southern (rear) areas surrounded by a shaded walkway supported by pillars, and a hypostyle in the rear where there were three rows of three columns on both sides of the central walkway.

Probably during sequence 2 the exterior of the old talatat Pylon III was re-clad in large blocks. Extensions were made to the left and right (west and east) sides of that pylon to accommodate the new addition of B 502. Pianchy's temple (and B 502 in particular) was the first major work of Kushite architecture. More traditional and largely irregular sized sandstone blocks were used. According to Wilson the modification was radical, and it reflected "a complete change in the temple's political direction (see Fig. 2)."[18] Major innovations – the expansion, the fresh building materials, and the massive columns on bases – all point to the new outlook of the indigenous kingship.

With regard to the floor of sequence 2, Reisner's interpretations seem to hold; namely, that the column bases were installed as soon as the floor was laid. The deposition of the floor can be identified because two *in situ* blocks are of the same size and level as the capping layer, Wilson's WCB10 and WCB 11, which certainly belonged to sequence 2.[19] Finally, the mortar and plaster found in B 502 are representative of the Kushite reconstruction and additions to the Great Temple. The differences between the earlier (pre-B 502) and the later plaster are significant.

In the hypostyle area to the rear (north) there were originally fifty-six columns. They were decorated with abaci, which were later reused (see Figs. 4 and 9). The two major excavations failing to find large stone beams, concluded that the roof had been made of wood rather than stone and had degraded over time.[20]

17 Wilson, Construction Sequences of B 502 Gebel Barkal, 40.

18 Wilson, Construction Sequences of B 502 Gebel Barkal, 47.

19 Wilson, Construction Sequences of B 502 Gebel Barkal, 51, 54, 59, 67, and 76.

20 But there are difficulties with the date of the roof. As Angelika Lohwasser indicated to me, the original plan for B 502 was that of an open area hall, one that was later transformed into a hypostyle hall.

All of the first column alignments in B 502 had been completed, and not abandoned partly through the construction. Moreover, the levels and types of fill indicate that B 502 was finished and functioned as an outer hall to the refurbished B 500. Therefore, its purpose was well-established before its reliefs were designed on papyri, approved, if not begun to be carved.

By sequence 3 the present architectural layout becomes apparent.[21] It began with demolition of the original column alignment followed by a new arrangement (Figs. 5–6). This significant alteration opens the issue of dating the wall reliefs. Except for the bases of the columns of sequence 2, a new arrangement of twenty-eight columns was erected in which the central aisle bifurcated two sets, right and left, each having two columns apiece. Seven rows were set up leaving the rear of Hall B 502 alone. There, the original three columns per side were left intact. According to WILSON "this re-configuration was carried out relatively soon after the initial building of the hall by Pianchy."[22] No specific historical cause can be presently argued. The older method of employing large solid bases for the columns was now altered to a "hastily" erected order utilizing some of the pre-existing stone features of sequence 2 with, however, unsupported alignments.

The span of the roof must have been increased by this reconstruction even though the covering probably did not envelope the entire hall. The unsupported columns of sequence 3 ought to have provided the substructure of a wooden roof. The new columns had bronze sheathing, first recognised by REISNER. Gebel or mud filling had to have been used as column support for this second stage arrangement because the new columns straddled the space between the older two and were placed directly on the floor. In addition, the columns directly flanking the central corridor were erected in this way. Incidentally, the demolition layer can be distinctly observed. Of equal importance, the level of the hall was raised. The talatat floor level was definitely lower than the new floor created during the third sequence. Elevation is distinct towards B 503.

Yet the entire new columnar set up was poorly constructed. The reworking was hasty, and oriented to the central and front (southern) area of B 502. Was clearance being done to make room for Tanwetamani's kiosk, which belongs to sequence 4? But there is a definite temporal gap between these modifications and the future edifice (Figs. 7–8).

WILSON also points out that the raising of the floor of Hall B 502 was to avoid flooding. Bronze sheathing placed around the lower drums of the columns is, perhaps, one of the most distinctive elements in this new reconstruction. It allows us to separate those columns of the preceding sequence 2 from the following sequence. Yet the internal architectural layout still retained the peristyle arrangement in the rear or south. The entire hall was now more effectively covered and the central corridor is smaller: c. 7.2m in width instead of the earlier c. 12.7m.

The progress with the modifications within the hall was relatively rapid. The archaeological debris from the demolition of sequence 2 was predominately pristine. The shards are still sharp and undisturbed. However, as WILSON points out, because no C14 dates could be obtained from this level, this evidence is subjective.

---

21 WILSON, Construction Sequences of B 502 Gebel Barkal, 95–134.

22 WILSON, Construction Sequences of B 502 Gebel Barkal, 97.

Given that Pianchy later extended his Great Temple further by completing and decorating Hall B 501, it would have been up to his successors to revamp B 502.[23] The Tanwetamani kiosk was built separately and thus after sequence 3.[24]

Based upon reliefs in B 501 we can date the building to Pianchy's major northern campaign if not earlier. There are no depictions of warfare in this hall. Only the submission of the king's opponents can be connected to Pianchy's Egyptian military actions. Hence, the decorative program in B 501 had already begun when he went north to Thebes in his twentieth regnal year. Hall B 501 must have been planned and in progress by then.

3 War Scenes of B 502[25]

Pianchy's military reliefs are located at the front of B 502. Cultic reliefs in B 502 are located at the back, thereby indicating the design was conceived to be close to the sanctuary of the temple deity, Amun of Napata. This dichotomy between religious and secular is not surprising. The representations are arranged in this manner:[26]

1. D1 and D2: horse representations. Inner right side, front.
2. E1 and E2: major battle and possible triumph depictions.
   Inner left and right side of Pylon II.
3. Destroyed portions of the front area of the inner left side.
   Here, one can argue for symmetry with D1–D3.

Two side entrances break the two side walls not quite evenly. Of D1, on the southern right side of the forecourt, nothing remains except horse legs and a man (pharaoh?) who faces to the rear. The depiction is not overly martial, but it may commemorate a departure to war. Some may feel that this scene depicts reverence to Amun, but I disagree because the placement is not appropriate.

D2 carries the action forward and therefore may be connected to E1 if not E2. The two horses of D2 imply a chariot, now gone. I believe that it may have been carved in the missing portion between D1 and D2. A groom stands in front of the animals. The space between him and the right front corner of Hall B 502 is very small. Nothing else could have been added. An outwardly directed representation of war preparations logically could have belonged there.[27]

It is scene E1 which helps us to analyse the purport of these reliefs.[28] Again, the flow of action is to the centre. Fine horses trot to the entrance way from the south-eastern tower of

23 Török, Image of the Ordered World, 65–69; and Wilson, Construction Sequences of B 502 Gebel Barkal.

24 Wilson, Construction Sequences of B 502 Gebel Barkal, 6, 14–15, 19, 42, 58, 83, 96, 99, 112, 114–116, 122, 125, 129, and 134.

25 See Spalinger, The Persistence of Memory in Kush, Chapters 2 ("Enemies in the Reliefs") and 3 ("The Visual Record"), in press.

26 As I indicate in the acknowledgements, all of the photographs included in this chapter were taken by H. Wilson.

27 With regard to the "reading" of registers in the later temples of the Meroitic Kingdom, E. Winter, Untersuchungen zu den ägyptischen Tempelreliefs der griechisch-römischen Zeit, DÖAW 98, Vienna 1968, is useful for scholarly analysis. Yet Török pointed out the difficulty with respect to these Nubian temples in Török, Image of the Ordered World, 195–196, note 685.

28 I found Török, Sacred Landscape, Historical Identity and Memory: Aspects of Napatan and Meroitic Urban Architecture, in: T. Kendall (ed.), Nubian Studies 1998. Proceedings of the Ninth International Conference of the International Society of Nubian Studies, August 21–26, 1998, Boston 2004, 157–175,

Pylon II. There are no battle scenes. Pianchy is not extant but he may originally have been carved at the extreme right.[29]

Because I have already discussed these reliefs in detail in a separate publication, let me summarise here. Note as well the Kushite/Nubian iconography of altars and trussed bulls at the bottom in a narrow register, all for Amun,[30] and established for a victory celebration in this very temple. This is non-Egyptian in outlook, as is the "dangling young man." The only Egyptian environment is the water, presumably the Nile River.

The Egyptian method of narrative has been supplanted by a Kushite ideological interpretation of events. The scene presents a triumphal "return to home," as I have maintained, and thereby diverges considerably from the Egyptians outlook. Within the representations no Egyptian may be found. If one reads from bottom to top – a supposition that may not correctly represent the Kushite outlook – promenading horses separate three detailed pictorial registers.[31]

1. Altars and bulls: bottom. This small register can be interpreted as a static, repetitive base frieze. A thin horizontal line separates 1 from 2.
2. Horse procession. As with D1 and D3 no chariots are shown.
3. Water, perhaps the Nile. This second frieze is as narrow as the first. Another thin line separates 3 from 4.
4. Second horse procession. Details of the captured or killed enemies are clear. This scene parallels those in the so-called Sun Temple at Meroe,[32] but the

---

the best overall presentation of the overall structure of the structure of the reliefs in Nubian (Kushite-Napatan-Meroitic) temples in connection with a descriptive evaluation.

29 See note 33 below for an additional reference to a second, indeed closer, parallel from Beg. N 19. This icon is a key piece of evidence in my analysis in Spalinger, The Persistence of Memory in Kush, Chapter 3 ("The Visual Record"), in press. One important parallel to it is that of the prisoner whom Apedemak offers to the king: F. Hintze/U. Hintze/K.-H. Priese, Musawwarat es Sufra I.2. Der Löwentempel. Tafelband, Berlin 1971, Plates 17 and 25 (outer west front, southern half).
I remarked in my forthcoming study, "He is a young Nubian, alive and manacled somewhat, but dangling, or at least held off the ground. His two hands, caught in a wooden device, are not quite bound together even though they are prevented from moving much at all. He is controlled by a scissor-shaped wooden constraint with an uraeus on its top and an open end. Moreover, the prisoner is being offered by Apedemak to the king and not vice-versa. The captive does not seem to be a seasoned war veteran. In scene E1 the young man is definitely held off the ground."

30 Note as well the study of bull and cow offerings, among other items, in C. Rilly, Les inscriptions d'offrandes funéraires. Une première clé vers la comprehension du méroïtique, in: RdE 54, 2003, 167–175.

31 In addition to my earlier comments on these scenes in Spalinger, The Persistence of Memory in Kush, in press; add Török, Image of the Ordered World, 54–70; and T. Kendall, Gebel Barkal Epigraphic Survey: 1986 Preliminary Report of First Season's Activity: Observing the Cliff Inscription and Bridge Replacement, and Recovering the Piye Reliefs in the Great Amun Temple, Boston 1986.

32 Some time ago M. Zach/H. Tomandl, Bemerkungen zu den Amunheiligtümern im Süden des meroitischen Reiches, in: BzS 7, 2000, 129–158, here: 132, stressed the fact that the oldest and most important Amun cult at Meroe is temple M 250.
For the important reliefs at the so-called Sun Temple, we now have the definitive edition of F. W. Hinkel, Der Tempelkomplex Meroe 250. Mit Beiträgen von B. Dominicus, J. Hallof, The Archaeological Map of the Sudan, Supplement 1, 2, Berlin 2001. For the boats (I.2b), C 10 (113 shows the head of the ram of Amun); and B. Dominicus in the same work, (I.1), 176–178. The more over-arching study remains that

"dangling man" belongs to an image in the Lion Temple at Musawwarat es-Sufra, wherein the god presents the king with the same figure. Even closer is the representation of Arkeniwal wherein the king holds the young male enemies off the ground.[33]A thin line separates 4 from 5.

5. Third horse procession. No men are evident, but the picture is fragmentary.

The attention paid to the royal horses is an immediate clue to the totally Kushite interpretation pf these grandiose scenes of the triumphal march home. Other images that are at odds with Egyptian attitudes involve the king. Piancy is not there *in media res*. He remains outside of his army's success. Moreover, neither he nor his soldiers seem to do much fighting. The dead and captive enemies are relegated to the read of the third register. We are faced with a rather static procession that appears to reveal an official triumph.

The centre aisle of B 500 is the vantage point that straightforwardly reveals the import of the entire scene. The god is assumed to be at the centre. The pictorial account of the war's results, superbly rendered by a triumphal military procession, concludes at the roofed alley, the core pathway to the cultic rear of B 500.

To "read" this section of the inner pylon is somewhat problematical. If the break between registers four and six is minor, then we should be able to connect them and to interpret them together. A more serious issue exists as we confront all of them. If we are "à l'égyptien", then, as I have remarked above, then the narrative would have begun at the lowest register. Can we make this assumption?

In the bottom, first, register the horses are returning in pairs, lead, as well as shown in the fifth register, by a groom in what can only be a return home. The parade is the final act of some bellicose activity. The altars represent the setting: Amun's temple at Gebel Barkal. (NB: in Piancy's Great Stela the return narrative ended in Thebes.)

There is no overt demarcation between the second register and the third, the waterway, which may refer to the arrival at Thebes and perhaps indicates the triumphant army's entrance into Karnak. Alternatively, and I follow this interpretation, it could be interpreted as the successful army's advance inwards from the quay at Napata, reminiscent of Kamose's arrival at Thebes as recorded on his second Victory Stela. The altars would therefore stand schematically for temple B 500, and the upper level ships would represent the return of Piancy's flotilla to his capital. At any rate, the last image illustrates the nature of the Kushite army. Like the earlier Egyptian military, Piancy's army was marine based because the Nile

---

of L. Török, Archaism and Innovation in 1st Century BC Meroitic Art: Meroe Temple M 250 Revisited, in: Azania 39, 2004, 203–224. Earlier, see Török, Image of the Ordered World, 210–225.

33 See note 29 above.
The location is on the left outside wall of the pylon of Beg. N 19 at Begrawiah: K.-R. Lepsius, Denkmaeler aus Aegypten und Aethiopien V, Berlin 1849–1859, Pl. 49 = Beg. A 31. I thank Olaf Kaper for showing me this scene during the conference in which this chapter was presented. Kendall, Gebel Barkal Epigraphic Survey: 1986, fig. 9, probably followed this paradigm. The depiction is a smiting scene, but in B 502 it is carved on the *inside* of the pylon whereas this parallel is on the outside.
The important depiction has also been reproduced in S. Chapman/D. Dunham, Decorated Chapels of the Meroitic Pyramids at Meroe and Barkal, The Royal Cemeteries of Kush III, Boston 1952, 4 with Pl. 22 C (cf. also Pl. 32 D). Add D. Dunham, Royal Tombs at Meroë and Barkal, Boston 1957, 175; and P. Lenoble, Le rang des inhumés sous tertre à enceinte à El Hobagi, in: Meroitic Newsletter 25, 1994, 89–124, here: 98.

localities were its stomping grounds. In the Kushite case the land-based sector of the military also included horses, not to mention chariots, as we shall see in E2.

The differences between the chariotry and the infantry are not delineated here.[34] Furthermore, Piancy never subdivides the latter into archers and foot soldiers, not to mention runners and other specialists. E1, D1, and D 2 showcase his horses, as does his Great Stela. E1 stands as an embodiment of the Kushite mentality. All of the registers belong together. Finally, there is no historical development as we see in the New Kingdom snapshots of war. The difficulty for us is determining the timing of the event – whether it is to be separated from the accompanying picture to the left on wall E2.

Török discovered divisions between the left and right sides of Kushite, Napatan, and Meroitic temples.[35] The geographic centre of both areas was different. In the case of B 500, the left side seemed to correspond to "north" and the right to "south." If so, then we should view both sides as a whole. Nevertheless, with regard to B 502 his argument can be questioned. E2 on the left depicts conflict whereas E1, on the right, displays the homecoming. Therefore I tend to associate the scenes on the respective inner walls of Pylon II with the same campaign, each side a tableau. This supposition, however, may be queried.

E1 is an idealised culmination spectacle, one that does not quite enter the cultic arena. With E2 the direction is again to the centre of the temple, and there are only two registers present, with the same thin dividing line used in E1. The inner left wall perpendicular to it is destroyed. Nevertheless, I strongly feel that it must have been linked to E2 just as D1 and D2 appear to connect to E1.

The method of depiction in E2 is identical to that in E1. Both do not draw upon the earlier pharaonic interpretative modes. In a previous, longer study of the war scenes in Piancy's Great Temple, I discussed the Kushite motif of combat between a single warrior and his opponent. Art reveals an aspect of cultural values.

The Kushite-Egyptian patterns can be schematically listed:[36]

Egyptian	*Kushite*
1. King fighting.	1. King not at battle.
2. King in chariot as hero.	2. King absent, hence not a *Feldherr*
3. Embattled chariots and infantry.	3. Individual engagements.
4. Sequential segments: departure, combat, return.	4. Panoramas and processions, often depicting triumphs
5. Processions to centre except on side walls.	5. Progress is to the centre.

34 I have covered this in detail in Spalinger, The Persistence of Memory in Kush, passim, and especially in Chapter 7 ("War in the Royal Narrative Inscriptions"), in press.

35 In general, see L. Török, Space, temple and society. On the built worldview of the Twenty-Fifth Dynasty in Nubia, in: I. Caneva/A. Roccati (eds.), Acta Nubica. Proceedings of the X International Conference of Nubian Studies, Rome 9–14 September 2002, Rome 2006, 231–238. There is a summary on pages 233–234, which he expanded in Török, Image of the Ordered World, 55–65; Török disagrees with Kendall's concept of an overt wish to follow Egypt's imperial past. I also observed Priese's more gradualist argument that the Kushites (Napatans in the vocabulary of Török and Priese) tended to lose their "Egyptianness" over time.

36 Here, I am restating my analyses in A. Spalinger, Icons of Power. A Strategy of Interpretation, Prague 2011.

These salient points describe the Kushite way of interpreting warfare. From New Kingdom Egypt was derived the impetus to emblazon the walls of a temple with war motifs; but beyond the medium there was a fresh approach, initiated by Pianchy and continued at Napata and Meroe. E2 separated chariotry, infantry, and perhaps cavalry. The absence of a mass of enemies is striking to anyone expecting a resemblance to New Kingdom war scenes. Likewise, no clash between chariot-driven opponents is present.

Nevertheless, the readings of the two extant registers in E2 can be combined to produce the following narrative outlook:

1. Battlefield melee involves the chariots although without strategy.
2. One-on-one iconography is featured.
3. There is no movement of any troops; all is static.
4. The denouement belongs to the infantry, one Kushite soldier versus one enemy.

If we examine these scenes, it appears that the design and use of spears and bows and arrows did not significantly change from second millennium BC Egypt to first millennium Kush. But other weapons and defence accoutrements diverged from those employed during the New Kingdom. As was recognised decades ago, the round shields are the most obvious example of a discontinuity – if that may be the correct word.

But the conical helmets (or encased caps) are the most important innovation. This means of head protection is not known from Egypt or the Near East. It did not originate in the Nile Delta or in Ionia. Quite to the contrary, such headgear is Nubian, even if we cannot yet confirm a southern locality. It is the key to the entire historical interpretation of the military scenes carved on the walls of Hall B 502.

We can now eliminate any Assyrian connection. The foes of Pianchy are Nilotic in appearance, especially in their beardless faces.

Similarly, they are not Egyptians or Libyans. The conical helmets absolutely rule out this possibility. Moreover, observe the absence of feathers in the hair (for the Libyans, a point stressed very early by Karl-Heinz Priese),[37] while there are chevrons on the chest of one warrior.[38] Although the chariots with six spokes per wheel could equally argue for Egyptian manufacture, the round shields, known from Pianchy's Great Stela, direct us to Kushites. Ultimately, the date of the reliefs provides the conclusive evidence.

Wilson's archaeological research establishes that Hall B 502 was constructed very early in the reign of Pianchy. For this reason, notwithstanding the timing of the decoration, I view the depicted events as having occurred during the monarch's early years, if not his first or second. The physical setting is poorly represented in the carving: there is no fortress, citadel, city, or urban centre. E2 presents a neutral background virtually devoid of extant environment save for one rather pathetic overgrown shrub, or better a small tree. Pictorially, nothing justifies the assumption that Pianchy was fighting in Egypt or against Egyptians.

---

37 Priese, ZÄS 98, 1972, 16–32.

38 If one argues that the man is an enemy, then why the prominent position on the horse? It appears better to consider him to be in the Kushite army. Indeed, the one-on-one (friend defeating enemy) arrangement of the triumphal scene indicates that the rider is a Kushite.

From Napatan historical sources and from Tanwetamani's Dream Stela, it is apparent that the southern rulers frequently spent their first year on warfare.[39] A conflict is often predicated to have begun just before the king has taken the throne. The timing should be no surprise. Thutmose I, II, Thutmose III (after the death of Hatshepsut), Amunhotep II (as coregent in his third regnal year), Seti I, and Ramesses II all faced the same situation. The liminal phase encompassing the death of a monarch and the accession of an untested beginner threatened stability, whereupon an immediate show of force presented a successful image. Such, I feel, was the case here. We may not have sufficient material for a statistically precise conclusion (neither do we for Egypt); nevertheless, in Kush and Napata, an opening year war was frequent enough. Whatever the date of this conflict, it is evident that the war scenes in B 502 are definitely not to be connected to Pianchy's major campaign in his twentieth regnal year.

4 Dating the Narrative Warfare in B 502 and B 501

The historically pictorial evidence of Pianchy's extension of the Great Temple is relatively meagre. Only scene F, on the left inner front wall of Hall B 501, can be specifically linked to his warfare in year twenty.[40] Here, it is somewhat surprising that only one portion of the available space has been used for that campaign, and no military action has been specified. To the contrary, the Kushite monarch overtly, strongly, and impressively presented the submission of his opponents. I have called this the "Athribis Scene" as it can only refer to Pianchy's resolution of his northern invasions and resolution of the contested issues of Hermopolis and Middle Egypt. He had already taken Memphis and then attempted to set up a political machine in the far north, including parts of the Delta. In Pianchy's written account, he also made Tefnacht of Sais a dependent, even though in reality terms this was never the case.

The absence of a battle from the program of B 501 is less than satisfying. If we consider all of the other scenes in B 501, and exclude, of course, the outer walls of B 502 (C1 and C2), everything than remains is religious or cultic in nature. This evidence led me to conclude that a major portion of the inner wall surfaces in B 501 had already received decoration before the Great War took place. Indeed, observe the fact that scene F, the significant depiction of the capitulation of Pianchy's foes, was inserted into the area at the front of the side entrance on the left. The corresponding segment I is cultic-religious. For the sake of argument, let me avoid discussing the possible *heb sed* representations, although I must stress that no convincing argument for its occurring in the king's thirtieth regnal year can be proposed. This speculation must remain moot.[41]

39 Cairo JE 48863. See now M. ZACH, The Army and Military Dictatorship in Meroe?, in: J. R. ANDERSON/ D. A. WELSBY (eds.), The Fourth Cataract and Beyond. Proceedings of the 12th International Conference for Nubian Studies, British Museum Publications on Egypt and Sudan 1, Leuven/Paris/Walpole, MA, 2014, 557–571. The situation is covered in SPALINGER, The Persistence of Memory in Kush, Chapters 6 ("Textual Analysis"), 7 ("War in the Royal Narrative Inscriptions"), and 8 ("Pictorial Analysis and the Temple Program"), in press.

40 SPALINGER, The Persistence of Memory in Kush, Chapter 9 ("Hall 501 and the Meaning of the Great Temple"), in press.

41 TÖRÖK, Image of the Ordered World, 59, 66, and 68; add T. KENDALL, The Origin of the Napatan State: El Kurru and the Evidence for the Royal Ancestors, in: St. WENIG (ed.), Studien zum antiken Sudan. Akten der 7. Internationalen Tagung für meroitistische Forschung vom. 14. bis 19. September 1992 in Gosen/bei Berlin, Meroitica 15, Wiesbaden 1999, 3–117, here: 75–76 and Fig. 20.

The outer face of Pylon II (C1 and C2) was, as might be expected if we adhere to an Egyptological viewpoint, traditional. At the bottom one can still make out the carvings of the foreign captives, with their hands tied behind the back, above the names of their respective countries. The designations of the enemies of Kush are also standard, albeit not exactly parallel to New Kingdom examples. On both sides, two flagpole recesses serve as divisions, on which the king is portrayed in a smiting pose.[42] He is in the centre, adjacent to the aisle of the temple. The king's legs and feet are planted at the bottom, there being no row of captives surrounding the crenelated walls of their lands. The same was so for C2, although the upper portions in which the king would have appeared are missing. All in all, the outer faces of the original first pylon in the Great Temple do not help us much in analysing historical events, especially since the upper sections of the building have been eroded and then lost.

The work on B 501 was probably begun sometime within Pianchy's second decade, whereas that for B 502 would have commenced earlier. Indeed, I think that the commitment to the plan for the earlier hall was made upon Pianchy's accession. Nevertheless, the extent of bank wall space available for the carving of his Nubian campaign or campaigns must have been tempting. Indeed, it could not have been otherwise than pristine because these scenes are in the front. As an aside, it is unfortunate that we cannot determine any of the reliefs on the outside walls of B 502.

5 Type of Warfare

Despite chariots and horses and the ubiquitous round shields, the tactics employed by the Kushites cannot be reconstructed. The Kushite (not Egyptian) artistic methods of dwelling on tableaux of one-on-one combats and the denouement of victory processions should not be taken at face value. They are stereotypical icons. In another depiction, E1, the royal armada is present, albeit during its voyage home. However, none of these parameters are indicative of the relatively backward nature of the king's army in comparison to that of the Neo-Assyrians. The Kushite armaments appear weaker than those possessed by later Near Eastern enemies, but Pianchy's Egyptian opponents may not have been any more advanced.

An overriding question is how these bellicose portrayals compare to what we known from Pianchy's extensive account on his Great Stela.[43] From this document something can be learned with regard to his tactical accomplishments.

Pianchy was forced to besiege Hermopolis and Memphis because the Egyptian polity was divided and each local ruler, native or of Libyan descent, was in a position to hinder the royal advance.[44]

D. Redford, Pharaonic King-Lists, Annals and Day Books: A Contribution to the Study of the Egyptian Sense of History, SSEA 4, Mississauga 1986, 179–186, demonstrates that the "year 30" requirement was, as most of us realise, not always followed. Always recourse must be had to E. Hornung/E. Staehelin, Neue Studien zum Sedfest, AegHelv 20, Basel 2006.

42 It is useful to add here the comments of Zach, The Army and Military Dictatorship in Meroe?.

43 Spalinger, The Persistence of Memory in Kush, Chapter 8 ("Pictorial Analysis and the Temple Program"), in press.

44 Classically, see J. C. Darnell, Two Sieges in Aethiopic Stelae, in: D. Mendel/U. Claudi (eds.), Ägypten im Afro-orientalischen Kontext. Aufsätze zur Archäologie, Geschichte und Sprache eines unbegrenzten Raumes. Gedenkschrift Peter Behrens, Afrikanistische Arbeitspapiere, Sondernummer 1991, Cologne 1991, 73–93.

The situation was parallel to Anchtify's during the First Intermediate period and Kamose's during the Second. Piancy enumerated his advances, crossing of the Nile, battles, and siege operations.

Piancy mentioned his archers but not the equipment of his other footsoldiers. We can state categorically that iron weapons were not used effectively, or at all. Military technology had developed little since New Kingdom Egypt. The reliefs in B 502 indicate that the troops had no armour and only rudimentary helmets.

The Great Stela acknowledged horses, but without the pictorial evidence from B 502 it would have been impossible to see that Piancy (and presumably the Egyptians) used the light New Kingdom chariot having six spokes per wheel. No matter how often we notice Piancy's interest in horses and Kushite horse breeding, none of the extant equid representations in the Great temple is a familiar portrait of an individual animal. At best, one could argue that these warhorses were taller at the withers than those of New Kingdom. However, they did not display the considerably more massive aspect of the later Neo-Assyrian cavalry contingents.

A key excerpt from Piancy's war narrative was first addressed by Alan GARDINER in 1935.[45] His very useful analysis is pertinent because this segment describes Piancy's ideal warfare encounter. Here are the norms of battle:

1. Take action during daylight. Night is prohibited.
2. Fight within visual distance.
3. Challenge the enemy.
4. Remain steady if the foe awaits infantry and chariotry support from another city. *T-nt-ḥtrw* is used here.
5. Fight when an opponent wishes to do so.

There are additional stipulations:

6. If the enemy has allies, await them as well. This is similar to the fourth in the epreceding list.
7. With regard to the local leaders or Libyans – the distinction and the equality of treatment are significant – "challenge them to battle in advance" (to quote GARDINER).
8. Demand that the enemies prepare their horses (for chariot warfare) and form a battle line.

Provided that these directives were followed, the combat between armies would be just. Because allies were members of the opponent's forces, it was not permitted to attack until all of them were completely prepared. To the defenders belonged the choice of when to initiate the battle. Surprise attacks, or any actions under cover of darkness, were forbidden. Nothing underhanded was acceptable; nothing cowardly was condoned. Individual physical combat and repression appears to have been iconised in art, especially within a triumphal depiction. Was integrity not a mere personal value?

45 A. GARDINER, Piankhy's Instruction to His Army, in: JEA 21 1935, 219–223, reveals how greatly Piancy's attitudes differed from an Egyptian's. There are some useful background remarks in PRIESE, ZÄS 98, 1972, 16–32.

Piancy's northern aggression brought him into a cultural setting that was different from his homeland. His rules of engagement nevertheless represent the scenario of Kushite warfare. Moreover, his planned course of action suited his enthusiasm for horses and the anticipated need to subjugate fortified cities before moving farther into the Delta. Pianchy's words were *sui generis* (*e.g.*, the "right way" to deal with Namlot of Hermopolis). His methods were his own. Any resemblance to the warrior-aristocratic rules of European feudalism is merely perceived.[46]

We can envisage troops drawn up on both sides of a relatively plat plain within sight of each other. Nevertheless, they probably could not hear one another's challenges, which would have been issued by envoys. The artificiality might have been constricting to other practitioners of warfare, who would have criticised the lack of tactical arrangements. To take a case in point, why are the charioteers not assigned an initial battlefield position? Was strategy assumed, and thus no commentary need have been made; or rather was Pianchy not interested in details? In his short speech, he enjoined his troops to mass (prepare for combat) and wait.

Given the limited nature of the source, can we believe that this military practice was typical of the Kushites elsewhere? Later Napatan royal narratives help us little.[47] In truth, the army often did the fighting while the king remained at the capital. Furthermore, none of the later hieroglyphic inscriptions give much detail as to tactics and combat. We are forced back upon the war scenes of B 502. There the imagery spotlights horses in triumphal return, but chariots are also present. With respect to scene E2, the one in which combat is experienced by the viewer, the lower extant register likewise underlines the nature of chariot warfare. (NB: cavalry cannot be assumed here.) Neither is there any memorial of battle, but rather a confrontation of pairs of individuals. The chariot encounters in the lower of two registers are stark, indeed unmoving. The chariots do not rush at the enemy's troops. They do not shoot a flight of arrows or hurl a string of javelins in the dramatic manner of a New Kingdom combat scene. The Kushite chariots *appear* not to be not a major component of the army and do not act as a unit. It is as if they are more decorative than instrumental.

There are no heroic stands of individual soldiers. The same may be said with regard to the king himself. Considering the royal ideology, no one else would be singled out. Nevertheless, the absence of tension is not characteristic of battle. The engagement of two armies, typical of the Egyptian narrative program, is missing. Certainly, chariot clashes happened often enough. However, the absence of imagery, while disconcerting, may very well be due to Kushite preferences; *i.e.*, what they wished to depict.

In my historical reconstruction, the wall reliefs of B 502 recount a conflict with southerners, Nubians who were a threat somewhere to the north of Gebel Barkal, or to the east of Pianchy's kingdom. One should not expect them to have a chariot industry, nor a large supply of horses, although the possibility has to be considered. From the slim evidence in later Napatan royal accounts, nothing can be argued supporting or against such a hypothesis. Regardless of the speculations, Pianchy, at least, did employ chariots.

---

46 The idea that Pianchy's social or cultural milieu, or more specifically, his attitudes, were tainted by "feudalism" is not valid. The argument is based upon his conceptions of horses, battles, sieges, and especially his relations with Hermopolis both before and after the city's capture. See SPALINGER, Pianchy/Piye. Between Two Worlds.

47 SPALINGER, The Persistence of Memory in Kush, Chapter 6 ("Textual Analysis"), in press.

Do Pianchy's military reliefs explicate the Kushite military influence in Egypt? Unfortunately no. Even his Great Stela is laconic with respect to this situation, especially in comparison to Thutmose III or Ramesses II's lengthy accounts.

In B 502 we are at the final phases of a campaign, and the pictorial account on the right (E1) specifically indicates the king's narrative program: a triumph of some sort is presented. We are unable to prove that the Kushite army was engaged in a minor dispute, yet we can argue that this local war (if E1 and E2 are to be combined) was small in comparison to the later campaign in Egypt. The conflict may have been a result of the Kushite state's difficulties in controlling incursions from without, especially from the east. By no means do these representations refer to a major power, nor is there any indication that they reflect a rebellion in the kingdom. The publication of the war scenes in Hall B 502 allows us to penetrate further into an early time during Pianchy's rule.

We are left with an illustration of the war materiel and weaponry, as well as the accoutrements of combat. The mechanics of combat can be barely discussed on the basis of E1 and E2. This is due to the singular nature of the icon of friend versus foe. Nevertheless, the strategy was quite similar to earlier cases in Egypt: use the flotilla to transport the army, then march the troops to meet the enemy at a fateful destination where the terrain was flat and the sun had arisen. Anything more specific belongs to a lengthier study of Kushite warfare, an interest which I intend to pursue.

Acknowledgements

This study is highly dependent upon a series of photographs taken by Heather Wilson, University of Auckland. The analyses of the figures are hers. All of the nine figures in this study are taken from her unpublished study with great appreciation.

Finally, I refer frequently to my yet unpublished work, A. SPALINGER, The Persistence of Memory in Kush: Pianchy and his Temple, Prague, P. ONDERKA (ed.), Proceedings of the 12th International Conference for Meroitic Studies 2016, Prague, forthcoming. There the reader will find ample references as well as discussion of specific subtopics, all of which relate to the presentation given here. Finally, I must recommend the various comments by C. SARGENT, The Napatan Royal Inscriptions; Egyptian in Nubia, Yale University PhD Thesis, New Haven 2004, for specific grammatical remarks on the king's Great Stela.

The significant work of N.-C. GRIMAL, La stèle triomphale de Pi(ᶜankh)y au Musée du Caire: JE 48882 et 47086–47089, Études sur la Propagande Royale Égyptienne I, MIFAO 105, Cairo 1981, covering the Great Stela, remains a standard.

Beneath the '*talatat*' floor block from which Charcoal was obtained for C14 Dating.
Chisel marks (hollows) created to hold wall plaster.
Note: The block had been reused. There are 'pocking' indentations underneath the block (where the sample was obtained) indicating that this was a surface initially plastered for a vertical wall.

Fig. 1: Carbon 14 Source

Construction of Inner Northern Wall of B502 from the external '*Talatat*' Pylon of B503
Extension to the '*talatat*' Pylon
Evidence of '*Talatat*' deliberately cut
Remains of outer '*talatat*' pylon of B503
Remains today.
Later facing (remnants only)

Fig. 2: Construction of Inner Northern Wall of B 502 from the External 'talatat' Pylon of B 503

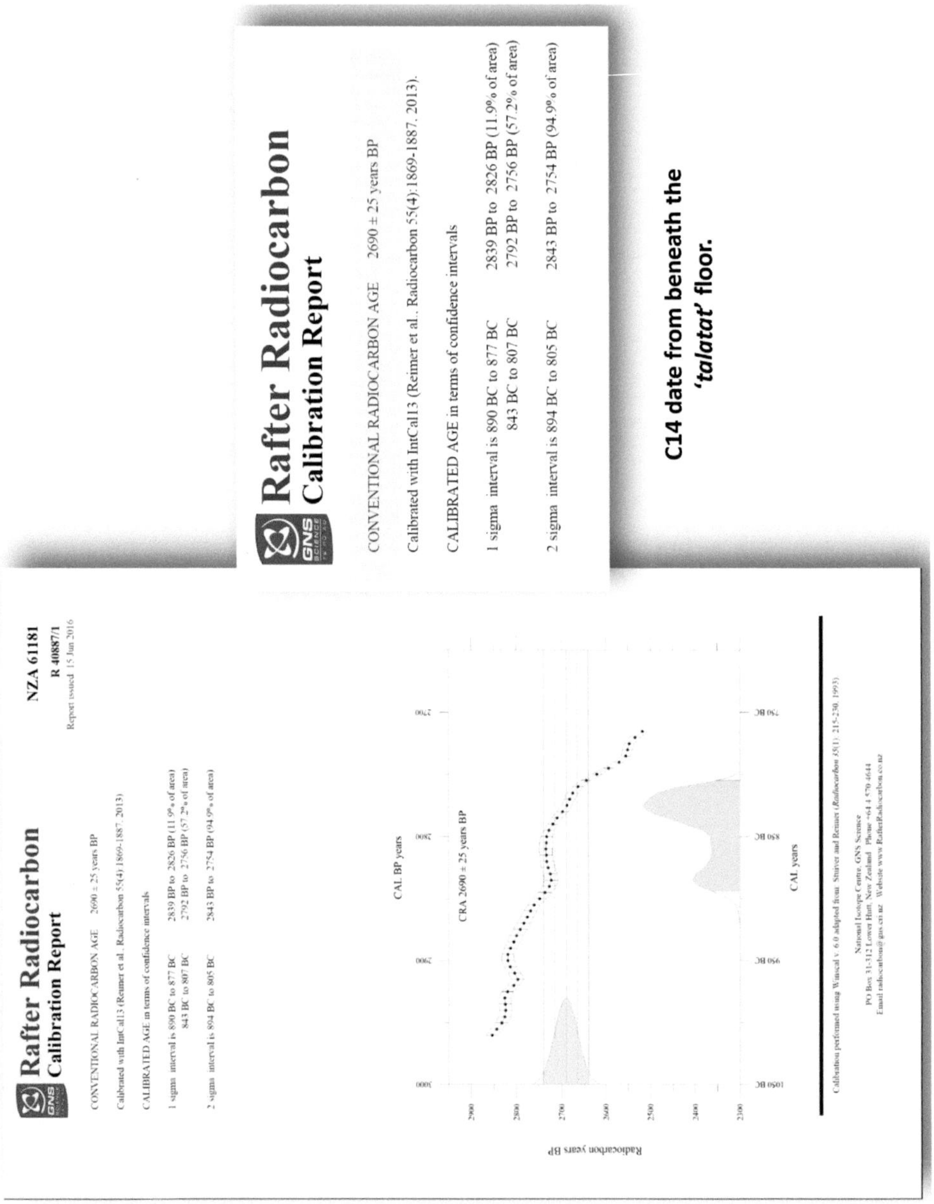

Fig. 3: Carbon 14 Date

Fig. 4: The Single Row of Columns and Bases of sequence 2 Directly inside Pylon 2. WCB 27/28

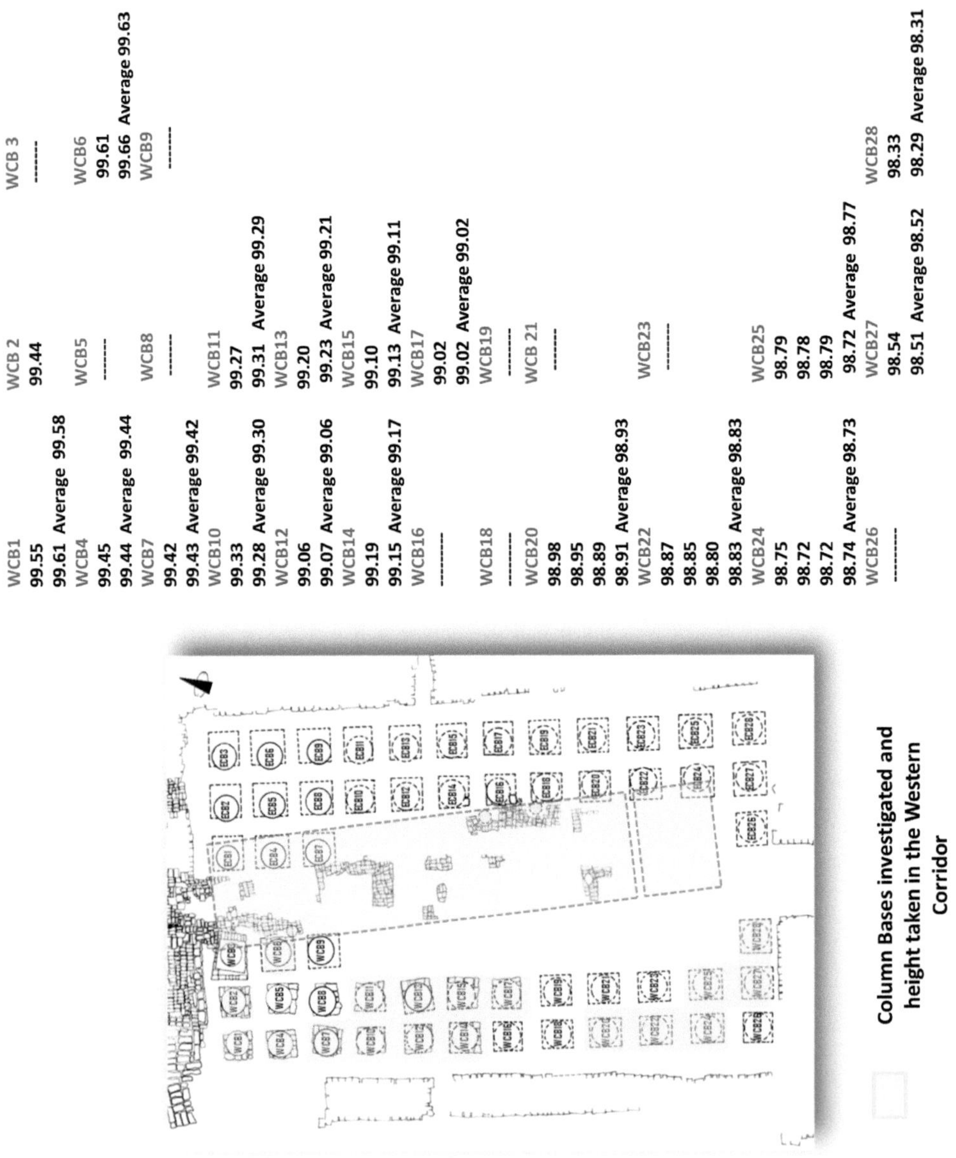

Fig. 5: Increasing Height of the Column Bases of sequence 2 from South to North

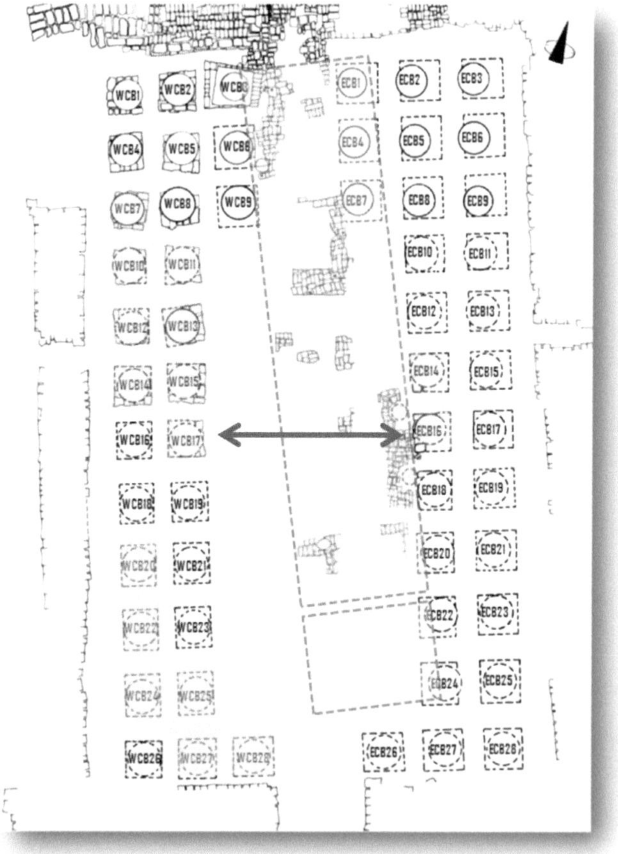

Column Bases investigated and height taken in the Eastern Corridor

ECB14
98.69
ECB16
99.00
99.03 Average 99.01

Fig. 6: Increasing Height of the Column Bases of sequence 2 from South to North in the Eastern Corridor

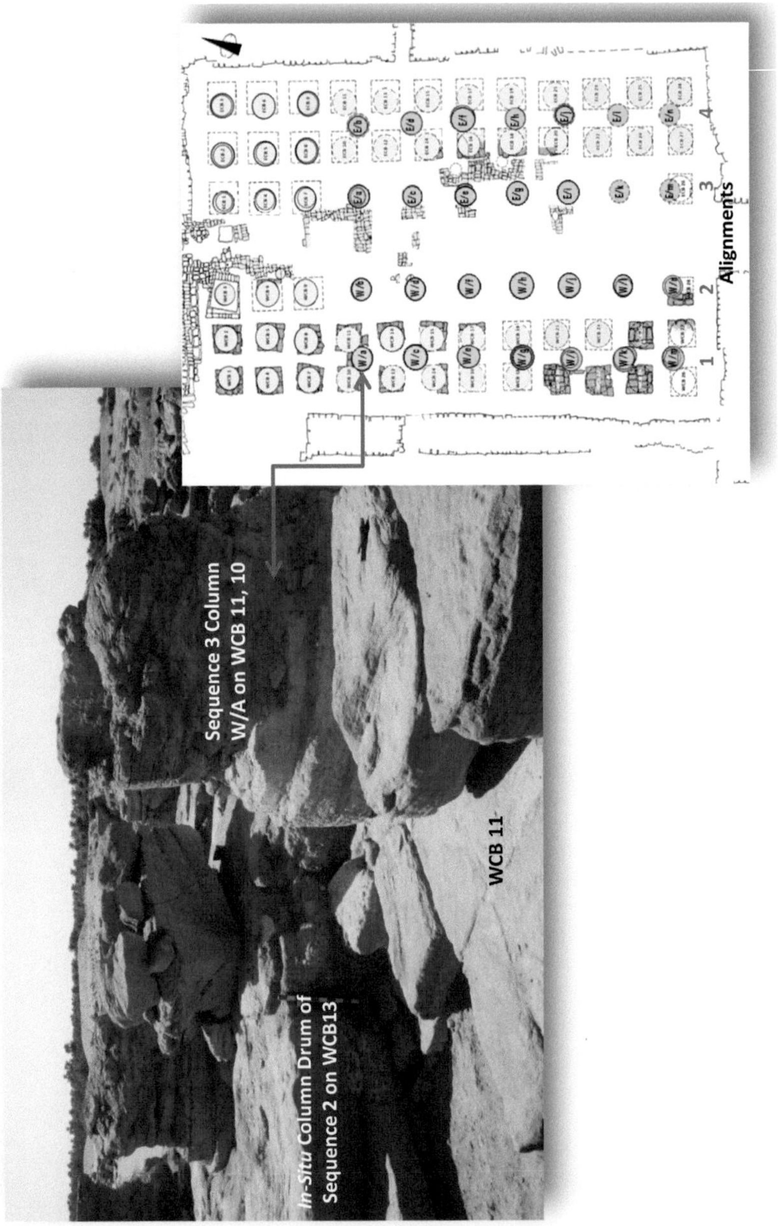

Fig. 7: New Column Alignment (W/A) placed on Old Column Base in Western Corridor. Facing South-West

Fig. 8: Sequence 3 Column in Alignment 2 (W/B) showing the Absence of a Base Plinth and Stepped Profile. Western Corridor Facing East

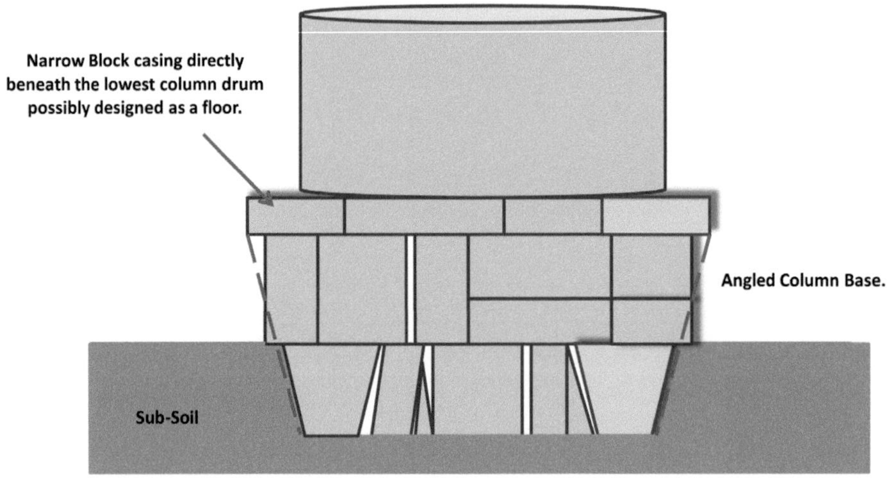

Fig. 9: Sequence 2. Configuration of the Column Bases

Doubling the Double Kingdom:

Taharqo's creation of a religio-political landscape

Angelika Lohwasser

Abstract

The Kushite pharaoh who left abundant sources in Egypt and Nubia was Taharqo (690–664 BC). Several stelae provide us with texts about various events of his reign – like the enormous inundation in his 6th regnal year or the training of the soldiers in Dahshur. Even more impressive is the intensive construction program, covering Egypt as well as Nubia. His name is present on many buildings in the Thebaid, but also in Edfu and Athribis, perhaps Memphis, and in Nubia in Qasr Ibrim, Semna, Kawa, Jebel Barkal and Sanam. His burial in Nuri is exceptional, since its substructure is similar to the Osireion of Seti I in Abydos.

Looking closer to the building activities in Nubia the overall structure of the sacral landscape resembles somewhat Egypt: The religious centre of Egypt at that time was Karnak, and it is mirrored by Jebel Barkal as 'Southern Karnak'. Nuri, although finally the burial place of Taharqo, may have acted as 'Southern Abydos' in the original strategy of the king, since the topography of the area and the ground plan of the subterranean installation are parallels to this old holy place. In Kawa, one mentions the copy of the relief of mortuary temples of the Old Kingdom in Saqqara. Taharqo himself orders craftsmen from Memphis to decorate this temple. Temple T of Kawa is the only temple of Taharqo so far which includes a cult for Ptah. Thus, with Barkal/Nuri/Kawa we find the Nubian versions of the most holy places in Egypt, namely Karnak/Abydos/Memphis.

Taharqo was the most Egyptian pharaoh of the Kushite Twenty-Fifth Dynasty. His investments into the theological evolution of what became the cultic traditions of the Late Period are more than noteworthy – the Edifice at the Lake in Karnak is the best example. The central deities of Egyptian kingship are tied to their main sanctuaries Karnak (Amun), Abydos (Osiris) and Memphis (Ptah). These deities – and their topographical anchorage in the sacral landscape – are the pillars of the ideology of kingship in Egypt of that time. They were transferred to Kush by Taharqo to establish the Nubian version of the Egyptian kingship.

Introduction

The Kushite Twenty-Fifth Dynasty ruled for about 60 years in Egypt as well as in their homeland, in Kush.[1] The heyday of this period was the reign of king Taharqo (690–664 BC),

1 For a concise history of the Twenty-Fifth Dynasty see R. Morkot, The Black Pharaos – Egypt's Nubian Rulers, London 2000.

and it is this king who will be in the focus of this contribution.[2] He developed an innovative way to shape Nubia as counterpart to Egypt, and this approach is based in his understanding and implementation of kingship which differed from his predecessors.

The comprehension of the dominion by Pi(ankh)y and Taharqo

The Triumphal Stela of king Pi(ankh)y that tells the story of his triumphal journey to the north, lacks the mention of Kush, Nubia or any Kushite place.[3] Even Napata, the capital of the kingdom, does not occur in the text. Did Pi(ankh)y conquer Egypt as a foreign ruler? Why did he not speak about his own empire? Or was Upper Egypt already merged with Nubia and therefore one single dominated region? In general, how was his understanding of his territory? In recent years, several studies were published which interpret the reign of Pi(ankh)y as either continuing the Libyan form of rule of the Third Intermediate Period[4] or a 'Sudanic king, dominating a segmentary state'[5]. It is true that according to the Triumphal Stela, Pi(ankh)y did not present himself as the only king, but the overlord over a number of minor kings.[6] This is shown in the lunette: Pi(ankh)y as overlord is standing, all the other kings pay their homage – although their name is in cartouche and they are called *nsw*, king. Libyan rulership is based on the Libyan tribal system, where several chiefs of equal rank can coexist, although one king is *primus inter pares*.[7] Looking to the later Napatan state which was organised as ambulatory kingship, we learn that the king had to travel to the centres of his empire to be accepted by the sacral and political authorities there.[8] Thus, the ideological foundations of Kushite kingship seem to be based in the political system of a 'segmentary state'. The core aspect of a 'segmentary state' is that there is not just one, but numerous centres of political power. The king as overlord needs the acceptance of all these local chiefs,

2 For Taharqo and the evidence of his reign see K. Dallibor, Taharqo – Pharao aus Kusch. Ein Beitrag zur Geschichte der 25. Dynastie, Achet. Schriften zur Ägyptologie A 6, Berlin 2005.

3 Primary edition N.-C. Grimal, La stèle triomphale de Pi(ʿankh)y au Musée du Caire: JE 48882 et 47086–47089, Études sur la Propagande Royale Égyptienne I, MIFAO 105, Cairo 1981; a recent edition of the stela is A. El Hawary, Wortschöpfung. Die Memphitische Theologie und die Siegesstele des Pije – zwei Zeugen kultureller Repräsentation in der 25. Dynastie, OBO 243, Freiburg/Göttingen 2010.

4 A. Leahy, The Libyan Period in Egypt: An Essay in Interpretation, in: Libyan Studies 16, 1985, 51–65; E. Lange, Legitimation und Herrschaft in der Libyerzeit. Eine neue Inschrift Osorkons I. aus Bubastis (Tell Basta), in: ZÄS 135, 2008, 131–141. For the Triumphal Stela, see also J. Moje, Herrschaftsräume und Herrschaftswissen ägyptischer Lokalregenten. Soziokulturelle Interaktionen zur Machtkonsolidierung vom 8. bis zum 4. Jahrhundert v. Chr., Topoi. Berlin Studies of the Ancient World 21, Berlin/Boston 2013, 44.

5 K. Howley, Sudanic Statecraft? Political Organization in the Early Napatan Period, in: Journal of Ancient Egyptian Interconnections 7, 2015, 30–41.

6 The same is true for the self-presentation of the king in the Sandstone Stela from Jebel Barkal (Khartoum, SNM 1851; G. A. Reisner, Inscribed monuments from Gebel Barkal, in: ZÄS 66, 1931, 76–100), which might reflect the situation before the reign of Pi(ankh)y (for a possible earlier date see A. Lohwasser, Deconstructing early Kushite ideology: On the unknown king of the so-called coronation stela of Pi(ankh)y, in: P. Onderka (ed.), Proceedings of the 12th International Conference for Meroitic Studies 2016, Prague, forthcoming.

7 Lange, Legitimation und Herrschaft, 139.

8 L. Török, Ambulatory Kingship and Settlement History. A Study on the Contribution of Archaeology to Meroitic History, in: C. Bonnet (ed.), Études nubiennes. Conférence de Genève. Actes du VIIe Congrès international d'études nubiennes 3–8 septembre 1990, Volume 1: communication principales, Geneva 1992, 111–126.

and he tightly ties their loyalty to the kingdom with the distribution of exotic or luxurious gifts.[9] Although, of course, the Meroitic system of government is historically much younger than the reign of Pi(ankh)y, we can assume that the basic idea of rulership was not only one single king ruling over the whole territory alone, but a number of local chiefs with a king on the top of this group. The texts of the Napatan Period, that recount the coronation journey to the local centres, are a strong argument for the existence of such an idea even before the Meroitic Period, and therefore this form of rulership might have been valid even already for Pi(ankh)y. He did not aspire to be the exclusive king over all of Egypt and Kush, but to be accepted as overlord, while leaving the minor kings unrestricted in their exercise of power.

The most prominent Kushite pharaoh was Taharqo. As far as we can judge from the texts, Taharqo wanted himself to be seen and understood as *Egyptian* pharaoh. He was crowned in Memphis and he ruled over both Egypt and Kush – it is the first time in the Twenty-Fifth Dynasty, that we learn about an empire extending over two 'states', namely Egypt and Kush. Pi(ankh)y, although coming from Nubia, did not comment on a unified kingdom including both Egypt and Nubia. While there is no proof of such an idea of a double kingdom before, Taharqo refers to the two integral parts of his empire in several texts. For example, he mentions Nubia and Egypt in the account of the big inundation in year 6 (Kawa V: l. 9): "The sky rained in *Nubia* and adorned the hills. Every man in *Nubia* was inundated with an abundance of everything, *Egypt* was in beautiful festival."[10] Or, even more specific, he mentions that he had been in *Nubia*, while he was chosen by Shebitqo to join the king in *Thebes*.[11] And he was crowned in *Memphis* and called for his mother, who was in *Nubia*.[12] All this suggests that he understood his territory of rule and power as a union of two parts, Egypt and Nubia/Kush.

Jebel Barkal in the reign of Taharqo

Taharqo implemented an enormous building program.[13] This activity of temple building covered both Egypt and Kush. Focusing on Nubia, he is engaged at Jebel Barkal at the Kushite capital of Napata. Taharqo was not the first king to build a temple there; on the contrary, already the kings of the New Kingdom started to build temples at this very spot.[14] We have evidence for Thutmose III, Thutmose IV, Akhenaton or Semenkhkare, Seti I and Ramesses II as commissioning temples at this mountain.

---

9 D. N. Edwards, The Archaeology of the Meroitic State. New perspectives on its social and political organisation, BAR International Series 640, Oxford 1996.

10 Stela Kawa V: l. 9, M. F. L. Macadam, The Temples of Kawa I: The Inscriptions, Part I: Text and Part II: Plates, Oxford University Excavations in Nubia, London 1949, 27, pl. X. Translation after T. Eide/T. Hägg/R. H. Pierce/L. Török (eds.), Fontes Historiae Nubiorum. Textual Sources for the History of the Middle Nile Region between the Eighth Century BC and the Sixth Century AD. Volume I: From the Eighth to the Mid-Fifth Century BC, Bergen 1994, 151.

11 Kawa IV: l. 7–9, Macadam, Kawa I, 15, pls. 7–8.

12 Stela Kawa V: l. 16–18 (Macadam, Kawa I, 28, pl. X).

13 See the compilation in Dallibor, Taharqo.

14 T. Kendall/E. A. Mohammed/H. Wilson/J. Haynes/D. Klotz, Jebel Barkal in the New Kingdom: An emerging picture in: N. Spencer/A. Stevens/M. Binder (eds.), Nubia in the New Kingdom. Lived experience, pharaonic control and indigenous traditions, British Museum Publications on Egypt and Sudan 3, Leuven 2017, 159–192.

The Jebel Barkal is a prominent landmark in a rather flat topographical surrounding, a table top mountain with a natural rock-needle at its south-western cliff. The shape of this needle seems to have been regarded as monumental uraeus which could be interpreted as the icon of pharaonic kingship, but has also several other connotations.[15] Jebel Barkal was interpreted as the mythological birthplace of the god Amun. It was a holy place for the Egyptians at least since Thutmose I visited Jebel Barkal.[16] It was a centre of Amun-worship since Thutmose III at the latest, who refers to the 'Pure Mountain' in his Jebel Barkal stela.[17] The Egyptian designation for the area of Jebel Barkal is *Jp.t-sw.t*, which is in fact the same name as Karnak.[18] Thus, it seems that the temple site of Jebel Barkal was conceptualised as 'Southern Karnak' and both places share the same toponym 'Southern Heliopolis'.[19] As in Karnak, several pharaohs of the New Kingdom erected sacral buildings at Jebel Barkal. And as in Karnak, the main temple was constructed for the cult of Amun.

During the later Ramessides, there are no more building activities attested here. The threat posed by the Sea People and internal problems with famine and some political and economic crises made the Egyptians concentrate on their homeland.

In the early Twenty-Fifth Dynasty, the Amun Temple at Jebel Barkal was the first structure to be rebuilt after the passing of several hundred years.[20] Pi(ankh)y did not only restore it, but enlarged it extensively. Temple B 500 then measured 156m in length, which is 300 Egyptian cubits. His huge construction work seems to have had two phases, while later kings only integrated kiosks, or installed statues and stelae in the temple. It was in use even in the Meroitic time, when king Natakamani made some restorations. All in all, the Amun Temple at Jebel Barkal was the main cult place of Amun for the Kushite kings, as was the Amun Temple in Karnak for the Egyptian pharaohs.

15 See the extensive study by T. Kendall, The Monument of Taharqa on Gebel Barkal, in S. Wenig (ed.), Neueste Feldforschungen im Sudan und in Eritrea, Akten des Symposiums vom 13. bis 14. Oktober 1999 in Berlin, Meroitica 21, Wiesbaden 2004, 1–45; but also T. Kendall, Why did Taharqa Build his Tomb at Nuri?, in: W. Godlewski/A. Łajtar/I. Zych (eds.), Between the Cataracts. Proceedings of the 11th Conference of Nubian Studies, Warsaw University, 27 August – 2 September 2006. Part One: Main Papers, PAM, Supplement Series 2,1 Warsaw 2008, 117–147.

16 Critical L. Gabolde, Karnak, Amon-Rê : la genèse d'un temple, la naissance d'un Dieu, BdE 167, Cairo 2018, 408–410. I. Guermeur, Les cultes d'Amon hors de Thèbes. Recherches de géographie religieuse, BEHE, Science religieuses 123, Thurnhout 2005, 538, suggests a veneration of the remarkable mountain already prior to the Egyptian presence. Nevertheless, the association of Amun with the Jebel Barkal was inaugurated by Thutmose III, as this is the earliest source.

17 Urk. IV, 1238.

18 Jebel Barkal is called the first time *Jp.t-sw.t* by Thutmose III (Urk. IV, 1238). See also Kendall, Why did Taharqa Build his Tomb at Nuri?, 124–125; T. Kendall, Reused Relief Blocks of Piankhy from B 900: Toward a Decipherment of the Osiris Cult at Jebel Barkal, in: J. R. Anderson/D. A. Welsby (eds.), The Fourth Cataract and Beyond. Proceedings of the 12th International Conference for Nubian Studies, British Museum Publications on Egypt and Sudan 1, Leuven/Paris/Walpole 2014, 663–686, see 672–673.

19 Gabolde, Karnak, 487; Kendall, Why did Taharqa Build his Tomb at Nuri?, 125 and n. 16. Tanis acted as 'Northern Thebes' in the Third Intermediate Period (see Guermeur, Cultes d'Amon, 298).

20 G. A. Reisner, The Barkal Temples in 1916, in: JEA 4, 1917, 213–227. For a summary on the restoration, enlargement and later installations in B 500 see T. Kendall/E. A. Mohammed, A Visitor's Guide to The Jebel Barkal Temples, Khartoum 2016. Online: http://www.jebelbarkal.org/frames/VisGuide.pdf, 47–52. Accessed on 30.04.2018.

Taharqo contributed to the sacral landscape at Jebel Barkal as well. In his engagement, we can identify a parallel to Karnak: In Karnak, he extended the Mut Temple. This may be associated with the significance on the festival of the decades, which gained importance under Taharqo.[21] The construction work in the Mut temple could also be seen in connection with the emphasis on female aspects of Kushite kingship ideology, especially since Taharqo erected a kind of 'birth house' (Mammisi) in front of the Mut Temple.[22] The focus on the Mut temple may lastly be connected with the 'Myth of the Distant Goddess'.[23] This myth is of extraordinary importance for the Kushite kings and Mut of Karnak, called Mut of Isheret (*nb.t-jšrw*), is in fact the returning Distant Goddess referred to in the myth. As the furious Eye of Ra, she journeys to Nubia. She is calmed down by male gods, namely Thot, Bes, Shu and Onuris and brought back to Egypt. Reunited with the sun god Ra, she was put as rearing up uraeus snake on his forehead. This myth is integrated into the royal ideology of the Napatan kings since there are many references to it in the relief programs of temples and in texts.[24] Even from the Meroitic Period, we know several allusions to this myth.[25]

At Jebel Barkal, Taharqo founded a temple for Mut.[26] It is dedicated to Mut, the Eye of Ra (*jr.t Rˁ*) and thus Mut as the Distant Goddess.[27] B 300 is a semi-rock cut temple, exactly beneath the uraeus-pinnacle – a precisely elected position (Fig. 1). Besides being a sign of kingship, the uraeus is also the final form of the Eye of Ra or the Distant Goddess. It is thus a more than appropriate spot to establish a temple for exactly this aspect of Mut. Taharqo is depicted several times with the four-feathered crown of Onuris,[28] thus one of the gods who

---

21 The temple of Mut in Karnak is one station in the festival of the decades. The most instructive building in this respect is the so-called Edifice at the Holy Lake in Karnak, built by Taharqo (R.A. Parker/J. Leclant/J.-C. Goyon, The Edifice of Taharqa by the Sacred Lake of Karnak, Brown Egyptological Studies 8, London 1979). For the festival of decades as visualised in the Edifice see K. M. Cooney, The Edifice of Taharqa by the Sacred Lake: Ritual Function and the Role of the King, in: JARCE 37, 2000, 15–47, see 26 and n. 86; K. Demuss, *Ḏsr-s.t.* Studien zum Kleinen Tempel von Medinet Habu, Göttingen 2010, 175–177 (Online publication, PhD Thesis). <http://webdoc.sub.gwdg.de/diss/2010/demuss/> Accessed on 12.11.2018.

22 R. Fazzini/W. Peck, The precinct of Mut during Dynasty XXV and early Dynasty XXVI: a growing picture, in: JSSEA 11(3), 1981, 115–126, see 122–126.

23 Although most of the written evidence on this myth derives from later periods in Egypt, there are several allusions to it already in the Twenty-Fifth Dynasty. For the myth see H. Junker, Die Onurislegende, DAWW 59,1–2, Vienna 1917; D. Inconnu-Bocquillon, Le mythe de la Déesse Lointaine à Philae, BdE 132, Cairo 2001; for the earlier allusions see A. von Lieven, Fragments of a Monumental Proto-Myth of the Sun's Eye, in: G. Widmer/D. Devauchelle (eds.), Actes du IXe congrès international des études démotiques, BdE 147, Cairo 2009, 173–181.

24 For a discussion on this myth acting as legitimatory reference see A. Lohwasser, Herrschaft und Heil – Macht und Mythos. Die politische und religiöse Legitimation der nubischen Pharaonen Pi(anch)y und Taharqo, in: M. Becker/A. I. Blöbaum/A. Lohwasser, Inszenierung von Herrschaft und Macht im ägyptischen Tempel: Religion und Politik im Theben des frühen 1. Jahrtausends v. Chr., ÄUAT 95, Münster, forthcoming, Chapter II.4.1.

25 E. Kormysheva, Evidences of the Sun-Eye Legend in the Meroitic Kingdom, in: M. Zach (ed.). The Kushite World. Proceedings of the 11th International Conference for Meroitic Studies, Vienna, 1–4 September 2008, BzS. Beiheft 9, Vienna 2015, 343–358.

26 C. Robisek, Das Bildprogramm des Mut-Tempels am Gebel Barkal, Veröffentlichungen der Institute für Afrikanistik und Ägyptologie der Universität Wien 52, Beiträge zur Ägyptologie 8, Vienna 1989.

27 Kendall, Why did Taharqa Build his Tomb at Nuri?, 125.

28 Robisek, Bildprogramm des Mut-Tempels, 69.

calms down the furious Eye of Ra in Nubia. On the rear wall of the sanctuary, we can see Taharqo again with the crown of Onuris, offering to Amun and the lion-headed Mut, the Eye of Ra (Fig. 2).[29] Taharqo also (re-)built another temple, just beside the Mut Temple. B 200 is dedicated to Hathor-Tefnut,[30] again one of the appearances of the Distant Goddesses. Thus to my mind, in founding especially the Mut Temple here, he copies once more the complex of Karnak, confirming Jebel Barkal as being understood as the 'Southern Karnak'.

Fig. 1: Jebel Barkal: Temples B 200 and B 300 directly beneath the pinnacle (Photo: A. Lohwasser)

29 The decoration of this wall is published for the first time in Kendall /Mohammed, Visitor's Guide, 14, fig. 3.

30 P. M. Wolf, Die archäologischen Quellen der Taharqozeit im nubischen Niltal, PhD Thesis, unpublished, Berlin 1990, 144–147.

Fig. 2: Rear wall in the sanctuary of B 300
(Photo: B. WHITNEY)

The temple of Sanam

Opposite the temple area of Jebel Barkal the temple of Sanam is situated.[31] Probably a New Kingdom temple existed there already, although definite proof is currently lacking.[32] However, Taharqo definitely built a temple there for 'Amun-Re, Bull of Nubia'.[33] Since the situation of this temple on the other bank of the Nile – and in fact this is the only known Kushite temple on the 'left' bank of the Nubian Nile known so far – resembles the situation of Medinet Habu, László TÖRÖK proposed to understand the cultic connection between Jebel Barkal and Sanam in the same way as between Karnak and Medinet Habu.[34] He supports this

31 F. L. GRIFFITH, Oxford Excavations in Nubia VIII–XVII. Napata, Sanam Temple, Treasury and Town, in: AAA 9, 1922, 67–124.

32 A. LOHWASSER, Aspekte der napatanischen Gesellschaft. Archäologisches Inventar und funeräre Praxis im Friedhof von Sanam – Perspektiven einer kulturhistorischen Interpretation, Contributions to the Archaeology of Egypt, Nubia and the Levant 1, Vienna 2012, 299. In 2018 new excavations started in the temple area which will shed light on the earlier phases of the temple of Taharqo (Sanam Temple Project, see https://www.ees.ac.uk/sanam-temple-project).

33 For the discussion of the name, see J. POPE, The Double Kingdom under Taharqo. Studies in the History of Kush and Egypt, c. 690–664 BC, Culture and History of the Ancient Near East 69, Leiden/Boston 2014, 90–91 with n. 289.

34 L. TÖRÖK, The Image of the Ordered World in Ancient Nubian Art. The Construction of the Kushite Mind (800 BC–300 AD), PÄ 18, Leiden/Boston/Cologne 2002, 35–39. This interpretation is followed by GUERMEUR, Cultes d'Amon, 524.

hypothesis with the argument that Sanam was dedicated to Amun as bull and that the focus of the rituals in the Small Temple at Medinet Habu was on Amun Kamutef – Bull of his Mother. The Small Temple of Medinet Habu existed since the early Eighteenth Dynasty and was in use until the end of the Pharaonic empire because of its strong links to the ideology of kingship.[35] It is one of the places of the 'primordial mound' and a place of worship of the Hermopolitan Ogdoad in the Late Period. On the occasion of the decades festival, the king merged with Osiris and Amun to regenerate and renew creation and kingdom. The god Amun travelled from Karnak to Luxor, then to Medinet Habu, where the main rituals were executed in the Small Temple. There, the union of Amun, Osiris and the king took place which granted the rebirth and especially the rejuvenation of kingship. Then, Amun travelled back to the Mut Temple in Karnak and finally to his main temple complex in Karnak. It is Taharqo who not only finalised the restauration of the Small Temple in Medinet Habu,[36] but who also built an unusual sanctuary in the compound of Amun in Karnak as final destination of the procession of the decades festival. Although this so-called 'Edifice of Taharqo' at the Holy Lake is only partly preserved, we can interpret the decoration of the subterranean rooms as portraying the journey of the king – merged with Amun and Osiris – through the night and his regenerated appearance, together with the renewal of the creation as well as the renewal of the gods.[37]

The relief decoration in the temple of Sanam is largely destroyed and can thus not be investigated further.[38] The distance between Jebel Barkal and Sanam is far greater than between Karnak and Medinet Habu, thus a similar bark procession seems less plausible. But as we do not have evidence about bark processions at the Nubian Nile at all, the existence of different rituals, executed in Nubia only, is conceivable. Since there was already a New Kingdom temple situated at Sanam, the position was chosen to link the kingdom of Taharqo to the reign of the Egyptian pharaohs. The hypothesis that Sanam functioned for Jebel Barkal like the Small Temple in Medinet Habu functioned for Karnak seems plausible for the time of Taharqo. The arguments are the topographical situation as well as the unusual name of Amun – Bull of Nubia.[39] In other words: Sanam could have been the destination of the Nubian version of the decades festival during the reign of Taharqo and could therefore be understood as southern Medinet Habu.

Kawa and Taharqo

At the site of Kawa, again a place with New Kingdom engagement, Taharqo built a new temple for Amun of Kawa. Since five stelae of Taharqo with detailed lists of endowments and offerings for every year, starting from year 3 up to the opening of the temple in year 10, were discovered here, we know a lot about the equipment and personnel of a temple in

35 For the Small Temple, its chronology and rituals see DEMUSS, *Dsr-s.t.*

36 See the detailed discussion in A. I. BLÖBAUM, „Denn ich bin ein König, der die Maat liebt". Herrscherlegitimation im spätzeitlichen Ägypten. Eine vergleichende Untersuchung der Phraseologie in den offiziellen Königsinschriften vom Beginn der 25. Dynastie bis zum Ende der makedonischen Herrschaft, AegMon 4, Aachen 2006, 136–139.

37 See note 21.

38 TÖRÖK, Image of the Ordered World, 37–38, interprets the presentation of a barque procession as the procession of Amun of Napata to Sanam.

39 In such names, typically the locality is used, like Amun of Napata, Amun of Kawa, Amun of Pnubs.

Kush in general.[40] Kawa is interpreted as a major place for the early Kushites, it might have been a powerbase for the advance into Egypt.[41] With the excavations of Derek Welsby,[42] we got a broader and more nuanced picture of this site. Today, a town with different quarters, a cemetery and several temples are known. Since the name of Taharqo occurs repeatedly, his reign must have been a phase of intensive construction or occupancy of this site.

Taharqo rebuilt the temple for Amun in stone, after the former sanctuary had fallen into ruin. He visited the site during his journey to the north, to Egypt, when the ruling pharaoh sent for Taharqo to accompany him. After his coronation in Memphis, Taharqo remembered that he promised to rebuild this temple[43] and he thus arranged for the construction work with the words: "His Majesty sent his army to Kawa, together with numerous gangs of workmen and good craftsmen, the number of which is unknown. An overseer of works being there with them to direct the work in this temple, while his Majesty was still in Memphis."[44] This sentence is usually understood that Taharqo sent specialised craftsmen and an architect from Memphis down to Kawa.[45] Although it might be interpreted in this way, it is only mentioned that the king sent specialists, while he himself stayed in Memphis, thus not going to Kawa personally. However, it is intriguing that Taharqo states that he sent the specialists directly after his coronation in Memphis, while he was staying in the capital. Although we cannot be sure that there were indeed Memphite craftsmen, some scenes in the relief decoration resemble Memphite patterns.[46] Most prominent is of course the scene with the sphinx, presented on the west wall of the festival court in Temple T at Kawa. There, a sphinx is shown trampling Libyan enemies, and in front of the motive, the so-called 'Libyan family' is depicted. The whole composition is a close copy of a relief in the Old Kingdom mortuary temples of Sahure and Niuserre in Saqqara (Fig. 3).[47] Although some details are omitted, perhaps due to the limited space in Kawa, even the names of the members of the Libyan family are the same. Therefore, it is not unlikely that the designer of the temple or at least its decoration had a Memphite background.

---

40 All stelae are published in Macadam, Kawa I. Pope, Double Kingdom, 51, stated that only with the great effort of Taharqo the cult in Kawa gained greater prominence.

41 Morkot, Black Pharaohs, 157.

42 D. A. Welsby, Kawa. The Pharaonic and Kushite Town of Gematon. History and archaeology of the site, London 2014. Booklet produced for the Qatar-Sudan Archaeological Project. http://www.qsap.org.qa/images/doc/kawa_ qsap_english_booklet.pdf. Accessed on 12.11.2018.

43 The narrative of the idea to reconstruct the temple is recounted on stelae Kawa IV and VI (Macadam, Kawa I).

44 Kawa IV: 20–22. Translation after Eide/Hägg/Pierce/Török, Fontes Historiae Nubiorum I, 142.

45 On the basis of the interpretation of Macadam, Kawa I, 21.

46 Already mentioned in M. F. L. Macadam, The Temples of Kawa II: History and Archaeology of the Site, Part I: Text and Part II: Plates, Oxford University Excavations in Nubia, London 1955, 63–64. The unpublished M.A. Thesis of Sara Bock, Ägyptische Vorbilder und kuschitische Innovationen am Tempel T von Kawa, Berlin 2006, deals with these adoptions in detail. I am grateful to her for sending the text to me.

47 In Kawa: Macadam, Kawa II, pl. IX; at the causeway of Sahure: L. Borchardt, Das Grabdenkmal des Königs S'aḥu-Re. Band II: Die Wandbilder, Wissenschaftliche Veröffentlichungen der Deutschen Orient-Gesellschaft 26, Leipzig 1913, pl. 1; at the causeway of Niuserre: L. Borchardt, Das Grabdenkmal des Königs Ne-user-re^{c}, Wissenschaftliche Veröffentlichungen der Deutschen Orient-Gesellschaft 7, Leipzig 1907, pls. 8–11.

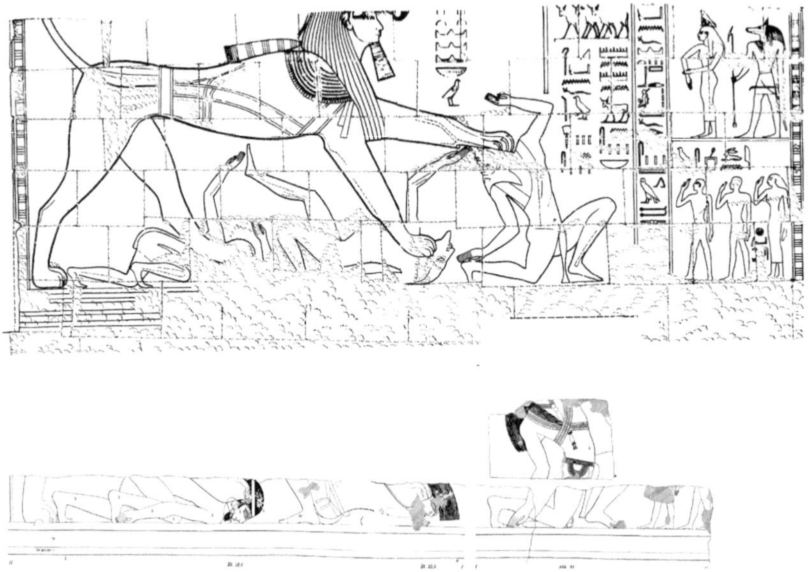

Fig. 3: Kawa T, interior wall of pylon (MACADAM, Kawa II, pl. IX) and pyramid causeway of Niuserre (BORCHARDT, Grabdenkmal des Königs Ne-user-re^c^, pl. 10)

There is another hint to Memphis in Temple T at Kawa: it is the only Kushite temple known where a cult of the god Ptah has been integrated. The temple is dedicated to Amun, who is the primary god of Kushite kingship. This is expressed most obviously in the 'covenant of Alara', attested in two versions on stelae from Kawa:[48] Alara initiated a very close (personal and cultic) connection with Amun, who in turn granted him the kingdom; Taharqo links himself to Alara and this covenant to secure the kingdom for himself and his family.[49] Therefore, the main god in Kawa is Amun as guarantor of kingship. As such, he was worshipped in two forms, as Amun of Napata who is responsible for the coronation, and as the local form Amun of Kawa.[50] But it is likely that a third god was worshipped in Kawa, namely Ptah. He is depicted right above the two forms of Amun on the southern jamb of the pylon (Fig. 4). The northern jamb is partly destroyed, but the preserved lower part corresponds to the southern jamb, thus one can imagine that Ptah was depicted there also.[51] Therefore, the three gods – Amun of Kawa, Amun of Napata and Ptah – welcome the king and are presented as lords of the temple. On the shrine of Taharqo, a small installation in the temple court, the unusual form of Ptah *nwn-wr*, Ptah-Nun the Great,[52] is depicted. He is presented in community with his consort Sakhmet and their son Nefertem.[53] Török already pointed out the significance

48 Kawa IV: l. 16–19 (MACADAM, Kawa I, 16) and Kawa V: l. 22–25 (MACADAM, Kawa I, 36).

49 A detailed analysis of this passage in the text of the stelae from Kawa is K. JANSEN-WINKELN, Alara und Taharka: Zur Geschichte des nubischen Königshauses, in: Or 72, 2003, 141–158.

50 See the discussion in TÖRÖK, Image of the Ordered World, 99–100.

51 MACADAM, Kawa II, pls. XXIIIa, XXIVd.

52 LGG III, 173. Ptah-Nun the Great is attested from the New Kingdom to the Roman Period.

53 MACADAM, Kawa II, pl. XVII b, c.

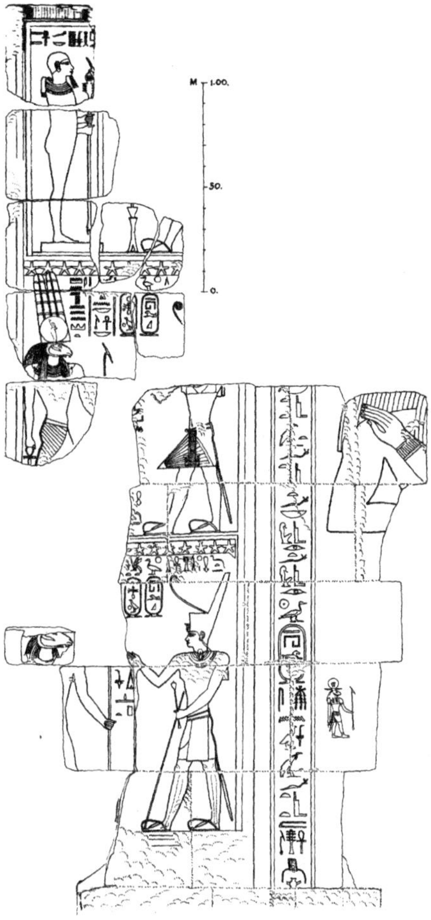

Fig. 4: Kawa T, doorjamb of pylon (MACADAM, Kawa II, pl. XXIIIa)

of Ptah in Kawa, where this god is also called Taharqo's father: "The incorporation of Ptah (...) within the iconographic program of the Kawa temple may be sufficiently explained by the Dynasty's close contacts with Memphis and the political concept of its legitimacy in Memphis."[54]

Apart from the incorporation of Memphite deities, such as Ptah, and the decoration copied from Memphite models, Taharqo installed people of the north as priestesses and servants at Kawa.[55] They were neither prisoners of war nor slaves, but "men who know their spells", thus ritual specialists. Although the provenance of these people is not reported except being from *t3 mḥw*, *i.e.* Lower Egypt, it is intriguing to speculate that these people also originated from the region of Memphis, and were thus familiar with Memphite rituals.

Taharqo indeed had a special connection to Memphis, which was not only the place of his coronation, but also of his palace in Egypt proper. A sporting race of his elite troops started in Memphis as written in the so-called 'Dahshur stela' (l. 13).[56] The Assyrian sources describe that Taharqo fled from the royal palace in Memphis.[57] Taharqo manifested his connection to Memphis even in his name: he chose the throne-name *Nfrtm-ḫwj-Rʿ*, 'protected by Nefertem and Ra' or 'Nefertem is protector of/protected by Ra'. The integration of Nefertem into the throne name of an Egyptian pharaoh is attested only for one ephemeral king of the Fourteenth Dynasty and it is unlikely that Taharqo constructed his name based on that model. It is more probable that he chose Nefertem as particularly local Memphite deity to relate himself with Memphis.[58] This emphasis on Memphis is mirrored in the temple of Kawa: the possible origin of the architect and craftsmen, the detailed copy of

54 TÖRÖK, Image of the Ordered World, 92.

55 Kawa VI: l. 15, 20–21. See the discussion in POPE, Double Kingdom, 53, 273.

56 H. ALTENMÜLLER/A. M. MOUSSA, Die Inschriften der Taharkastele von der Dahschurstraße, in: SAK 9, 1981, 57–84.

57 Assurbanipal, Prisma E (H.-U. ONASCH, Die assyrischen Eroberungen Ägyptens. Teil 1: Kommentare und Anmerkungen. Teil 2: Texte in Umschrift, ÄUAT 27, Wiesbaden 1994, 97) and Large Egyptian Tablets (ONASCH, Assyrische Eroberungen, 105).

58 J. LECLANT, Recherches sur les monuments Thébains de la XXVe dynastie dite éthiopienne, BdE 36, Cairo 1965; DALLIBOR, Taharqo, 30.

Memphite temple decoration, the incorporation of Memphite deities and the installation of northern ritual personal hint to a very close connection of Kawa with the Egyptian residence of Taharqo and one of the most important religious centres of Egypt. Therefore, Kawa can be interpreted as Taharqo's 'Southern Memphis'.

The Osireion of Nuri

George A. REISNER excavated the site of Nuri in 1916–1918 and since then it is known as pyramid cemetery of the kings and queens of the Napatan Period.[59] The inauguration of the necropolis can again be attributed to Taharqo. His pyramid is the first and biggest, situated on the highest point of the bedrock terrace. When REISNER excavated the pyramid of Taharqo, he discovered that the substructure did not have the usual and expected Kushite form. In El Kurru, where all the predecessors of Taharqo were buried, the graves consist of a burial chamber and sometimes an antechamber.[60] In Nu. 1, however, the substructure resembles the Osireion of Seti I in Abydos (Fig. 5).[61] This circumstance has been discussed several times already, while most recently Timothy KENDALL pointed out that "... Nuri I – like Seti's Osireion – seems to have been designed to assert that Taharqa had truly and literally become

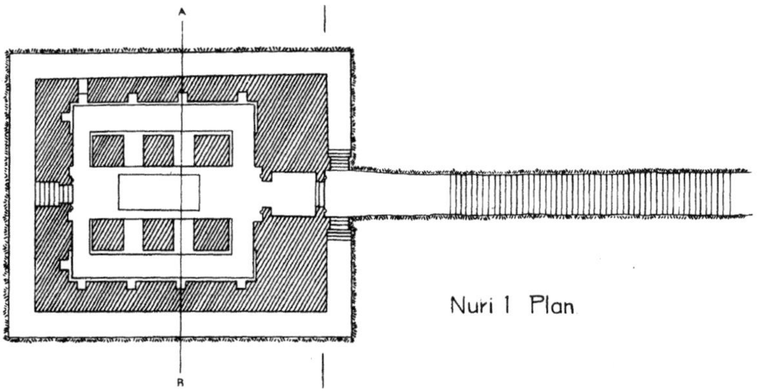

Fig. 5: Substructure of pyramid Nu. 1 (DUNHAM, Nuri, fig. 1)

the god, and that the primeval kingship, fertility, and the continuity of the state emanated from the sainted being of that king, who had become the eternal king".[62] That Taharqo built his pyramid exactly at Nuri, and not in the royal cemetery of El Kurru, is explained by KENDALL with its location at the exact point where the sun rises on New Year's Day when seen from Jebel Barkal.[63]

The fusion of Taharqo and Osiris is obvious, since Nu. 1 was the burial place of Taharqo, where Taharqo merged with and transformed into Osiris Taharqo. But I think that there is

59 D. DUNHAM, Nuri. Royal Cemeteries of Kush 2, Boston 1955.

60 D. DUNHAM, El Kurru. Royal Cemeteries of Kush 1, Cambridge 1950, 128–131.

61 As already pointed out by Jean LECLANT: J. LECLANT, Taharqa, in: W. HELCK/W. WESTENDORF (eds.), Lexikon der Ägyptologie VI, Wiesbaden 1986, 156–184.

62 KENDALL, Why did Taharqa Build his Tomb at Nuri?, 120.

63 KENDALL, Why did Taharqa Build his Tomb at Nuri?, 120–125. TÖRÖK, Image of the Ordered World, 39, interprets the relationship between Sanam and Nuri as parallel to Jebel Barkal and El Kurru.

also another aspect of Nuri, which has not been considered so far. In contemporaneous Egypt, the Osirian cult in Abydos experienced a revival, if not a new orientation. For the Twenty-Fifth Dynasty, Julia BUDKA recognised a peak in the deposition of so-called *qaab*-vessels, special ritual vessels for the Osirian cult in Abydos.[64] Why this increase of interest in the Twenty-Fifth Dynasty? Apart from the general shift towards the cult of Osiris as regenerative power in the Third Intermediate Period, there was a link between the myth of Osiris and the ancestor cult of the Kushites, as Julia BUDKA as well as Ute and Andreas EFFLAND have already pointed out.[65] With the connection to Osiris as the predecessor of Horus and thus the living pharaoh, every ruling king links himself to the line of ancestors. That the Kushites were extremely interested in Abydos is recorded not only by the thousands of *qaab*-vessels, but also by the creation of a cemetery for Kushite royal women.[66] Moreover, at least one fragment of a stone shabti of the Kushite God's Wife Amenirdis I. is known from Abydos.[67] Since we know that the God's wives were not buried in Abydos, but in the Thebais, this shabti has to be seen as a relic of another ritual. It may be a substitute of Amenirdis, to attend the mystical performances at Abydos, or it may be a remnant of a ritual deposition as well.

The links between Abydos and Nuri are manifold. Taharqo not only constructed a tomb substructure in striking resemblance with the Osireion of Abydos, Nuri it is also the first site with stone shabtis. Shabtis are found in the tombs in El Kurru, but all of them are made of faience, the usual material also in contemporaneous Egypt. In the tombs of Taharqo and Senkamanisken, a later king, a huge number of stone shabtis were found. Brigitte BALANDA investigated the Kushite use of shabtis, stating that they may have been regarded as guardian demons, placed in rows at the walls to protect the dead.[68] Also in the grave of Taharqo, REISNER reconstructed that they "had originally been ranged standing in at least three rows around the walls of the main chamber B, but the majority were found scattered in various parts of the chamber. Others were found about the entrance and in the corridors N1, S1 and S2."[69] Thus, we do in fact not know whether they were arranged in the same way as in the other royal burial chambers or whether just some of them were deposited in rows, while the others have just 'been there'.

The main ritual relict in contemporary Abydos are the *qaab*-vessels. BUDKA pointed out that the only place with *qaabs* apart Abydos is Nuri![70] Nevertheless, there is no evidence

64 A. EFFLAND/U. EFFLAND, Abydos. Tor zur ägyptischen Unterwelt; Antike Welt Beigaben; Darmstadt/Mainz 2013, 78–79; J. BUDKA, Kushites at Abydos: A view from Umm el-Qaab, in: C. JURMAN/D. A. ASTON/B. BADER (eds.), A True Scribe of Abydos. Essays on First Millennium Egypt in Honour of Anthony Leahy, OLA 265, Leuven 2017, 54–63.

65 J. BUDKA, Kuschiten in Abydos: Einige Überlegungen zur Nutzung von *Cemetery D* (Mace) während der 25. Dynastie, in: GM 232, 2012, 29–51, see 31; EFFLAND/EFFLAND, Abydos, 78–79.

66 A. LEAHY, Kushites at Abydos: The Royal Family and Beyond, in: E. PISCHIKOVA/J. BUDKA/K. GRIFFIN (eds.), Thebes in the First Millenium BC, Cambridge 2014, 61–95.

67 U. EFFLAND, Funde aus dem Mittleren Reich bis zur Mamlukenzeit aus Umm el-Qaab, in: MDAIK 62, 2006, 131–150, see 135; EFFLAND/EFFLAND, Abydos, 79–80, fig. 6.

68 B. BALANDA, Protecting the Mummy – A Reinterpretation of *Shabtis* in the Napatan Funerary Customs, in: J. R. ANDERSON/D. A. WELSBY (eds.), The Fourth Cataract and Beyond. Proceedings of the 12th International Conference for Nubian Studies, British Museum Publications on Egypt and Sudan 1, Leuven/Paris/Walpole 2014, 655–662.

69 DUNHAM, Nuri, 10.

70 J BUDKA, Kushite Pottery in Egypt: An Update from Thebes and Abydos, in: E. PISCHIKOVA/J. BUDKA/K. GRIFFIN (eds.), Thebes in the First Millennium BC: Art and Archaeology of the Kushite

for a *qaab* vessel in the tomb of Taharqo, but several *qaabs* have been found in foundation deposits of later tombs.[71] As a hypothesis we can reconstruct that the *qaabs* were deposited near the Osireion like in Egypt in the time of Taharqo, and they have been used secondarily as vessels in these later foundation deposits. The same can be true for the newly introduced stone shabtis: if they were in fact ritual relics in or at the Osireion in Nuri, could they not have been rearranged at the walls later to act as Kushite guardians in the tomb? Therefore I suggest that Taharqo built the complex in Nuri as 'Southern Abydos'. Apart from the arguments about its location and the connection to Osiris already put forward by Kendall, also the Nuri landscape resembles somewhat that of Abydos. The pyramid itself is built on an elevation at the Wadi at-Tarbul, but there is a larger wadi in the hinterland, Wadi ad-Dagawwed, which reaches the Nile near Nuri.[72] Although the dominance of the wadi is not as impressive as in Abydos, it was perhaps one additional aspect of establishing the Osireion exactly here.[73]

If Taharqo intended to map Nuri out as 'Southern Abydos' and establish an Osirian ancestor cult there, the substructure of Nu. 1 originally cannot have been projected as his tomb. The today visible superstructure of Nu. 1 was built in two stages, the first pyramid was enlarged later. It is the only royal pyramid in Kush without chapel on the east side. If a chapel for the first and smaller pyramid existed, has never been proven, additional excavations would therefore be necessary.[74] If the Osireion of Nu. 1 was not planned to be a tomb, it is even possible that Nuri was originally not established as cemetery, since Tanwetamani was buried in El Kurru, the traditional cemetery of the Kushite kings.[75] It is likewise possible that Taharqo planned to be buried in Egypt – which failed because of the withdrawal by the Assyrians. Of course, in the end, Nu. 1 *was* the tomb of Taharqo, since three canopic jars with his name were found there, as well as some remains of an interment.[76] This may be motivated by the fact that the planned tomb of Taharqo (in Memphis or elsewhere) was beyond the zone of influence and the Osireion was a suitable – and available – structure for the burial of this very king. But if we consider the religious and political strategy of Taharqo, we can understand Nuri as 'Southern Abydos', as a cult place for the Osirian rituals in Nubia which aimed at incorporating the living king into the series of all kings and also linking him with his divine predecessor.

Conclusion

With the development of the temple area of Jebel Barkal as 'Southern Karnak/Heliopolis', the conceptualisation of the temple of Sanam as 'Southern Medinet Habu', the construction of Kawa as 'Southern Memphis' and the establishment of Nuri as 'Southern Abydos', Taharqo emulated the four main Egyptian cult places of his time in Nubia. These places are linked with the main deities of the Kushite kingdom and their rituals: Amun(-Re), Mut, Osiris and

Period and Beyond, GHP Egyptology 27, London 2018, 357–371, see 364.

71 Budka, Kushite Pottery, 364, with n. 45, fig. 7.

72 I am grateful to Mohammed el Toum who helped me to gain the names of these wadis.

73 Since the inhospitable area of the Fourth Cataract starts directly north of Nuri, a position further to the north would not have been possible.

74 Dunham, Nuri, 7: "No trace of any chapel associated with superstr. B. Whether one was built in connection with superstr. A cannot be ascertained without further excavation."

75 Ku. 16 (Dunham, El Kurru, 60–63).

76 G. A. Reisner, Known and Unknown Kings of Ethiopia: Excavation of the Royal Cemetery at Nuri, 1916–1918, in: BMFA 16, 1918, 67–82, see 72.

Ptah. These deities and their topographical anchoring points in the landscape are the pillars of kingship ideology. Amun-Re of Karnak is the state god, who travelled with the king to Medinet Habu for regeneration rituals. He is also the god who is responsible for the coronation of the king. Mut has a double role in the Twenty-Fifth Dynasty: she is the divine consort of Amun, whereas female members of the Kushite court act as Amun's human consorts, as so-called God's Wives with both cultic and economic power.[77] And Mut is one of the Distant Goddesses whose mythology and ritual verbalise strong links between Nubia and Egypt, since she escapes to Nubia and comes back to Egypt.[78] Osiris is the divine predecessor of all pharaohs and the god who regenerates kingship. And Ptah, although his exact position in the kingdom of the early first millennium is not clear yet, becomes prominently visible at least in the context of the 'Shabaqo Stone', a Memphite ritual text of the Twenty-Fifth Dynasty.[79] This king, the predecessor of Taharqo, enlarged the Ptah Temple in Karnak,[80] thus we can attribute a dominant position to this god. All these deities were favoured by Taharqo's building and cultic investments in Egypt. He contributes substantially to the Amun- as well as to the Mut-complexes in Karnak, he restores and extends the Small Temple at Medinet Habu, and in his reign, we see a peak in the rituals in Abydos and we know that his palace and of course other cultic activities were intensive in Memphis. This sacral landscape is mirrored in Nubia by Taharqo to project Egyptian religious and royal ideology onto the heartland of the Napatan state in Nubia, thus emulating Egyptian models while customising royal ideology according to Kushite ideas. Taharqo is the most Egyptian of the Kushite pharaohs. And it was his plan to 'Egyptianise' Nubia and its main religious places. He is the first of the Kushite rulers to postulate a kingship in Kush oriented along Egyptian essentials. He did so in establishing an intensive building program in Nubia, and in projecting the Egyptian sacral landscape unto Nubia. Of course, the 'real' Double Kingdom in Egyptian state ideology is the unification of Upper and Lower Egypt. The pharaohs bear the title 'King of Upper and Lower Egypt, Lord of both lands', meaning Upper and Lower Egypt. With doubling the Egyptian sacral landscape in Kush, Taharqo however created a real territorial Double Kingdom comprising both Egypt and Kush. In contrary to Pi(ankh)y, who seems to include Kush into the mental map of Egypt, Taharqo differentiated both territories as two different lands. He labels them 'Kemet' and 'Ta-seti' in several texts, thus explicitly speaking of two different domains. His ideology of kingship deals with these two distinct territories of his rulership, combined in the pharaonic realm. In the same time, however, he mirrors the Egyptian sacral landscape in Kush and integrates the main Egyptian royal rituals into the Kushite royal ideology. He implements these Egyptian cults in establishing buildings at specific places which will last for the whole Napatan Period. Although temples and cults were modified, the Osireion was re-designated as tomb and the Egyptian conception altered to a Kushite one, Taharqo was the pharaoh who created the sacred landscape in Nubia initially as a reflection of the Egyptian royal cultic topography.

77 A. Lohwasser, 'Nubianess' and the God's Wives of the 25th Dynasty. Office Holders, the Institution, Reception and Reaction., in: M. Becker/A. I. Blöbaum/A. Lohwasser (eds.), "Prayer and Power". Proceedings of the Conference on the God's Wives of Amun in Egypt during the First Millennium BC, ÄUAT 84, Münster 2016, 121–136.

78 Inconnu-Bocquillon, Mythe de la Déesse Lointaine, 197–203.

79 El Hawary, Wortschöpfung.

80 Leclant, Monuments Thébains, 36–41.

The inefficient communication of kingship in the Twenty-fifth Dynasty

Shih-Wei Hsu

Abstract

The kingship of the Twenty-fifth Dynasty has been up to now repeatedly studied from different points of view, such as of its succession, legitimation, theory, reality and so on. Actually, royal inscriptions of this period contain many so-called "archaising" phrases, which imitated from the inscriptions of the Eighteenth or Nineteenth Dynasties. This paper aims to discuss the use of figurative language in royal inscriptions of the New Kingdom and the Twenty-fifth Dynasty, and focus on its function, and purpose, particularly on its differences and development. It will show that power of images has still a strong effect in these propagandistic inscriptions. The kingship and its ideology can spread between the two kingdoms with the use of these images.

I Introduction

In comparison to other periods, kingship in the Late Period of ancient Egypt was not treated for a long time.[1] During the last two decades, studies focusing on kingship of the Late Period have increased. Kingship has been studied from different points of views, such as succession, legitimation, theory, reality etc. The Twenty-fifth Dynasty, or so-called Kushite Dynasty, is one of the "foreign rulerships" in Egyptian history.[2] Due to their Egyptianisation, they left a lot of references and sources behind, *e.g.* they rebuilt and restored temples and tombs, and they cast reliefs in a similar style to those of the Old Kingdom.

At the same time, they also imitated many phrases from the royal inscriptions of the Eighteenth and Nineteenth Dynasties. The use of figurative language for royal inscriptions is very common from the Middle Kingdom onwards, and it reached its peak during the Ramesside Period. The Kushite royal inscriptions certainly adopted this tradition; kings still used some images to describe themselves, their enemies and even their deeds. The usage of figurative language in royal inscriptions changed in some ways between the New Kingdom and the Kushite Dynasty in terms of its development, function and purpose. According to the

1 A. I. Blöbaum, „Denn ich bin ein König, der die Maat liebt". Herrscherlegitimation im spätzeitlichen Ägypten. Eine vergleichende Untersuchung der Phraseologie in den offiziellen Königsinschriften vom Beginn der 25. Dynastie bis zum Ende der makedonischen Herrschaft, AegMon 4, Aachen 2006, 3–4.

2 K. Jansen-Winkeln, Die Fremdherrschaften in Ägypten im 1. Jahrtausend v. Chr., in: Or 69, 2000, 1–20, here: 13–16.

results of my doctoral dissertation,[3] the main function of figurative language is as a written decoration in royal inscriptions. The combination of written and visual images was the best way to reinforce the kingship and its ideology. Figurative language was still used in the royal inscriptions of the Twenty-fifth Dynasty, but it appeared less frequently and aimed mostly to reinforce the relationship between the kings and gods. In this paper, inscriptions have mainly been selected from those of Pi(ankh)y, Shebitku, Shabako, Taharqa and Tanutamun.[4] The usage of figurative language will be divided by topics in the following section.

II Usage of figurative language

II.1 Royal names and titularies

Royal names and titularies are the first clues to understand the ideological concerns and emphases of the Egyptian ruling elite.[5] Naming kings after strong wild animals already had a long tradition since the Predynastic Period.[6] In particular, the "bull" is the most significant animal that the kings always used in their names, for example *k3 nḫt* "strong bull" represents almost all the kings from the Eighteenth Dynasty onwards. In comparison to preceding periods, however, Kushite kings were not named after animals quite so often. One of the few examples is the Horus Name of Pi(ankh)y, which he had simply borrowed from Thutmose III, *k3 nḫt ḫꜥ m W3st* "Strong Bull, who has appeared in Thebes",[7] with a very minor change to *k3 nḫt ḫꜥ m Npt* "Strong Bull, who has appeared in Napata".[8] The alternative to his Horus Name is *k3 t3wj=fj* "the Bull of his two Lands".[9] Besides the images from animals, Pi(ankh)y also adopted his Nebty and Golden Horus Names from Thutmose III's. Thus, he took on same images as Thutmose III did: *w3ḥ nsyt mj Rꜥ m pt* "Enduring of kingship like Re in heaven"[10] and *ḏsr ḫꜥw sḫm pḥtj ꜥnḫ ḥr nb n m3=f mj 3ḫtj* "Sacred of appearances, powerful of strength, at the sight of whom every one lives like He-of-the-Horizon".[11] The relationship to the sun-god is also expressed by phrases after titularies, such as *ꜥnḫ mj Rꜥ* "may he live like Re" and *ꜥnḫ mj Rꜥ ḏt* "may he live like Re forever".[12]

3 S.-W. Hsu, Bilder für den Pharao: Untersuchungen zu den bildlichen Ausdrücken des Ägyptischen in den Königsinschriften und anderen Textgattungen, PÄ 36, Leiden 2017.

4 For the sources of the inscriptions see annex 1. Abbreviation of kings in this paper: Pi(anky)y = P, Shebitku = She, Shabako = Shabako = Sha, Taharqa = T, Tanutamun = TN. The following cross-references refer to annex 1 and abbreviations, *e.g.* P_1_L 26 = Pi(ankh)y, Stela Khartoum SNM 1851, line 26.

5 T. A. H. Wilkinson, What is a King is This: Narmer and the Concept of the Ruler, in: JEA 86, 2000, 23–32, here: 24.

6 L. D. Morenz, Zoophore Herrschernamen: auf Spurensuche nach neuen proto-dynastischen Potentaten, in: WZKM 95, 2005, 119–137.

7 J. von Beckerath, Handbuch der ägyptischen Königsnamen, MÄS 49, Mainz am Rhein 1999, 206–207 3 H3, 208–209 5 H5; T. Eide/T. Hägg/R. H. Pierce/L. Török (eds.), Fontes Historiae Nubiorum. Textual Sources for the History of the Middle Nile Region between the Eighth Century BC and the Sixth Century AD. Volume I: From the Eighth to the Mid-Fifth Century BC, Bergen 1994, 49 8a; 50 9a.

8 R. J. Leprohon, The Great Name. Ancient Egyptian Royal Titulary, Writings from the Ancient World 33, Atlanta 2013, 160 Horus; Eide/Hägg/Pierce/Török (eds.), Fontes Historiae Nubiorum I, 48 1a.

9 Von Beckerath, Handbuch, 206–207 3 H2; Leprohon, Great Name, 161 Horus 5; Eide/Hägg/Pierce/Török (eds.), Fontes Historiae Nubiorum I, 49 8a.

10 Leprohon, Great Name, 161 Two Ladies; Eide/Hägg/Pierce/Török (eds.), Fontes Historiae Nubiorum I, 48 1b.

11 Leprohon, Great Name, 161 Golden Horus.

12 Blöbaum, Herrscherlegitimation, 220–221.

II.2 Legitimation and divine relationships

Besides the royal titularies, the kings of the Twenty-fifth Dynasty always emphasise their relationships to gods, particularly their legitimacy as the son of GN, especially as *z3 Imn* "son of Amun" or *z3 Imn-Rꜥ* "son of Amun-Re" (T_5_L 1).[13] This pattern recalls the epithet of *z3 Rꜥ* "son of Re", which already appeared starting in the Fourth Dynasty[14] and continued to be used in the Twenty-fifth Dynasty (P_2_L 2/60–61).[15] *z3 Rꜥ* "son of Re" represents the divine origin of kings from the sun god, whether as a titulary or as an epithet, sometime even in expanded form; for example, the king Shebitku was called *z3 Rꜥ m3ꜥ mrj* "the true and beloved son of Re",[16] and *z3 Rꜥ m3ꜥ ḫꜥ ḥr nst=f* "the true son of Re, who appeared on his throne".[17] Taharqa declared that *jnk p3=k šrj* "I am your child" to Amun (T_2_L 7). The proclamation of the divine legitimation of the king was necessary, so that he could officially receive the permission and power to rule the land. The father-son-relationship indicates that the king is the earthly incarnation of the god of creation, and exists as an image of his likeness:[18]

> *ꜥn jrw mj Rꜥ n pt*
> "whose form is beautiful like (that of) Re in heaven". (P_1_L 26)
> *tjt nṯr šzp ꜥnḫ Itm prj m ẖt*
> "image of god, living likeness of Atum, who came forth from the body". (P_2_L 1)
> *tjt 3ḫt nt Itm*
> "splendid image of Amun". (T_5_L 1)

Basically, in the father-son-relationship, the king is regarded as the legitimate heir to the god. The god allotted or appointed the position to the king and made him as an official ruler:

> *ḏj n=j Imn n Npt jr ḥq3 n ḫ3st nbt*
> "Amun of Napata appointed me to be ruler of every foreign land". (P_1_L 17–18)
> *ḏj n=j Imn m W3st jr ḥq3 n Kmt*
> "Amun in Thebes appointed me to be ruler of Egypt". (P_1_L 19)
> *wḏ n=k jt=k jwꜥ=f*
> "your father (Amun) allotted you his inheritance". (P_2_L 84)
> *sꜥḥꜥ.n=f wj m nswt*
> "He (Amun) elevated me as king". (T_4_L 19)

The other method of appointment is expressed by the image "egg". *swḥt* "egg" replaces *z3* "son" from the Eighteenth Dynasty onwards; in late time "egg" referred to the unborn child in the Ramesside Period. The kings were meant to be rulers before their birth. "In the egg" is an expression of predestination for the future kingship, which appeared already from the Middle Kingdom onward.[19]

---

13 L. Török, The Kingdom of Kush. Handbook of the Napatan-Meroitic Civilization, HdO 31, Leiden/New York/Köln 1997, 207; Blöbaum, Herrscherlegitimation, 181.

14 Hsu, Bilder für den Pharao, 159 with n. 86.

15 Blöbaum, Herrscherlegitimation, Dok. 25-T-020.

16 Blöbaum, Herrscherlegitimation, Dok. 25-ST-015.

17 Blöbaum, Herrscherlegitimation, Dok. 25-ST-010.

18 B. Ockinga, Die Gottebenbildlichkeit im Alten Ägypten und im Alten Testament, ÄUAT 7, Wiesbaden 1984.

19 Hsu, Bilder für den Pharao, T/a/III/1.

ḏd=j r=k m ẖt n mwt=k jw=k r ḥqꜣ n Kmt rḫ=j tw m mw wnn=k m swḥt jw=k r nb jr.n=j
"I said to you, while you were still in the body of your mother, that you would be the ruler of Egypt. I recognised you as seed, while you existed still in the egg. You would be the lord I made". (P_1_L 2–6)
jnk ms m ẖt sḫpr m swḥt nṯr mtwt nṯr jm=j
"I was born in the body, appeared as divine egg. I am the seed of god".[20] (P_2_L 68–69)
jw=f ḥqꜣ m swḥt
"He will be a ruler, when he is still in the egg". (P_2_L 2)

Other similar images, such as *mw*/*mtwt* "water", and *prt* "seed" have the same function of indicating a descendant relationship between the king and the god:
prt wꜥbt pr ḫnt=f
"the pure seed that came forth in front of him". (T_5_L 1)

In addition, *mrjj GN* "beloved of a god" can still be found both in royal titularies and titles and in inscriptions.[21] This expression also evokes a kind of selection of the kings by the gods. *mrjj Ꞽmn* "beloved of Amun" or *mrjj Ꞽmn-Rꜥ* "beloved of Amun-Re"[22] appear mostly in royal names, because the Kushite kings desired an official legitimation in Gebel Barkal and Thebes. However, the other term *mrjj mj GN* "beloved like GN", which was used very frequently in the New Kingdom, was not found in these selected texts.

II.3 The kings' descriptions and royal deeds
Apart from legitimation, royal descriptions usually contain battle scenes. But reports concerning the battlefield are less common in royal inscriptions from the Twenty-fifth Dynasty. Nevertheless, some images used preferentially to describe the battlefield still appear in this period. The term "bull", for example, always portrays the power and strength of the kings: Pi(ankh)y was praised as *Ḥr nswt nḫt kꜣ hd kꜣw* "Horus, victorious king, bull who prevails over bulls" (P_2_L 72), and *js ntk nbwtj ḫntj tꜣ šmꜥw Mntw kꜣ nḫt-ꜥ* "O, you are Ombite (Seth), foremost of Upper Egypt, Montu, bull with strong arms" (P_2_L 129). The expression here "Bull who prevails over bulls" is an uncommon one, which may recall Sinuhe's comparison of himself to a bull in the midst of other herds.[23] This metaphor implies that Pi(ankh)y has an equal ability to challenge other rulers (*i.e.* bulls) of the Lower Egypt.[24] In this period, Egypt was seen as a field in which many contenders could fight for their own power and territory. Regarding the battle scenes in general, the inscriptions of this period really lack of rhetorical stylistics. They are just images such as *ꜣbj* "panther",[25] *gp n mw* "cloudburst",[26] and *ṯꜣww* "wind"[27] or *ḏrtjw* "kite"[28] depicting royal rage and speed.

20 Wb 2, 2:2. I express my gratitude to Dieter Kurth for this reference.
21 Blöbaum, Herrscherlegitimation, 227–238.
22 There are totally 82 references from Pi(ankh)y, Shebitku, Shabako, Taharqa and Tanutamun. See Blöbaum, Herrscherlegitimation, 233.
23 Sinuhe B 118–120. http://aaew.bbaw.de/tla/servlet/GetCtxt?u=guest&f=0&l=0&tc=842&db=0&ws=1474&mv=4. Accessed on 10.05.2019.
24 H. Goedicke, Pi(ankh)y in Egypt. A Study of the Pi(ankh)y Stela, Baltimore 1998, 71.
25 P_2_L 23, 31, 92.
26 P_2_L 27, 93, 96.
27 T_1_L 9.
28 T_1_L 9.

The kings of the Twenty-fifth Dynasty still used the title *nṯr nfr* "the perfect god",[29] and identified themselves with a deity. The kings attempted to ascribe to themselves the special quality of a god. Horus is a symbol not just of kingship, but also of strength, as his figure is as falcon. The kings are identified as Horus: […] *Ḥr nb ꜥḥ* "[…] Horus, lord of palace" (P_2_L 56); *nfr.wj Ḥr ḥtp m nꜥt=f* "how wonderful is Horus who is pleased with his town" (P_2_L 60–61); *Ḥr mrj Ỉwnw* "beloved Horus of Heliopolis" (P_2_L 105); *Ḥr ṯmꜣ-ꜥ* "Horus, with strong arm" (TN_5_L 3) and *pr pw jr.n ḥm=f m bw wnn=f jm mj pr Ḥr m Ḫbyt* "Forthcoming was what his majesty did from the place he had been, as Horus came forth from Khemnis" (TN_5_L 6).

Montu is a warlike god from the New Kingdom,[30] while Atum stands for the creative power of the primal god,[31] and Thoth represents wisdom and intelligence.[32]

> *nswt ḏs=f mj Mnṯw* "the king himself is like Montu". (T_1_L 10–11)
> *nb qnw mj Mnṯw* "Lord of strength like Montu". (TN_5_L 2)
> *Ỉtm pw n rḫyt* "Atum is he for the people". (TN_5_L 1)
> *ḥqꜣ mj Ỉtm* "A ruler is like Atum". (T_4_L 2)
> *rḫ ḫt pw qn m kꜣt nb snnw Ḏḥwtj* "he is a knowledgeable and capable in every work, a second Thoth". (T_1_L 11–12)
> *mꜣꜥ jb mj Ḫntj Ḥsrt* "whose heart is true like that of presiding over Hesret (Thoth)". (TN_5_L 1)

The sun-god still played an important role in this period. The kings identified themselves with Re to receive his creative strength:

> *mrwt=f ḥr pḫr tꜣw mj Rꜥ ḫꜥꜥ=f m pt*
> "love of him pervades the lands like (that of) Re when he appears in heaven". (T_4_L 3)
> *pr pw jr.n ḥm=f m ꜥḥt=f […] mj psḏ Rꜥ m ꜣḫt*
> "Forthcoming was what his majesty did from his palace […] like Re shined in the horizon". (TN_1_L 32)

One interesting image is the deity Mahes (or Miysis) whose strength the king Tanutamun compared with (TN_1_L 2). The name of Mahes *mꜣj ḥzꜣ* "the wild lion", was a popular metaphor for the kings from the Eighteenth Dynasty,[33] and this term persists through to the Ptolemaic Period. This lion-cult, obviously, transformed into the cult of Apedemak, the war god worshipped by the Meroitic people.[34]

In royal dedications, the gods often grant eternity to the king in the form of different gifts, sometime in comparison to that of a deity.

> *nswt=f m ḥḥ m Tꜣ-tnn*
> "his kingship will be millions (of years) like (that of) Tatenen". (T_4_L 3)

29 Blöbaum, Herrscherlegitimation, 198–199; Hsu, Bilder für den Pharao, 188 with n. 226.

30 N. Grimal, Les termes de propagande royale égyptienne de la XIXe dynastie à la conquête d'Alexandre, MAIBL 6, Paris 1986, 409 with n. 1397.

31 Grimal, Propagande royale égyptienne, 380–381.

32 Grimal, Propagande royale égyptienne, 430–432.

33 Hsu, Bilder für den Pharao, 193–194.

34 F. Breyer, Tanutamani. Die Traumstele und ihr Umfeld, ÄUAT 57, Wiesbaden 2003, 89 with n. 235.

dj ꜥnḫ mj Rꜥ ḏt
"given life like Re forever". (TN_1_Label of King)[35]

The death of a king is always written in figurative language. With the concept of an "ascent to heaven", the king is compared to a falcon rising to heaven.[36] For example, Taharqa describes the death of his predecessor as follows:

šzp.n=j ḫꜥ(.w) m Jnb-ḥḏ m-ḫt ḥr bjk r pt
"I have received the crown in Memphis, after the falcon had departed to heaven". (T_5_L 15)

II.4 Descriptions of enemies and orientational metaphors

It is still very doubtful whether the kings of the Twenty-fifth Dynasty really mounted a campaign against foreign lands. Nevertheless, the kings make an attempt to present how they conquered the foreign lands: *e.g.* the Golden Horus Name of Shebitku is *ꜥꜣ ḫpš ḥwj pḏwt psḏt* "the one with great of strength who has struck down the Nine Bows"; Pi(ankh)y described how *šfyt ḥm=f r pḥ Sṯtjw* "the dignity of his majesty reaches to Asiatics" (P_2_L 30), while Taharqa declared himself *jṯt tꜣw wꜥf pḏwt psḏt* "the one who seized all lands and defeated the Nine Bows" (T_5_L 3). However, if we observe the relationship between the king and his enemies, there are two motifs "smiting the enemies" and "under the king's feet (sandals)", which correspond to the theory of UP-DOWN orientational metaphors.[37] These motifs juxtapose the contrasting postures of the king and his enemies: UP = GOOD – The king stands erect, is dominant and prevails, DOWN = BAD – his enemies are laying, squatting, kneeling, fallen and humiliated.[38] The relief of Temple T of Taharqa in Kawa offers a very good example. Taharqa is depicted as an androcephalic griffin with the additional epithet *ptpt ḫꜣswt nbwt* "trampling all foreign lands" (T_3_label for left hand [south] scene), while he tramples three enemies under his feet.[39] This was clearly inspired by the Old Kingdom Memphite reliefs of Sahure.[40] The clay stamp seals of Shabako (Sha_1) offer another clear example of "smiting the enemies". This UP-DOWN orientational metaphor is also found in the written material:

35 For more see S.-W. HSU, "The Pharaoh lives forever": Royal Eternal Life in Ancient Egyptian Royal Inscriptions, in: Or 86.2, 2017, 274–285, here: 280–283.

36 S.-W. HSU, The Use of Figurative Language Concerning in the Death of the King, in: ArOr 82.2, 2014, 201–209, here: 206.

37 G. LAKOFF/M. JOHNSON, Metaphors we live by, Chicago/London 1980, 14–19.

38 S.-W. HSU, Captured, Defeated, Tied and Fallen: Images of Enemies in Ancient Egypt, in: GM 252, 2017, 71–87; A. DAVID, Devouring the Enemy: Ancient Egyptian Metaphors of Domination, in: BACE 22, 2011, 83–100, here: 86 with n. 16; R. NYORD, Breathing Flesh: Conceptions of the Body in the Ancient Egyptian Coffin Texts, CNIP 37, Copenhagen 2009, 10.

39 R. K. RITNER, Libyan vs. Nubian as the Ideal Egyptian, in: S. E. THOMPSON/P. DER MANUELIAN (eds.), Egypt and Beyond. Essays Presented to Leonard H. Lesko upon his Retirement from the Wilbour Chair of Egyptology at Brown University June 2005, Providence, RI, 2008, 305–314.

40 HSU, Bilder für den Pharao, 178–181; M. F. L. MACADAM, The Temples of Kawa I: The Inscriptions, Part I: Text, Oxford University Excavations in Nubia, London 1949, 63–65.

rḏ.n=f ḥsq n pḏwt pḏwt psḏt dmꜣ.w ẖr ṯbwt=j
"He (Amun) has caused beheading of the Bow-People, and the Nine Bows being tied up beneath my sandals". (T_1_L 6)
wḏ n=j jt=j Ỉmn ḏj tꜣ nb ḫꜣst nb ẖr ṯbwt=j
"My father Amun commanded me to place every land and foreign land beneath my sandals". (T_5_L 15)
ḏj.n(=j) n=k tꜣw nb(w) m [ksw] ḫꜣswt nbwt ẖr ṯbwt=k
"I have given to you all lands in [bowing], with all foreign lands beneath your sandals". (She_1_west wall label for Amun L 4)[41]
ḏj.n(=j) n=k tꜣw nb(w) ḫꜣswt nbwt pḏwt psḏt dmḏ ẖr ṯbwt=k ḏt
"I have given to you all lands, all foreign lands, and Nine Bows gathered beneath your sandals forever". (TN_1_Label of Amun)

The battle scenes contain some metaphors for king's enemies, *i.e.* the opponents: People reported Pi(ankh)y that Tefnakhte had united the north-western part of Egypt and people are subjected to him like *ṯsmw m jrj rdwj* "dogs at his feet" (P_2_L 3). Although "dog" is a typical symbol of obedience, loyalty and humility, the "dog"-usage in Pi(ankh)y's text refers instead to the motif of "flattering subjugations". In addition, the opponents of Pi(ankh)y are designated as "bulls". In the end of his text, Pi(ankh)y made *kꜣw m ḥmwt* "bulls into women" (P_2_L 157–158), because these local rulers were afraid of Pi(ankh)y and *rd.wj=sn m rd.wj ḥmwt* "their posture was like the posture of women" (P_2_L 149–150).[42] It is obviously that woman symbolises the weakness and defencelessness. For the characteristic of helplessness, Tanutamun uses a very unclear image *jnḥw*, which might be translated as "mouse", "gecko" or lizard",[43] to describe to the Chiefs of Lower Egypt and how they were afraid of his Majesty. This image was probably borrowed from the inscription of the second stela of Kamose.[44]

II.5 Special metaphors

There are some special usages of metaphors in the Triumphal Stela of Pi(ankh)y:

- *sd m rꜣ* "tail in the mouth":[45] this expression is reminiscent of the ouroboros, which is a serpent eating its own tail.[46] Nicholas Grimal translated it as "il s'est enroulé comme le serpent".[47] This term is actually a metaphorical symbol for an "unbroken ring of siege around a city".[48] It means that Pi(ankh)y has encircled Heracleopolis completely.[49]

41 Cf. Sha_1_label.

42 This reference indicates that these rulers were not pure (*i.e.* *ꜥmꜥ*, uncircumcised people) and have eaten fishes, therefore they were not allowed to enter the king's palace. J. F. Quack, Zur Beschneidung im Alten Ägypten, in: A. Berlejung/J. Dietrich/J. F. Quack (eds.), Menschenbilder und Körperkonzepte im Alten Israel, in Ägypten und im Alten Orient, Orientalische Religionen in der Antike 9, Tübingen 2012, 561–651, here: 590 with n. 202. I express my gratitude to Karl Jansen-Winkeln for this hint.

43 Hsu, Bilder für den Pharao, 449 with n. 26.

44 L. Habachi, The Second Stela of Kamose and his Struggle against the Hyksos Ruler and his Capital, ADAIK 8, Glückstadt 1972, 34–35 L9 with n. f.

45 P_2_L 5.

46 http://aaew.bbaw.de/tla/servlet/S02?wc=868135&db=0. Accessed on 01.12.2018.

47 N.-C. Grimal, La stèle triomphale de Pi(ꜥankh)y au Musée du Caire: JE 48882 et 47086–47089, Études sur la Propagande Royale Égyptienne I, MIFAO 105, Cairo 1981, 14 with n. 38: "il s'est fait en qualité de queue-dans-la-gueule".

48 Wb 4, 364:6: "bildlich vom rückenlosen Ring der Belagerung um eine Stadt".

49 Goedicke, Pi(ankh)y in Egypt, 14 with n. 31.

- *wj3 n mw n ḥm=f* "reject the water of his majesty" (P_2_L 7): this term can be traced back to *ḥr mw(=f)* "on (someone's) water", *i.e.* "depending on someone" or "surrendering to someone" (TN_1_L 30).[50] A plausible explanation involves of the relationship between the water consumer downstream and the water supplier upstream.[51] The water supplier is in the up-position and could cut off the water anytime. Therefore, this expression is always used for loyalty.[52] *wj3 n mw n ḥm=f* could be understood as "someone is disloyal to his majesty".[53]

- *dp ḏbꜥ=j* "taste of my fingers" (P_2_L 26): this is a conceptual metaphor from a physical experience. It refers to haptic-tactile perception:[54] THE HAND STANDS FOR CONTROL; CONTROL IS HOLDING SOMETHING IN THE HAND.[55] Already in the inscription of the Kadesh Battle, Ramesses II said that *ḏjw=j dp=sn ḏrt=j m km n 3t* "I cause them to taste my hand immediately",[56] which means that he has punished his enemies. In the case of Pi(ankh)y, fingers serve as a metonymic device for the hand and bear the same meaning.[57]

- *ẖr ḏbꜥ* "under someone's finger" (P_2_L 78; P_2_L 131): On the one hand, this expression could be regarded as a spatial metaphor referring to the width of a finger:[58] Pi(ankhy)'s opponents are so tiny in front of his greatness. On the other hand, it is a metonymic expression for being 'under the control' of someone, *i.e.* "in someone's hand".[59]

III Conclusion

The figurative language in the royal inscriptions of the Twenty-fifth Dynasty is mainly used to emphasise two themes:

1. divine legitimation
2. kings and opponents in battle scenes

All in all, the images come mostly from the divine world and animal world. They represent different functions as follows (see Tab. 1 below).

---

50 Wb 2, 52–53.

51 W. Westendorf, „Auf jemandes Wasser sein" = „von ihm abhängig sein", in: GM 11, 1974, 47–48, here: 47.

52 Hsu, Bilder für den Pharao, 261–262.

53 Wb 1, 272:14; Goedicke, Pi(ankh)y in Egypt, 20.

54 E. Steinbach, „Ich habe seinen Anblick geschmeckt...": Verben der Wahrnehmung und die semantischen Beziehungen zwischen Perzeption und Kognition, in: G. Neunert/H. Simon/A. Verbovsek/K. Gabler (eds.), Text: Wissen – Wirkung – Wahrnehmung. Beiträge des vierten Münchner Arbeitskreises Junge Aegyptologie (MAJA 4), 29.11. bis 1.12.2013, GOF IV/59, Wiesbaden 2015, 209–225, here: 216–217.

55 Z. Kövecses, Metaphor. A Practical Introduction, Oxford 2010, 243.

56 KRI II, 52:1–4 (§ 155).

57 D. A. Werning, Der ‚Kopf des Beines', der ‚Mund der Arme' und die ‚Zähne' des Schöpfers. Zu metonymischen und metaphorischen Verwendungen von Körperteil-Lexemen im Hieroglyphisch-Ägyptischen, in: K. Müller/A. Wagner (eds.), Synthetische Körperauffassung im Hebräischen und den Sprachen der Nachbarkulturen, AOAT 416, Münster 2014, 107–161, here: 119.

58 Werning, ‚Kopf des Beines', 150.

59 Wb 4, 565:3.

Characteristic	Category	Image
Legitimate	Animal world	Egg
	Divine world	Amun/Amun-Re
		Atum
		Re
	Human relationship	Child
		Son
	Natural world	Water
	Plant world	Seed
Strong, powerful	Animal world	Bull
	Divine world	Atum
		Harachte
		Horus
		Mahes
		Montu
		Re
		Seth
Wise, intelligent	Divine world	Thoth
Speed	Animal world	Kite
	Natural world	Cloudburst
		Wind
Rage, angry	Animal world	Panther
Eternal	Divine world	Re
		Tatenen
Death of the king	Animal world	Falcon
Descriptions of opponents	Animal world	Bull
		Mouse?
	Human relationship	Women

Tab. 1: Overview of metaphorical images

However, in comparison to the inscriptions of the New Kingdom, the usage of figurative language has been strongly reduced here. The reasons why royal inscriptions of Twenty-fifth Dynasty did not contain many figurative expressions are as follows:

1) Due to the political background of occurrences of civil insurrection and war, Egypt was divided into many local powers. Thebes served mainly as a religious place, where the Kushite kings had a strong connection with the god Amun. Compared to earlier periods, Thebes did not possess real political power. As a result, there are fewer references of the so-called *pr-ꜥnḫ* "the house of life".[60] Poorly trained Nubian scribes made an effort to use Egyptian language and writing in order to reproduce the affairs of kings on monuments.[61] They adopted and imitated the concepts of Egyptian kingship ideology. The usurpation of former monuments saved time as well as costs and energy.[62] In addition, it represents a typical archaising movement. These

60 A. H. Gardiner, The House of Life, in: JEA 24, 1938, 157–179, here: 165–167.

61 Török, Kingdom of Kush, 57–58.

62 R. S. Bianchi, Daily Life of the Nubians. Daily Life Through History, London 2004, 156.

former monuments serve as sources of inspiration for a contemporary age. The Kushite kings could show their kingship very succinctly and achieve the same propagandistic intention as the brilliant Egyptian Pharaohs of the past. Therefore, they borrowed only a few images for certain purposes and did not create any new images of their own.

2) Most still remaining and legible inscriptions of the Twenty-fifth Dynasty recorded events about enthronement, dedications to gods, restoration of temples, inundations etc. These details were written in a precise manner, without exaggerating or extra emphasis. Furthermore, the content of royal inscriptions does not refer to battle events very much. Although Pi(ankh)y's inscriptions are constructed similarly to those of the New Kingdom, a lot of rhetorical stylistics are lacking. The royal inscriptions of the New Kingdom contain uncountable images to emphasise the "strong" kings and the "weak" enemies. This kind of written "communication" aimed to spread Egyptian kingship to all of Egypt and to foreign lands. In the Twenty-fifth Dynasty, however, the kings did not battle with foreigners, but only with local opponents of Lower Egypt instead,[63] nor did they actually extend their border into foreign lands. They were even not able to overcome the threat of Assyria.[64] As a result, it seemed not necessary to have extra images to emphasise the kings and their opponents. The written "communication" of kingship in the Twenty-fifth Dynasty is inefficient in the figurative sphere.

In conclusion, these monumental messages represent the ruler's legitimation and play the role of an "elevated, explicit, and central manifestation of political thought".[65] Although the figurative language becomes rare in this period, it still functions as decoration in these inscriptions and highlights certain attributes of royal authority. With this minor form of "Egyptianisation", the Kushite kings could claim that they were more Egyptian than other chiefs, whether native Egyptians accepted this or not. At least, they attempted to maintain their ideological basis for a unified rule over Egypt and Kush.

63 Török, Kingdom of Kush, 208 with n. 83.

64 D. Kahn, Taharqa, King of Kush and the Assyrians, in: JSSEA 31, 2004, 109–128.

65 Török, Kingdom of Kush, 59.

Annex: Sources of the selected inscriptions

Kings	Inscriptions	Reference
Pi(ankh)y	1. Stela of Khartum SNM 1851 Sandstone Stela	• K. JANSEN-WINKELN, Inschriften der Spätzeit. Teil II: Die 22.–24. Dynastie, Wiesbaden 2007, 350–351 §35.2 • GRIMAL, Propagande royale égyptienne, 217–219 • EIDE/HÄGG/PIERCE/TÖRÖK (eds.), Fontes Historiae Nubiorum I, 55–62 (8) • R. K. RITNER, The Libyan Anarchy: Inscriptions from Egypt's Third Intermediate Period, Writings from the ancient world 21, Atlanta 2009, 461–464 (143)
	2. Triumphal Stela (Cairo JE 48862 [+47086–47089])	• JANSEN-WINKELN, Inschriften der Spätzeit II, 337–350 §35.1 • GRIMAL, La stèle triomphale de Pi(ᶜank)y • EIDE/HÄGG/PIERCE/TÖRÖK (eds.), Fontes Historiae Nubiorum I, 62–118 (9) • RITNER, Libyan Anarchy, 465–492 (145) • GOEDICKE, Pi(ankh)y in Egypt
Shebitku	1. Karnak Chapel (Berlin 1480)	• K. JANSEN-WINKELN, Inschriften der Spätzeit. Teil III: Die 25. Dynastie, Wiesbaden 2009, 46–50 §47.7 • RITNER, Libyan Anarchy, 501–505 (154)
Shabako	1. Stamp Seals (BM 84527 + 84884)	• JANSEN-WINKELN, Inschriften der Spätzeit III, 24 §46.50 • RITNER, Libyan Anarchy, 499 (151)
Taharqa	1. Dahshur Stela	• JANSEN-WINKELN, Inschriften der Spätzeit III, 59–61 §48.12 • EIDE/HÄGG/PIERCE/TÖRÖK (eds.), Fontes Historiae Nubiorum I, 158–163 (23) • H. ALTENMÜLLER/A. M. MOUSSA, Die Inschriften der Taharkastele von der Dahschurstraße, in: SAK 9, 1981, 57–84

Kings	Inscriptions	Reference
Taharqa	2. North-Court of Pylon VI of Amun Temple	• JANSEN-WINKELN, Inschriften der Spätzeit III, 84–87 §48.33 • EIDE/HÄGG/PIERCE/TÖRÖK (eds.), Fontes Historiae Nubiorum I, 181–190 (26) • A. SPALINGER, The Foreign Policy of Egypt Preceding the Assyrian Conquest, in: CdE 53, 1978, 22–47, here: 28–33 • KAHN, JSSEA 31, 2004, 109–128 • RITNER, Libyan Anarchy, 505–511 (155)
	3. Kawa Relief	• RITNER, Libyan Anarchy, 524–527 (159) • M. F. L. MACADAM, The Temples of Kawa II: History and Archaeology of the Site, Part II: Plates, Oxford University Excavations in Nubia, London 1955, pl. IXb
	4. Kawa IV	• JANSEN-WINKELN, Inschriften der Spätzeit III, 132–135 §48.74 • EIDE/HÄGG/PIERCE/TÖRÖK (eds.), Fontes Historiae Nubiorum I, 135–145 (21) • MACADAM, Kawa I Text, 14–21
	5. Kawa V	• JANSEN-WINKELN, Inschriften der Spätzeit III, 121–123 §48.60; 135–138 §48.75 • RITNER, Libyan Anarchy, 539–545 (162) • EIDE/HÄGG/PIERCE/TÖRÖK (eds.), Fontes Historiae Nubiorum I, 145–158 (22) • MACADAM, Kawa I Text, 23–26; 32–41
Tanutamun	1. Dream Stela (Cairo JE 48863)	• JANSEN-WINKELN, Inschriften der Spätzeit III, 236–240 §49.8 • EIDE/HÄGG/PIERCE/TÖRÖK (eds.), Fontes Historiae Nubiorum I, 193–209 • RITNER, Libyan Anarchy, 566–573 (169) • BREYER, Tanutamani

Religion and Power during the Twenty-fifth Dynasty

The building activities of the Kushite kings in Karnak

Essam Nagy

Abstract

The Kushite kings built a number of monuments within the precincts of the Karnak temples, such as columns, gateways, walls, chapels, and individual temples. They also added and renovated the monuments of their predecessors, including the temples of Amun-Re, Khonsu, Ptah, Opet, Mut and Montu as well as numerous chapels of Osiris. The architectural activities of the rulers of the Kushite Dynasty mirror their religious and political power in Egypt. An examination of the extensive work conducted by these kings at the temples of Karnak reveals that their structures and scenes imitated those of the earlier New Kingdom rulers. This paper investigates the political and religious situation during the Twenty-fifth Dynasty, in the context of the concept of kingship. Did the architectural programme reflect the Kushite understanding of kingship? Additionally, how can we determine the relationship between the Kushite rulers and the God's Wives through their monuments?

This paper will give an update on the Kushite building activities in Karnak with a special focus on the Osiris chapels and highlight the recent work carried out by the team of the Osiris-Ptah Neb-ankh Research Project (OPNARP) at the area south of the Tenth Pylon of the Amun-Re precinct.

Introduction

This paper will present a short summary of an investigation of the relationship between religious concepts and building activities in the early first millennium BC at Thebes, focusing on the architectural works of the Twenty-fifth Dynasty at Karnak.

The building activities of the Kushite kings can help to understand Kushite royal ideology and aspects of specific approaches to self-representation and the chosen official appearance for the Egyptian society. The rulers of the Twenty-fifth Dynasty started a massive building program at Karnak. Every Kushite king is attested by means of architectural building at Karnak, especially at the main precincts of Amun-Re, Mut and Montu.

Kushite buildings at Karnak

The Twenty-fifth Dynasty kings executed a massive building program. A number of structures were added to the precinct of Amun-Re and some of their predecessors' buildings were renewed. The Kushites also carried out building activity at the temples of Montu and Mut. All in all, their building works include the temples of Amun-Re, Khonsu, Ptah, Opet,

Mut and Montu.[1] Because of the state of preservation and several destruction events it is still challenging to reconstruct the full building programme of the Kushites at Karnak.[2] Nevertheless, the following are clearly Kushite contributions within the Amun-Re precinct (Fig. 1):

King Shabitka built a small sandstone chapel for Amun-Re, located to the southeast of the Sacred Lake.[3] Richard Lepsius moved blocks from this chapel to the Egyptian Museum in Berlin.[4]

King Shabaka renewed the Fourth Pylon,[5] originally built by Thutmose IV.[6] Shabaka also built a small sandstone colonnaded hall at the north side of the great hypostyle hall of the Amun-Re temple, still visible are remains of three rows of columns, each row consisted of five columns, now in very bad conditions.[7] Furthermore two gates were added by the king in front of the Ptah temple, gates number two[8] and four[9] after the modern numbering system. East of the Ptah temple the king built the so-called Treasury of Shabaka. Recent excavations conducted by Nadia Licitra showed a remarkable extension of this building, so far only known by two rows of six cylindrical sandstone columns with well-preserved different colours.[10]

1 E. Nagy, The Architectural Activity of the Napatan Kings at the Temples of Karnak during 701–656 BC: Historical and Archaeological Study in the Light of Recent Archaeological Excavations, Cairo University, unpublished MA thesis, Cairo 2016.

2 G. Legrain, Les temples de Karnak. Fragment du dernier ouvrage de Georges Legrain, Bruxelles 1929, 5–12.

3 See Fig. 1, no. 7.

4 J. Leclant, Recherches sur les monuments Thébains de la XXVe dynastie dite éthiopienne, BdE 36, Cairo 1965, 59–60; PM II^2, 223; TIP^2, 345–55; K.-R. Lepsius, Denkmaeler aus Aegypten und Aethiopien, Text III, Leipzig 1900, 40–42; A. Masson, Offering Magazines on the Southern Bank of the Sacred Lake in Karnak: The Oriental Complex of the Twenty-fifth–Twenty-sixth Dynasty, in: E. Pischikova/J. Budka/K. Griffin (eds.), Thebes in the First Millennium BC, Newcastle upon Tyne 2014, 587–602, here: 594–595.

5 See Fig. 1, no. 2.

6 F. Larché, Architecture, in: B. Letellier/F. Larché, La cour à portique de Thoutmosis IV, Études d'égyptologie 12, Paris 2013, 19–127, here: 19 (online edition, http://www.soleb.com/livres/thoutmosis-iv/karnak-evolution.html). Accessed on 06.09.2019. See also TIP^2, 379–380; J. Leclant, Les inscriptions 'éthiopiennes' sur la porte du IVe pylône du grand temple d'Amon à Karnak, in: RdE 8, 1951, 101–120, here: 104–113.

7 See Fig. 1, no. 3; P. Barguet, Le temple d'Amon-Rê à Karnak. Essai d'exégèse, RAPH 21, Cairo 1962, 17; H. Chevrier, Rapport sur les travaux de Karnak (1937–1938), in: ASAE 38, 1938, 567–608, here: 596–598; E. Blyth, Karnak. Evolution of a Temple, London/New York 2006, 194.

8 See Fig. 1, no. 5; PM II^2, 197–202; Leclant, Recherches sur les monuments Thébains de la XXVe dynastie, 36–40; Ch. Thiers, Le temple de Ptah à Karnak. Remarques préliminaires, in: H. Beinlich (ed.), 9. Ägyptologische Tempeltagung. Kultabbildung und Kultrealität, KSG 3,4, Wiesbaden 2013, 319–342; G. Legrain, Le temple de Ptah Rîs-Anbou-f dans Thèbes, in: ASAE 3, 1902, 38–66; S. Biston-Moulin/Ch. Thiers, Le temple de Ptah à Karnak I. Relevé épigrahique, BiGen 49, Cairo 2016, 233–238.

9 See Fig. 1, no. 6; G. Legrain, Le temple de Ptah Rîs-Anbou-f dans Thèbes (suite), in: ASAE 3, 1902, 97–114.

10 See Fig. 1, no. 4; N. Licitra, The Treasury of Shabaka, Centre franco-égyptien d'étude des temples de Karnak, Rapport 2012, Rapport d'activité du CFEETK, Luxor 2013, https://www.nakala.fr/nakala/data/11280/9b1ffb73, 47–49. Accessed on 06.09.2019; Blyth, Karnak, 194.

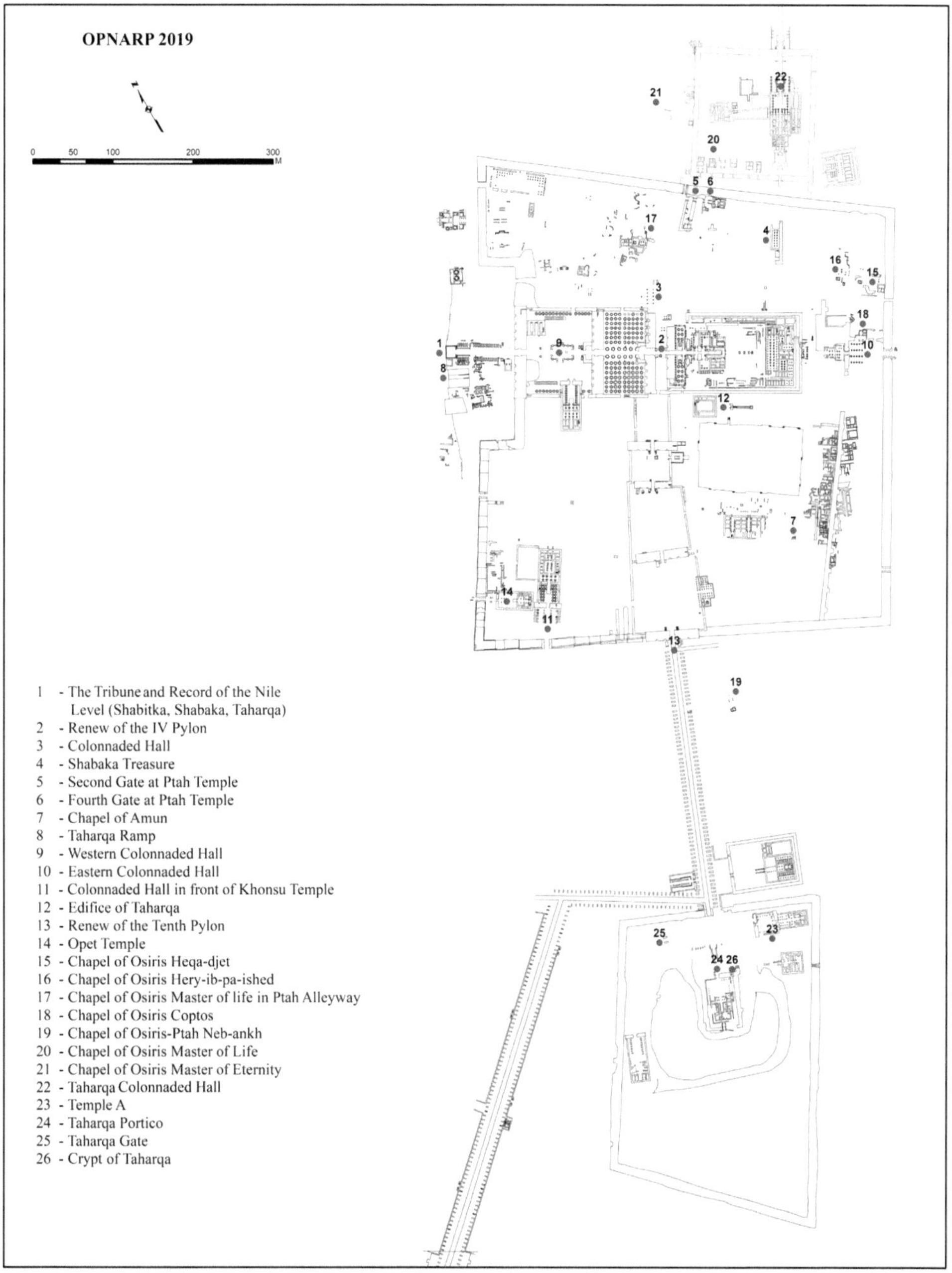

Fig. 1: General Map of Karnak with indication of the Twenty-fifth Dynasty building activities (© CFEETK with modifications by Essam NAGY)

King Taharqa was the most active Kushite king at Karnak. He ordered several structures within the Amun-Re precinct, he built the middle ramp in front of the temple, at its western entrance,[11] first excavated by Jean LAUFFRAY (Fig. 2), and recently fully exposed by Mansour BORAIK (Fig. 3).[12]

Fig. 2: King Taharqa, middle ramp, excavated by J. LAUFFRAY (© CFEETK)

11 See Fig. 1, no. 8; J. LAUFFRAY, Abords occidentaux du premier pylône de Karnak. Le dromos, la tribune et les aménagements portuaires, in: Kêmi 21 (Cahiers de Karnak 4), 1971, 77–144, here: 87–95; M. BORAIK/A. GRAHAM, Geomorphological investigations in the Western part of Karnak Temple (Quay and Ancient Harbour). First Results, in: Cahiers de Karnak 13, 2010, 101–109, here: 102–104; S. AUFRÈRE/J.-C. GOLVIN, L'Égypte restituée III. Sites, temples et pyramides de Moyenne et Basse Égypte. De la naissance de la civilisation pharaonique à l'époque gréco-romaine, Paris 1997, 82–83. 86–87.

12 M. BORAIK, Excavations of the Quay and the Embankment in front of Karnak Temples. Preliminary Report, in: Cahiers de Karnak 13, 2010, 65–78, here: 69–70.

Fig. 3: King Taharqa, middle ramp, excavated by M. Boraik (© Mansour Boraik)

The so-called kiosk of Taharqa in front of the Second Pylon is a colonnade constructed of two rows of colums with five columns in each row (Fig. 4).[13]

Fig. 4: Taharqa, colonnaded hall in front of the Second Pylon (©CFEETK)

The so-called Edifice of Taharqa,[14] located at the northwest corner of the Sacred Lake, consists of two floors. Unfortunately, the upper floor is much destroyed, but the lower, kind of subterranean part survived with a complex division of rooms,[15] its scenes portray the journey of Re through the underworld during the night.[16] At the eastern side of the Amun-Re temple

13 See Fig. 1, no. 9; Blyth, Karnak, 196–197; Leclant, Recherches sur les monuments Thébains de la XXVe dynastie, 8–13. J. Hourdin, The Kushite Kiosks of Karnak and Luxor: A Cross-over-Study, in: E. Pischikova/J. Budka/K. Griffin (eds.), Thebes in the First Millennium BC: Art and Archaeology of the Kushite Period and Beyond, GHP Egyptology 27, London 2018, 255–270, here: 256.

14 See Fig. 1, no. 12; PM II^2, 219–221; R. A. Parker/J. Leclant/J.-C. Goyon, The Edifice of Taharqa by the Sacred Lake of Karnak, Brown Egyptological Studies 8, London 1979, 81; K. M. Cooney, The Edifice of Taharqa by the Sacred Lake: Ritual Function and the Role of the King, in: JARCE 37, 2000, 15–47; R. H. Wilkinson, The Complete Temples of Ancient Egypt, New York 2000, 160; Leclant, Recherches sur les monuments Thébains de la XXVe dynastie, 75; see also B. von Bothmer, Egyptian Sculpture of the Late Period. 700 B.C. to A.D. 100, The Brooklyn Museum, New York 1960, 7–18; E. Russmann, Kushite headdresses and 'Kushite' style, in: JEA 81, 1995, 227–232.

15 Cooney, JARCE 37, 2000, 15–47.

16 Wilkinson, The Complete Temples, 160; Parker/Leclant/Goyon, The Edifice of Taharqa, 81.

the king erected another colonnaded hall, located in front of the Ramesses II temple and close to the eastern gate leading into the Amun-Re precinct (Fig. 5).[17]

Fig. 5: Taharqa, colonnaded hall, eastern side of the Amun-Re temple (©Essam NAGY)

Taharqa built another colonnaded hall in front of Khonsu temple, which is today nearly completely destroyed.[18] This colonnaded hall consisted originally of four rows of columns with five columns each, exactly like the one at the eastern side of the Amun-Re precinct.[19] All in all, Taharqa therefore erected four colonnaded halls in the four main directions of the Karnak temples.[20] Furthermore, the king added structures to the Opet temple,[21] which is located at the western side of Khonsu Temple. A number of stone blocks with the name of Taharqa have been found by Henri CHEVRIER, and were probably part of a chapel.[22]

17 See Fig. 1, no. 10; PM II², 71; LECLANT, Recherches sur les monuments Thébains de la XXVe dynastie, 56–58.

18 See Fig. 1, no. 11; LECLANT, Recherches sur les monuments Thébains de la XXVe dynastie, 84; PM II², 227–228.

19 J. LECLANT, Les colonnades-propylées de la XXVᵉ Dynastie a Thèbes, in: Les Cahiers Techniques de l'art IV.1. Numéro special publié à l'occasion du dixième anniversaire de leur fondation, 1957, 27–45.

20 H. CHEVRIER, Plan d'ensemble de Karnak, in: ASAE 36, 1936, 77–87, here: 84–85. 1936.

21 LECLANT, Recherches sur les monuments Thébains de la XXVe dynastie, 82–83; PM II², p. 245.

22 H. CHEVRIER, Rapport sur les travaux de Karnak (1947–1948), in: ASAE 47, 1947, 161–183, here: 170–178; LECLANT, Recherches sur les monuments Thébains de la XXVe dynastie, 181; G. CHARLOUX (ed.), Le parvis du temple d'Opet à Karnak. Exploration archéologique (2006–2007). Travaux du Centre franco-égyptien d'étude des temples de Karnak, BiGen 41, Cairo 2012, 400–404.

Another block was found re-used under the foundation below the northern wall of the Opet temple,[23] maybe part of a small hall was built at the Opet temple court.[24] In the southwestern corner outside of the enclosure wall of Amun-Re the excavations of the Supreme Council of Antiquities have revealed part of the sandstone embankment, datable to the Kushite period and built during the reign of Taharqa (Fig. 6).[25] Furthermore the king ordered reconstruction and renovation work at the Amun-Re temple, traceable are inscriptions at the Second Pylon and the renewal of the gate of the Tenth Pylon.[26]

Fig. 6: Embankment extension behind the recumbent rams in front of Khonsu temple (©Mansour Boraik, Cahiers de Karnak 14, 2013, 29, fig. 23)

In the Montu temple in the northern side of the Karnak complex, king Taharqa built another colonnaded hall consisting of four rows of columns with five columns each.[27] During earlier

23 C. Traunecker, Les cryptes du temple d'Opet à Karnak, Mémoire de l'EPHE, inédit, 1975, 41; E. Laroze/G. Charloux, Premiers résultats des investigations archéologiques de la mission d'étude du temple d'Opet à Karnak (2006–2008), in: CRAIBL octobre 2008, 2008, 1305–1359; E. Laroze, Osiris et le temple d'Opet. Apports de l'étude architecturale, in: L. Coulon (ed.), Le culte d'Osiris au Ier millénaire av. J.-C. Découvertes et travaux récents. Actes de la table ronde internationale tenue à Lyon. Maison de l'Orient et de la Méditerranée (université Lumière-Lyon 2) les 8 et 9 juillet 2005, BdE 153, Cairo 2010, 219–238.

24 See Fig. 1, no. 14; the author worked as a member of the archaeological team of the Franco Egyptian Center working in the excavation, restoration and conservation project at Opet temple.

25 M. Boraik, The Sphinx Avenue Excavations. Second Report, in: Cahiers de Karnak 14, 2013, 13–32, here: 29; Boraik, Cahiers de Karnak 13, 2010, 69–70.

26 See Fig. 1, no. 13; Leclant, Recherches sur les monuments Thébains de la XXVe dynastie, 80–81; PM II^2, 62; Nagy, The Architectural Activity of the Napatan Kings at the Temples of Karnak, 46.

27 See Fig. 1, no. 22; Leclant, Recherches sur les monuments Thébains de la XXVe dynastie, 85; J. Leclant, Une statuette d'Amon-Rê-Montou au nom de la divine adoratrice Chepenoupet, MIFAO 66.4, Mélanges

excavations remains of a temple foundation built by Taharqa were found.[28] In addition, the king renewed the entrance gate of the Montu temple.[29]

In the Mut complex, Taharqa erected red granite sphinxes located near the temple entrance, which are nowadays in a bad state of preservation. Within the Mut temple, Temple A (Fig. 7), located in the north-eastern corner of the Mut temple, was largely modified by Taharqa as the king renewed most of this temple.[30]

Fig. 7: Temple A, Mut temple
(©Essam NAGY)

A monumental gate of Taharqa is located to the northwest of the temple in the same axis as Temple A. It consists of two small towers (the northern and southern tower) and was discovered by the Brooklyn Museum Archaeological Mission.[31] Furthermore, the king built a portico to the south of the open court of the Mut temple.[32] Within the temple proper the

Maspero I, Orient Ancien, Paris 1961, 74–98; PM II², 5, P. BARGUET/J. LECLANT, Karnak-Nord IV (1949–1951). Fouilles conduites par Cl. Robichon. Rapport de P. Barguet et J. Leclant. Fascicule 1 (texte), Fascicule 2 (planches), FIFAO 25, Cairo 1954, 5–6, 68.

28 BARGUET/LECLANT, Karnak-Nord IV, 6–36.

29 BARGUET/LECLANT, Karnak-Nord IV, 68.

30 See Fig. 1, no. 23; R. FAZZINI/W. PECK, Excavating at the Temple of Mut, in: Archaeology (An official Publication of the Archaeological Institute of America) 36.2, 1983, 16–23.

31 See Fig. 1, no. 25; R. FAZZINI, The Brooklyn Museum's 2010 Season of Fieldwork at the Precinct of the Goddess Mut at South Karnak. Online version expedition report 2010, 1–38. <https://www.brooklynmuseum.org/features/mut_expedition_reports>. Accessed on 06.09.2019; R. FAZZINI/M. MCKERCHER, The Brooklyn Museum's 2013 Season of Fieldwork at the Precinct of the Goddess Mut at South Karnak, 2–3. Online version expedition report 2013, 1–29. <https://www.brooklynmuseum.org/features/mut_expedition_reports>. Accessed on 06.09.2019.

32 See Fig. 1, no. 24; R. FAZZINI/W. PECK, The precinct of Mut during Dynasty XXV and early Dynasty XXVI: a growing picture, in: JSSEA 11(3), 1981, 115–126, here: 116–119. FAZZINI/PECK, Archaeology (An official Publication of the Archaeological Institute of America) 36.2, 1983, 16–23, 80.

so-called Crypt of Taharqa or Crypt of Montuemhat was built by Montuemhat, the governor of Thebes during Taharqa's reign. The walls of this small room are decorated with religious scenes and texts. The eastern wall shows the king standing, presenting offerings and adoring the goddess Mut, behind the king, Montuemhat with his father and son, both named Nesptah, are depicted.[33] According to the inscriptions the king renewed and added elements in the temples of the goddess in Upper Egypt.[34]

Osirian chapels during the Kushite Period in Karnak

The Osirian chapels at Karnak represent complicated aspects of the late building programme at the site because their building phases and dating are partly still unclear. Especially a fine dating of these chapels to specific reigns within the Twenty-fifth Dynasty is a challenge. Recent work has provided much additional information, but the research on these chapels is still ongoing.[35]

Within the Amun-Re temple, Shabitka has built as an extension the outer room of the chapel of Osiris Heqa-djet located at the east of Amun-Re temple, near the enclosure wall.[36] This chapel consists of two parts: the inner part is dating to the Libyan Period, the outer part to the Kushite Period. Relief scenes are showing the king with the God's Wife Amenirdis I, most of the scenes show however Amenirdis I and Shepenwepet I presenting offerings independently to the gods.[37]

The chapel of Osiris Hery-ib-pa-ished is located at the northeast of the Amun-Re temple along the way of the enclosure wall and is nowadays unfortunately in a very bad condition. Nevertheless the lintel of its stone gate preserves the name of the chapel itself, and the name of Shepenwepet II. In the entrance the Divine Adoratrices Shepenwepet II and Amenirdis I are depicted (Fig. 8).[38] Among the decoration an interesting relief is to highlight, showing the singer of Amun and sister of Montuemhat, governor of Thebes, standing behind

33 PM II^2, 258; Leclant, Recherches sur les monuments Thébains de la XXVe dynastie, 114.

34 See Fig.1, no. 26; R. Fazzini, Two Semi-Erased Kushite Cartouches in the Precinct of Mut at South Karnak, in P. Brand/L. Cooper (eds.), Causing His Name to Live: Studies in Egyptian Epigraphy and History in Memory of William J. Murnane, Culture and History of the Ancient Near East 37, Leiden/Boston 2009, 95–101; M. Benson/J. Gourlay, The Temple of Mut in Asher. An Account of the Excavation of the Temple and of the Religious Representations and Objects Found Therein, as Illustrating the History of Egypt and the Main Religious Ideas of the Egyptians, London 1899, 264–265.

35 See, *e.g.* L. Coulon/A. Hallmann/F. Payraudeau, The Osirian Chapels at Karnak: An Historical and Art Historical Overview Based on Recent Fieldwork and Studies, in: E. Pischikova/J. Budka/K. Griffin (eds.), Thebes in the First Millennium BC: Art and Archaeology of the Kushite Period and Beyond, GHP Egyptology 27, London 2018, 271–293.

36 See Fig. 1, no. 15; G. Lefebvre, Histoire des grands prêtres d'Amon de Karnak jusqu'à la XXIe dynastie, Paris 1929, 205; Leclant, Recherches sur les monuments Thébains de la XXVe dynastie, 47–54.

37 M. Ayad, God's Wife, God's Servant: The God's Wife of Amun (c. 740–525 BC). London/New York 2009, 39–42; M. Ayad, Gender, Ritual, and Manipulation of Power. The God's Wife of Amun (Dynasty 23–26), in: M. Becker/A. I. Blöbaum/A. Lohwasser (eds.), "Prayer and Power". Proceedings of the Conference on the God's Wives of Amun in Egypt during the First Millennium BC, ÄUAT 84, Münster 2016, 89–106.

38 See Fig. 1, no. 16; the author has the approval from the Ministry of Antiquities to start the study and documentation for this chapel; Leclant, Recherches sur les monuments Thébains de la XXVe dynastie, 43–44; R. Fazzini, Egypt Dynasty XXII–XXV, Iconography of Religions, Section 16, Egypt 10, Leiden 1988, 20; Coulon/ Hallmann/Payraudeau, The Osirian Chapels at Karnak, 277.

Fig. 8: Chapel of Osiris Hery-ib-pa-ished, located at the northeast of the Amun-Re temple (©Brigitte BALANDA)

Shepenwepet II. Unfortunately, it remains unclear when exactly the chapel was built, maybe it belongs already to the period of the Assyrian invasions.[39]

The chapel of Osiris Neb-ankh 'Lord of life' is located along the way to the Ptah temple and was erected by Taharqa and the God's Wife Shepenwepet II. Because of its very small size, this chapel is generally regarded as the smallest among the Osirian chapels in Karnak,[40] consisting of only two rooms. Room I is small, an entrance of only 36cm in its northern wall leads to Room II. Reliefs within the chapel attest the name and also the representations of Taharqa and the Divine Adoratrice Shepenwepet II.[41]

The chapel of Osiris of Coptos is located at the eastern part of the Amun-Re temple. At present, the building is destroyed, but it was built out of re-used blocks with depictions of Amenirdis I or II, dating to the Kushite period.[42] The chapel was probably built during the reign of Shabaka.[43]

---

39 NAGY, The Architectural Activity of the Napatan Kings at the Temples of Karnak, 74–75.

40 See Fig. 1, no. 17; L. CHRISTOPHE, Karnak-Nord III (1945–1949). Fouilles conduites par C. Robichon. Rapport de Louis A. Christophe, FIFAO 23, Cairo 1951, 12–13.

41 NAGY, The Architectural Activity of the Napatan Kings at the Temples of Karnak, 75–76; G. LEGRAIN, Le temple et les chapelles d'Osiris a Karnak, III. La chapelle d'Osiris, maître de la vie, in: RecTrav 24, 1902, 208–214, here: 209–210.

42 See Fig. 1, no. 18; NAGY, The Architectural Activity of the Napatan Kings at the Temples of Karnak, 78.

43 COULON/HALLMANN/PAYRAUDEAU, The Osirian Chapels at Karnak, 276.

In the Montu precinct, North Karnak, the Kushite kings also built Osirian chapels. The chapel of Osiris Neb-ankh is located to the north of the enclose wall of Amun-Re within the Montu precinct. This chapel was already excavated by Auguste MARIETTE in 1858 and can be dated in the reign of Shabaka. Texts and reliefs attest the name of Amenirdis.[44]

The chapel of Osiris Neb-djet/Padedankh is also located at North Karnak. Although it is also very destroyed, several building blocks were discovered re-used in other buildings in Montu temple. Some of these blocks show Shepenwepet II and Amenirdis I, and the chapel was built during the reign of Taharqa.[45]

Fig. 9: Amenirdis, block discovered during the recent excavations at the front façade of Amun-Re temple under the supervision of M. BORAIK

Additional blocks with Amenirdis were discovered during the recent excavation at the front façade of the Amun-Re temple under the supervision of BORAIK (Fig. 9),[46] further fragments were found during the Sphinx avenue excavations.[47]

In Karnak South, the chapel of Osiris-Ptah Neb-ankh is noteworthy. This chapel is located to the south of the Tenth Pylon of the Amun-Re temple to the east of the ram-headed sphinxes avenue[48] between the temple of Amun-Re and Mut.[49] This chapel was built by Taharqa and completed by Tanutamani as both kings were represented in the scenes of the chapel. It is remarkable that no scenes of Divine Adoratrices are attested. The monument was discovered by locals in 1875, when it was in a poor condition. In 1921–1922, Maurice PILLET undertook some cleaning and restoration work, building a wooden ceiling and a door in order to protect it from the rain.[50] Prior to this, the first scientific work conducted on the chapel was by MARIETTE,

44 LECLANT, Recherches sur les monuments Thébains de la XXVe dynastie, 194–195; NAGY, The Architectural Activity of the Napatan Kings at the Temples of Karnak, 78; COULON/HALLMANN/PAYRAUDEAU, The Osirian Chapels at Karnak, 275; see Fig. 1, no. 20.

45 NAGY, The Architectural Activity of the Napatan Kings at the Temples of Karnak, 80–81; COULON/HALLMANN/PAYRAUDEAU, The Osirian Chapels at Karnak, 276; see Fig. 1, no. 21.

46 BORAIK, Cahiers de Karnak 13, 2010, 74–75.

47 J. HOURDIN, À propos de la chapelle d'Osiris-Padedankh de Chapenoupet II. Un apport à sa reconstitution épigraphique et architecturale, in: Cahiers de Karnak 14, 2013, 401–423.

48 E. NAGY, The Chapel of Osiris-Ptah Neb-ankh: A Report on the Fourth Season of Work, in: E. PISCHIKOVA/J. BUDKA/K. GRIFFIN (eds.), Thebes in the First Millennium BC: Art and Archaeology of the Kushite Period and Beyond, GHP Egyptology 27, London 2018, 294–303, here: 294; LECLANT, Recherches sur les monuments Thébains de la XXVe dynastie, 278; BLYTH, Karnak, 207; see Fig. 1, no. 19.

49 M. JORDAN/S. BICKEL/J.-L. CHAPPAZ, La porte d'Horemheb du Xe pylône de Karnak, CSEG 13, Geneva 2015, 204.

50 M. PILLET, Rapport sur les travaux de Karnak (1921–1922), in: ASAE 22, 1922, 235–260, here: 259.

who made an epigraphic survey of the walls.[51] Its location was noted and briefly commented upon by Jean Leclant,[52] while the inscriptions were published by Francis Breyer,[53] and later Karl Jansen-Winkeln.[54] However, since its discovery, no excavation of the site had been undertaken until the author of this paper started a new project. This project conducts excavations and carries out documentation, restoration, and reconstruction work of the chapel and the surrounding area.

Finally, recent excavations carried out at the temples of Karnak have yielded several blocks and fragments dating to the Twenty-fifth Dynasty. The large building program of the Kushite kings becomes more and more obvious and is especially notable by means of the Osirian chapels. A number of these small chapels are still standing in the Karnak precincts, but some of them cause problems in fine dating them to specific Kushite kings and Divine Adoratrices. Without doubt, the Kushite building work at Karnak mirrors aspects of religious structures but also of political power and networks.

Conclusion

The Twenty-fifth Dynasty kings have contributed to the Karnak Temples and their architectural buildings comprise a variety of forms like colonnaded halls, chapels and other structures. The Kushites renewed older buildings but also erected new buildings and added new elements to the monuments of their predecessors. All of this complex building program reflects religious aspects and clearly attests to the political dimension of these religious believes. The temples of Karnak kept their position as the main cult centre for most Egyptian gods and goddesses during the Kushite time. The Kushite buildings partly imitated earlier works of royal ancestors and paid in particular attention to the cult of Osiris, well attested with the Osirian chapels. The kings of the Twenty-fifth Dynasty appointed their daughters as 'chief wives of Amun' as one aspect to take control over Thebes and its religion, political, and administration power, and they created the adoption for the first time when Shepenwepet I had to adopt Amenirdis I.[55]

Within the Osirian chapels the absence of the king in the reliefs of some chapels may point to a period when the Kushite royal power was weakened, which was the case during the Assyrian invasions between 670–660 BC. It may also prove that the Divine Adoratrices had strong religious and political power during the Twenty-fifth Dynasty, and played an important role in this period. Some scenes showing high officials and their family members also attest to strong power structures for these elite people like Montuemhat.

I would like to propose that the explanation for the absence of the God's Wife in the chapel of Osiris-Ptah Neb-ankh, built by Taharqa and completed by Tanutamani, may be found in

51 A. Mariette, Monuments divers recueillis en Egypte et en Nubie I (texte), II (tables), Paris 1889, 27, pls. 79–87.

52 Leclant, Recherches sur les monuments Thébains de la XXVe dynastie, 110–113.

53 F. Breyer, Tanutamani. Die Traumstele und ihr Umfeld, ÄUAT 57, Wiesbaden 2003, 373–404.

54 K. Jansen-Winkeln, Inschriften der Spätzeit. Teil III: Die 25. Dynastie, Wiesbaden 2009, 229–234; Nagy, The Architectural Activity of the Napatan Kings at the Temples of Karnak, 282.

55 Nagy, The Architectural Activity of the Napatan Kings at the Temples of Karnak, 92; R. Meffre, Political Changes in Thebes during the Late Libyan Period and the Relationship Between Local Rulers and Thebes, in: M. Becker/A. I. Blöbaum/A. Lohwasser (eds.), "Prayer and Power". Proceedings of the Conference on the God's Wives of Amun in Egypt during the First Millennium BC, ÄUAT 84, Münster 2016, 47–60, here: 48.

aspects of the royal ideology, influenced by real political events and a new situation. The king seems to have tried to show his religious and political power, presenting offerings to different gods and goddesses, imitating the New Kingdom kings, and sending a message in times of Assyrian invasions.

Acknowledgements

I would like to warmly thank Julia Budka for her support, encouragement, advice, and also for reading this text, further thanks go to the organising committee of the Conference, especially to Veronica Hinterhuber. Thanks also to Kenneth Griffin.

I would like to thank Mostafa Waziri (Secretary General of the Supreme Council of Antiquities), Ayman Eshmawi (Head of Egyptian Antiquities Sector), Mohamed Abdel Badee (Under Secretary of Upper Egypt), Mohamed Yehia (General Director of Upper Egypt), Khazafi Abdel Raheem (General Director of Luxor), Mostafa AlSaghir (General Director of Karnak), Fawzy Helmy (Director of Karnak), Ghada Ibrahim (Director of Foreign Missions Affairs) and Warda El Nagar, Hagag Rabee, (Karnak Inspectors), Rais Mahmoud Farouk, Rais Ayman Farouk, and all the colleagues at the Karnak Inspectorate for their support and assistance throughout our work at the site. In particular, I am indebted to the Centre franco-égyptien d'étude des temples de Karnak (CFEETK) directed by Christophe Thiers. Thanks are also due to John Sherman, Director of the American Research Center in Egypt (ARCE) in Luxor for his generous support. Finally, special thanks go to the team members Haytham Mohamed Saad Eldin (Inspector of Antiquities & Site Manager), Ali Mohmaed Earfan, Ahmed Sayed El Naseh, Mona Ali Abady, (Egyptologists), Mohamed Abd El Baset (director of survey team), Ahmed Hassan (surveyor and GIS specialist), for their efforts in working hard in excavation, documentation, and the mapping of the site. We are very grateful to all for their generous support for the project.

Das Ende der Zivilverwaltung?

Das Wesirat von der 21. bis zur 26. Dynastie

Carola Koch

Abstract
Due to rich and valuable source material from the New Kingdom as well as extensive preliminary work, the position of the vizier as the king's representative from the Old to the New Kingdom is well documented. However, the vizier's position after the New Kingdom was widely assumed to have been marginalized and reduced to a function as a judicial officer. As a consequence the analysis of the vizier's situation during the First Millennium was hitherto neglected. This study aims to the examination of all viziers of the First Millennium, their position, their place of origin and employment to conclude that the duties of the vizier in dynasties 21 to 26 exceeded the assumed function of a judge by far. The title *ṯ3tj* still denoted a person of high executive powers. Furthermore, the analysation of the vizier position enables to draw conclusions as to the organisation of the Egyptian state in times of changing powers and territories.

Dank relativ vielseitiger Quellenbefunde aus dem Neuen Reich und den darauf basierenden umfassenden Arbeiten von Wolfgang HELCK und Guido VAN DEN BOORN ist die Position des Wesirs als Stellvertreter des Königs und zweiter Mann im Staat vom Alten bis zum Neuen Reich unumstritten.[1] „Alles was hineingeht in, alles was hinausgeht aus dem Palast wird ihm gemeldet".[2] Die Botschaften des Königshauses an *ḥ3tjw-ʿ* und *ḥḳ3w ḥwwt* wurden auf sein Geheiß weitergeleitet.[3] Er setzte Beamte und Schreiber ein,[4] versammelte auf des Königs Geheiß die Armee.[5] Er war der Vorgesetzte der Arbeiter von Deir el-Medineh,[6]

1 W. HELCK, Zur Verwaltung des Mittleren und Neuen Reichs, PÄ 3(a), Leiden 1975, 17–64; G. VAN DEN BOORN, The Duties of the Vizier: Civil Administration in the Early New Kingdom, Studies in Egyptology, London/New York 1988.

2 Urk. IV, 1105.

3 Urk. IV, 1113.

4 Urk. IV, 1112, 9; Graffito Cerny 1111: G. DRESBACH, Zur Verwaltung in der 20. Dynastie: das Wesirat, Königtum, Staat und Gesellschaft früher Hochkulturen 9, Wiesbaden 2012, 240 (3).

5 Urk. IV, 1112, 12–13.

6 oBerlin P 10663 (DRESBACH, Wesirat, 246–247 [17]); oBM EA 65933 (DRESBACH, Wesirat, 263 [29]); oBM EA 50744 (DRESBACH, Wesirat, 264 [30]); oKairo CG 25274 (DRESBACH, Wesirat 284 [54]); oKairo CG 25290 (DRESBACH, Wesirat, 284 [56]); oKairo CG 25291 (DRESBACH, Wesirat 285 [57]); oKairo CG 25537 (DRESBACH, Wesirat, 287 [62]); oKairo CG 25565 (DRESBACH, Wesirat 289 [64]); oKairo JE 72452 (DRESBACH, Wesirat, 296); oOIM 16991 (DRESBACH, Wesirat, 303 [79]); pDeM 28 (DRESBACH,

kontrollierte die Getreideabgaben und war sowohl für die Lebensmittelversorgung der Arbeiter verantwortlich,[7] als auch für das Entgegennehmen von Abgaben.[8] Auch die Aufsicht des Versiegelns und Öffnens von Räumlichkeiten lag in seiner Zuständigkeit.[9] Er war mit der Einsetzung von bestimmten Priestern betraut[10] und saß dem Richtergremium der *ḳnbt* vor.[11] Ihm oblag es zu bestrafen[12] und zu begnadigen.[13] Auch im Tempel führte der Wesir in der Regel die Befehle Pharaos aus[14] und leitete die dort anfallenden Bauarbeiten.[15]

Die Position des Wesirs im ersten Jahrtausend ist dagegen nur schwer fassbar, weil wir über weit weniger Material verfügen, und das vorhandene ist recht einseitig. Für die Zeit nach der Aufgabe von Deir el-Medineh zu Beginn der 21. Dynastie steht uns kein vergleichbarer Materialfund an administrativen Dokumenten zumindest bis in die griechisch-römische Epoche zur Verfügung. Gleiches gilt für Königs- und Tempeldekrete. Weil die überkommenen Quellen aus der Dritten Zwischenzeit im großen Maße aus dem Tempelbereich stammen, und es sich eben nicht um Verwaltungstexte handelt, in denen hohe Verwaltungsbeamte eine herausgehobene Rolle spielen, verschiebt sich unsere heutige Wahrnehmung und entsprechend auch das Bild, das wir uns von der ägyptischen Gesellschaft machen. Karl Jansen-Winkeln ist einer der prominentesten Befürworter der These, dass es nach dem Neuen Reich praktisch keine zivile Administration mehr gegeben habe, und die ursprünglich dort angesiedelten Zuständigkeiten von Tempeln und Militär übernommen wurden.[16] Der Wesir wäre demzufolge seiner ursprünglichen umfangreichen Kompetenzen enthoben, was nach Diana Pressl eine zwingende Konsequenz des Wegfalls eines zentralistischen Herrschaftssystems war.[17] Als einziges Relikt seiner bis ins Neue Reich belegten Funktion wird die Zuständigkeit des Wesirs als Oberhaupt der Judikativen gesehen.[18]

Wesirat, 345–348 [95]); pDeM 29 (Dresbach, Wesirat, 349 [96]); pTurin Kat.1880 (Dresbach, Wesirat, 373–379).

7 oKairo CG 25562 (Dresbach, Wesirat, 288–289); oOIM 16991 (Dresbach, Wesirat, 303–304 [79]); pTurin Kat.1880 (Dresbach, Wesirat, 373–379); pTurin Kat. 2074 (KRI VI, 609: 3–4).

8 oTurin N. 57047 (Dresbach, Wesirat, 306 [81]).

9 Urk. IV, 1105, 1106; zur Inspektion von Gräbern: pAbbott (pBM 10221) (Dresbach, Wesirat, 307 [83]); pTurin 2029 (KRI VI, 572: 13–14, 580) und die Umbettungsvermerke unter Herihor (z.B. Sarg Kairo CG 61019 von Sethos I.: KRI VI, 838; Sarg Kairo CG 61020 von Ramses II.: KRI VI, 838).

10 pTurin Kat. 1887 (RAD 75:9).

11 pAbbott (pBM 10221); pBM 10052; pBM 10053 (pHarris A); pBM 10054 (Dresbach, Wesirat, 309–319, 324–332); pBM 10383 (Pap. De Burgh) (Dresbach, Wesirat, 339); pLeopold II-Amherst (Dresbach, Wesirat, 365–369); pMayer A (Dresbach, Wesirat, 371–372); pTurin Kat. 2021 + pGenf D 409 rto (KRI VI, 738–742).

12 pBM 10055 (pSalt 124) (Dresbach, Wesirat, 334–335).

13 oBerlin P 12654 (Dresbach, Wesirat, 252).

14 KRI V, 430: 11–13.

15 KRI V, 231: 1–4.

16 K. Jansen-Winkeln, Die Fremdherrschaften in Ägypten im 1. Jahrtausend v.Chr., in: Or 69, 2000, 1–20, hier: 11; K. Jansen-Winkeln, Die Entwicklung der genealogischen Informationen nach dem Neuen Reich, in: M. Fitzenreiter (Hrsg.), Genealogie – Realität und Fiktion von Identität. Workshop am 04. und 05. Juni 2004, IBAES 5, London 2005, 137–145, hier: 143; K. Jansen-Winkeln, Die Libyer in Herakleopolis magna, in: Or 75, 2006, 297–316, hier: 299.

17 D. A. Pressl, Beamte und Soldaten. Die Verwaltung in der 26. Dynastie in Ägypten (664–525 v. Chr.), Europäische Hochschulschriften – Reihe III 779, Frankfurt am Main 1998, 97.

18 U.a. Pressl, Beamte und Soldaten, 107–112; O. Perdu, Psammétique Séneb. Un vizir d'Héliopolis avant la conquête d'Alexandre, in: Égypte, Afrique & Orient 42, 2006, 41–52, hier: 50–51; F. Payraudeau,

Auf einem Würfelhocker der 22. Dynastie trägt der Wesir *Ns-pꜣ-kꜣ-šwtj* A die seit alters her für sein Amt signifikante Tracht und präsentiert dem Gott Amun ein Abbild der Göttin Maat.[19] Das Reichen der Maat durch eine Privatperson ist selten und in der Regel auf bildliche Darstellungen zu Funerärtexten beschränkt.[20] In diesem Fall wird das Motiv auf der Tempelstatue in Zusammenhang mit der Position des Wesirs als Oberhaupt der Jurisdiktion gedeutet. Bereits seit dem Alten Reich war der Titel *ḥm-nṯr Mꜣꜥt* fester Bestandteil der Wesirstitulatur, und er bleibt es bis zum Ende der Libyerzeit.[21] In der auf dem Würfelhocker angebrachten Inschrift bestätigt *Ns-pꜣ-kꜣ-šwtj* A seine richterliche Funktion, indem er angibt: „Ich saß auf der Matte in den sechs großen Häusern, indem ich zwei Menschen richtete, so dass sie zufrieden waren."[22] Ein weiteres Beispiel für die Tätigkeit des Wesirs als Richter kann in der Inschrift des Hor gelesen werden, der sich als absolut unparteiisch bezeichnet „während er auf der Matte saß".[23] Und auf der Basis einer Wesirsstatue aus der 30. Dynastie bezeichnet sich der Stifter als derjenige, der richtet, indem er nicht parteiisch und gerecht in seinem Urteil ist.[24] Dass es sich bei den angeführten Beispielen eben nicht nur um überkommende Phrasen

---

Administration, société et pouvoir à Thèbes sous la XXIIe dynastie bubastite, BdE 160, Kairo 2014, 173–190.

19 Kairo CG 42232/Luxor J.152: G. LEGRAIN, Statues et statuettes de rois et de particuliers III (CG 42192–42250), Kairo 1914, 78–80, pl. XL, XLI.

20 E. TEETER, The presentation of Maat: Ritual and Legitimacy in Ancient Egypt, SAOC 57, Chicago 1997, 42.

21 HELCK, Verwaltung, 56, bezeichnete die Göttin sogar als „Bürogottheit" für das Wesirbüro. Siehe auch W. HELCK, Maat, in: W. HELCK/W. WESTENDORF (Hrsg.), Lexikon der Ägyptologie III, Wiesbaden 1980, 1110–1119, hier: 1112. Zu der Titelverbindung in der Libyerzeit siehe PAYRAUDEAU, Administration, 186. Die Verknüpfung der Titel *ṯꜣtj* und *ḥm-nṯr Mꜣꜥt* wurde jedoch seit der 25. Dynastie aufgehoben. Nur noch wenige Wesire waren fortan auch *ḥm-nṯr Mꜣꜥt*, und in der Regel waren die Maatpriester nicht länger Wesire. Zum Maatanhänger beim Wesir siehe B. GRDSELOFF, L'insigne du grand juge égyptien, in: ASAE 40, 1940, 185–202. In der 26. Dynastie trägt ein Priester aus Herakleopolis das Maatsymbol um den Hals, ohne dass einer seiner Titel eine juristische Funktion bestätigen würde: Kairo CG 48632 (J. A. JOSEPHSON/M. M. ELDAMATY, Catalogue général of Egyptian antiquities in the Cairo Museum. Nrs. 48601–48649: Statues of the XXVth and XXVIth Dynasties, Kairo 1999, 74–76, pl. 32; K. JANSEN-WINKELN, Inschriften der Spätzeit. Teil IV: Die 26. Dynastie. Band 1, Psametik I.–Psametik III., Wiesbaden 2014, 207 (342) (hier und im Folgenden: bei Quellenangaben aus JANSEN-WINKELN, Inschriften der Spätzeit siehe dort für weiterführende Literatur).

22 K. JANSEN-WINKELN, Inschriften der Spätzeit. Teil II: Die 22.–24. Dynastie, Wiesbaden 2007, 205–207 (44), g, 2–3.

23 Kairo JE 37512: JANSEN-WINKELN, Inschriften der Spätzeit II, 449–450 (100). H. KEES, Der Vezir Hori, Sohn des Jutjek, in: ZÄS 83, 1958, 129–138, hier: 132 hatte die Inschrift, die wörtlich lautet „Ich wurde eingeführt als *ṯꜣjtj sꜣb ṯꜣtj jmj-rꜣ ḥwwt wrwt*, ohne dass es einen Bruder, Sohn meiner Mutter (?) mir gegenüber auf der Matte gab" (Übersetzung nach K. JANSEN-WINKELN, Ägyptische Biographien der 22. und 23. Dynastie. Teil 1: Übersetzung und Kommentar, ÄUAT 8, Wiesbaden 1985, 219) dahingehend gedeutet, dass es keinen leiblichen Bruder gegeben hätte, der ihm das Recht auf die Richtertätigkeit streitig gemacht haben könnte. Dagegen wandte JANSEN-WINKELN, Ägyptische Biographien 1, 222 ein, „Daß ein bestimmter Sohn wie der Vater zum Wesir ernannt wurde, war doch kaum ein einklagbares Recht", weshalb er meint, dass *Jwtk* dadurch vielmehr betonen wollte, wie unparteiisch er war, dass er auf der Richtermatte keinen Bruder kannte. Hier ist wohl JANSEN-WINKELN zuzustimmen. Ein Amtsantritt aus Mangel an Mitbewerbern (hier Brüdern) ist sicher nichts, dessen man sich rühmen konnte und wollte.

24 J.-C. GOYON/M. GABOLDE, Trois pièces de Basse Époque et d'Époque Ptolémaïque au Musée des Beaux-Arts de Lyon (1), in: Bulletin des musées et monuments lyonnais 1991 (3–4), 2–27.

älterer Zeit handelt und der Wesir auch nach dem Neuen Reich als rechtsprechende Instanz wahrgenommen wurde, findet sich im Papyrus Rylands 9 bestätigt, in welchem darüber berichtet wird, dass *P3-dj-3st* II. am Ende der Regierungszeit von Psammetich II. Klage vor dem Wesir im Haus des Richtens erhob.[25] Ein bisher unveröffentlichter, nur fragmentarisch erhaltener Papyrus aus Sakkara, der nach John Tait möglicherweise in die zweite Hälfte des 5. oder in das 4. Jh. v. Chr. zu datieren ist, nennt einen Anruf an einen Wesir, der ebenfalls in Zusammenhang mit Richtern und deren Tätigkeit steht.[26] Und auch auf pBerlin P 23757 aus dem 3. Jh. v. Chr. wird der Wesir in Zusammenhang mit juristischen Vorgängen aufgeführt.[27] Eine juristische Tätigkeit des Wesirs ist offensichtlich und unumstritten.

Die überkommenen Quellen zum Amt im ersten Jahrtausend lassen allerdings ein breiteres Spektrum an Wesirszuständigkeiten erkennen als es eine Gleichsetzung mit dem obersten Richter vermuten ließe, wie im Folgenden dargelegt werden soll. So werden in den biographischen Inschriften der Libyerzeit noch die seit alters her mit dem Wesirat in Verbindung gebrachten Kompetenzen zum Ausdruck gebracht. Der Wesir Hor weist ganz allgemein darauf hin, dass man sich an den Wesir wendet, wenn einem Unrecht wiederfährt: „‚Wesir Hor, gerechtfertigt', sollt ihr sagen, wenn man euch Böses antun will".[28] Der Text des bereits angesprochenen Würfelhockers des *Ns-p3-k3-šwtj* A zieht zahlreiche Parallelen zwischen dem Wesir und dem Gott Thot in seiner Funktion als Wesir und rechter Hand von Horus und Re und stellt damit den Wesir auch weiterhin an die Seite des Königs und irdischen Horus: „Der König empfing den Schmuck des Horus, während ich bei ihm war wie Thot." und „…während ich mit der Maat geschmückt war und als *jmj-r3 njwwt* amtierte wie Thot im Hofstaat des Re".[29] Auf seiner Schreiberstatue Kairo CG 48613/JE 36948 bezeichnet sich der Wesir *Ns-p3-mdw* als *sš nswt m3ʿ* sowie als „Binse des Herrn der beiden Länder in den Tempeln" (*ʿrt pw n nb t3wj m r3w-prw*), „Schreibpalette des Königs bei seinen Angelegenheiten" (*gstj*[30] *nswt m-m ḫt=f*) und derjenige, der die Gottesopfer der Götter von Ober- und Unterägypten inspiziert" (*šnj ḥtpw-nṯr n nṯrw šmʿw mḥw*).[31] Der Wesir *Nḫt=f-Mwt* C rühmt sich in seiner Inschrift, das *pr-wnḫ* in Ordnung gebracht zu haben.[32] Auch wenn

25 G. Vittmann, Der demotische Papyrus Rylands 9. Teil I: Text und Übersetzung. Teil II: Kommentare und Indizes, ÄUAT 38, Wiesbaden 1998, 166–167, 510–512.

26 J. Tait, A demotic list of temple and court occupations: P. Carlsberg 23, in: H.-J. Thissen/T. Zauzich, Grammata Demotika, Festschrift für Erich Lüddeckens zum 15. Juni, Würzburg 1984, 211–233, hier: 220; S. L. Lippert, *ṯ3ty* statt *tb-m-mšʿ*: Neues zum Wesir im Demotischen, in: ZÄS 130, 2003, 88–97, hier: 92.

27 Lippert, ZÄS 130, 2003, 93.

28 Kairo JE 37512, b,1: Jansen-Winkeln, Inschriften der Spätzeit II, 449–450.

29 Kairo CG 42232, g, 2 und i, 4: Jansen-Winkeln, Inschriften der Spätzeit II, 205–207 (44). Übersetzung aus Jansen-Winkeln, Ägyptische Biographien 1, 212. Die Benennung von Thot als Wesir des Sonnengottes findet sich in Tb 145.

30 Zu dieser Lesung verweist K. Jansen-Winkeln, Biographische und religiöse Inschriften der Spätzeit aus dem Ägyptischen Museum Kairo. Teil 1: Übersetzungen und Kommentare, ÄUAT 45, Wiesbaden 2001, 8 (2) auf P. Wilson, A Ptolemaic Lexikon: A Lexicographical Study of the Texts in the Temple of Edfu, OLA 78, Leuven 1997, 1113–1114.

31 K. Jansen-Winkeln, Inschriften der Spätzeit. Teil III: Die 25. Dynastie, Wiesbaden 2009, 492–493 (256); Jansen-Winkeln, Biographische und religiöse Inschriften 1, 7.

32 Kairo CG 42229: Jansen-Winkeln, Inschriften der Spätzeit II, 309–310 (24), c 9–11; Übersetzung nach Jansen-Winkeln, Ägyptische Biographien 1, 206–207.

die genaue Deutung dieses *pr-wnḫ* nach wie vor unklar ist (Zeughaus?[33]), standen Gebäude offensichtlich immer noch unter der Aufsicht des Wesirs. *Nḫt=f-Mwt* C fährt fort indem er klassische, von alters her dem Wesir zugeschriebene Aufgaben nennt: „Ich gab Gesetze gemäß den alten Schriften; mein Sprechen (=Richtspruch) bedeutete Atem des Lebens." Natürlich lässt sich bei der Verwendung von biographischen Inschriften immer einwenden, es handele sich um Traditionsliteratur, die sich bestimmter Vorlagen älterer Zeit bediente und daher keinerlei Aussagekraft über die Zustände zum Erstellungszeitpunkt der Kopie besäße. Zur Position des Wesirs im ersten Jahrtausend sind diese biographischen Angaben allerdings auch nur ein erster Hinweis, der noch durch weiteres Quellenmaterial ergänzt werden kann.

Die Nähe des Wesirs zum König und eine Tätigkeit in dessen unmittelbarem Umfeld wird in dem Onomastikon Papyrus Carlsberg 23,31 zum Ausdruck gebracht,[34] das zwar in die Ptolemäerzeit datiert, allerdings auf Vorlagen aus der saitisch/persischen Zeit zurückzuführen ist.[35] Es handelt sich dabei um eine Auflistung der Ämter des Palastes. Wenn Sandra Lippert mit ihrer Identifizierung des demotischen Wortes für Wesir recht behält, dann steht der *ṯ3tj* in dieser Zeit an der Spitze der Palastverwaltung, gefolgt vom *jmj-r3 ꜥwj*, dem *jmj-r3 ḫtmw*, dem *jmj-r3 sš ḫnt wr*, dem *jmj-r3 pr wr* sowie den Herolden zur Linken und zur Rechten des Königs.[36]

Eine der wenigen Darstellungen eines Wesirs in Ausübung seiner Tätigkeit im ersten vorchristlichen Jahrtausend findet sich auf dem sogenannten Orakelpapyrus aus Brooklyn.[37] Auf diesem stehen der göttlichen Barke mit dem Schrein des Amun acht Personen gegenüber, u.a. die hohen Funktionäre Monthemhet, sein Sohn *Ns-Ptḥ* sowie der kuschitisch-stämmige Hohepriester und Königssohn Horachbit. Dass der ebenfalls abgebildete Wesir *Ns-p3-ḳ3-šwtj* D erst an siebter Stelle vor dem vom Orakel betroffenen Bittsteller abgebildet wurde, führte Richard Parker zu folgendem knappen und harten Urteil: „Nothing can illustrate the relatively low estate at this time of the Vizier, formerly the first in the kingdom under Pharao, than the ranking of the priests in the vignette where the Vizier follows all but the last man.".[38] In diesem Fall macht man es sich allerdings zu leicht, wenn man einfach nachzählt und anhand der Disposition auf den allgemeinen Rang der abgebildeten Person schließt. Es gibt andere, sogar plausiblere Deutungsoptionen für das Dargestellte, die sich mit der These, bei dem Wesir handele es sich auch noch in der frühen 26. Dynastie um einen hohen Beamten, vereinbaren

---

33 Wb 1, 323–4.

34 pCarlsberg 23, 31.x+9-x+15: J. Tait, A demotic list of temple and court occupations, 214–216.

35 Der ebenfalls in diesem Onomastikon genannte Titel *jmj-r3 sš ḫnt wr* ist nur aus dieser Zeit belegt: G. Posener, La première domination perse en Égypte. Recueil d'inscriptions hiéroglyphiques, BdE 11, Kairo 1936, 8.

36 Lippert, ZÄS 130, 94: zur Identifizierung des lange als *tb-n-mšꜥ* (z.B. G. R. Hughes, Preface, additional notes and glossary to G. Mattha, The Demotic legal code of Hermopolis West, BdE 45, Kairo 1975, 68 und H. J. Thissen, Die Lehre des Anchscheschonqi (P. BM 10508): Einleitung, Übersetzung, Indices, PTA 32, Bonn 1984, 131), *wḥm* (Tait, A demotic list of temple and court occupations, 220–222) oder *tḏme/tbme* (M. Smith, Review Thissen, Heinz Josef, Die Lehre des Anchscheschonqi, in: JNES 48,1, 1989, 51–54, hier: 53 folgte der Lesung S. R. K. Glanvilles, The instructions of Onchsheshonqy [British Museum Papyrus 10508] part I: introduction, translation, notes, and plates. Catalogue of Demotic Papyri in the British Museum 2. London 1955, 70 [73]) gelesenen demotischen Wort für *ṯ3tj*.

37 R. A. Parker, A Saite oracle papyrus from Thebes in the Brooklyn Museum (Papyrus Brooklyn 47.218.3), Brown Egyptological Studies 4, Providence 1962; Jansen-Winkeln, Inschriften der Spätzeit IV,1, 218–231 (363).

38 Parker, Oracle papyrus, 34.

lassen. Der Papyrus ist ein Zeugnis für eine Orakelprozession des Amun-Re anlässlich derer der Stifter den Gott zu einer Entscheidung bezüglich der Einsetzung seines Vaters, einem Wab-Priester des Amun, im Monthkult befragte. Entsprechend sind die dargestellten hohen Priester aus dem Month- und Amunkult direkt betroffen und bei der Befragung des Gottes die ersten Entscheidungsträger. Es handelte sich um eine reine Tempelangelegenheit, deren Gewicht wir heute nicht mehr nachvollziehen können, die allerdings bedeutend genug war, ein derartiges Zeugnis dafür mit 50 Zeugen für die Nachwelt festhalten zu wollen. Die Abbildung des Wesirs an der Stelle hinter allen direkt von der Entscheidung Betroffenen kann auch bedeuten, dass er das Gesamtereignis beaufsichtigte. Wie Anthony Leahy bereits 1979 feststellte bedeutete der Umstand, dass der Wesir in diesem Zusammenhang überhaupt präsent ist, nicht seinen Bedeutungsverlust sondern drückt viel eher das Gegenteil aus: wie seit dem Neuen Reich üblich, war der Wesir in der frühen 26. Dynastie ein Beamter der Zivilverwaltung, der auch in die wichtigen Abläufe und Entscheidungen im Tempel involviert war.[39] Neben der Option, dem Wesir als Vertreter Pharaos die Aufsicht über das Gesamtereignis zuzuschreiben, bestünde aber auch die Möglichkeit, das Abgebildete mit der im Neuen Reich gut belegten Funktion des Wesirs als Mittler zwischen Bittsteller und Gottheit zu sehen.[40] Beide Interpretationen stellen den Wesir in die Tradition seiner Vorgänger im Amt zur Zeit des Neuen Reiches. Mit der postulierten Rolle des Wesirs als oberster Richter ist die Darstellung hingegen nicht zu vereinen.

Nicht zuletzt deuten die assyrischen Annaleninschriften darauf hin, dass mindestens ein Wesir der 25. Dynastie als Beamter in der Funktion eines Gebietsoberhauptes wahrgenommen wurde.[41] Der auf dem Rassam-Zylinder des Assurbanipal genannte „König“ IS-pi-ma-a-tu von Thinis konnte von Leahy und Herman de Meulenaere etwa zeitgleich als der Wesir *Ns-p3-mdw* A identifiziert werden.[42] Dieser steht in der Wahrnehmung des Assyrerkönigs damit neben einflussreichen Persönlichkeiten wie Necho I. und Monthemhet von Theben.

Etwas später amtierte der Wesir *Ḥr-s3-3st* R, der in seiner Titulatur Priestertitel aus Memphis, Heliopolis und Letopolis vereinigt.[43] Dieser *Ḥr-s3-3st* wird von Günter Vittmann als der Vater der königlichen Gemahlin Psammetich I., Mehitemusechet, gedeutet.[44] In

39 A. Leahy, Nespamedu, “King” of Thinis, in: GM 35, 1979, 31–39, hier: 39 (28).

40 C. Raedler, Die Wesire Ramses’ II. – Netzwerke der Macht, in: R. Gundlach/A. Klug (Hrsg.), Das ägyptische Königtum im Spannungsfeld zwischen Innen- und Außenpolitik im 2. Jahrtausend v. Chr., Wiesbaden 2004, Königtum, Staat und Gesellschaft früher Hochkulturen 1, 277–416, hier: 373–375; P. Pamminger, Magistrale Intervention: der Beamte als Mittler, in: SAK 23, 1996, 281–304.

41 H.-U. Onasch, Die assyrischen Eroberungen Ägyptens. Teil 1: Kommentare und Anmerkungen. Teil 2: Texte in Umschrift, ÄUAT 27, Wiesbaden 1994, 36.

42 Leahy, GM 35, 1979, 31–39; H. De Meulenaere/W. Clarysse, Notes de prosopographie thébaine, in: CdE 53, 1978, 226–253, hier: 231.

43 Sarg Kairo TN 21/11/16/10 und Stele Kairo TN 27/1/25/17: Jansen-Winkeln, Inschriften der Spätzeit III, 429–430 (154); Sarg einer Nachfahrin aus der 26. Dynastie im Handel: K. Jansen-Winkeln, Inschriften der Spätzeit. Teil IV: Die 26. Dynastie. Band 2, Gottesgemahlinnen/26. Dynastie insgesamt, Wiesbaden 2014, 1016 (473); Stelophor Philadelphia E.16025: Jansen-Winkeln, Inschriften der Spätzeit III, 374 (49).

44 Filiationsangabe laut Kapelle der Mehitemusechet in Medinet Habu, Jansen-Winkeln, Inschriften der Spätzeit IV,1, 28–33: G. Vittmann, Die Familie der saitischen Könige, in: Or 44, 1975, 375–387, hier: 376–377; G. Vittmann, Priester und Beamte im Theben der Spätzeit: Genealogische und prosopographische Untersuchungen zum thebanischen Priester- und Beamtentum der 25. und 26. Dynastie, Veröffentlichungen der Institute für Afrikanistik und Ägyptologie der Universität Wien 3,

Anbetracht der zuvor bereits thematisierten hohen politischen Stellung des Wesirs *Ns-Mnw* A von Thinis am Ende der 25. Dynastie ist es verlockend, die Heirat Psammetichs I. mit der Tochter des memphitischen Wesirs *Ḥr-s3-3st* R als eine Maßnahme zur Machtübernahme durch Anbindung an das neue Königshaus von Sais zu deuten. Der Wesir am Übergang von der 25. zur 26. Dynastie wäre entsprechend nicht nur ausnahmsweise und in Thinis mit einem erheblichen Maß an Macht und Einfluss jenseits der bloßen Rechtsprechung ausgestattet gewesen.

In eben diese Richtung deutet auch der Umstand, dass nachweislich zwei Wesire aus der späten Libyerzeit Vorfahren von Lokalherrschern waren. Der Großvater des bekannten Fürsten Tefnacht, Basa, war als Wesir in Sais tätig.[45] Und der Wesir *P3j=f-t3w-m-ʿ-B3stt* war Großvater des *P3-sn-n-Ḫnzw*, der als Lokalherrscher in Mostai (*njwt rn=s*) im Zentraldelta amtierte.[46] Es ist vorstellbar, dass die Wesirsposition durchaus maßgeblich für die dominante Stellung ihrer Enkel war.[47]

Und schließlich findet der Wesir auch im Buch vom Tempel Erwähnung als rechte Hand des Königs und Oberhaupt der Verwaltung. Der Text stammt aus der Römerzeit, nimmt allerdings Bezug auf eine vermeintliche Vorlage aus der 2. Dynastie.[48] Sollte die Wesirsposition nach dem Neuen Reich der Bedeutungslosigkeit anheimgefallen sein, ist nicht ohne weiteres ersichtlich, warum man ihn fast 1000 Jahre später in seiner angestammten, nahezu staatstragenden Funktion erwähnt. Natürlich bestünde auch beim Buch vom Tempel ebenso wie bei den biographischen Texten die Möglichkeit, dass es sich um bloße Reproduktion von Traditionsliteratur handelt, so dass der Aussagewert dieser Quellen immer unter Vorbehalt zu betrachten ist.

* *
*

Die politische Landschaft Ägyptens hatte sich nach dem Neuen Reich verändert. Mehrere Machthaber amtierten nebeneinander, als Könige in Tanis und Hohepriester in Theben in der 21. Dynastie oder sogar mit bürgerkriegsähnlichen Zuständen und der Herrschaft eines Gegenkönigs innerhalb des Gebietes von Oberägypten in der 22./23. Dynastie.[49] Mit der zunehmenden Differenzierung der jeweiligen Machtgebiete gehen erwartungsgemäß eine Verkleinerung des Zuständigkeitsbereichs der Wesire, sowie ein paralleles Wirken mehrerer Amtsinhaber einher.

Eine Teilung des Wesirats ist bereits in der 21. Dynastie wahrscheinlich, weil sich im Norden und Süden zwei politische Systeme nebeneinander entwickeln. Das oberägyptische

---

Beiträge zur Ägyptologie 1), Wien 1978, 43; TIP², §490–492. Dagegen: H. De Meulenaere, La statue d'un vizir thébain: Philadelphia, University Museum E. 16025, in: JEA 68, 1982, 139–144.

45 Bronzestatuette des Amun Florenz 1777: Jansen-Winkeln, Inschriften der Spätzeit II, 270–271 (11).

46 Würfelhocker des Sohnes, Verbleib unbekannt und Stele Kairo o.Nr. (?), dort allerdings nur als *jmj-r3 njwt* bezeichnet: Jansen-Winkeln, Inschriften der Spätzeit IV,1, 47–48 (86) 65–66 (119). Zu der Stellung des Enkels am Übergang von der 25. zur 26. Dynastie siehe O. Perdu, Documents relatifs aux gouverneurs du delta au début de la XXVIe dynastie, in: RdE 57, 2006, 151–188, hier: 154–162.

47 Anders Pressl, Beamte und Soldaten, 121, die eine Bindung an ein bestimmtes Gebiet als Indiz für eine „Provinzialisierung" und eine damit einhergehende Abwertung des Wesirstitels wertet.

48 J. F. Quack, Das Buch vom Tempel und verwandte Texte: ein Vorbericht, in: Archiv für Religionsgeschichte 2, 2000, 1–20.

49 R. K. Ritner, The End of the Libyan Anarchy in Egypt: P. Rylands IX. cols. 11–12, in: Enchoria 17, 1990, 101–109, hier: 102, spricht von einer „Balkanization of Egypt".

Wesirsamt wird von den lokalen Machthabern Pianch, Herihor und Pinodjem I. abgedeckt. Zwei weitere Titelträger sind unter Vorbehalt im Anschluss zu identifizieren.[50] Nur wenige nicht-königliche Quellen sind aus Unterägypten in der 21. Dynastie überliefert. Deshalb ist die Teilung in dieser Zeit schwer nachweisbar. Der Zusammenstellung unterägyptischer Wesire im Anhang (Tab. 1) ist jedoch zu entnehmen, dass spätestens zu Beginn der 22. Dynastie unterägyptische Wesire im Amt waren.[51] Nimmt man nun nicht an, dass die 21. Dynastie in Unterägypten alles Bisherige verworfen hat und alle Aufgaben von ebenfalls nicht belegten anderen Funktionären durchführen ließ, um dann unter Scheschonk I. wieder zu alten Strukturen zurückzukehren, ist die Hypothese von der Existenz unterägyptischer Wesire in der 21. Dynastie nur folgerichtig. Die lokalen Machthaber Pianch und Herihor waren trotz ihres Lokalherrscherstatus dem ägyptischen König rein formell untergeordnet.[52] Und auch Pinodjem I. führt den Wesirstitel ausschließlich dort, wo er nicht selber als König bezeichnet wird (Tab. 2). Der Titel Wesir kennzeichnete die drei entsprechend als die rechte Hand des Königs,[53] vor allem bei Tätigkeiten, die sie als dessen Vertreter durchführten:[54] Bau- und Restaurierungsarbeiten am Tempel[55] sowie Umbestattungen der Könige des Neuen Reiches.[56] Die rundbildliche Darstellung Kairo CG 42190 zeigt Herihor sogar ausschließlich in seiner Funktion als Wesir,[57] und auf dem Ostrakon Kairo CG 25744 schreibt der Wesir Herihor an Pharao, seinen Herrn.[58] Eine etwaige juristische Tätigkeit wird hier im Übrigen nicht zum Ausdruck gebracht.

Werden für die 21. Dynastie zwei Wesire mit Sitz in Theben und Tanis oder Memphis angenommen, so ist vorstellbar, dass sich deren Anzahl mit einer Zunahme „echter" Könige

50 Der Papyrus Berlin 23098, der einen Wesir […]-*nfr* nennt, ist derartig stark zerstört, dass ihm keine weiteren Informationen zu entnehmen sind: H.-W. Fischer-Elfert, Zwei Akten aus der Getreideverwaltung der XXI. Dynastie (P. Berlin 14.384 und P. Berlin 23098), in: H. Altenmüller/ R. Germer (Hrsg.), Miscellanea aegyptologica: Wolfgang Helck zum 75. Geburtstag, Hamburg 1989, 39–65, hier; 63–65. Der von K. Kitchen (TIP², table 15) mit Fragezeichen nach Pinodjem I. datierte Wesir *Jmn-pꜣ-mšꜥ* ist bei H. Kees, Das Priestertum im ägyptischen Staat vom Neuen Reich bis zur Spätzeit. PÄ 1, Leiden 1953, 318 ohne Quellenangabe genannt.

51 Die Behauptung Pressls „Im Fall des Wesirats ist zu bedenken, daß für eine Zeitspanne von fast 400 Jahren lediglich in Oberägypten Wesire nachgewiesen sind" (Pressl, Beamte und Soldaten, 120) ist vor dem Hintergrund der aktuellen Beleglage schlicht falsch.

52 TIP², Preface 1995, XIV weist darauf hin, dass es sich bei Herihor nur um ein auf Karnak bezogenes Königtum handelt.

53 Ob es sich dabei um den tanitischen König oder Amun-Re handelt, kann und soll an dieser Stelle nicht entschieden werden.

54 Siehe auch M. Römer, Gottes- und Priesterherrschaft in Ägypten am Ende des Neuen Reiches. Ein religionsgeschichtliches Phänomen und seine Grundlagen. ÄUAT 21, Wiesbaden 1994, 37, 44, 60.

55 Pianch nennt auf oKairo CG 25745 explizit auf den König bezogene Titel, u.a. auch Wesir: KRI VI, 849 (2); Herihor trägt den Wesirstitel auf einem Block, der in der Hypostylenhalle von Karnak gefunden wurde: K. Jansen-Winkeln, Inschriften der Spätzeit. Teil I: Die 21. Dynastie, Wiesbaden 2007, 4 (1); Pinodjem I. bezeichnet sich als Wesir in einer Inschrift im Luxortempel: Jansen-Winkeln, Inschriften der Spätzeit I, 17 (22b) und in einer Restaurationsinschrift in Medinet Habu: Jansen-Winkeln, Inschriften der Spätzeit I, 18–20 (24) (25).

56 Herihor trägt den Titel auf den Särgen von Sethos I. und Ramses II.: KRI VI, 838, 5–6 und 9–10; Pinodjem I. wird als Wesir in den Graffiti im Grab des Haremhab bezeichnet: Jansen-Winkeln, Inschriften der Spätzeit I, 35–36 (61).

57 Abbildung siehe http://www.ifao.egnet.net/bases/cachette/. Zugriff am: 23.04.2019.

58 KRI VI, 847–848.

in Ägypten vergrößerte. Für die Zeit des Übergangs von der 22. zur 23. Dynastie ist dies tatsächlich nachvollziehbar. Wie die Priesterannalen von Karnak berichten, wurde im 8. Jahr von Petubastis I. ein *Pꜣ-ntj-jw=f-ꜥnḫ* als Wesir eingesetzt.[59] Der Hohepriester Osorkon B berichtet, dass es sich bei Petubastis I. um den Gegenkönig zu Takeloth II. in Oberägypten handelt.[60] Es wird mit *Pꜣ-ntj-jw=f-ꜥnḫ* demnach ein lokaler, nur für den Herrschaftsbereich des Petubastis zuständiger Wesir ernannt. Das Wesirat dieser Zeit war entsprechend nicht nur zwei- sondern wohl mindestens dreigeteilt. Denn auch Takeloth II., der andere oberägyptische König hatte mutmaßlich einen Wesir an seiner Seite. Interessanterweise gibt es mehrere Wesire, die sicher, wenn auch zeitlich später als Takeloth II., in Herakleopolis belegt sind, das als mögliche Hauptstadt des Herrschaftsbereichs von Takeloth II. gilt (Tab. 2[61]).[62] Es wäre denkbar, dass sich die Stadt unter Takeloth II. nicht nur zur „Königsstadt" sondern auch zu einem Wesirssitz wandelte.[63] Ein weiteres Annalenfragment, das in etwa zeitgleich wie das soeben besprochene Fragment mit der Nennung des Petubastis anzusetzen ist und

59 Kairo JE 36494: J.-M. Kruchten, Les annales des prêtres de Karnak (XXI–XXIIImes dynasties) et autres textes contemporains relatifs à l'initiation des prêtres d'Amon, OLA 32, Leuven 1989, 36–44, pl. 2, 16; Jansen-Winkeln, Inschriften der Spätzeit II, 213 (16).

60 R. A. Caminos, The chronicle of prince Osorkon, AnOr 37, Rom 1958.

61 *Ppnh* (Gruppenfigur Kairo CG 882: Jansen-Winkeln, Inschriften der Spätzeit IV,2, 965–966 [404]; M. Zecchi, Prosopografia dei sacerdoti del Fayyum. Dall'Antico Regno al IV secolo a.C., Archeologia e storia della civiltà egiziana e del vicino Oriente antico – Materiali e studi 4. Imola 1999, 4–6) ist zwar nach Maßgabe seiner anderen Titel und dem Fundort der fragmentarisch erhaltenen Gruppenfigur, die ihn nennt, mit dem Fayum assoziiert. Wie allerdings bereits der Papyrus Rylands 9 zeigt, sind Priestertitel des Fayum bei einem Oberhaupt von Herakleopolis nicht ungewöhnlich: Vittmann, Papyrus Rylands 9, II, 713. Siehe auch Kairo CG 48632 (Jansen-Winkeln, Inschriften der Spätzeit IV,1, 207 [342]); R. Meffre, D'Héracléopolis à Hermopolis: la Moyenne Égypte durant la Troisième Période intermédiaire (XXIe – XXIVe dynasties), Paris 2015, 235–238.

62 Zu einer Verbindung von Takeloth II. mit Herakleopolis siehe D. A. Aston, Takeloth II, a king of the Herakleopolitan/Theban Twenty-Third Dynasty revisited: the chronology of Dynasties 22 and 23, in: G. P. F. Broekman/J. Demarée/O. E. Kaper (Hrsg.), The Libyan period in Egypt: historical and cultural studies into the 21st–24th Dynasties, Proceedings of a conference at Leiden University, 25–27 October 2007, EU 23, Leuven 2009, 1–28, hier: 18; C. Jurman, From the Libyan dynasties to the Kushites in Memphis: historical problems and cultural issues, in: G. P. F. Broekman/J. Demarée/O. E. Kaper (Hrsg.), The Libyan period in Egypt: historical and cultural studies into the 21st–24th Dynasties, Proceedings of a conference at Leiden University, 25–27 October 2007, EU 23, Leuven 2009, 113–138, hier: 122; Meffre, D'Héracléopolis à Hermopolis, 311, 334 weist darauf hin, dass Takeloth II. weder in Herakleopolis noch überhaupt im nördlichen Mittelägypten belegt ist und daher die Annahme einer Residenz in Herakleopolis rein hypothetisch sei; so auch Payraudeau, Administration, 360–361, 368–369. Dass dies jedoch nicht zwingend dazu führen muss, von der u.a. von David Aston vertretenen These abzuweichen, merkt K. Jansen-Winkeln, Review: Meffre, Raphaële 2015. D'Héracléopolis à Hermopolis: la Moyenne Égypte durant la Troisième Période intermédiaire (XXIe – XXIVe dynasties), in: BiOr 73 (1–2), 2016, 85–94, hier: 89–90, FN 14 zu Recht an. Eine Assoziation mit Herakleopolis ergibt sich schon zwingend aus dem Umstand, dass der Vater von Takeloth II., *Nmrṯ* C, seinen Sitz in dieser Stadt hatte. Siehe auch TIP[2], Preface 1995, xxiii, wo Kitchen auf die wenigen Belege für Takeloth II. in Theben verweist und ihn vielmehr als tanitischen König deutet.

63 Auf pKöln 5632 werden drei Personen aufgelistet, die Söhne eines namentlich nicht genannten Wesirs waren. Aufgrund der erhaltenen Namen hält Vittmann eine Herkunft aus Herakleopolis oder Abusir el-Meleq für wahrscheinlich: G. Vittmann, Eine „protodemotische" Abrechnung aus der Dritten Zwischenzeit (Papyrus Köln 5632), FS NN. Der Papyrus datiert wahrscheinlich in die 2. Hälfte des 8. Jahrhunderts.

welches nach Scheschonk III. datiert, berichtet von der Einsetzung eines *ṯ3tj n njwt rsj*.[64] Vor allem mit Blick auf den singulären Zusatz „*n njwt rsj*" wäre vorstellbar, dass auch der in Unterägypten residierende König einen Vertreter in Theben hatte, womit sich die Zahl allein der oberägyptischen Wesire auf drei erhöhen würde. Nachdem schließlich die Teilung von Oberägypten aufgehoben worden war, ernannte der Hohepriester und Königssohn Osorkon B wieder einen eigenen thebanischen Wesir mit herakleopolitanischen Wurzeln.[65] Fragment 7 der Annalen berichtet, dass ein *Ḥr-s3-3st*, Sohn eines Herischef-Priesters aus dem Fayum im 39. Regierungsjahr von Scheschonk III. zum Wesir ernannt wurde.[66] Dass gleichzeitig der Wesir in Herakleopolis im Amt blieb, es also auch nach dem Ende der Teilung Oberägyptens mehrere Wesirssitze gab, ist angesichts der später belegten, bereits genannten Wesire aus Herakleopolis plausibel. Zusammenfassend geben die genannten Priesterannalen Auskunft darüber, dass der Zuständigkeitsbereich der Wesire entsprechend der jeweiligen Herrschaftsgebiete der Könige kleiner geworden war. Hier lohnt sich im Übrigen der Blick auf das Amt des *jmj-r3 šmꜥ(t)*. Auch hier gibt es nachweislich zwei Amtsinhaber während der Teilung Oberägyptens. *Ḥr-s3-3st* B war der Amtsinhaber im Gefolge von Petubastis I.[67], während Osorkon B als „Vorsteher von Oberägypten" seines Vaters Takeloth II. auftrat.[68]

Unter der Prämisse, dass das oberägyptische Wesirat spätestens seit der 23. Dynastie geteilt war, wie es im Übrigen bereits DE MEULENAERE erwogen hatte,[69] ist eine chronologische Auflistung der oberägyptischen Wesire wie sie Kenneth KITCHEN erstmals aufstellte, nicht länger plausibel.[70] Würde die bereits angesprochene Zuordnung des in den Annalen des Assyrerkönigs belegten Wesirs *Ns-Mnw* A nach Thinis eben nicht als Ausnahme gedeutet, dann müssten keine komplizierten und hochspekulativen Überlegungen zu einer außerplanmäßigen Verlegung des Wesirssitzes von Theben nach Abydos/Thinis angestellt werden.[71] Zudem wäre erklärt, warum die Abfolge von Wesiren aus einflussreichen Familien wie die der thebanischen Monthemhet-Familie scheinbar immer wieder unterbrochen wird. Mindestens sechs Mitglieder der Familie tragen den Wesirstitel.[72] Geht man von nur einem

---

64 Priesterannalen, Fragment 5: KRUCHTEN, Annales des prêtres, 54; JANSEN-WINKELN, Inschriften der Spätzeit II, 203 (37).

65 PAYRAUDEAU, Administration, 368.

66 Kairo JE 36493 (KRUCHTEN, Annales des prêtres, 59–85; JANSEN-WINKELN, Inschriften der Spätzeit II, 203–204 [38]).

67 Priesterannalen 2; Karnak (JANSEN-WINKELN, Inschriften der Spätzeit II, 213 [16]).

68 Monumentalinschrift Bubastidentor, Karnak (JANSEN-WINKELN, Inschriften der Spätzeit II, 161–168 [7]).

69 DE MEULENAERE/CLARYSSE, CdE 53, 1978, 231. Dagegen hatte sich noch zuletzt PAYRAUDEAU, Administration, 175 ausgesprochen.

70 TIP^2, table 15.

71 M. BIERBRIER, The Late New Kingdom in Egypt (c. 1300 – 664 B.C.). A Genealogical and Chronological Investigation, Warminster 1975, 105 hatte eine gegen den zu mächtig gewordenen Monthemhet gerichtete Aberkennung des Wesirsamtes durch den kuschitischen König gemutmaßt. Und LEAHY, GM 35, 1979, 35, erklärte den Umzug des Wesirssitzes als eine Maßnahme, Macht innerhalb von Oberägypten zu verteilen. Beiden Erklärungsversuchen steht allerdings die scheinbar ungebrochen große Machtposition des Monthemhet in der Folgezeit entgegen.

72 Als erster Amtsinhaber der Familie wird in der Regel *Ḥr-s3-3st* F bezeichnet. Auf dem Würfelhocker Kairo CG 42250 (JANSEN-WINKELN, Inschriften der Spätzeit IV,1, 155 [282]) sind drei Amtsinhaber in der Genealogie des Stifters genannt. Harsiese F ist Sohn eines Amun-Priesters *P3-dj-3st* und dieser wiederum ist ein Sohn eines *mj nn ꜥnḫ-wn-nfr*. Worauf bezieht sich dieses *mj nn*? In der Regel würde

oberägyptischen Wesir aus, müssen zwei nicht mit der Familie verbundene Wesire in die chronologische Auflistung eingefügt werden: *ꜥnḫ-Ḥr*[73] und *Ns-pꜣ-ḳꜣ-šwtj* B.[74] Dieses Problem wäre gelöst, wenn man von mehreren Wesiren an unterschiedlichen Orten in Oberägypten ausginge. Macht und Einfluss der einzelnen Wesire variierten offensichtlich. Während etwa der thinitische Wesir vom Assyrer Assurbanipal als König wahrgenommen wurde, verloren Titel und Amt des thebanischen Amtsinhabers ihre Bedeutung angesichts der Ämterakkumulation des Monthemhet, die ihn auch ohne den Wesirstitel zum „König" von Theben machten.[75]

Die von Kitchen als oberägyptische Wesire in die Abfolge der Wesire der Monthemhet-Familie eingefügten *ꜥnḫ-ḥr* und *Ns-pꜣ-ḳꜣ-šwtj* B müssten entsprechend einem anderen Dienstort zugeordnet werden. Anhand der einzigen Hinterlassenschaft, die ihn bezeugt, ist es sogar denkbar, dass *ꜥnḫ-Ḥr* ein unterägyptischer Wesir war. Immerhin ist in Zusammenhang mit den auf der Osirisstatue seiner Tochter *Dj-ꜣst-ḥb-sd* genannten Personen auch eine Tochter eines Deltafürsten Akanosh genannt. Ob es sich bei dieser Tochter um die Mutter oder Adoptivmutter der *Dj-ꜣst-ḥb-sd* handelt, ist in diesem Zusammenhang zunächst einmal unerheblich. Fest steht, dass die Familie eine wie auch immer geartete Verbindung zu einem *wr n Mšwš* und damit nach Unterägypten hatte. Für unterägyptische Lokalherrscher war es durchaus üblich, Töchter im Gottesstaat unterzubringen.[76] Beispiele sind *Ns-Ḫnzw*, Tochter

---

man annehmen, dass es sich auf die Titel des zuvor Genannten bezieht. *ꜥnḫ-wn-nfr* wäre entsprechend ein *ḥm-nṯr Jmn* gewesen. Anders als zahlreiche andere zeitgenössische Objekte verwendet die Inschrift *mj nn* an keiner anderen Stelle obwohl drei Personen *ḥm-nṯr Jmn jmj-rꜣ njwt* und *ṯꜣtj* sind. Ein *mj nn* an letzter Stelle kann mit Platzproblemen des Schreibers in Zusammenhang gebracht werden. Hier verhält es sich hingegen so, dass das *mj nn* genauso viel Platz beansprucht wie das vermeintlich zu wiederholende *ḥm-nṯr Jmn*. Ich stelle daher die These auf, dass sich das *mj nn* auf die Titel von Enkel, Urenkel und Ur-urenkel beziehen und dass auch *ꜥnḫ-wn-nfr* ein *ṯꜣtj* war. Interessanterweise ist ein zeitgenössischer Wesir namens *ꜥnḫ-wn-nfr* überliefert: Jansen-Winkeln, Inschriften der Spätzeit II, 232 (28); P. Lacau, Note sur la tombe No. 3 de Tehneh, in: ASAE 26, 1926, 38–41. In seinem Grab ist bedauerlicherweise nichts erhalten, was ihn familiär zuordnen ließe. Vor dem Hintergrund aber, dass *ꜥnḫ-wn-nfr*, der Großvater des Harsiese F möglicherweise ein Wesir war, wäre es durchaus denkbar, dass er mit diesem identisch ist.

73 Der Vater der *Dj-ꜣst-ḥb-sd*, genannt auf der Statue Kairo CG 38238 aus Medinet Habu: Jansen-Winkeln, Inschriften der Spätzeit III, 302 (66).

74 Der Sohn des *Pꜣ-dj-Jmnt* II., genannt auf einem Sarg, dessen Verbleib unbekannt ist: Payraudeau, Administration, 522 (169C); Jansen-Winkeln, Inschriften der Spätzeit III, 360 (22).

75 Die Aufteilung Oberägyptens in mehrere (Verwaltungs-)Einheiten besaß eine lange Tradition. Bereits im Alten Reich gliederte sich Oberägypten in die drei Verwaltungsbezirke *tp šmꜥ*, *ḥrjw-jb* und die nördlichen Gaue des Landesteils, deren Sammelbezeichnung nicht erhalten ist: H. Goedicke, Zu imj-rA Sma und tp-Sma im Alten Reich, in: MIO 4, 1956, 1–10. Auch nach der Verwaltungsreform im Neuen Reich blieben zumindest die beiden südlichen Einheiten erhalten, wie den Inschriften im Grab des Rechmire entnommen werden kann (Urk. IV, 1120, 1129). Und auch in der Römerzeit werden die südlichen 15 Gaue als die beiden Einheiten Thebais und Heptanomia (H. Gauthier, Les nomes d'Égypte depuis Hérodote jusqu'à la conquête arabe, MIE 25, Kairo 1935, 176) beziehungsweise Obere und Untere Thebais (W. Helck, Die altägyptischen Gaue, Beihefte zum Tübinger Atlas des Vorderen Orients, Reihe B [Geisteswissenschaften] 5, Wiesbaden 1974, 47) geführt. Eine Aufteilung Oberägyptens war entsprechend über viele Jahrhunderte gewachsen und wurde erhalten. Im Zuge von Machtstreitigkeiten wäre ein Rückzug der streitenden Parteien in einen bereits vororganisierten Verwaltungsbereich nur folgerichtig.

76 J. Yoyotte, Les vierges consacrées d'Amon thébain, in: I. Guermeur (Hrsg.), Histoire, géographie et religion de l'Égypte ancienne: opera selecta par Jean Yoyotte, OLA 224, Leuven/Paris/Walpole, MA, 2013, 149–157.

des *wr Mꜥ Ḥr-wḏꜣ*,[77] eine Tochter des *wr ꜥꜣ n rbjw ꜥnḫ-Ḥr* C namens *Nbt-jmꜣw-m-ḥꜣt*[78] und *Jꜥḥ-tꜣj=s-nḫt*, Tochter des *ḥrj M Ns-nꜣ-jswt*.[79]

Für Unterägypten hatte Kitchen ebenfalls eine chronologische Auflistung der belegten Wesire zusammengestellt, die mittlerweile erheblich erweitert werden kann (siehe Tab. 1).[80] Dass aber besonders in Unterägypten mit seinen zahlreichen Lokalherrschern auch mehrere zeitgleich amtierende Wesire im Amt waren, klingt unter anderem in der Piye-Stele an: „Da kamen diese Kleinkönige, die *ḥꜣwtjw* von Unterägypten, alle Großen, die die Feder tragen, alle Wesire, alle Großen und Königsbekannten im Westen, im Osten und auf den Inseln, um die Schönheit seiner Majestät zu sehen".[81] Dass dabei nicht nur „richtige" Könige, sondern auch Lokaloberhäupter wie der *jrj-pꜥt* von Athribis einen Wesir unter sich hatten, bestätigt pQueen's College. Der Wesir *Pꜣ-dj-ꜣst* wird in dem Text als oberster Befehlsempfänger des *jrj-pꜥt* präsentiert.[82] Unter den Kuschiten wurde das System der Teilung des Wesirats auf mehrere Amtsinhaber nicht nur beibehalten. Auch das wohl in die Libyerzeit zurückreichende Phänomen der Bildung ganzer Wesirsdynastien an bestimmten Orten hatte weiterhin Bestand. Dass das Amt des höchsten Zivilverwalters und Königsvertreters tatsächlich erblich wurde, lässt sich in der späten 22./23. Dynastie in der *Pꜣ-mjw*-Familie nachweisen. *Pꜣ-mjw* II. trägt den Titel ebenso wie seine Söhne *Pꜣ-dj-Jmnt* II. und *Pꜣ-ḫꜣr* sowie der Enkel *Ns-pꜣ-ḳꜣ-šwtj* B.[83] Seit der 25. Dynastie dann treten die großen Wesirsfamilien in Theben, Abydos und Unterägypten in Erscheinung. Neben den bereits genannten Familien von Theben ([*ꜥnḫ-wn-nfr*], *Ḥr-sꜣ-*

77 Berlin 7478: Jansen-Winkeln, Inschriften der Spätzeit II, 416–417 (40); C. Koch, „Die den Amun mit ihrer Stimme zufriedenstellen": Gottesgemahlinnen und Musikerinnen im thebanischen Amunstaat von der 22. bis zur 26. Dynastie, SRAT 27, Dettelbach 2012, 240 (44).

78 Stele Kairo JE 40716: Jansen-Winkeln, Inschriften der Spätzeit III, 302 (65); Koch, Gottesgemahlinnen, 234 (17).

79 Stele Verbleib unbekannt: Jansen-Winkeln, Inschriften der Spätzeit IV,1, 66 (121); Koch, Gottesgemahlinnen, 230 (3).

80 Im Gegensatz zur Libyerzeit, wenn die Titelfolge *tꜣjtj sꜣb* eng mit dem *ṯꜣtj* verbunden ist, treten in der 26. Dynastie Titelträger *sꜣb* (ohne *tꜣjtj*) auf, die diese Titelfolge mit einem anderen Titel in Verbindung tragen, nämlich dem *ꜥḏ-mr*. Dieses in der Saitenzeit als Rückgriff auf das Alte Reich wieder eingeführte Amt wird als eine Art Oberhaupt eines Gaus gedeutet. Überlieferte Titelträger sind mit Unterägypten assoziiert. Ein *sꜣb ꜥḏ-mr* wurde offenbar von einem (*tꜣjtj*) *sꜣb ṯꜣtj* unterschieden und entsprechend in der Zusammenstellung nicht berücksichtigt. Die Titelkombination tritt bei nachfolgenden Personen auf: *Psmṯk*, Sohn des *Gm.n=f-ḥr-bꜣk* und der *Ṯꜣrt*: Stele Florenz 2551 (Jansen-Winkeln, Inschriften der Spätzeit IV,1, 536–537 [243]); *Pꜣ-jrj-jꜥḥ*, Sohn des *Pꜣ-dj-ꜣst* und der *Šsp-Jmn-tꜣj=s-ḥrt*: Würfelhocker Berlin 11482 (Jansen-Winkeln, Inschriften der Spätzeit IV,2, 778–779 [62]); *Pꜣj=f-ṯꜣw-šrj*, Vater des *Ḥj* (?): Stele des Sohnes Yverdon 83.2.1 (Jansen-Winkeln, Inschriften der Spätzeit IV,2, 781 [73]). Ebenfalls in der 26. Dynastie tritt der *sꜣb* auch noch ganz ohne *ṯꜣtj* und *ꜥḏ-mr* auf. Dieser Titel steht eher am Anfang der Titulatur: *Pꜣ-kꜣp rn=f nfr Wꜣḥ-jb-Rꜥ-m-ꜣḫt* (Campbell's tomb, Giza: Jansen-Winkeln, Inschriften der Spätzeit IV,2, 881–882 (259); *Ḥr-nb-ḫꜣst*, Sohn des *Ḫnmw-m-ḥꜣt* und der *Šsmtt* (Statue London BM 21478, Herkunft unbekannt: Jansen-Winkeln, Inschriften der Spätzeit IV,2, 962–963 [398]).

81 Kairo JE 48862, Zeile 107: Jansen-Winkeln, Inschriften der Spätzeit II, 347 (1); N.-C. Grimal, La stèle triomphale de Pi(ᶜankh)y au Musée du Caire. JE 48862 et 47086–47089, Études sur la Propagande Royale Égyptienne I, MIFAO 105, Kairo 1981.

82 H.-W. Fischer-Elfert, Papyrus Queen's College recto: A narrative in abnormal hieratic, in: R. Enmarch/V. M. Lepper, Ancient Egyptian literature. Theory and practice, Proceedings of the British Academy 188, 2013, 143–151, hier: 148.

83 Genealogie der Familie bei Payraudeau, Administration, 157.

ꜣst F, *Ns-Mnw* A, *Pꜣ-dj-ꜣst*, *Ḫꜥm-Ḥr* I/A, *Ns-Mnw* B und *Pꜣ-hrr*/*Ḥr-sꜣ-ꜣst* G) und Abydos (*Ns-pꜣ-ḳꜣ-šwtj* C, *Ns-pꜣ-mdw- Ns-pꜣ-ḳꜣ-šwtj* D) etablierten sich in Unterägypten mindestens zwei Wesirsfamilien, die allerdings keinem Amtssitz zweifelsfrei zugeordnet werden können: a) *ꜥnḫ-Ššnḳ*, *Ḥr-sꜣ-ꜣst*, *Pꜣ-šrj-n-ꜣst*; b) *Ḥr-sꜣ-ꜣst* R, *Ḏd-kꜣ-Rꜥ* (Memphis?). Wenn ein hohes Amt erblich wird, steigen damit automatisch Macht und Einfluss des Amtsinhabers. Auch dies könnte ein Grund für die zuvor festgestellte hohe Position der abydenischen und einiger unterägyptischen Amtsinhaber sein. Für keine dieser mächtigen Familien reicht die Beleglage über die Regierungszeit von Psammetich I. hinaus. Es wäre vorstellbar, dass die Vergabe von Wesirsamt und -titel wieder faktisch auf den König überging. Aus dem Umstand, dass der hier als thinitischer Wesir vermutete *Ns-pꜣ-ḳꜣ-šwtj* D auf dem bereits angesprochenen Orakelpapyrus in Theben belegt ist, könnte man schließen, dass Theben und Abydos unter Psammetich I. wieder unter einem Wesir vereinigt wurden, möglicherweise als Gegengewicht zu Monthemhet und in der Position eines Vertrauten des Königs aus Sais.[84] Ob der Wesir *Jry*[85] sowie die beiden anderen „neuen" oberägyptischen Wesire, die beide den Namen *Ḏd-Bꜣstt-jw=f-ꜥnḫ* trugen und von Nashat Alzohary als Großvater und Enkel gedeutet werden[86] vor *Ns-pꜣ-ḳꜣ-šwtj* D oder direkt nach diesem amtierten, lässt sich nicht mit Bestimmtheit sagen.[87] Im Verlauf der 26. Dynastie, hier mutmaßlich mit Amtsantritt der Gottesgemahlin Nitokris und ihres *jmj-rꜣ pr wr* Ibi, wurden in Theben anfallende ursprüngliche Wesirsaufgaben durch den *jmj-rꜣ pr wr* der Gottesgemahlin übernommen. Bezeichnenderweise trägt die Gottesgemahlin Anchnesneferibre den Titel *tꜣjtj-sꜣb* einmal sogar selbst.[88]

Auch in Unterägypten scheint es einen „weichen Übergang" während der Herrschaft von Psammetich I. gegeben zu haben. Aus seiner Regierungszeit sind noch mindestens acht Wesire belegt. Dieser Befund ließe auf mehrere Wesirssitze in Unterägypten noch in der frühen 26. Dynastie schließen.

Papyrus Rylands 9[89] liefert möglicherweise einen Hinweis darauf, wie und wann sich das Wesirat im weiteren Verlauf der 26. Dynastie gewandelt hat. Als sich *Pꜣ-dj-ꜣst* II. direkt an Psammetich II. wendet, um das ihm zugefügte Unrecht zu melden, wird er aufgrund dessen schlechten Gesundheitszustandes wieder weggeschickt. Daraufhin erstattet er dem Wesir und den Richtern Meldung. Diese sind offensichtlich die nach Pharao Ranghöchsten und stehen auch über dem lokalen Oberhaupt in Herakleopolis (XV,9). Etwas später im Text von Papyrus Rylands 9 und zeitlich am Ende der 26. Dynastie wird diese Position von dem *jmj-rꜣ rwt* eingenommen (XIX). Und in der Perserzeit dann muss *Pꜣ-dj-ꜣst* III. dem *sntj* Rede und

84 So bereits G. Vittmann, Neues zu Pabasa, Obermajordomus der Nitokris, in: SAK 5, 1977, 244–264, hier: 262.

85 Sarg Wien 3941 und Stele Kairo JE 4886 des Sohnes: Jansen-Winkeln, Inschriften der Spätzeit IV,2, 597–598 (6), 598 (7); TIP², table 15, §489; G. Vittmann, Ein neuer Wesir der Spätzeit, in: GM 15, 1975, 47–52.

86 *Ḏd-Bꜣstt-jw=f-ꜥnḫ* auf der Sitzfigur Kairo JE 27749 aus Theben/Achmim (N. Alzohary, The lower part of the statue of a new vizier *Ḏd-Bꜣstt-iw.f-ꜥnḫ* (Cairo JE 27749), in: MDAIK 68, 2012, 31–41) wäre demnach der Großvater des *Ḏd-Bꜣstt-jw=f-ꜥnḫ* von der Stele Kairo TN 18/2/25/2 aus Abydos (Jansen-Winkeln, Inschriften der Spätzeit IV,1, 124–125 [242]): Alzohary, MDAIK 68, 2012, 40.

87 Angesichts seines Titels *sꜣb ꜥḏ-mr* wäre sogar vorstellbar, dass der ältere *Ḏd-Bꜣstt-jw=f-ꜥnḫ* mit Unterägypten assoziiert werden muss (siehe oben, Fußnote 80).

88 Kairo CG 42205: Jansen-Winkeln, Inschriften der Spätzeit IV,2, 732 (98); Koch, Gottesgemahlinnen, 107–108 (i.1).

89 G. Vittmann, Papyrus Rylands 9, I, 120–123, 166–167, 180–183.

Antwort stehen (II, 16ff).[90] Alle drei Institutionen werden mit ähnlichen Kompetenzen und in vergleichbarer Position angeführt. Es wäre denkbar, hier den Wandel in der Zuständigkeit bei einer Beschwerde an oberster Stelle widergespiegelt zu sehen: Bis zu den bereits von Diodor genannten Reformen des Amasis[91] wäre der Wesir in einer ähnlichen Position wie im Neuen Reich als rechte Hand des Königs beziehungsweise Lokalherrschers auch für Recht und Ordnung zuständig gewesen. Unter Amasis gingen dessen Zuständigkeiten an den *jmj-r3 rwt* über, bis schließlich in der Perserzeit der *sntj* übernahm. Dieser wäre demnach der Nachfolger des Wesirs.[92]

Nach der ersten Perserzeit sind schließlich noch vier oder fünf[93] ägyptische und zwei griechisch stämmige Wesire überliefert. Angesichts der bescheidenen Quellenlage ist allerdings keine fundierte Aussage darüber möglich, ob mit dem wiedereingeführten Wesirstitel nach der 27. Dynastie bestimmte Aufgaben verknüpft waren. Im Archiv des Hor werden den griechischen Titelträgern sowohl militärische als auch zivile Autoritäten bescheinigt, so dass Mark SMITH sogar einen Vergleich mit den *strategoi* für angebracht hält.[94] Ohne die Bedeutung des Titels festlegen zu können, hatte bereits Stephen GLANVILLE erkannt: „The context requires an important title or office. As so does the determinative."[95]

Alles in allem scheinen die genannten Belege einige gute Gründe für die Annahme zu liefern, dass das Amt des Wesirs als Stellvertreter des Königs und damit höchster Beamter der sogenannten Zivilverwaltung auch nach dem Neuen Reich bis in die 26. Dynastie als solches fortbestand. Das ausgerufene Ende der Zivilverwaltung nach dem Untergang des Neuen Reiches kann entsprechend nicht bestätigt werden.

90 J. YOYOTTE, Les vierges, 193; M. CHAUVEAU, Titres et fonctions en Égypte perse d'après les sources égyptiennes, in: P. BRIANT/M. CHAUVEAU (Hrsg.), Organisation des pouvoirs et contacts culturels dans les pays de l'empire achéménide, Persika 14, Paris 2009, 123–131, hier: 127. G. VITTMANN, Rupture and continuity: on priests and officials in Egypt during the Persian period, in: P. BRIANT/M. CHAUVEAU (Hrsg.), Organisation des pouvoirs et contacts culturels dans les pays de l'empire achéménide, Persika 14, Paris 2009, 89–121, hier: 100–101, spricht sich für eine Einführung des *sntj* bereits in der Regierungszeit des Amasis aus.

91 DIODOR I, 95, 1.

92 Ähnlich bereits W. HUSS, Die Verwaltung des ptolemaiischen Reichs, MBP 104, München 2011, 33.

93 Es ist unklar, ob der in das traditionelle Wesirsgewand gekleidete *ʿš3-jḫt* tatsächlich als Wesir amtierte, da er an keiner Stelle auch nur einen der spezifischen Wesirstitel trägt.

94 Texte 7 (5–8), 26 (recto, 1–3) und 60 (x + 1–2): SMITH, JNES 48,1, 1989, 53–54.

95 GLANVILLE, Onchsheshonqy, 70 (73).

Anhang: Wesire im ersten Jahrtausend

Name und Filiationsangabe (Weil/TIP²/Vittmann)	**Datierung**	**Hinterlassenschaft**
Ḥr, Sohn des *P3-ḥm-nṯr*, Vater des *Ḳ3j-Jn-ḥrt* A. Weil, Die Veziere des Pharaonenreiches, Straßburg 1908, 157 (§37)	21. Dyn. (Perdu) Mitte 22. Dyn. (Jansen-Winkeln)	Stele mit Ptah-Figur Berlin 8169 (Jansen-Winkeln, Inschriften der Spätzeit II, 230–231 [25])/ Würfelhocker Paris Louvre E.20368 (Jansen-Winkeln, Inschriften der Spätzeit II, 263–264 [7]; O. Perdu, Les statues privées de la fin de l'Égypte pharaonique [1069 av. J.-C. – 395 apr. J.-C.]. Tome I, Hommes, Paris 2012, 198–207)
P3-n-Jmn	späte 21. oder frühe 22. Dyn.	Würfelhocker eines Nachkommen Kairo JE 65843 (Jansen-Winkeln, Inschriften der Spätzeit IV,2, 826 [165])
Jkn, Sohn der *Jyw*	Osorkon I.	Bestattung in Tell el-Belamun (Jansen-Winkeln, Inschriften der Spätzeit II, 60 [37])
B3s3, Vater des *Gmj.n=f-st-k3pw*, Großvater des Tefnacht	22. Dyn.	Bronzestatuette des Amun Florenz 1777 (Jansen-Winkeln, Inschriften der Spätzeit II, 270–271 [11])
Hrrm Weil, Veziere, 149 (§26)	22./23. Dyn.	Stele Paris Louvre IM 3113 (Jansen-Winkeln, Inschriften der Spätzeit II, 397 [34])
Ḏd-ḫy, Sohn des *Ḫnzw*-[...]	Datierung unklar, da die Verbindung zum Stifter nicht eindeutig ist	Würfelhocker eines Nachkommen, ehem. Privatsammlung (Jansen-Winkeln, Inschriften der Spätzeit IV,2, 819–821 [154])
Ṯ3j-nfr, Sohn des *Grg-t3wj*[96]	späte 25. Dyn.?	Gruppenfigur eines Nachkommen Alexandria 435 (Jansen-Winkeln, Inschriften der Spätzeit IV,1, 507 [220])
P3j=f-ṯ3w-m-ꜥ-B3stt, Vater des *ꜥnḫ-sm3-t3wj*	späte 25. Dyn.	Würfelhocker des Sohnes, Verbleib unbekannt (Jansen-Winkeln, Inschriften der Spätzeit IV,1, 47–48 [86])/ Stele Kairo o.Nr. (?) (Jansen-Winkeln, Inschriften der Spätzeit IV,1, 65–66 [119])
Ḥr-3ḫ-bjt	25. Dyn.	Sitzfigur Neapel 237 (Jansen-Winkeln, Inschriften der Spätzeit III, 374 [48])
P3-dj-3st[97]	späte 25. Dyn.?	pQueen's College (Fischer-Elfert, Papyrus Queen's College recto, 143–151)

96 *Ṯ3j-nfr* trägt nur die Titelfolge *t3jtj s3b*.

97 Dieser Wesir *P3-dj-3st* wird ohne Filiationsangabe in einem literarischen Text genannt. Es könnte sich um einen fiktiven Wesir oder ein Pseudonym handeln.

Name und Filiationsangabe (Weil/TIP^{2}/Vittmann)	**Datierung**	**Hinterlassenschaft**
ꜥnḫ-Ḥr, Vater der *Dj-ꜣst-ḥb-sd* Weil, Veziere, 139–140 (§10) TIP^{2}, table 15 Vittmann, Priester und Beamte, 149	25. Dyn. ca. 730 v. Chr. (TIP^{2})	Osirisstatue Kairo CG 38238 (Jansen-Winkeln, Inschriften der Spätzeit III, 302 [66])
Ḥr-wḏꜣ, Sohn des *Pꜣ-ꜥꜣ-pnj* Identisch mit?	späte 25. Dyn.?	Würfelhocker eines Nachkommen New York MMA 1993.161 (Jansen-Winkeln, Inschriften der Spätzeit IV,2, 829–830 [175])
Ḥr-wḏꜣ, Vater des *Pꜣ-n-P* (*Ḥr-wḏꜣ* [Enkel]) Weil, Veziere, 148 (§23)	späte 25. Dyn.?	Würfelhocker eines Nachkommen Cleveland 1932.204 (Jansen-Winkeln, Inschriften der Spätzeit IV,2, 848 [202])
Mnṯw-ḥtp, Ehemann der Königstochter Amenirdis TIP^{2}, §490a, table 15 Vittmann, Priester und Beamte, 145	späte 25. Dyn. ca. 685–675 v. Chr. (TIP^{2})	Stele Kairo o.Nr.(?) (Jansen-Winkeln, Inschriften der Spätzeit III, 564–565 [404])/ Skarabäus Moskau I.a.2398 (Jansen-Winkeln, Inschriften der Spätzeit III, 564 [403])
ꜥnḫ-Ššnḳ, Vater des *Ḥrj* und des Wesirs *Ḥr-sꜣ-ꜣst* Weil, Veziere, 142 (§13)	22./23. Dyn. (Weil) späte 25. Dyn. (A. Leahy, 'May the King Live': The Libyan Rulers in the Onomastic Record, in: A. Lloyd [Hrsg.], Studies in Pharaonic Religion and Society in Honour of J. Gwyn Griffiths, EES Occasional Publications 8, London 1992, 146–163, hier: 150)[98]	Stele eines Nachkommen Paris Louvre IM 4097 (J. Labudek, Late Period stelae from Saqqara. A socio-cultural and religious investigation University of Birmingham Research Archive e-theses repository: http://etheses.bham.ac.uk/913/, 2010, 290. Zugriff am: 23.04.2019; É. Chassinat, Textes provenant du Sérapéum de Memphis [suite], in: RecTrav 23, 1901, 76–91, hier: 79)/ Fragment einer Stele RB 18395 (A. M. Ibrahim/R. Nageb/D. Devauchelle/F.-R. Herbin, Présentation des stèles nouvellement découvertes au Sérapéum, in: BSFE 106, 1986, 31–44; eine Publikation durch Ibrahim und Devauchelle ist in Vorbereitung;[99] erwähnt von de Meulenaere gegenüber F. Payraudeau, Harsiésis, un vizir oublié de l'Époque Libyenne? in: JEA 89, 2003, 199–205, hier: 205 [9])

98 Arthur Weil legte eine Generationenlänge von 30 Jahren zugrunde, Leahy hingegen 25 Jahre.

99 Ich danke Didier Devauchelle für die freundliche Erlaubnis, die auf dem Fragment genannten Wesire an dieser Stelle mit aufzunehmen. Ebenfalls danken möchte ich Günter Vittmann für den Hinweis auf das Objekt.

Name und Filiationsangabe (WEIL/TIP²/VITTMANN)	**Datierung**	**Hinterlassenschaft**
Ḥr-s3-3st, Sohn des *ʿnḫ-Ššnḳ*	frühe 26. Dyn. (zur Datierung siehe Erläuterungen bei *ʿnḫ-Ššnḳ*)	Fragment einer Stele RB 18395 (IBRAHIM/NAGEB/DEVAUCHELLE/HERBIN, BSFE 106, 1986, 31–44; eine Publikation durch IBRAHIM und DEVAUCHELLE ist in Vorbereitung; erwähnt von DE MEULENAERE gegenüber PAYRAUDEAU, JEA 89, 2003, 205 [9])
P3-šrj-n-3st, Sohn des *Ḥr-s3-3st*, Enkel des *ʿnḫ-Ššnḳ*	frühe 26. Dyn. (zur Datierung siehe Erläuterungen bei *ʿnḫ-Ššnḳ*)	Fragment einer Stele RB 18395 (IBRAHIM/NAGEB/DEVAUCHELLE/HERBIN, BSFE 106, 1986, 31–44; eine Publikation durch IBRAHIM und DEVAUCHELLE ist in Vorbereitung; erwähnt von DE MEULENAERE gegenüber PAYRAUDEAU, JEA 89, 2003, 205 [9])
Ḥr-s3-3st R, Vater der königlichen Gemahlin *Mḥjt-m-wsḫt* TIP², §490b–492, table 15 VITTMANN, Priester und Beamte, 39–43	späte 25. Dyn./ frühe 26. Dyn. ca. 675–660 v. Chr. (TIP²)	Sarg Kairo TN 21/11/16/10 der Tochter (JANSEN-WINKELN, Inschriften der Spätzeit III, 429–430 [154])/ Stele Kairo TN 27/1/25/17 der Tochter (JANSEN-WINKELN, Inschriften der Spätzeit III, 429–430 [154])/ Sarg einer Nachfahrin aus der 26. Dynastie im Handel (JANSEN-WINKELN, Inschriften der Spätzeit IV,2, 1016 [473])/ Stelophor Philadelphia E.16025 (JANSEN-WINKELN, Inschriften der Spätzeit III, 374 [49])
Ḏd-k3-Rʿ, Sohn des *Ḥr-s3-3st* R, Vater des *Šp-n-jw-s-ʿ3-s*, Vorfahr der *Jrtj-r-w* WEIL, Veziere, 148 (§24) TIP², §493c, table 15 VITTMANN, Priester und Beamte, 148	frühe 26. Dyn. ca. 660ff v. Chr. (TIP²)	Kanopensatz ehem. Wien 3580–3583, derzeitiger Aufenthaltsort unbekannt (Auktionskatalog GORNY & MOSCH GIESSENER MÜNZHANDLUNG GMBH vom 18.12.2018. https://www.gmcoinart.de/templates/images/muenzen/Kataloge/gm_auktion_260_katalog.pdf. Zugriff am 23.04.2019; JANSEN-WINKELN, Inschriften der Spätzeit III, 564 [402])/ Sarg einer Nachfahrin, im Handel (JANSEN-WINKELN, Inschriften der Spätzeit IV.2, 1016 [473])
S3-Sbk, Vater des *Ḥr-wḏ3*, Großvater des *Mrj-Ptḥ* WEIL, Veziere, 146 (§20) TIP², 493d, table 15 VITTMANN, Priester und Beamte, 147	Psammetich I.	Kniefigur des Sohnes Baltimore WAG 22.79 (JANSEN-WINKELN, Inschriften der Spätzeit IV.1, 87 [146])/ Sarkophagdeckel London BM 17 (881) (JANSEN-WINKELN, Inschriften der Spätzeit IV,1, 41–42 [73])

Name und Filiationsangabe (WEIL/TIP²/VITTMANN)	**Datierung**	**Hinterlassenschaft**
N3-sẖpr-n-Sḫmt, Sohn der *Šsp-Jmn-t3j=s-ḥrt* WEIL, Veziere, 144 (§17) TIP², 493d, table 15 VITTMANN, Priester und Beamte, 145–146	Psammetich I.	Würfelhocker Frankfurt IN 1449 (JANSEN-WINKELN, Inschriften der Spätzeit IV,2, 265 [389])
B3k-n-rn=f WEIL, Veziere, 145 (§19) TIP², 493d, table 15 VITTMANN, Priester und Beamte, 146	Psammetich I.	Kniefigur Brooklyn 82.23 + Brüssel E.7049 (JANSEN-WINKELN, Inschriften der Spätzeit IV,1, 76 [141])/ Grab Sakkara LS 24 (JANSEN-WINKELN, Inschriften der Spätzeit IV,1, 76–81 [143])/ Sarkophag Florenz 2182 (1705) (JANSEN-WINKELN, Inschriften der Spätzeit IV,1, 82–87 [145])
Gmj-n=f-ḥr-b3k, Sohn des *Jw=f-ʿ3* und der *J-nw* WEIL, Veziere, 146 (§21) TIP², 493d, table 15 VITTMANN, Priester und Beamte, 147	Psammetich I.	Sarkophag Turin 2201 (JANSEN-WINKELN, Inschriften der Spätzeit IV,2, 789–791 [88])
Ḥr-sm3-t3wj-m-ḥ3t TIP², 493d, table 15 VITTMANN, Priester und Beamte, 148	Psammetich I.	Würfelhocker Privatsammlung Mailand (JANSEN-WINKELN, Inschriften der Spätzeit IV,1, 40 [71])/ Türsturzfragment Kairo JE 88213/JE 88215 (JANSEN-WINKELN, Inschriften der Spätzeit IV,1, 65 [118])/ Kanopenkrug Wien 5182 (JANSEN-WINKELN, Inschriften der Spätzeit IV,1, 65 [119])
Psmṯk-mrjj-Nt WEIL, Veziere, 150 (§28) TIP², 493e, table 15 VITTMANN, Priester und Beamte, 147	Amasis	Uschebti aus dem Kunsthandel (JANSEN-WINKELN, Inschriften der Spätzeit IV,1, 582 [323])/ Stele Paris Louvre IM 4076 (E. JELINKOVA, Un titre saïte emprunté à l'Ancien Empire, in: ASAE 55[1], 1958, 79–125, hier: 113 [21])/ Siegelabdruck (JANSEN-WINKELN, Inschriften der Spätzeit IV,1, 560 [291])
Jw=f-ʿ3	26. Dyn.	Unterteil Kniefigur Privatsammlung Kairo (JANSEN-WINKELN, Inschriften der Spätzeit IV,2, 974 [411])

Name und Filiationsangabe (Weil/TIP²/Vittmann)	Datierung	Hinterlassenschaft
ʿnḫ-wn-nfr, Sohn des *P3-šrj-n-Ptḥ*	26. Dyn..	Unterteil Theophor ehem. Sammlung Sameda (Kairo) (Jansen-Winkeln, Inschriften der Spätzeit IV,2, 1171 [817])
Nfr-ḏd-Nfr-jb-Rʿ	26. Dyn.	Statuensockel London UC 14626 (Jansen-Winkeln, Inschriften der Spätzeit IV,2, 879–880 [254])
Nicht erhalten, Sohn (?) des *Ns-šw-[Tfnwt]*	26. Dyn.	Würfelhocker Basel 19782 (Jansen-Winkeln, Inschriften der Spätzeit IV,2, 957–958 [387])
B3k-n-nfj (Großvater der *Š3w-Jmn-n-jm=s*)	26. Dyn.	Stele Mataria 3885 (unpubliziert/A. M. W. Moustafa, Die saitische Nekropole in Heliopolis. Archäologische und architektonische Studie, unveröff. Dissertation Leipzig, den 28.12.2017)[100]

Tab. 1: Wesire in Unterägypten

Name und Filiationsangabe (Weil/TIP²/Vittmann)	Datierung/ Möglicher Dienstsitz	Hinterlassenschaft
Pianch	späte 20. Dyn.	oKairo CG 25745 (KRI VI, 849 [2])
Herihor TIP², table 15	ca. 1075 v. Chr. (TIP²)	Sarg Sethos I. (KRI VI, 838: 5–6)/ Sarg Ramses II. (KRI VI, 838: 9–10)/ Block Karnak (Jansen-Winkeln, Inschriften der Spätzeit I, 4 [1])/ Statue Kairo CG 42190 (KRI VI, 843–844)/ oKairo CG 25744 (KRI VI, 847–848)
Pinodjem I. Weil, Veziere, 129–130 (§1) TIP², table 15	ca. 1070 v. Chr. (TIP²)	Beischrift Luxortempel (Jansen-Winkeln, Inschriften der Spätzeit I, 17 [22 b])/ Restaurationsinschriften (Jansen-Winkeln, Inschriften der Spätzeit I, 18–20 [24] [25])/ Graffito 2144 (Jansen-Winkeln, Inschriften der Spätzeit I, 37 [64])/ Graffito Grab des Haremhab (KV 57) (Jansen-Winkeln, Inschriften der Spätzeit I, 35–36 [61])

100 Ich danke Günter Vittmann für die Auskunft.

Name und Filiationsangabe (Weil/TIP²/Vittmann)	**Datierung/ Möglicher Dienstsitz**	**Hinterlassenschaft**
Jn-ḥr-pꜣ-mšꜥ TIP², table 15 (bezieht sich auf Kees, Priestertum, 318, der die Quelle nicht nennt)	ca. 1040 v. Chr. (TIP²) 21. Dyn. (?) (Kees)	
[...]-*nfr*		pBerlin 23098 (Jansen-Winkeln, Inschriften der Spätzeit I, 203 [35])
Thebanische Wesire der 22./23. Dynastie nach Payraudeau, Administration 180–181		
Ḥr-sꜣ-ꜣst (möglicherweise identisch mit *Ḥr-sꜣ-ꜣst* D?) Weil, Veziere, 158 (§38a)	frühe 22. Dyn.? (Payraudeau)	Kartonage der Tochter Brooklyn 34.1223/ Uschebti Ramesseum 54 (Jansen-Winkeln, Inschriften der Spätzeit II, 254 [67];Payraudeau, Administration II, 568)
J-ꜥꜣ Weil, Veziere, 139 (§9) TIP², table 15	Scheschonk I. (Payraudeau) ca. 925 v. Chr. (TIP², table 15)	Kartonage Cambridge E 8.1896 (Jansen-Winkeln, Inschriften der Spätzeit II, 101 [27])
Pꜣ-dj-Mwt A/ I (Genealogie: TIP², 220) identisch mit dem von Kitchen (TIP², table 15) verlesenen Rudpamut	Osorkon I. (Payraudeau) ca. 940 und ca. 880 v. Chr. (Rudpamut) (TIP², table 15)	Würfelhocker Kairo CG 42215/ Kairo CG 42214/ Priesterannalen Karnak (Jansen-Winkeln, Inschriften der Spätzeit II, 239 [45], 240 [46]; Kruchten, Annales des prêtres, 94)
Ns-r-Jmn VII/A, Sohn des *Nb-nṯrw* II. (Stammbaum: TIP², §177; F. Kampp, Die thebanische Nekropole: zum Wandel des Grabgedankens von der 18. bis zur 20. Dynastie I, Theben 13, Mainz am Rhein 1996, 404) Weil, Veziere, 131–134 (§3) TIP², table 15	frühe 22. Dyn. (Payraudeau)	Würfelhocker Kairo CG 42225/ Kartonage aus dem Ramesseum/ Grabinschrift TT 117/ Block Kairo JE 29248 (Jansen-Winkeln, Inschriften der Spätzeit II, 135–139 [75], 250 [55], 461–462 [123], 302–303 [18])
Ḥr XXVI, Sohn des *Jwtk* A TIP², table 15	22. Dyn. (Payraudeau) ca. 845? v. Chr. (TIP², table 15)	Statue Kairo JE 37512 (Jansen-Winkeln, Inschriften der Spätzeit II, 449–450 [100])
Jwtk B, Sohn des *Ḥr* XXVI.	22. Dyn. (Payraudeau)	Papyrus Kairo JE 95718/ Kanopen Kairo CG 4371–4374/ Statue Kairo JE 37512 (A. Niwiński, Studies on the illustrated Theban funerary papyri of the 11th and 10th centuries B.C., OBO 86, Freiburg [Schweiz]/Göttingen 1989, 262 [Cairo 28]; Jansen-Winkeln, Inschriften der Spätzeit II, 449–450 [100], 466 [134], 470 [149])

Name und Filiationsangabe (Weil/TIP²/Vittmann)	**Datierung/ Möglicher Dienstsitz**	**Hinterlassenschaft**
Nb-nṯrw IX.	Mitte 22. Dyn. (Payraudeau)	Sarkophag eines Nachkommen (25. Dyn.) Kairo CG 41001 (Jansen-Winkeln, Inschriften der Spätzeit III, 415–416 [143])
Ḥr XVIII. Weil, Veziere, 143 (§14) TIP², table 15	Osorkon II. – Takeloth II.? (Payraudeau) ca. 820 und ca. 876 v. Chr. (TIP², table 15)	Karnak Priesterannalen 1 (Kruchten, Annales des prêtres, 36–44)/ wohl auch Papyrus Berlin 3048 (Jansen-Winkeln, Inschriften der Spätzeit II, 170–171 [12]; Payraudeau, Administration, 555 [196])
Ns-pꜣ-ḳꜣ-šwtj A, Sohn des *Ḏd-Ḏḥwtj-jw=f-ꜥnḫ* A (Stammbaum TIP², §166) TIP², table 15	Osorkon II. – Scheschonk III. (Payraudeau) ca. 835 v. Chr. (TIP², table 15)	Würfelhocker Kairo CG 42232/ Stele Liverpool M.13916 (Jansen-Winkeln, Inschriften der Spätzeit II, 205–207 [44]; Jansen-Winkeln, Inschriften der Spätzeit III, 410–411 [137])
Name nicht erhalten (*Ḥr* XVIII. oder *Pꜣ-ntj-jw=f-ꜥnḫ*?) Weil, Veziere, 136 (§6)	Scheschonk III. (Payraudeau)	Karnak Priesterannalen (Kruchten, Annales des prêtres, pl. 2; Payraudeau, Administration, 614 [284])
Ḥr-sꜣ-ꜣst D, Sohn des *Ns-pꜣ-ḳꜣ-šwtj* A (Stammbaum: K. Kitchen, A lost stela of the Third Intermediate Period, in: C. Berger/G. Clerc/N.-C. Grimal (Hrsg.), Hommages à Jean Leclant 4, BdE 106,4, Kairo 1994, 163–167, hier: 165) TIP², table 15	Scheschonk III. (Payraudeau) ca. 825 v. Chr. (TIP², table 15)	Stele Liverpool M.13916 (Jansen-Winkeln, Inschriften der Spätzeit III, 410–411 [137])/ Kanopen Louvre E. 21339–40, MG 23094 (Jansen-Winkeln, Inschriften der Spätzeit II, 234 [35]; F. Gombert-Meurice/F. Payraudeau [eds.], Servir les dieux d'Égypte. Divines adoratrices, chanteuses et prêtres d'Amon à Thèbes, Catalogue Musée de Grenoble 2018, 161 [80])/ Relief Elephantine (Jansen-Winkeln, Inschriften der Spätzeit II, 254–255 [68])
Pꜣ-ntj-jw=f-ꜥnḫ, Sohn des *Ḥr* XVIII. Weil, Veziere, 143 (§15) TIP², table 15	Petubast I. (Payraudeau) ca. 815 v. Chr. (TIP², table 15)	Karnak Priesterannalen 1 (Kruchten, Annales des prêtres, 36–44; Jansen-Winkeln, Inschriften der Spätzeit II, 213 [16])
Nḫt=f-Mwt C, Sohn von *Nb-nṯrw* VI. Weil, Veziere, 136–137 (§7) TIP², table 15	Takeloth II. ? (Payraudeau) ca. 775 v. Chr. (TIP², table 15)	Stelophor Kairo CG 42229/ Sargensemble Berlin 20132/ Würfelhocker Kairo JE 37851/ Würfelhocker Kairo JE 36733/ Sarg Privatsammlung Lieblein 1113 (Jansen-Winkeln, Inschriften der Spätzeit II, 309–310 [24], 391–392 [20]; Jansen-Winkeln, Inschriften der Spätzeit III, 411 [138], 417 [144])

Name und Filiationsangabe (Weil/TIP²/Vittmann)	**Datierung/ Möglicher Dienstsitz**	**Hinterlassenschaft**
Ḥr-sꜣ-ꜣst E, Sohn des *Pꜣ-shn-ꜣst* TIP², table 15	Scheschonk III. (Payraudeau) ca. 790 v. Chr. (TIP², table 15)	Karnak Priesterannalen (Kruchten, Annales des prêtres, 59–85)
Jw=f-fꜣy (Genealogie TIP², 225) Weil, Veziere, 149 (§25)	? (Payraudeau)	Sarg der Urenkelin Paris Louvre E.3913 (Jansen-Winkeln, Inschriften der Spätzeit III, 436 [163])
ꜥnḫ-wn-nfr, Vater der *Krm*	Osorkon III. ? (Payraudeau)	Uschebtis Kairo JE 49639–49651/ Kanopen seiner Tochter (Jansen-Winkeln, Inschriften der Spätzeit II, 232 [28], 399 [41])
Pꜣ-mjw, Sohn des *Pꜣ-dj-Jmnt* I Weil, Veziere, 134–135 (§4) TIP², table 15	Osorkon III.? (Payraudeau) ca. 765 v. Chr. (TIP², table 15)	Sargensemble Kairo CG 41036/ Sargdeckel Paris Louvre E.3863/ Grabausstattung Luxormuseum R 845/ Stele Kopenhagen 3545/ Osirisfigur London BM 22913/ Sarg des Urenkels/ Würfelhocker Kairo JE 36940/CG 42275 (Jansen-Winkeln, Inschriften der Spätzeit III, 359 [21], 361 [24]; Jansen-Winkeln, Inschriften der Spätzeit II, 398 [37], 398 [38])
Ḥr X., Sohn des *Nḫt=f-Mwt* C Weil, Veziere, 136–137 (§8) TIP², table 15	Osorkon III. (Payraudeau) ca. 770 v. Chr. (TIP², table 15)	Stelophor Kairo CG 42229 (Jansen-Winkeln, Inschriften der Spätzeit II, 309–310 [24])
Ḥr XXIV., Sohn des *Nb-nṯrw* IV. (?)	Osorkon III. ? (Payraudeau)	Kanopen Topol'cianky 979–982/ Statue Kairo JE 37344 eines Nachkommen/ Würfelhocker des Enkels Kairo JE 37413/ Würfelhocker des Urenkels Kairo JE 37848 aus Theben (Jansen-Winkeln, Inschriften der Spätzeit II, 469 [143]; Jansen-Winkeln, Inschriften der Spätzeit III, 524, 521–522 [311], 522–523 [312])
Ḏd-Ḫnzw-jw=f-ꜥnḫ E Weil, Veziere, 144 (§16) TIP², table 15	? (Payraudeau) ca. 780 v. Chr. (TIP², table 15)	Skarabäus/ Sargensemble und Uschebtikästen der Enkelin, Verbleib unbekannt (Jansen-Winkeln, Inschriften der Spätzeit II, 400 [42]; Jansen-Winkeln, Inschriften der Spätzeit III, 493–494 [258])
Pꜣ-dj-Jmnt II., Sohn des *Pꜣ-mjw* TIP², table 15	Osorkon III. oder Piye (Payraudeau) ca. 750 v. Chr. (TIP², table 15)	Kartonage Deir el-Bahari 30/ Sargfragment Deir el-Bahari 38/ Sarg eines Nachkommen Luxormuseum R 845/ Sarg des Enkels Luxor R 844 (Payraudeau, Administration, 471–473 [109])

Name und Filiationsangabe (Weil/TIP^2/Vittmann)	**Datierung/ Möglicher Dienstsitz**	**Hinterlassenschaft**
ʿnḫ-Wsrkn, Sohn des *Ḏd-Ptḥ-jw=f-ʿnḫ* TIP^2, table 15	Takeloth III. (Payraudeau) ca. 755 v. Chr. (TIP^2, table 15)	Statue Kairo JE 91300 + Musée Rodin Co. 3386/ Sarg Boston MFA 72.4824 (Jansen-Winkeln, Inschriften der Spätzeit II, 479–480 [25]; Jansen-Winkeln, Inschriften der Spätzeit III, 361–362 [30.13a]; Payraudeau, Administration, 430 [34])
Ḥr-sꜣ-ꜣst, Sohn des *Ḏd-jʿḥ*	ca. 775–750 v. Chr. (Payraudeau[101])	Stele Kairo JE 43197 (Jansen-Winkeln, Inschriften der Spätzeit II, 463–464 [126])
Pꜣ-ẖꜣr, Sohn des *Pꜣ-mjw* Weil, Veziere, 134–135 (§5) TIP^2, table 15	ca. 760–735 v. Chr. (Payraudeau) ca. 760 v. Chr. (TIP^2, table 15)	Sargensemble Kairo CG 41036/ Sargdeckel Paris Louvre E.3863/ Sarkophag Paris Louvre E 18846 des Sohnes (Jansen-Winkeln, Inschriften der Spätzeit III, 359 [21]; Payraudeau, Administration, 467 [101])
Nb-nṯrw X., Sohn des *Ḥr* XXIV.	ca. 750–725 v. Chr. (Payraudeau)	Kanopen Kairo SR 15912/ Würfelhocker des Urenkels Kairo JE 37344/ Sarg (Jansen-Winkeln, Inschriften der Spätzeit II, 399 [40]; Jansen-Winkeln, Inschriften der Spätzeit III, 524 [315]; Payraudeau, Administration, 486 [127])
Ns-pꜣ-ḳꜣ-šwtj B, Sohn des *Pꜣ-dj-Jmnt* II. TIP^2, table 15	ca. 750–725 v. Chr. (Payraudeau) ca. 725 v. Chr. (TIP^2, table 15) Abydos?	Sarg, Verbleib unbekannt aus Deir el-Bahari (Jansen-Winkeln, Inschriften der Spätzeit III, 360 [22])/ Sargfragment Deir el-Bahari 37 (Payraudeau, Administration, 521 [169 A])/ Sarg Luxor R 844 (F. Payraudeau, Administration, 522 [B])/ Uschebtikasten, Verbleib unbekannt (Payraudeau, Administration, 523 [D])/ Sarkophag und Särge des *Ns-pꜣ-ḳꜣ-šwtj* VI. Luxor R 845 (Payraudeau, Administration, 523 [E–G])

101 Der von Payraudeau, Administration, 181, als Wesir der Libyerzeit (ca. 775–750 v. Chr.) aufgeführte *Ḥr-sꜣ-ꜣst*, Sohn des *Ḏd-jʿḥ* ist unter Vorbehalt und mit großem Fragezeichen zu datieren. Die Stele, die ihn als Teil der Familiengenealogie aufführt, wurde vom Erstbearbeiter R. El-Sayed, Deux monuments du Musée du Caire, in: BIFAO 85, 1985, 173–185, hier: 176–178, in die 22. Dynastie datiert. Namen und Titel deuten auf die Libyerzeit (siehe Jansen-Winkeln, Inschriften der Spätzeit II, 464). *Ḥr-sꜣ-ꜣst*, der fünf Generationen vor dem Stifter amtierte, wäre entsprechend in die frühe 21. Dynastie oder sogar an das Ende des Neuen Reiches zu setzen. Ikonographische Kriterien führten Payraudeau, JEA 89, 2003, 204, zu einer Datierung der Stele in die 25. oder sogar 26. Dynastie. Zu weiteren Titeln des *Ḥr-sꜣ-ꜣst* und deren Wert für eine genauere Datierung siehe C. Koch, Datieren und Identifizieren: Vom Nutzen der Titelkunde, FS NN.

Name und Filiationsangabe (Weil/TIP²/Vittmann)	**Datierung/ Möglicher Dienstsitz**	**Hinterlassenschaft**
Ḥr-s3-3st F, Vater des *P3-dj-3st* C, *Ns-Mnw* A und des *Ḫ*ʿ*m-ḥr* A (TIP², 231) Weil, Veziere, 151–152 (§29) TIP², table 15 Vittmann, Priester und Beamte, 149–150	ca. 750–725 v. Chr. (Payraudeau) ca. 745 v. Chr. (TIP², table 15) Theben	Sarkophage der Urenkelin Kairo CG 41058 (Jansen-Winkeln, Inschriften der Spätzeit III, 422 [149])/ Sarkophag des Sohnes Kairo CG 41029 (Jansen-Winkeln, Inschriften der Spätzeit III, 447 [183])/ Würfelhocker eines Nachkommen Kairo CG 42250 (Jansen-Winkeln, Inschriften der Spätzeit IV,1, 155 [282])/ Würfelhocker eines Nachkommen Kairo CG 48629 (Jansen-Winkeln, Inschriften der Spätzeit III, 489 [250])
Ns-Mnw A, Sohn des *Ḥr-s3-3st* F (Genealogie TIP², 231) Weil, Veziere, 153–154 (§32) TIP², table 15 Vittmann, Priester und Beamte, 150	ca. 740 v. Chr. (TIP², table 15) Theben	Sarg Kairo CG 41058 (Jansen-Winkeln, Inschriften der Spätzeit III, 422–423 [149])
P3-dj-3st, Sohn des *Ḥr-s3-3st* F und der *B3b3jw* (Genealogie TIP², 231) TIP², table 15 Vittmann, Priester und Beamte, 150	ca. 720 v. Chr. (TIP², table 15) Theben	Sarkophag Kairo CG 41029 (Jansen-Winkeln, Inschriften der Spätzeit III, 447 [183])
Ppnḥ, Sohn des *Ns-nbw* (*Sm3-t3wj* [Sohn] *Ppnḥ* [Enkel])	25. Dyn. oder früher[102] Herakleopolis	Gruppenfigur Kairo CG 882 (Jansen-Winkeln, Inschriften der Spätzeit IV,2, 965–966 [404])
Nicht namentlich genannt, Vater von *Wḏ3-sm3-t3wj*, *P3-sn-n-Ḥr* und *Wsjr-nḫt*	2. Hälfte 8. Jh. v. Chr. (Vittmann) Herakleopolis	Papyrus Köln 5632 (G. Vittmann, FS NN)
Wsjr-nḫt, Vater des ʿ*nḫ-p3-ẖrd*	25. Dyn.[103] Herakleopolis[104]	Würfelhocker des Urenkels Kairo CG 8632/ JE 38012/ Torso Stehfigur ehem. Schweizer Privatsammlung (Jansen-Winkeln, Inschriften der Spätzeit IV,1, 207 [342]; Jansen-Winkeln, Inschriften der Spätzeit IV,2, 963–964 [400])

102 Zecchi, Prosopografia dei sacerdoti, 4–6, datierte irrtümlich in die Ptolemäerzeit: siehe H.G. Fischer, An Eleventh Dynasty couple holding the sign of life, in: ZÄS 100, 1973, 16–28, hier: 27, n.56.

103 *Wsjr-nḫt* trägt auf beiden Hinterlassenschaften nur den Titel *t3jtj s3b*.

104 Die Zuordnung des *Wsjr-nḫt* nach Herakleopolis erfolgte aufgrund mehrerer Indizien: a) Fundort der Stehfigur (Jansen-Winkeln, Inschriften der Spätzeit IV.2, 963–964 [400]) in Herakleopolis; b) Obwohl Würfelhocker Kairo CG 48632 in der Cachette von Karnak gefunden wurde, führen *Wsjr-nḫt* und seine Nachkommen auf diesem herakleopolitanische Priestertitel; c) Der Name *Wsjr-nḫt* ist vor allem im nördlichen Ägypten nachweisbar: siehe Vittmann, FS NN.

Name und Filiationsangabe (Weil/TIP²/Vittmann)	**Datierung/ Möglicher Dienstsitz**	**Hinterlassenschaft**
ꜥnḫ-pꜣ-ẖrd, Sohn des *Wsjr-nḫt* (*Ḥrj-šf-ḥtp* [Sohn] *Jmn-jr-dj-sj* [Enkel])	25. Dyn. Herakleopolis	Würfelhocker des Enkels Kairo CG 48632/ JE 38012 (Jansen-Winkeln, Inschriften der Spätzeit IV,1, 207 [342])
Ḫꜥm-ḥr I/A, Sohn des *Ḥr-sꜣ-ꜣst* (*Pꜣ-dj-Jmn* [Sohn]) (Genealogie TIP², 231; J. Leclant, Montouemhat: Quatrième prophète d'Amon, Prince de la ville, BdE 35, Kairo 1961, 263) Weil, Veziere, 153 (§31) TIP², table 15 Vittmann, Priester und Beamte, 150–151	ca. 715 v. Chr. (TIP², table 15) Theben	Sarg der Enkelin Kairo CG 41058 (Jansen-Winkeln, Inschriften der Spätzeit III, 422 [149])/ Würfelhocker Kairo CG 42234 (Jansen-Winkeln, Inschriften der Spätzeit III, 446–447 [180])/ Stehfigur des Enkels Kairo CG 42236 (Jansen-Winkeln, Inschriften der Spätzeit III, 454–456 [198])/ Sargensemble des Sohnes aus Theben (Jansen-Winkeln, Inschriften der Spätzeit III, 448–449 [185])/ Mumienleinen des Sohnes New York MMA 25.3.214 (Jansen-Winkeln, Inschriften der Spätzeit III, 450 [187])/ Pavianskulptur des Sohnes, Magazin Kairo (Jansen-Winkeln, Inschriften der Spätzeit III, 450 [189])/ Stele der Tochter Paris Louvre E.20092 (Jansen-Winkeln, Inschriften der Spätzeit III, 451 [192])/ Würfelhocker des Urenkels Kairo CG 42250 (Jansen-Winkeln, Inschriften der Spätzeit IV,1, 155–156 [282])/ Sargensemble des Urenkels Kairo CG 41008/CG 41057 (Jansen-Winkeln, Inschriften der Spätzeit IV,1, 158 [285])/ pBrooklyn 47.218.3 (R.A. Parker, Saite oracle papyrus, 24)
Pꜣ-hrr/*Ḥr-sꜣ-ꜣst* G, Sohn des *Ḫꜥm-Ḥr* I/A (Genealogie TIP², 231) Weil, Veziere, 140 (§11) TIP², table 15 Vittmann, Priester und Beamte, 152	ca. 700 v. Chr. (TIP², table 15) Theben	Würfelhocker des Sohnes Kairo CG 42249 (Jansen-Winkeln, Inschriften der Spätzeit III, 488–489 [249])/ Sargdeckel des Enkels Kairo CG 41068 (Jansen-Winkeln, Inschriften der Spätzeit IV.1, 156 [283])

Name und Filiationsangabe (Weil/TIP²/Vittmann)	**Datierung/ Möglicher Dienstsitz**	**Hinterlassenschaft**
Ns-Mnw B, Sohn des *Ḫ3m-Ḥr* I/A (Genealogie TIP², 231) Weil, Veziere, 153 (§32) TIP², table 15 Vittmann, Priester und Beamte, 152–153	ca. 690 v. Chr. (TIP², table 15) Theben	Sargfragment Frankfurt 800 (Jansen-Winkeln, Inschriften der Spätzeit III, 450 [188])/ Sarg der Ehefrau Kairo CG 41020 (Jansen-Winkeln, Inschriften der Spätzeit III, 450–451 [190])/ Sarg des Sohnes Kairo CG 41022 (Jansen-Winkeln, Inschriften der Spätzeit III, 486–487 [246])
Ns-p3-k3-šwtj C, Vater von *Ns-p3-mdw* und *Dd-Jnj-ḥrt-jw=f-ʿnḫ* (Genealogie P. Munro, Die spätägyptischen Totenstelen, ÄF 25, Glückstadt 1973, 118) Weil, Veziere, 154–155 (§34) TIP², table 15 Vittmann, Priester und Beamte, 154–159	ca. 680 v. Chr. (TIP², table 15) Abydos	Osirophor des Urenkels Kairo CG 48649 (Jansen-Winkeln, Inschriften der Spätzeit IV,2, 1059 [561])/ Pyramidion Glasgow 13.176 (Jansen-Winkeln, Inschriften der Spätzeit III, 395–396 [102])/ Stehfigur des Sohnes Kairo CG 48608/ JE 37416 (Jansen-Winkeln, Inschriften der Spätzeit III, 491–492 [255])/ Osirophor des Sohnes Kairo CG 48647/ JE 37447 (Jansen-Winkeln, Inschriften der Spätzeit III, 507 [283])/ Stele eines Nachkommen Kairo CG 22141 (Jansen-Winkeln, Inschriften der Spätzeit IV,2, 976–977 [414])/ Stele eines Nachkommen London BM 624 (Jansen-Winkeln, Inschriften der Spätzeit IV,2, 974–976 [412])
Ḥr-3ḫ-bjt, Sohn des *Ḥr-s3-3st* (*Ḥr-s3-3st* [Sohn])	späte 25. Dyn.	Würfelhocker des Enkels New York MMA 35.9.1 (Jansen-Winkeln, Inschriften der Spätzeit III, 493 [257])
Ḥr-s3-3st, Sohn des *Ḥr-3ḫ-bjt*	späte 25. Dyn.	Würfelhocker des Sohnes New York MMA 35.9.1 (Jansen-Winkeln, Inschriften der Spätzeit III, 493 [257])
Ns-p3-mdw, Sohn des *Ns-p3-k3-šwtj* C und der *T3-ḫ3ʿ-n-B3stt* Weil, Veziere, 140–141 (§12) TIP², table 15 Vittmann, Priester und Beamte, 154–159	ca. 670 v. Chr. (TIP², table 15)	Stehfigur Kairo CG 48608/JE 37416/ Schreiberfigur Kairo CG 48613/JE 36948/ pBrooklyn 47.218.3/ Sistrophor London BM 1132/BM 1225/ Pyramidion Berlin 2090 (Jansen-Winkeln, Inschriften der Spätzeit III, 491–492 [255], 492–493 [256], 396–397 [103]; R. A. Parker, Saite oracle papyrus, 27; Jansen-Winkeln, Inschriften der Spätzeit IV,1, 180–181 [316])

Name und Filiationsangabe (WEIL/TIP²/VITTMANN)	**Datierung/ Möglicher Dienstsitz**	**Hinterlassenschaft**
Ns-p3-k3-šwtj D, Sohn des *Ns-p3-mdw* A und der *Jrtj-r-w* (*T3-h3ʿ-n-B3stt* [Ehefrau] *T3-h3ʿ-n-B3stt* [Tochter] *Ns-p3-mdw* [Sohn]) WEIL, Veziere, 155 (§35) TIP², table 15 VITTMANN, Priester und Beamte, 154–159	ca. 660 v. Chr. (TIP², table 15)	pBrooklyn 47.218.3/ Stele London BM 1333/ Stele Wien ÄS 189/ Hockfigur Kairo JE 37000/ Schreiberstatue Kairo CG 48634/JE 36662/ Sistrophor London BM 1132/BM 1225/ Würfelhocker der Söhne Kairo JE 37849/ Kairo JE 36963/ Stele des Enkels London BM 1333 (R. A. PARKER, Saite oracle papyrus, 15; JANSEN-WINKELN, Inschriften der Spätzeit IV,1, 179 [314], 180–181 [316]; JANSEN-WINKELN, Inschriften der Spätzeit IV,2, 1012 [466]; H. SATZINGER, Kunsthistorisches Museum Wien, Ägyptisch-Orientalische Sammlung. Lieferung 17: Hieroglyphische Inschriften aus der ägyptischen Spätzeit, CAA, Darmstadt 2012, 131–138)
Jrj, Vater des *Dd-B3stt-jnk-t3t-swt* TIP², table 15 VITTMANN, Priester und Beamte, 159–160	ca. 650–640 v. Chr.? (TIP², table 15)	Sarg des Sohnes Wien 3941/ Stele des Sohnes Kairo JE 4886 (JANSEN-WINKELN, Inschriften der Spätzeit IV,2, 597–598 [6], 598 [7]; G. VITTMANN, GM 15, 1975, 47–52)
Dd-B3stt-jw=f-ʿnh, Sohn des *Hr-s3-3st* (Genealogie ALZOHARY, MDAIK 68, 2012, 39)	wohl 26. Dyn.[105] Unterägypten?[106]	Sitzfigur Kairo JE 27749 (ALZOHARY, MDAIK 68, 2012, 31–41)
Dd-B3stt-jw=f-ʿnh, Sohn des *P3-dj-3st* (*Ns-pr-nbw* (Sohn) *T3-nšt* [Ehefrau]) WEIL, Veziere, 159 (§39) VITTMANN, Priester und Beamte, 160	Psammetich I. Abydos?	Stele des Sohnes Kairo TN 18/2/25/2 (JANSEN-WINKELN, Inschriften der Spätzeit IV,1, 124–125 [242])

Tab. 2: Wesire in Oberägypten

105 Ikonographische Kriterien erlauben einen Datierungsspielraum von der späten 22./23. Dynastie bis in die frühe 26. Dynastie (R. A. FAZZINI, Several Objects, and some Aspects of the Art of the Third Intermediate Period, in: E. GORING/N. REEVES/J. RUFFLE (Hrsg.), Chief of Seers. Egyptian Studies in Memory of Cyril Aldred, Studies in Egyptology, London/New York/Edinburgh, 1997, 113–137, hier: 123; B. VON BOTHMER, Egyptian Sculpture of the Late Period 700 B.C. to A.D. 100. The Brooklyn Museum, New York 1960, 2, 11; PERDU, Les statues privées, 46). Allerdings ist der archaisierende Titel *ʿd-mr*, den *Dd-B3stt-jw=f-ʿnh* trägt, nur in der 26. Dynastie belegt (siehe Fußnote 79).

106 *Dd-B3stt-jw=f-ʿnh* trägt nur den Titel *t3jtj-s3b*. Dass er zudem die Bezeichnung (*s3b*) *ʿd-mr* trägt, könnte auf eine Herkunft aus Unterägypten deuten (siehe Fußnote 80).

Name und Filiationsangabe	**Datierung**	**Hinterlassenschaft**
Psmṯk-snb Weil, Veziere, 149–150 [§27])	Saitenzeit (?) (Weil) 29. Dyn. (?) L. Borchardt, Statuen und Statuetten von Königen und Privatleuten im Museum von Kairo, Nr. 1–1294, Teil 3: Text und Tafeln zu Nr. 654–950. Catalogue général des antiquités égyptiennes du Musée du Caire. Berlin 1930; R. El-Sayed, Un document relatif au culte dans Kher-aha (statue Caire CG. 682), in: BIFAO 82, 1982, 187–204) 30. Dyn. (?) (Perdu, Égypte, Afrique & Orient 42, 2006, 41–52)	Statue CG 682/JE 29877/ Statue Louvre E 17379/ Statue Turin suppl. 9/Florenz 8708/ einige Statuenfragmente in Privatsammlungen: zusammengestellt von O. Perdu, Égypte, Afrique & Orient 42, 2006, 41–52
Pꜣ-šrj-tꜣ-jḥt rn=f nfr Pꜣ-dj-Nt, Sohn des *Ḥr-jr-ꜥꜣ* und der *Nt-jjtj* (Ehemann der *Bꜣstt-jr-dj-s*)	26. Dyn. (?) (Vittmann) 27. Dyn. (?) (Jørgensen) 30. Dyn. (?) (H. De Meulenaere, Le surnom égyptien à la Basse Époque [deuxième série d'addenda et corrigenda], in: H. Győry [Hrsg.], Mélanges offerts à Edith Varga. „le lotus qui sort de terre“, BMH Supplèment-2001, Budapest 2002, 381–394, hier: 390)	Statuenbasis Kopenhagen AEIN 101 (M. Jørgensen, Catalogue Egypt IV: Late Egyptian sculpture 1080 BC – AD 400. Translated by Neil Martin Stanford. Ny Carlsberg Glyptotek: Katalog, Kopenhagen 2009, 137–138; Vittmann, Priester und Beamte, 147)
Ḥr-sꜣ-ꜣst, Sohn des *Wn-nfr*	30. Dyn.	Sarkophagfragment Kairo TN 28/5/25/5/ Naophor Berlin 21596/ Statue ehem. Sammlung Golénischeff 83/ Moskau 5320/ Basis Lyon E.G. 1748: zusammengestellt von H. de Meulenaere, Le vizir Harsiêsis de la 30e dynastie, in: MDAIK 16, 1958, 230–236. Aufgrund der fehlenden Filiationsangaben besteht auch die, wenn auch geringe, Möglichkeit, dass es sich um unterschiedliche Wesire mit Namen *Ḥr-sꜣ-ꜣst* handelt.
ꜥnḫ=f-n-Ḫnzw, Sohn der *Ḏd-Ḫnzw*	30. Dyn.?	Basis London BM EA 14340 (J. H. Taylor, The vizier Ankhefenkhonsu, in: GM 116, 1990, 97–101, hier: 97–99, fig. 1–4)

Name und Filiationsangabe	**Datierung**	**Hinterlassenschaft**
ʿš3-jẖt, Vater des *P3-šrj-n-t3-jsw*[107]	30. Dyn.	Kairo JE 36576 (I. GUERMEUR, Le groupe familial de Pachéryentaisouy: Caire JE 36576, in: BIFAO 104, 2004, 245–289)
Tmpn	Ptolemäerzeit	Archiv des Hor, Text 7 (J. D. RAY, The Archive of Ḥor. Texts from Excavations 2. Excavations at North Saqqâra: Documentary Series 1, London 1976, 36)
Ariston	Ptolemäerzeit[108]	Archiv des Hor, Text 26 (RAY, The Archive of Hor, 93–96)

Tab. 3: Wesire nach der ersten Perserherrschaft

107 Die Gruppenstatue seines Sohnes zeigt *ʿš3-jẖt* im Wesirsgewand. Den Titel trägt er aber nicht. Es wäre vorstellbar, dass die Verwendung dieses speziellen Gewandes zu diesem späten Zeitpunkt auch anderen Gruppen offenstand. Vergleichbares erfolgte mit dem Emblem der Maat, das nur bis in die 26. Dynastie den Wesiren vorbehalten war: PERDU, Les statues privées, 396–397, n.5. *ʿš3-jẖt* wäre dann aus der Liste zu streichen.

108 In pParis 65 wird ein hoher Beamter namens Ariston genannt, der im Jahr 146 v.Chr. per Rundschreiben Anweisungen an die gesamte Landesverwaltung gibt. Könnte dieser „important officer", wie ihn P. W. PESTMAN, Registration of Demotic contracts in Egypt, P.Par.65, in: H. ANKUM (Hrsg.), Satura Roberto Feenstra oblata sexagesimum quintum annum aetatis complenti ab alumnis collegis amicis oblata, Freiburg (Schweiz) 1985, 17–26 nennt, mit unserem Wesir identisch sein? Ich danke Wolfgang Wegner für den entsprechenden Hinweis.

All the king's men.

Networks of high officials in the late Saite Period

Alexander Schütze

Abstract

The famous biographical inscription of Udjahorresnet is still the most important historical source for the political history of Egypt under Persian rule in the late sixth and early fifth century BC. However, Udjahorresnet was also a typical representative of high officials in the late Twenty-sixth Dynasty: He held several archaizing titles with ambiguous meaning, erected a statue in the temple of Neith at Sais depicting him in the so-called Persian costume and was buried in a monumental shaft tomb in a Memphite cemetery. This article discusses Udjahorresnet's titles like chief physician, overseer of the *kbnt*-ships of the king, director of the scribes of the council or overseer of the great hall within the context of the development of the Egyptian administration in the later Saite Period. While it is still difficult to determine the exact functional context of these titles, a comparison with other officials holding the same titles like Udjahorresnet reveals a close network of members of the highest level of Egyptian administration. The very existence of such a network of officials is also confirmed by the proximity of their burial places as well as their common visual representation. The beginning of this development can be traced back to the reign of Psamtik II or Apries.

Introduction

This paper will focus on a sub-group of the Egyptian elite representing the highest level of administration in the late Twenty-sixth Dynasty. Starting point will be the well-known official Udjahorresnet who witnessed both the late Saite Period and the Persian conquest of Egypt as well as its aftermath being in office under Amasis, Psamtik III, Cambyses and Dareios I. In his famous biographical inscription on a naophorous statue in the Vatican (Museo Gregoriano Egizio 22690), he enumerates the milestones of his career:[1] Having been overseer of the

1 G. Posener, La première domination perse en Égypte. Recueil d'inscriptions hiéroglyphiques, BdE 11, Cairo 1936, 1–26. Scholarly literature on Udjahorresnet's biography and its historical implications is extensive. Cf. G. Vittmann, Ägypten zur Zeit der Perserherrschaft, in: R. Rollinger/B. Truschnegg/R. Bichler (eds.), Herodot und das Persische Weltreich. Akten des 3. Internationalen Kolloquiums zum Thema »Vorderasien im Spannungsfeld klassischer und altorientalischer Überlieferungen«, Innsbruck, 24.–28. November 2008, Wiesbaden 2011, 373–429, especially 377–381; F. Lopez, Democede di Crotone e Udjahorresnet di Saïs. Medici primari alla corte achemenide di Dario il Grande, Pisa 2015; K. Smoláriková, Udjahorresnet: the founder of the Saite-Persian cemetery at Abusir and his engagement as leading political person during the troubled years at

kbnt-vessels of the king under Amasis and Psamtik III, he was appointed to the office of the *wr swnw* "chief physician" by Cambyses after the Persian conquest. He oversaw the composition of the Persian king's royal titulatory, introduced to him the importance of the temple of Neith at Sais and organised the ritual cleaning of the temple having been occupied by foreigners. Later on, Udjahorresnet managed the rebuilding of the houses of life under Dareios I after having spent some time in the Persian heartland.

Udjahorresnet is a unique example for the agency of high officials in the reinterpretation of Egyptian royal ideology under foreign rule in the first millennium BC and thus perfectly fits into the subject of this volume. This paper will however focus on Udjahorresnet's career in the context of the development of the Egyptian administration in the Twenty-sixth Dynasty by discussing the following features that Udjahorresnet shared with other officials of the late Saite Dynasty: 1) Udjahorresnet held several archaising titles with ambiguous meaning reintroduced in the middle of the Twenty-sixth Dynasty. 2) He erected a statue in the temple of Neith in Sais showing him in a particular dress, the so-called Persian costume, covered with a biographical inscription praising his achievements for the temple. 3) Finally, he was buried in a monumental shaft tomb at Abusir, one of the Late Period cemeteries in the Memphite region.

In order to outline this development, I will discuss officials with titles also held by Udjahorresnet thus playing a similar role within the Egyptian administration. Then, I will look at their burial places in order to trace connections between these officials on a spatial level. Finally, I will shed light on their visual representation.

Udjahorresnet's titles

Besides traditional courtly offices, Udjahorresnet held a number of administrative titles like *wr swnw* "chief physician", *sḥḏ sẖw m ḏ3ḏ3t* "director of the scribes of the council", *jmj-r3 sẖw ḫn(r)t wr(t)* "overseer of the scribes of the great camp (?)", *jmj-r3 kbnwt nswt* "overseer of the *kbnt*-vessels of the king" and *jmj-r3 ḫ3swt ḥ3w-nbw* "overseer of the foreigners of the Haunebu".[2] The function of the offices behind these titles is subject to discussion. With other words, the very fact that an overseer of the royal fleet was later appointed to the office of the chief physician demands an explanation. Udjahorresnet himself gives us some hints: Having been overseer of the *kbnt*-vessels of the king under Amasis and Psamtik III, he was appointed to the office of the chief physician by the Persian king Cambyses. The biographical inscription on his naophorous statue also indicates a connection between his newly acquired offices and his deeds as the account of the composition of Cambyses' Egyptian royal names directly follows Udjahorresnet's appointment to the office of the chief physician.

There are extraordinarily good conditions for studying high officials' titles of the Twenty-sixth Dynasty: In the two decades after the publication of the last comprehensive study of the Egyptian administration in the Twenty-sixth Dynasty, Diana Pressl's *Beamte und Soldaten*, numerous new monuments were published and the whole material is easily accessible due

the beginning of the Twenty-Seventh Dynasty, in: J. M. Silverman/C. Waerzeggers (eds.), Political Memory in and after the Persian Empire, Ancient Near East Monographs 13, Atlanta 2015, 151–164; M. Wasmuth, Persika in der Repräsentation der ägyptischen Elite, in: JEA 103, 2018, 241–250; on the tomb of Udjahorresnet, see: L. Bareš, The shaft tomb of Udjahorresnet at Abusir, Abusir IV, Prague 1999.

2 The title *jmj-r3 ḫ3swt ḥ3w-nbw* "overseer of the foreigners of the Haunebu" is only to be found in Udjahorresnet's tomb at Abusir.

to the fourth volume of Karl JANSEN-WINKELN's *Inschriften der Spätzeit.*[3] While PRESSL collected 330 monuments belonging to about 180 officials, JANSEN-WINKELN's compilation includes over 1500 documents of non-royal persons with more than 343 monuments dating to the time of Psamtik I alone.[4] There are, however, methodological issues complicating the study of Egyptian administrative titles of the Twenty-sixth Dynasty: 1) High officials of the late Saite Dynasty often took over administrative titles well known from earlier periods, especially the Old and Middle Kingdoms. 2) Although the monuments often refer to the administrative titles of their owners, sometimes providing long chains of titles accumulated by a single official, we are principally lacking textual evidence putting these titles in their proper functional context. 3) The spatial and temporal disparity of monuments complicates their study. The archaeological context of these sources is often unknown, while their exact dating to a Pharaoh is subject to discussion.

In former studies of the administration of the Twenty-sixth Dynasty, the semantics of titles like "overseer of the ships of the king" or "chief physician" were often read literally thus projecting the functional context of offices in earlier periods directly onto the situation in the Twenty-sixth Dynasty. There are several examples that challenge the validity of this approach. This is especially the case for titles of Saite officials mentioned in the famous Petition of Peteese (Papyrus Rylands 9):[5] At the very beginning of the Twenty-sixth Dynasty, officials with the illustrious title "harbour master" (*ꜥꜣ n mrjt*) were active in the region of Heracleopolis Magna. While the title itself implies a nautical function of these officials, Papyrus Rylands 9 clearly shows that they were responsible for the collection of taxes in Upper Egypt. The nature of these taxes determines the connection between the office and tax collecting: the harbor master oversaw the ships that transported the harvest tax to the residence. Olivier PERDU proposes another approach in order to overcome these methodological issues: He dedicated a study to the title *jmj-rꜣ sẖw ḏꜣḏꜣt* "overseer of the scribes of the council" showing that the actual task of these officials was not jurisdiction as the term *ḏꜣḏꜣt* indicates but fiscal administration as several of the title holders were also accountant scribes.[6] In this paper, I will follow this approach comparing Udjahorresnet with other Egyptian officials holding the very same titles in the late Twenty-sixth Dynasty.

---

3 D. A. PRESSL, Beamte und Soldaten. Die Verwaltung in der 26. Dynastie in Ägypten (664–525 v. Chr.), Europäische Hochschulschriften – Reihe III 779, Frankfurt am Main 1998; K. JANSEN-WINKELN, Inschriften der Spätzeit. Teil IV: Die 26. Dynastie. Band 1, Psametik I.–Psametik III. Band 2, Gottesgemahlinnen/26. Dynastie insgesamt, Wiesbaden 2014; cf. G. VITTMANN, Priester und Beamte im Theben der Spätzeit: Genealogische und prosopographische Untersuchungen zum thebanischen Priester- und Beamtentum der 25. und 26. Dynastie, Veröffentlichungen der Institute für Afrikanistik und Ägyptologie der Universität Wien 3, Beiträge zur Ägyptologie 1, Vienna 1978; P.-M. CHEVEREAU, Prosopographie des cadres militaires égyptiens de la basse époque. Carrières militaires et carrières sacerdotales en Egypte du XIe au IIe siècle avant J.C., Paris 1985; D. AGUT-LABORDÈRE, The Saite Period: The Emergence of a Mediterranean Power, in: J. C. MORENO GARCÍA (ed.), Ancient Egyptian Administration, HdO 104, Leiden/Boston 2013, 965–1027.

4 Distribution of monuments of non-royal persons (after JANSEN-WINKELN, Inschriften der Spätzeit IV): Psamtik I: 343; Necho II: 23; Psamtik II: 49; Apries: 95; Amasis: 143; Twenty-sixth Dynasty: 760.

5 Cf. G. VITTMANN, Der demotische Papyrus Rylands 9. Teil I: Text und Übersetzung. Teil II: Kommentare und Indizes, ÄUAT 38, Wiesbaden 1998, 387–388; AGUT-LABORDÈRE, The Saite Period, 981–984.

6 O. PERDU, Le « directeur des scribes du Conseil », in: RdE 49, 1998, 175–194.

Chief physician

The functional context of the title *wr swnw* "chief physician" has been discussed controversially: Most scholars considered the chief physician as the personal doctor of the king.[7] But others went so far to interpret the *wr swnw* as a finance minister.[8] There are good reasons for both interpretations as the holders of this title besides Udjahorresnet illustrate (Tab. 1):

Name	**Date**	**Important titles**
Psamtikseneb[9]	Psamtik II	*wr swnw, wr jbḥ pr-ꜥꜣ, ḫrp Srkt, jmj-rꜣ qqt*
Paieftjauauineith[10]	Apries/Amasis	*wr swnw, jmj-rꜣ pr wr, jmj-rꜣ prwj ḥḏ, ꜥꜣ n ḫꜣ*
Psamtik[11]	Amasis	*wr swnw, jmj-rꜣ Ṯmḥw*
Horakhbit[12]	Amasis	*wr swnw, ḫrj-ḥb Pr-ꜥꜣ*
Udjahormehnet[13]	late 26th Dyn.?	*wr swnw Mḥw Šmꜥw*

Tab. 1: Chief physicians of the Twenty-sixth Dynasty

One of the better-known chief physicians is Paieftjauauineith who was in office under Apries as well as Amasis and held important offices like majordomo (*jmj-rꜣ pr wr*) and overseer of the two treasuries (*jmj-rꜣ prwj ḥḏ*). In an often-cited biographical inscription on the statue Louvre A 93 dating to the time of Amasis, Paieftjauauineith claims to have reorganised the financial situation of the temple of Khontamenti at Abydos by donating, for instance, one thousand aruras of arable land to the temple.[14] Several officials are known donating land to

7 G. Burkard, Medizin und Politik. Altägyptische Heilkunst am persischen Königshof, in: SAK 21, 1994, 35–57; H. Brandl/K. Jansen-Winkeln, Fünf Denkmäler des Obersten Arztes *Pꜣ-ꜥn-mnj* aus der 22. Dynastie, in: MDAIK 64, 2008, 15–34, here: 33; cf. P. Ghalioungui, The Physicians of Pharaonic Egypt, SDAIK 10, Mainz am Rhein 1983, 81–84; Pressl, Beamte und Soldaten, 22–24; Agut-Labordère, The Saite Period, 972–973.

8 Bareš, Shaft Tomb of Udjahorresnet, 37.

9 Rome, Museo Gregoriano Egizio 22687 (Jansen-Winkeln, Inschriften der Spätzeit IV.2, 60.100); sarcophagus from Heliopolis (Jansen-Winkeln, Inschriften der Spätzeit IV.2, 60.233), shabtis from Heliopolis (Jansen-Winkeln, Inschriften der Spätzeit IV.2, 60.234). The sarcophagus of Psamtikseneb is now housed in Norfolk, VA, Chrysler Museum of Art 71.2254; cf. J. Harrison, Collecting with Vision: Treasures from the Chrysler Museum of Art, London 2007, 17, fig. 5. Cf. niche stela London, British Museum 511 (Jansen-Winkeln, Inschriften der Spätzeit IV.2, 60.106).

10 Statue London, British Museum EA 83 (Jansen-Winkeln, Inschriften der Spätzeit IV.1, 56.125); statue in Tanta (Jansen-Winkeln, Inschriften der Spätzeit IV.1, 57.184); statue from Mit Rahina (Jansen-Winkeln, Inschriften der Spätzeit IV.1, 57.278); statue Paris, Louvre A 93 (Jansen-Winkeln, Inschriften der Spätzeit IV.1, 57.287); altar in Cairo (Jansen-Winkeln, Inschriften der Spätzeit IV.1, 57.312).

11 Shaft tomb at Saqqara (Jansen-Winkeln, Inschriften der Spätzeit IV.1, 57.234), stela Paris, Louvre IM 4048 (338) (Jansen-Winkeln, Inschriften der Spätzeit IV.1, 57.235); cf. L. Gestermann, Grab und Stele von Psametich, Oberarzt und Vorsteher der *Ṯmḥ.w*, in: RdE 52, 2001, 127–147. On the literary afterlife of Psamtik, see: J. F. Quack, Psammetich der Eunuch. Wie aus Geschichte Geschichten werden, in: A. I. Blöbaum/M. Eaton-Krauss/A. Wüthrich (eds.), Pérégrinations avec Erhart Graefe. Festschrift zu seinem 75. Geburtstag, ÄUAT 87, Münster 2018, 475–486.

12 Statue Alexandria 20950, 26532 (Jansen-Winkeln, Inschriften der Spätzeit IV.1, 57.216); sarcophagus from Sais (Jansen-Winkeln, Inschriften der Spätzeit IV.1, 57.217); alabaster vessel New York, Metropolitan Museum of Art 42.2.2 (Jansen-Winkeln, Inschriften der Spätzeit IV.1, 57.314).

13 Sarcophagus from Heliopolis (Jansen-Winkeln, Inschriften der Spätzeit IV.2, 60.226).

14 Paris, Louvre A 93 (Jansen-Winkeln, Inschriften der Spätzeit IV.1, 57.287); cf. H. Bassir, Image & voice in Saite Egypt. Self-Presentations of Neshor Named Psamtikmenkhib and Payeftjauemawyneith,

the temple or erecting new buildings especially at Sais, the residence of the Twenty-sixth Dynasty.[15] Another illustrious example is the majordomo Nakhthorheb, a contemporary of Paieftjauauineith who restored the temple of Neith at Sais.[16] Paieftjauauineith and Nakhthorheb probably conducted restoration work at Egyptian temples in their function as majordomo. Thus, there is no direct reference to the office of the chief physician. It is however striking that most of the hitherto known chief physicians also held other administrative titles without any obvious connection to the office of the *wr swnw*. This is not only the case for Paieftjauauineith but also for Psamtik who was *jmj-r3 Ṯmḥw* "overseer of the *Ṯmḥw*-Libyans" as well as Horakhbit who held the office of the *ẖrj-ḥb pr-ˁ3* "lector priest of the Pharaoh". The only exception is Psamtikseneb who probably served under Psamtik II (and Apries) and held the additional title *wr jbḥ pr-ˁ3* "chief dentist of the king". Like Udjahorresnet, he also held an archaising title referring to a fleet (*jmj-r3 qqt*). I will come back to this official at the end of this article.

Overseer of the ships of the king

The office *jmj-r3 kbnwt nswt* "overseer of the *kbnt*-vessels of the king" is also subject to discussion. The only other hitherto known official holding this title is Menekhibnekau, probably a contemporary of Udjahorresnet who was also buried in a shaft tomb at Abusir.[17] He was *jmj-r3 mšˁ* "overseer of the troop", *jmj-r3 ˁw* "overseer of the interpreters" but also *jmj-r3 ḫ3swt Ṯmḥw* "overseer of the *Ṯmḥw*-Libyans" like the chief physician Psamtik. Alan B. Lloyd considered the holders of the title *jmj-r3 kbnwt nswt* as admirals of a battle fleet consisting of triremes, but John Darnell was able to show that *kbnt*-vessels simply designated some kind of sea-going ships without necessarily being a battle ship.[18] Only a certain Hor (with the beautiful name Psamtik) who served under Psamtik II is explicitly designated as *jmj-r3 ˁḥˁw nswt n ˁḥ3 m W3ḏ-wr* "overseer of the royal battle ships on the great sea".[19] Interestingly, Hor was also *jmj-r3 ḫ3swt ḥ3w-nbw* "overseer of the foreigners of the Haunebu" like Udjahorresnet; and Greek mercenaries in the service of Apries were

---

Tucson 2014, especially 67–118.

15 N. Spencer, Sustaining Egyptian culture? Non-royal initiatives in Late Period temple building, in: L. Bareš/F. Coppens/K. Smoláriková (eds.), Egypt in Transition. Social and Religious Development of Egypt in the First Millenium BCE. Proceedings of an International Conference, Prague, September 1–4, 2009, Prague 2010, 441–490.

16 Berlin, Ägyptisches Museum und Papyrussammlung 1048 (Jansen-Winkeln, Inschriften der Spätzeit IV.1, 57.210).

17 Paris, Louvre E 13104 = Nantes 1255 (Jansen-Winkeln, Inschriften der Spätzeit IV.1, 57.207); Berlin, Ägyptisches Museum und Papyrussammlung 272 + Naples, Museo Archeologico Nazionale 181 (Jansen-Winkeln, Inschriften der Spätzeit IV.1, 57.208); shaft tomb at Abusir (Jansen-Winkeln, Inschriften der Spätzeit IV.1, 57.229); cf. L. Bareš/K. Smoláriková, The shaft tomb of Menekhibnekau. Volume 1: Archaeology, Abusir XXV, Prague 2011.

18 A. B. Lloyd, Triremes and the Saite Navy, in: JEA 58, 1972, 268–279; A. B. Lloyd, The inscription of Udjahorresnet. A Collaborator's Testament, in: JEA 68, 1982, 166–180, here: 168–169; J. C. Darnell, The *Kbn.wt* vessels of the Late Period, in: J. H. Johnson (ed.), Life in a multi-cultural society: From Cambyses to Constantine and beyond, SAOC 51, Chicago 1992, 67–89, especially 81–84; cf. Chevereau, Cadres militaires, 271–273, 324–325; Agut-Labordère, The Saite Period, 990–991.

19 Statue Manchester 3570 (Jansen-Winkeln, Inschriften der Spätzeit IV.1, 55.103); shabtis (Jansen-Winkeln, Inschriften der Spätzeit IV.1, 55.104); cf. R. B. Gozzoli, Psammetichus II. Reign, Documents and Officials, GHP Egyptology 25, London 2017, 179–180 (dos. 2); C. Price, The 'Admiral' Hor and his Naophorous Statue (Manchester Museum acc. no. 3570), in: C. Jurman/B. Bader/D. A. Aston (eds.),

transported with *kbnt*-vessels according to the victory stela of Amasis.[20] Moreover, the overseer of the *kbnt*-vessels of Menekhibnekau also held the title *jmj-rꜣ mšʿ* "overseer of the troop"; and the determinatives of the *kbnt*-vessels in the monuments of both Menekhibnekau and Udjahorresnet show a naval ram indicating the military nature of these ships.

In the time of Amasis, several officials are known holding the title *jmj-rꜣ ḥʿww nswt* "overseer of the *ḥʿw*-ships of the king" (Tab. 2):

Name	**Date**	**Important titles**
Hekaemsaf[21]	Amasis	*jmj-rꜣ ḥʿww nswt, jmj-rꜣ sẖw ḫn(r)t wr(t), jmj-rꜣ prwj ḥḏ nbw n ẖnw*
Tjanenhebu[22]	Amasis	*jmj-rꜣ ḥʿww nswt, jmj-rꜣ sẖw ḏꜣḏꜣt*
Psamtikmeriptah[23]	Amasis	*jmj-rꜣ ḥʿww nswt*
Iahmessaneith[24]	Amasis?	*jmj-rꜣ ḥʿww nswt*

Tab. 2: Overseers of the *ḥʿw*-ships of the king under Amasis

Already Jean-Claude Goyon pointed out that the other titles held by the overseers of the royal *ḥʿw*-ships, respectively the absence of any military titles, indicate that these officials were not admirals of a battle fleet.[25] Tjanenhebu, for instance, was *jmj-rꜣ sẖw ḏꜣḏꜣt* "overseer of the scribes of the council"; Hekaemsaf *jmj-rꜣ sẖw ḫn(r)t wr(t)* "overseer of the scribes of the great camp (?)" as well as *jmj-rꜣ prwj ḥḏ nbw n ẖnw* "overseer of the treasury in the residence". Maybe there is a connection between these officials and the harbour masters of the early Twenty-sixth Dynasty, Peteese and Sematauitefnakht, who actually had fiscal tasks as the well-known Papyrus Rylands 9 nicely illustrates.[26] The successor of Sematauitefnakht, Paakhraef held the office of *ḥrj ʿḥʿw n nb tꜣwj* "overseer of the *ʿḥʿw*-ships of the lord of the two lands".[27] The connection between the *ḥʿw*-ships and *kbnt*-vessels, both archaistic terms,

A True Scribe of Abydos. Essays on First Millennium Egypt in Honour of Anthony Leahy, OLA 265, Leuven/Paris/Bristol, CT 2017, 369–383.

20 Cairo, Egyptian Museum TN 13/6/24/1 (Jansen-Winkeln, Inschriften der Spätzeit IV.1, 57.97); cf. K. Jansen-Winkeln, Die Siegesstele des Amasis, in: ZÄS 141, 2014, 132–153.

21 Shaft tomb at Saqqara (Jansen-Winkeln, Inschriften der Spätzeit IV.1, 57.238).

22 Shaft tomb at Saqqara (Jansen-Winkeln, Inschriften der Spätzeit IV.1, 57.237).

23 Burial at Saqqara (Jansen-Winkeln, Inschriften der Spätzeit IV.1, 57.246); Stela IM 4019 (Jansen-Winkeln, Inschriften der Spätzeit IV.1, 57.247). Psamtikmeriptah also held several priestly titles.

24 Seal impression Birmingham, Museum and Art Gallery 1969W4363; C. Jurman, Impressions of What is Lost – A Study of Four Late Period Seal Impressions in Birmingham and London, in: C. Jurman/B. Bader/D. A. Aston (eds.) A True Scribe of Abydos. Essays on First Millennium Egypt in Honour of Anthony Leahy, OLA 265, Leuven/Paris/Bristol, CT, 2017, 239–272, here: 240–247, pls. 1–2.

25 J.-C. Goyon, La statuette funéraire I.E. 84 de Lyon et le titre saite 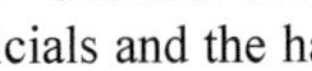, in: BIFAO 67, 1967, 159–171; cf. Agut-Labordère, The Saite Period, 997–999.

26 A. Leahy, Somtutefnakht of Heracleopolis: the art and politics of self-commemoration in the seventh century BC, in: D. Devauchelle (ed.), La XXVIe dynastie: continuités et ruptures. Actes du Colloque international organisé les 26 et 27 novembre 2004 à l'Université Charles-de-Gaulle – Lille 3. Promenade saïte avec Jean Yoyotte, Paris 2011, 197–223; J. Pope, The Historicity of Pediese, Son of Ankhsheshonq, in: RdE 66, 2015, 199–225.

27 Cairo, Egyptian Museum CG 48642 (Jansen-Winkeln, Inschriften der Spätzeit IV.1, 53.333); Paris, Bibliothèque Nationale 14 (Jansen-Winkeln, Inschriften der Spätzeit IV.1, 53.135); cf. Vittmann, Papyrus Rylands 9, II, 711–713.

remains however obscure and evidence for the military nature of the latter inconclusive. Interestingly, two of these officials, Tjanenhebu and Hekaemsaf, who were overseers of the scribes of the council respectively the great camp (?) like Udjahorresnet, were buried together with the chief physician Psamtik in a cluster of shaft tombs to the south and east of the pyramid of Unas at Saqqara.

Director of the scribes of the council and overseer of the great hall

Udjahorresnet's most obscure titles however are *sḥḏ sẖw m ḏ3ḏ3t* "overseer of the scribes of the council" and *jmj-r3 sẖ(w) ẖn(r)t wr(t)* "overseer of the great camp (?)". George POSENER discussed both titles in the commentary of his translation of the Naophoro Vaticano and noticed that these offices are not attested before the Saite Period giving some parallels.[28] He concluded that both offices must refer to some judicial functions as *ḏ3ḏ3t* is well known as a council of judges from the Old Kingdom onwards. Moreover, he directly linked the *ẖnrt wr(t)* to the well-known labour camps of the Middle Kingdom although the alternative translation *ẖnrt* "harim" would have been possible as well. Interestingly, his interpretation was based on the assumption that *ḏ3ḏ3t* designates some judicial institution. PRESSL followed POSENER's interpretation in her study of the administration of the Twenty-sixth Dynasty.[29] PERDU has however shown that *jmj-r3 sẖw ḏ3ḏ3t* "overseer of the scribes of the council" was not in charge of judicial tasks but of fiscal ones as some holders of the title where accountant scribes in earlier stages of their career.[30]

It might thus be worthwhile to have a closer look on officials of the Twenty-sixth Dynasty holding the title *jmj-r3 sẖ(w) ẖn(r)t wr(t)* "overseer of the great camp (?)" (Tab. 3):

Name	**Date**	**Important titles**
Harbes/Psamtiknefer[31]	Psamtik II	*jmj-r3 sẖ(w) ẖn(r)t wr(t)*
Udjahor/Psamtiksasekhmet[32]	Psamtik II	*jmj-r3 sẖ(w) ẖn(r)t wr(t), wḥm nswt*
Hekaemsaf[33]	Amasis	*jmj-r3 sẖw ẖn(r)t wr(t), jmj-r3 ḫʿww nswt, jmj-r3 prwj ḥḏ nbw n ẖnw*
Nesnaisut/Jahmes[34]	26th Dyn.	*jmj-r3 sẖ(w) ẖn(r)t wr(t), jmj-r3 sẖw nswt jwʿ-r3*
Wahibremeriptah[35]	26th/27th Dyn.	*jmj-r3 sẖ(w) ẖn(r)t wr(t), jmj-r3 šnwtj, jmj-r3 sẖw ḏ3ḏ3t*

Tab. 3: Overseers of the great camp (?) of the Twenty-sixth Dynasty

28 POSENER, La première domination perse, 8–9.

29 PRESSL, Beamte und Soldaten, 44–46.

30 PERDU, RdE 49, 175–194. Udjahorresnet is not included in PERDU's list of "overseers of the scribes of the council" because of his slightly different title. Cf. AGUT-LABORDÈRE, The Saite Period, 996–997.

31 Statue New York, MMA 19.2.2 (JANSEN-WINKELN, Inschriften der Spätzeit IV.1, 55.112); cf. GOZZOLI, Psammetichus II, 180–181 (Dos. 3).

32 Tomb LG 102 in Giza and shabtis (JANSEN-WINKELN, Inschriften der Spätzeit IV.2, 60.265); cf. GOZZOLI, Psammetichus II, 195 (Dos. 13).

33 On the monuments of Hekaemsaf, see no. 21. The title *jmj-r3 sẖw ẖn(r)t wr(t)* is only to be found on the sarcophagus.

34 Sarcophagus Cairo JE 57478 from Heliopolis (JANSEN-WINKELN, Inschriften der Spätzeit IV.2, 60.230).

35 Serapeum stela Paris, Louvre IM 4073: PERDU, RdE 49, 179 no. 3; statue fragment (?) Bremen, Übersee-Museum B04327: A. FELGENHAUER, Aus Gräbern, Heiligtümern und Siedlungen. Die altägyptische Sammlung des Übersee-Museums Bremen, Mainz 2015, 43 no. 66.

Claus Jurman recently pointed out that Saite writings of the title do not support a reading of the institution as *ḫnrt wr*(*t*) "great camp".[36] As Gardiner sign W17 (tall jars in rack) is used in most cases, the title might simply be translated as *ḫnt*(*j*) "entrance hall". In fact, Harbes (statue MMA 19.2.2, Thebes, Psamtik II) employs Gardiner sign F1 (ox head) substituting W17, while Gardiner sign U31 (baker's rake) is only to be found in the tomb of Udjahor (tomb LG 102, Giza, Psamtik II). All later attestations are written with W17 (tall jars in rack). Therefore, I would follow Jurman in understanding *ḫntj* "entrance hall" as an institution located at the royal residence, although not necessarily the royal harem. The other administrative titles held by the hitherto known officials like *jmj-r3 prwj ḥḏ nbw n ḫnw* "overseer of the two treasuries of the residence", *jmj-r3 sḫw nswt jwꜥ-r3* "overseer of the royal repast" or *jmj-r3 šnwtj* "overseer of the two granaries" fit well into this picture.

P. Carlsberg 23, a late demotic list from Tebtynis, provides supplementary evidence for the assumption that the title designated an important office at the royal court.[37] After the heading *n3 j3wt* (*n*) *pr pr ꜥ3* "the offices of the palace", the title *jmj-r3 sḫ*(*w*) *ḫnt wr* "overseer of the great entrance hall" is listed after the offices of the *ṯ3tj* "vizier", *jmj-r3 ꜥwj* "overseer of the house" and *jmj-r3 ḫtm* "overseer of the seal" (XXXI, x+9–12). Three other offices follow (XXXI, x+13–15): *jmj-r3 pr wr* "majordomo", *wḥm j3bj nsw* "herald to the left of the king", *wḥm wnmj nsw* "herald to the right of the king". The proximity of these titles is interesting because the *jmj-r3 sḫ*(*w*) *ḫnt wr* Horudja was also *wḥm nswt* "herald of the king"; the same is true for Pairkap another "overseer of the scribes of the great hall" (and *jmj-r3 sḫw ḏ3ḏ3t* "overseer of the scribes of the council") dating to the Thirtieth Dynasty.[38] Therefore, I would conclude that the "overseer of the scribes of the great hall" was responsible for the reporting system at the royal court while the "overseer of the scribes of the council" was in charge of the accountancy.

That the office of the "overseer of the scribes of the great hall" must have been an important one is also indicated by its prominent placement in funerary inscriptions of monumental shaft tombs. The office is mentioned at least three times in the tomb of Udjahorresnet. It is also unlikely that the office was a mere honorary title as the official Harbes only held this title. Udjahorresnet is not the only official holding the titles "overseer of the scribes of the council" and "overseer of the scribes of the great hall" in the same time. The same is true for Wahibremeriptah known through a hitherto unpublished Serapeum stela as well as a recently published statue fragment. The close connection of both offices is also confirmed by the "overseers of the royal ships" Hekaemsaf and Tjanenhebu, both buried in close vicinity next to the pyramid of Unas at Saqqara, each of them holding either one of the two titles.

Monumental tombs in Lower Egypt

The offices held by Udjahorresnet in the same time were distributed over several persons in the late Twenty-sixth Dynasty. The distribution of titles however forms a dense network connecting these officials with each other indirectly (Tab. 4). Several of the offices discussed

36 Jurman, Impressions of What is Lost, 245 n. 42.

37 J. Tait, A demotic list of temple and court occupations: P. Carlsberg 23, in: H.-J. Thissen/T. Zauzich (eds.), Grammata Demotika, Festschrift für Erich Lüddeckens zum 15. Juni, Würzburg 1984, 211–233.

38 Perdu, RdE 49, 183–184 no. 8. For another "overseer of the scribes of the great hall" of the Thirtieth Dynasty, see: I. Guermeur, Les monuments d'Ounnefer, fils de Djedbastetiouefânkh, contemporain de Nectanébo Ier, in: I. Régen/F. Servajean (eds.), Verba manent. Recueil d'études dédiées à Dimitri Meeks par ses collègues et amis, CENiM 2, Montpellier 2009, 177–199.

here are attested in the reign of Psamtik II for the first time in the Saite Period. Already PERDU thus suggested a reform of the administration under Psamtik II or Apries and not as late as Amasis as often assumed.[39]

	wr swnw	*jmj-r3 ḫ^cww*	*kbnwt nswt*	*jmj-r3 sḫw d3d3t*	*jmj-r3 sḫw ḫn(r)t wr*	*jmj-r3 ḫ3swt Tmḥw*	*jmj-r3 ḫ3swt ḥ3w-nbw*
Psamtik	X					X	
Tjanenhebu		X		X			
Hekaemsaf		X			X		
Wahibremeriptah				X	X		
Menekhibnekau			X			X	
Udjahorresnet	X		X	X	X		X

Tab. 4: Distribution of titles of some officials discussed above

The hitherto mentioned officials were not only associated with each other. The location of their burial places also indicates a network of people related to each other. Almost all these officials were buried in monumental shaft tombs of a new type in the Memphite cemeteries.[40] Udjahorresnet's tomb in the south of Abusir, for instance, was part of a cluster of shaft tombs subsequently excavated and published by a Czech mission in the last decades. Among the officials buried there are Menekhibnekau, overseer of the *kbnt*-vessels and overseer of the *Tmḥw*-Libyans as well as Iufaa who held the office of the "overseer of the foreign lands of the Haunebu" like Udjahorresnet.[41]

A similar situation is to be found in the south and west of the Unas pyramid at Saqqara: The shaft tomb of the chief physician Psamtik belongs to a cluster of tombs including the tombs of the overseers of the royal fleet Tjanenhebu and Hekaemsaf.[42] Psamtik can be dated to the reign of Amasis by means of a stela from the Serapeum at Saqqara; dated findings in the tombs of the two other officials indicate that they were contemporaries of Psamtik. While Psamtik was also "overseer of the *Tmḥw*-Libyans" like the "overseer of the *kbnt*-vessels" Menekhibnekau at Abusir, Tjanenhebu was also "overseer of the scribes of the council" and Hekaemsaf "overseer of the scribes of the great hall". Thus, we encounter the very same titles later on held by Udjahorresnet distributed over different officials in the late Twenty-sixth Dynasty. Saqqara and Abusir probably represent two subsequent generations of officials belonging to the highest level of Egyptian administration.

39 PERDU, RdE 49, 193; cf. AGUT-LABORDÈRE, The Saite Period, 1006–1009.

40 M. STAMMERS, The Elite Late Period Egyptian Tombs of Memphis, BAR-IS 1903, Oxford 2009; cf. BAREŠ, Tomb of Udjahorresnet, 21–28; L. GESTERMANN, Das spätzeitliche Schachtgrab als memphitischer Grabtyp, in: G. MOERS/H. BEHLMER/K. DEMUSS/K. WIDMAIER (eds.), *jn.t ḏr.w* – Festschrift für Friedrich Junge, Band 1, Göttingen 2006, 195–206; N. CASTELLANO I SOLE, L'arquitectura funerària al període saïta, Nova Studia Aegyptiaca, 4, Barcelona 2007.

41 Cf. STAMMERS, Late Period Egyptian Tombs, 156–158. On the tomb of Iufaa, see: L. BAREŠ/K. SMOLÁRIKOVÁ, The shaft tomb of Iufaa. Volume 1: Archaeology, Abusir XVII, Prague 2008; JANSEN-WINKELN, Inschriften der Spätzeit IV.1, 57.228. On the monuments of Menekhibnekau, see note 17.

42 Cf. STAMMERS, Late Period Egyptian Tombs, 162–165. Padienaset, another official buried there, was overseer of the treasury like Hekaemsaf.

Finally, it is noteworthy that two of the hitherto known chief physicians were buried at Heliopolis: The tomb of Psamtikseneb was closely located to the tombs of the "overseer of the scribes of the great hall" Nesnaisut as well as the royal scribe Hormaakheru/ Neferibresaneith.[43] The exact location of the tomb of the chief physician Udjahormehnet is hitherto unknown.[44] These examples however illustrate that high officials of the late Twenty-sixth Dynasty were not only related to each other through their titles but also through the location of their tombs. The monumentality of the up to 30m deep shaft tombs at Abusir and Saqqara illustrates the actual status of their owners and their supposed closeness to the king within the political economy of Late Period Egypt.

The "Persian costume"

Similarities of high officials of the late Saite Period are also observable in the case of their visual representation through statues, stelae etc. A specific feature of the representation of these officials is the so-called Persian costume. While priests adopted this particular dress in the Hellenistic Period, it was a privilege of high officials of the late Twenty-sixth and early Twenty-seventh Dynasty dynasties. Statues of officials dating to the Persian Period like Udjahorresnet (Rome, Museo Gregoriano Egizio 22960) and Ptahhotep (Brooklyn Museum 37.353) supported the assumption that the Persian costume actually was an import from the Persian Empire.[45] But a number of statues with the Persian costume like the statue of Paieftjauauineith in the Louvre (Paris, Louvre A 93), the statue of Psamtikseneb (Rome, Museo Gregoriano Egizio 22687) or the statues of Psamtiksaneith (Philadelphia, Pennsylvania Museum of Art 42-9-1), Wahibre (Cairo, Egyptian Museum CG 672) and Sematauitefnakht/Wahibramen (Cairo, Egyptian Museum TN 27/11/58/8) can securely be dated to the late Twenty-sixth Dynasty.[46] The chief physician Psamtik dating to the reign of Amasis is depicted in the Persian dress even on a Serapeum stela.[47]

Two-dimensional depictions of the Persian dress are also to be found on a number of niche stelae, *e.g.* the stela of the mayor of Sais, Wahibre.[48] Of particular interest is a stela now in the

43 S. Bickel/P. Tallet, La nécropole saïte d'Héliopolis. Étude préliminaire, in: BIFAO 97, 1997, 67–90, especially fig. 6; cf. Stammers, Late Period Egyptian Tombs, 152–155. Hormaakheru/Neferibresaneith: sarcophagus and shabtis (Jansen-Winkeln, Inschriften der Spätzeit IV.2, 60.231). On the sarcophagus of Nesnaisut, see note 34.

44 On the sarcophagus of Udjahormehnet, see note 13.

45 B. von Bothmer, Egyptian Sculpture of the Late Period. 700 B.C. to A.D. 100, The Brooklyn Museum, New York 1960; cf. J. A. Josephson, Egyptian Sculpture of the Late Period, in: JARCE 34, 1997, 10–14; G. Vittmann, Rupture and continuity: on priests and officials in Egypt during the Persian period, in: P. Briant/M. Chauveau (eds.), Organisation des pouvoirs et contacts culturels dans les pays de l'empire achéménide, Persika 14, Paris 2009, 89–121, especially 97–98. On the statue of Ptahhotep (Brooklyn Museum 37.353), see: Bothmer, Egyptian Sculpture, 76–77; K. Jansen-Winkeln, Drei Denkmäler mit archaisierender Orthographie, in: Or 67, 1998, 155–172, here: 163–168.

46 Philadelphia, Pennsylvania Museum of Art 42-9-1 (Jansen-Winkeln, Inschriften der Spätzeit IV.1, 57.212); Cairo, Egyptian Museum CG 672 (Jansen-Winkeln, Inschriften der Spätzeit IV.1, 57.185); Cairo, Egyptian Museum TN 27/11/58/8 (Jansen-Winkeln, Inschriften der Spätzeit IV.1, 57.211).

47 Paris, Louvre IM 4048 (338) (Jansen-Winkeln, Inschriften der Spätzeit IV.1, 57.235). On the monuments of Psamtik, see note 11.

48 Niche stela Edinburgh, National Museum of Scottland 1956.134 (Jansen-Winkeln, Inschriften der Spätzeit IV.1, 57.186); cf. statue Cairo, Egyptian Museum CG 672 (Jansen-Winkeln, Inschriften der Spätzeit IV.1, 57.185); donation stela London, British Museum EA 1427 (Jansen-Winkeln, Inschriften

British Museum, a monument dedicated by our chief physician Psamtikseneb for his family.[49] Nakhthorheb, the uncle of Psamtikseneb, as well as his brother Nekau are still visible and dressed in the Persian costume, while the figures of his father and mother are missing.

While Psamtikseneb and his father Padegihet were both *ḫrp Srkt*; the *ẖrj-ḥb ḥrj-tp* Nakhthorheb/Hormenekhibemakhet, who placed a number of partially large sized statues in temples all over the Nile delta, held the unusual title *ḫrp ḥrjw ḥkꜣwt m pr ꜥnḫ* "director of those who are above the magic forces in the house life".[50] Psamtikseneb, the first chief physician of the Saite Period we know of, thus belonged to a family of physicians with close ties to the house of life. This nicely fits to Udjahorresnet who reorganised the houses of life as a chief physician being an advisor of the Persian king in the same time. This double role of the chief physician is also reflected by the literary figure of Harsiese in the teaching of Ankhsheshonqi.[51]

Nakhthorheb is usually dated to the reign of Psamtik II, the heyday of basilophorous double names in the Twenty-sixth Dynasty, based on his beautiful name Hormenekhibemakhet.[52] Herman DE MEULENAERE who reconstructed the family tree of these officials suggested that Psamtikseneb and his brother Tefnakht were also active under Psamtik II.[53] Psamtik's II short reign of only six years however indicates that they probably served under his successor Apries later on. In any case, the niche stela discussed here as well as the statues of both officials are the hitherto earliest witnesses of the Persian costume.[54] It is certainly no coincidence that several chief physicians like Psamtikseneb, Paieftjauauineith, Psamtik and, last but not least, Udjahorresnet present themselves in this particular dress as a clear marker of the elite formation they belonged to.

Conclusion

The aim of this paper was to put titles of the famous Egyptian official Udjahorresnet in the context of the administration of the late Twenty-sixth Dynasty. His illustrious titles like "chief physician", "overseer of the *kbnt*-ships of the king", "overseer of the scribes in the council" or "overseer of the scribes of the great hall" still remain more or less elusive with regard to their functional context. The study of officials holding these titles in the late Saite Dynasty however

der Spätzeit IV.1, 57.187). On these niche stelae in general, see: H. I. M. MAHRAN, The Pseudo-naos of the Late Period. A Comparative View, in: L. BAREŠ/F. COPPENS/K. SMOLÁRIKOVÁ (eds.), Egypt in Transition. Social and Religious Development of Egypt in the First Millenium BCE. Proceedings of an International Conference, Prague, September 1–4, 2009, Prague 2010, 268–285.

49 London, British Museum EA 511 (JANSEN-WINKELN, Inschriften der Spätzeit IV.2, 60.106).

50 On the numerous monuments of Nakhthorheb see: JANSEN-WINKELN, Inschriften der Spätzeit IV.1, 55.91–93, 55.97, 55.99, 55.125–126; cf. GOZZOLI, Psammetichus II, 183–188 (Dos. 7). On the title *ḫrp Srkt*, see: F. VON KÄNEL, Les Prêtres-Ouâb de Sekhmet et les conjurateurs de Serket, Paris 1984.

51 P. BM 10508, Cols. 1–3; cf. AGUT-LABORDÈRE, The Saite Period, 972–973.

52 On Nakhthorheb's beautiful name, see: H. DE MEULENAERE, Le surnom égyptien à la Basse Époque, Istanbul 1966, 14 no. 44. On double names in the Twenty-sixth Dynasty, see: DE MEULENAERE, Le surnom, 27–34; GOZZOLI, Psammetichus II, 32–37.

53 H. DE MEULENAERE, Une famille de hauts dignitaires saïtes, in: H. DE MEULENAERE/L. LIMME (eds.), Artibus Aegypti. Studia in honorem Bernardi v. Bothmer a collegis amicis discipulis conscripta, Brussels 1983, 35–43, especially 40–41.

54 Tefnakht: statue Kairo CG 662 (JANSEN-WINKELN, Inschriften der Spätzeit IV.2, 60.108). Nakhthorheb and Nekau are still visible in the Persian costume on the niche stela. On the monuments of Nekau, see: statue Frankfurt a. M., Liebieghaus 715 (JANSEN-WINKELN, Inschriften der Spätzeit IV.2, 60.105); statue Bologna, Museo Civico Archeologico 1838 (JANSEN-WINKELN, Inschriften der Spätzeit IV.2, 60.107).

revealed that they were associated with each other indirectly through titles that were held by one person in the case of Udjahorresnet but were distributed over several officials in the late Twenty-sixth Dynasty. Additional evidence is provided by the fact that their burial places, *i.e.* monumental tombs in the Memphite necropoleis as well as at Heliopolis, were often located close together. In addition, the "Persian costume" was a characteristic feature of their visual representation as a distinct group in the Egyptian society of the late Twenty-sixth Dynasty.

Several archaizing titles like "chief physician", "overseer of the scribes of the council" or "overseer of the scribes of the great hall" were introduced in the reigns of Psamtik II or Apries. It is certainly no coincidence that the reign of Psamtik II was also the heyday of basilophorous double names held by high officials of the Egyptian administration. Moreover, officials were buried in a new type of tomb, the so-called Saito-Persian shaft tomb, in the Memphite necropoleis. Finally, the emergence of the "Persian costume" as a feature of elite representation can be traced back to the time of Psamtik II, too. Udjahorresnet thus was not only witness of the Persian conquest of Egypt and active political agent of the Achaemenid rule over the country but marks an ending point of the development of the Egyptian administration during the Twenty-sixth Dynasty. Pharaoh was certainly in the centre of this trend that might be described as a process of 'courtization' (*Verhöflichung*) to put it in the words of Norbert ELIAS.

Creative powers, royal authority and resurrection:

Identification of a non-royal person with the sun-god in the Late Period

Dana Bělohoubková and Jiří Janák

Abstract

This article represents a case study based on two sarcophagi from Late/Saite Period shaft tombs at Abusir where two variants of a single text are preserved. This so far unattested composition, which aims to help the deceased in reaching the afterlife, uses two liturgical means. At first praises the creative powers of the sun-god and enumerates the aspects of his royal duties in the created world, and then identifies particular parts of the deceased's body as well as his earthly duties with the sun-god and his activities. Besides presenting parts of the above-mentioned unpublished text, the work deals with the problem of the usage of seemingly royal religious concepts (as the corporeal identification of a person with the sun-god) in non-royal sphere during the Late/Saite Period.

Introduction

Large shaft tombs represent a very specific type of Late Period funeral architecture in Lower Egypt. The inscriptions on the walls of these monuments and on their sarcophagi thus constitute a key source for our understanding of religious concepts and notions of the Saite-Persian era, a period of tremendous changes and developments on the political, social and religious level. The site of Abusir, a necropolis of the Memphite area studied by the Czech Institute of Egyptology of the Charles University[1], is home to a cemetery of a unique group of shaft tombs built around 530–525 BC.

The Late Period shaft tombs at Abusir represent a well-defined group of funeral structures that is situated at the south-western outskirts of the Abusir pyramid field, at a distance of about 200m from the nearest pyramid complex, the unfinished tomb of King Raneferef. The whole group consists of five (or maybe six) larger and some five to eight medium-size structures of that specific type. So far, three large tombs had been excavated, namely those of Udjahorresnet,[2] Iufaa[3] and Menekhibnekau[4]. In addition to them, two smaller tombs had

---

1 M. Verner, Abusir: Realm of Osiris, Cairo 2002.

2 L. Bareš, The shaft tomb of Udjahorresnet at Abusir. With a chapter on pottery by Květa Smoláriková and an appendix by Eugen Strouhal, Abusir IV, Prague 1999.

3 L. Bareš/K. Smoláriková, The shaft tomb of Iufaa. Volume 1: Archaeology, Abusir XVII, Prague 2008.

4 L. Bareš/K. Smoláriková, The shaft tomb of Menekhibnekau. Volume 1: Archaeology, Abusir XXV, Prague 2011.

been unearthed, those of Padihor and an anonymous one (dubbed R 3).[5] All those tombs had been used for one person only, except for the complex structure of Iufaa, where four persons had been buried in addition to the tomb owner. All those tombs seem to have been built during a rather short span of time at the very end of the Twenty-sixth Dynasty, between 530 and perhaps 525 BC. Some of them might have been decorated or used even later, until as late as around 500 BC. Although, these tombs had been constructed and decorated by the same group of architects, workmen and craftsmen, they differ in a surprisingly considerable number of features, including even the orientation of the deceased and decoration. While the superstructures had been almost completely destroyed already in antiquity and only tiny fragments remain of their original decoration, the burial chambers are relatively well preserved.

The religious texts that cover the walls of these monuments have their sources in the Pyramid Texts of the Old Kingdom, on coffins of the Middle Kingdom and in tombs and on papyri of the New Kingdom. Buried in a shaft tomb, the deceased was completely surrounded by a complex system of religious-magical texts and images, which have been developing over millennia.[6] In the case of the Abusir tombs of the priest Iufaa and the general Menekhibnekau, one can observe compositions whose main concepts have been derived from much older texts, which in part were originally intended for the king.[7] The present paper focuses on such a composition, for which we lack an exact parallel yet.

Archaeological context

In the shaft tomb cemetery of the Saite Period located in the north-western part of the Abusir necropolis, an intact tomb of the priest Iufaa was uncovered by the team of the Czech institute for Egyptology in 1996[8] and the tomb of general Menekhibnekau was discovered several years later in 2002.[9] Both these tombs have a typical shape and lay-out of large Memphite shaft tombs of this period. They consist of a large burial chamber at the bottom of a deep main shaft, with most of the burial chamber filled with a huge sarcophagus. The mummy of the deceased was placed to its final resting place through a side shaft and then into an inner anthropoid sarcophagus laying within the outer one.

The textual composition in our focus is attested on the inner anthropoid sarcophagi of Menekhibnekau and Iufaa. The text was written on the outer side of the inner sarcophagus lid of general Menekhibnekau, but in the case of the inner sarcophagus of Iufaa, the text covers the inner side of its lid. Below, we shall first concentrate on the text recorded in the tomb of Menekhibnekau, taking Iufaa's version as a comparative material.

The inner anthropoid sarcophagus of general Menekhibnekau was made of greywacke and was buried oriented with its head pointing to the north. The complete chest of the sarcophagus and the upper part of the lid still remain *in situ*, deposited inside the outer sarcophagus in the

5 F. Coppens/K. Smoláriková, Lesser Late Period Tombs at Abusir. The tomb of Padihor and the Anonymous Tomb R3, Abusir XX, Prague 2009.

6 Bareš/Smoláriková, The shaft tomb of Menekhibnekau, 55–57.

7 R. Landgráfová/D. Míčková, Purification of the Whopper: The Royal Purification Ritual in the Shaft Tomb of Iufaa, in: F. Coppens/H. Vymazalová (eds.), XI. Tempeltagung: The Discourse between Tomb and Temple, KSG 3/6, Wiesbaden 2019, in press.

8 Bareš/Smoláriková, The shaft tomb of Iufaa.

9 Bareš/Smoláriková, The shaft tomb of Menekhibnekau.

burial chamber of Menekhibnekau. The anthropoid sarcophagus depicts a human face (of the owner) with a long tripartite wig. The lower outline of the wig is followed by a wide *wesekh*-collar, which actually marks both the end of the idealised depiction of the deceased and the beginning of the text that runs from the end of the collar to the feet. A beard was originally also modelled, but it, unfortunately, is now partly destroyed due to a forced opening of the sarcophagus during the ancient robbery. Part of the sarcophagus lid (from breast to feet) was smashed to small pieces and scattered around the tomb by ancient robbers, but its fragments have been carefully collected during the research on the tomb. These recovered fragments were then joined and connected to the parts of the inscription that still remained *in situ*.[10]

The text inscribed on the outside of the lid consists of 16 vertical columns, while the inner side of the sarcophagus is left blank without any decoration or inscription. During the excavation no traces of a wooden coffin were found, and it thus seems probable that Menekhibnekau's mummy rested in the inner sarcophagus without a coffin. The space between the inner and outer sarcophagi was partly filled with gypsum mortar, which was poured there in a liquid form, firmed instantly using small pebbles. The mortar was, however, poured over already existing texts and depictions on both the outer and the inner sarcophagi. This solid and presently very hard mortar mass thus still partly covers a frieze depicting demonic beings similar to the vignette of the Book of the Dead chapter 182 on the south end of Menekhibnekau's inner sarcophagus' chest (where the feet of deceased were) is. It is noteworthy that the same decoration covers also a lower part of Iufaa's inner sarcophagus. We can thus partly assume that also the decoration of the chest of both sarcophagi could have originally looked similarly.

Comparative material

The tomb of the priest Iufaa was found intact, with a huge outer sarcophagus taking almost all available space within the burial chamber. The inner anthropoid sarcophagus made of basalt was still holding the remains of a wooden coffin with the mummy of the deceased. The exterior of the coffin was covered with a thick layer of ochre-coloured stucco. The body of the deceased was covered by a faience bead net.[11]

The lid of the inner sarcophagus now still rests inside the tomb, placed on two wooden beams, making its documentation of both sarcophagi much easier than in the case of Menekhibnekau. The anthropoid inner sarcophagus, which also remains deposited within the tomb, is similar in shape and decoration to that of Menekhibnekau. It bears an idealised broad face of the deceased with a tripartite wig and an Osirian beard. A *wesekh*-collar is in this case supplemented by a rather large depiction of a scarab beetle. The whole outer side of the sarcophagus is covered with typical texts, consisting mainly of excerpts from the Pyramid Texts, the Coffin Texts and the Book of the Dead.[12] The inner side of the lid of the inner sarcophagus, however, contains the same, otherwise unknown text as was the one found on upper side of the lid of Menekhibnekau's inner sarcophagus. Unlike in Menekhibnekau's case, the composition was condensed into 14 columns here, probably from spatial reasons.

10 Bareš/Smoláriková, The shaft tomb of Menekhibnekau, 58.
11 Bareš/Smoláriková, The shaft tomb of Iufaa, 57–59.
12 Bareš/Smoláriková, The shaft tomb of Menekhibnekau, 55–57.

Both sarcophagi thus held the same composition, which rests in the focus of the present paper, on a very special place: it was located over the body and it was also intentionally created as the text nearest to the body of the deceased. The variant attested on the lid of Menekhibnekau's inner sarcophagus, partly destroyed by tomb robbers, can be in the most part reconstructed with help from Iufaa's inscription. There are, however, some significant differences in both versions. As Iufaa's edition is, for instance, more condensed due to the aforementioned lack of space, it omits some parts at the very end of the composition. The composition itself is written in a very interesting way. It has a form of a table with 14 in Iufaa's, or 16 columns in Menekhibnekau's case. The reading direction is left to right (in the case of Menekhibnekau) or right to left (in Iufaa's version) and downwards from chest to feet in both cases. There are also parts written not in columns but in lines, these line actually represent boxes of repetitive texts common to all columns they touch. Not only is such spatial layout very economical but it also provides information about the composition itself. It thus can be suggested that text could be intended to be recited from memory. Such structure and the repetitive use of certain parts of text could on the one hand show principles of an oral composition, and on the other point to ritual or magical use of the text. Could such composition be, for instance, recited over the body during the mummification ritual or at the final stage of the funeral?

Content

Every column of the textual composition focuses on and also begins with a particular body part of the sun-god Ra. In the version attested in the tomb of Menekhibnekau, the last four columns cover only two bodily parts of the god, the texts pertaining to each of those members of the divine body is stretched within two columns. The whole composition thus names 14 corporeal parts in the following order: the head, the ears, the radiant eyes, the tongue, the back of the head, the neck, the arms, the chest, the belly, the *ib*-heart, the *haty*-heart, the spine, the penis and the legs.

Such an entry is then followed by a declaration that all these respective parts of the body belong to Ra who himself is closely linked with the function of appropriate corporeal limbs by using a different epithet in every column. As these epithets are rather uncommon (He who has seven faces, He who hears petition of millions, He who sees eternity, He who overthrows the rebel, He who created the power of bulls, etc.), they were obviously chosen (or even newly formed) to create a direct semantic link the divine power and royal authority of the solar god with all parts of his divine body. The ears of Ra are, for instance, neatly linked with the god's ability (or royal function) to hear the petitions of millions. One can also observe a clear use of wordplays within the whole texts, as similar terms or even homophones are being used to mark intellectual links between terms, concepts and ideas. The torso (*št3.t*) can, thus, be directly connected to Ra's ability to cover, encompass or hide secrets (*sšt3*).

After these epithets a line of invocation to potential malevolent forces comes that should be read in all columns repeatedly: "*O people, gods, glorified spirits, dead, and so on, do not take power over* (or *do not control*) X". Directly after the invocation line the composition repeats the first element of the text, with X being a particular limb of Ra referred to also in his epithet. Then another brief line that is meant to be read in connection to every column individually is inserted and it bears an explicit warning to the all the aforementioned malevolent beings, as it says: *Beware!* For every column then there is a different threat to the malevolent beings, but warnings remain virtually the same. Should anyone take control over any part of Ra's body, the same or very similar action would then be turned against the attacker. The malevolent act would thus prevent the attacker from living or reaching the afterlife.

This negative, or rather apotropaic part of the composition is followed by an exclamation by which the deceased turns to Ra. This part is again written within a line that runs across all columns. It semantically and visually marks an opening of a second part of the composition, which describes the reciprocity between the deceased and Ra. Here, the deceased claims that he is the one who will protect the bodily parts of Ra and who, by doing so, enables the sun-god to perform his divine roles mentioned in the gods "royal" epithets. As the main goal of the composition is to enable the deceased to reach a blessed afterlife, these mutually beneficent actions are mainly connected to Ra's nightly journey through the Netherworld and to his role of the guarantor of universal resurrection. This crucial part is then followed be a final reciprocal claim of the deceased that Ra should (and will) provide him with the appropriate limbs and protect them for him. At several cases, a sentence is added at the end of the column as a postscript which strengthens the connection both between Ra and the deceased, and between the bodily parts of the two protagonists. It also clearly completes and concludes intellectual links and wordplays of the column, as for instance in the first column that at the beginning deals mainly with the head of Ra, and at the end with the head of Menekhibnekau: *Do not let control be taken over him by the one who seizes heads upon the executioner's block!* As a result, Iufaa and Menekhibnekau should regain the ability to live again and should be provided with protection against their enemies.

Translation[13]

This is the head of Ra, who has seven faces.
O people, gods, glorified spirits, the dead and so on,
do not take control over this head of Ra, who has seven faces!
Beware, lest your faces perish at your testing!
O Ra, this Menekhibnekau protects your head for you,
he attests your seven face for you.
May you protect the head of this Menekhibnekau,
may you attest his face for him.
Do not let control be taken over him
by the one who seizes heads upon the executioner's block!

These are the ears of Ra, who hears the petitions of millions.
O people, gods, glorified spirits, the dead and so on,
do not attack these ears of Ra who hears my name!
Beware, lest your petitions at the gates of the royal palace shall be turned back!
O Ra, this Menekhibnekau placed your ears onto your head,
so that they might hear the petitions of millions.

13 Translation of six of the fourteen parts of the text in our focus is presented here. The full translation will be published as an individual chapter in R. Landgráfová et al., The Tomb of Menekhibnekau. Volume 2: Texts and Inscriptions, Prague 2019 (in print). We are grateful to Renata Landgráfová and Filip Coppens for their cooperation, comments and suggestions on our translation of this interesting but intriguing text.

May you give his ears onto his head for this Menekhibnekau,
so that this evil deafness towards what came out of the mouth of Him who is in his sun-disk may not enter his ears,
and so that he might hear what Ra hears on this day.

These are the radiant eyes of Ra, who sees eternity.
O people, gods, glorified spirits, the dead and so on,
do not revert the sight of these radiant eyes of Ra!
Beware, lest darkness shall arise in your faces on the day of the procession of the god
and eternity shall be that which you do not know!
O Ra, this Menekhibnekau attested your radiant eyes for you,
so that you might see with them,
so that you see in the utmost darkness,
so that you might behold in the utmost darkness,
so that you might recognise eternity for you,
so that you might establish everlastingness for you.
May you cause this Menekhibnekau to see your beauty,
behold your joy and look at your four dazzling papyrus columns
when you arise within them.
May you recognise eternity for him,
may you establish everlastingness for him.
…
This is the belly of Ra, who hides his secrets.
O people, gods, glorified spirits, the dead and so on,
do not take control over this belly of Ra, who hides his secrets!
Beware, lest your forms are revealed unto the face of your enemy,
for it is your name that he will find!
O Ra, this Menekhibnekau has hidden your protection in his belly.
May you place his protection for this Menekhibnekau into your belly.

This is the *ib*-heart of Ra, the Lord of magical power.
O people, gods, glorified spirits, the dead and so on,
do not take control over this *ib*-heart of Ra, the Lord of magical power!
Beware, lest this magical power of yours be seized by your enemy!
O Ra, this Menekhibnekau placed your *ib*-heart in its proper place
and he assigned your magical power to you as your protection.
May you place his *ib*-heart in its proper place for this Menekhibnekau,
may you assign his magical power to him as his protection.
…
This is the penis of Ra, who brought the power of bulls into being.
O people, gods, glorified spirits, the dead and so on,
do not take control over this penis of Ra, who brought the power of bulls into being!
Beware, lest your see be feeble in the ground
and lest your semen be weak in the womb, so that it cannot conceive an heir!
O Ra, this Menekhibnekau has assigned your semen to you and has given your seed to you,

so that your family may be numerous and your flesh may live,
so that your body may prosper and your skin may be spotless,
so that your transformation may shine brightly and your form may be strong,
so that your dignity may be grant
and your name may be great in the faces of the living, the blessed spirits and the dead.
May you assign his semen to this Menekhibnekau,
so that his family may be numerous and his flesh may live,
so that his body may prosper and his skin may be spotless,
so that his transformations may shine brightly and his forms may be strong,
so that dignity may be grant
and his name may be great in the faces of the living, the blessed spirits and the dead.
…

Interpretation

As was briefly explained above, the first section of the composition, deals solely with the god Ra, as it enumerates and names individual 14 parts of his divine body, characteristics, epithets and roles; all connected to the god's supreme power and rule. The list of the corporeal parts does not, however, follow the order of earlier texts describing the so-called "deification of the body parts", attested in the Pyramid Texts, the Coffin Texts and the Book of the Dead, which differ in the number of limbs mentioned, in their sequence, as well as in the used terms.[14]

The words used to describe the corporeal parts in the two texts from the shaft tombs in Abusir combine three different meanings and can be interpreted from three different angles. Although they describe actual bodily parts of any human or divine being (like the head, the eyes, the ears etc.) and they point to the appropriates senses or functions of these parts, the used terms also reveal a symbolic meaning of the individual limbs and senses in relation to Ra's universal power and his ruling authority. In some cases, specific terms for some of the corporeal members were used, for instance, by the naming the *akhty*-eyes (the radiant eyes) instead of usual *irty*-eyes. Moreover, specific aspects of Ra's might and power related to Netherworld were stressed in his epithets (for example, *He who sees eternity*; *He who hears the petitions of millions*). Some of the terms used to refer to the parts of the divine body of Ra, as well as to his epithets represent intertextual or at least symbolic links to the Amduat and other so-called Underworld Books. They can thus be interpreted as references to the concept of the god's nightly journey through the Netherworld and to the notion of his death and resurrection.[15] However, the description of Ra's body and the use of epithets (*He who is in the faces [of humankind]*; *He who overthrows the rebel*; *He who unites the Two Lands*; etc.), on the one hand, stress the god's universal power and royal authority, but on the other they point also towards the weakest lap of his nightly journey, to potential dangers, and his need to constantly claim authority and reinforce power. The text thus shows both Ra's universal rule and his need for protection.

14 *E.g.*, PT 539 (§1303–1315), CT 761 (VI, 391–392) and BD 42 and 172. For more examples and references see, for instance, H. ALTENMÜLLER, Gliedervergottung, in: W. HELCK/W. WESTENDORF (eds.), Lexikon der Ägyptologie II, Wiesbaden 1977, 624–627.

15 For a brief overview, see, for instance, E. HORNUNG, Die Nachtfahrt der Sonne: eine altägyptische Beschreibung des Jenseits, Düsseldorf/Zürich 1998.

The second section of the composition enumerates these possible dangers and the opposing powers, and it seeks to provide protection against all thinkable enemies of Ra by identifying them by a broad scale phrase "people, gods, glorified spirits, the dead and so on". These beings are then immediately warned not to become hostile or oppose against the aforementioned corporeal part of Ra and against Ra himself in each of the ruling role of his (*e.g., O people, gods, glorified spirits, the dead and so on, do not take control over this head of Ra, who has seven faces!*). By linking the malevolent forces and their oppositions with deeds against the Creator's ruling power and authority, the ultimate thread is identified here as rebellion. Should any of these being fail to obey this command, he or she would be punished and effected in appropriate parts of his or her body (*e.g., Beware, lest your faces perish at your testing!*).

After describing the aspects of the ruling power of Ra connected to individual parts of his body and after enumerating threads from all possible hostile agents, a concluding section of the text occurs. There, a third and probably the most important protagonist is mentioned, as it is the deceased who acts in this final part of the text. The deceased himself offers Ra his ritual help and assures the god about the protection of his individual body parts (*e.g., O Ra, this Menekhibnekau placed your ib-heart in its proper place and he assigned your magical power to you as your protection*). By protecting Ra's corporeal parts, senses and aspects of power, the deceased magically ensures the god's very existence and, thus, also the order of the world. And for doing so he must and shall be adequately rewarded: by Ra's protection over the appropriate bodily parts of his own and by a successful acceptance into a blessed afterlife (*May you place his ib-heart in its proper place for this Menekhibnekau, may you assign his magical power to him as his protection*). The main intention of the concluding part (and thus of the whole composition) is to create ritually a relation of mutual dependency between Ra and the deceased. Such practise does not only take advantage of the typical *do ut des* principle of Egyptian cult and religion but also seeks its new enforcements by stressing Ra's own dependency on the deceased and by using the principles of magical extortion.

Ritual interdependency and mutual protection

The concept of interdependency and mutual efficacy between the creator god and the king (as the ultimate ritualist) has a long tradition in Egyptian religion and has developed into many forms, from the sun temples of the Old Kingdom and Mansions of Millions of Years and other temples of the New Kingdom (for example, Luxor) to the Mammisis of the Ptolemaic Period.[16] The idea that the ritualist and the gods are mutually beneficent has also found its way into non-royal sphere of afterlife beliefs. The closest parallel for how such mutual dependency of the ritualist and the solar god could move from the temple context into the sphere of personal afterlife comes from the papyrus Bremner-Rhind (BM EA10188; dated only 200 years after Iufaa). There, in the famous *Book of Knowing the Transformations of Ra and Overthrowing Apophis*,[17] Ra has been repeatedly described as the Creator, the Universal

16 F. Coppens/J. Janák/H. Vymazalová, The Fifth Dynasty 'sun temples' in a broader context, in: M. Bárta/F. Coppens/J. Krejčí (eds.), Abusir and Saqqara in the Year 2010, Prague 2011, 430–442 (with references).

17 R. O. Faulkner, The Papyrus Bremner-Rhind (British Museum No. 10188), Bibliotheca Aegyptiaca III, Bruxelles 1933 (col. 21–32); C. Carrier, Le papyrus Bremner-Rhind (BM EA 10188). Tome II. Le Livre du renversement d'Apophis, Paris 2015.

Lord and the Most Primeval One. However, even as a being of almost unlimited power, he is constantly endangered by hostile forces (both human and supernatural) represented by rebellious mankind and the Champion of Evil, Apophis. The cosmogonic introduction of this part of papyrus Bremner-Rhind provides explanation of where both Ra's cosmogonic and magical powers (*hekau* and/or *akhu*) come from, why the latter can be transferred from the Creator onto the king. And it also shows how – by imitating the king – any ritualist who magically destroys Apophis shall receive the ultimate protection from the Creator himself. It is due to such relation of mutual interdependency that Ra is actually forced to help the ritualist, since he has to act effectively for whom who has magically protected himself. The process of "acting effectively for someone who has been effective you" can be viewed as an ultimate definition of the mutual *akh*-effectiveness[18] and of the principle of (*do ut des*) reciprocity.

In the aforementioned case of the papyrus Bremner-Rhind, the king (or the ritualist) after providing ritual protection for Ra asks the god for destruction of his own enemies, in the texts from the two shaft tombs in Abusir, the deceased in the end seeks a ritual-magical protection over his body and for his transfigured being.

Solar and Osirian aspects

By connecting the afterlife fate of the deceased and the corporeal resurrection of Ra, the text also refers to ideas laying in the background of two Egyptian concepts of death and resurrection, the so-called *imitatio solis* and *imitatio Osiridis*.[19] According to the first, the deceased strives to ensure his afterlife existence by linking his posthumous journey to the journey of the sun, imitating the destiny of the sun-god and connecting his own rebirth into the afterlife with the daily resurrection of Ra. The second ties the fate of the deceased similarly with Osiris, his death, justification, restitution and resurrection.[20] In both cases, however, the deceased is not identified with these deities but he rather learns about their (and about his own) journey to the afterlife; he takes on the roles of the deities and only thus he partakes on their transfiguration and rejuvenation.[21]

Since the New Kingdom, these two principles partly merged into one composite concept where Osiris would become Ra's body in the Underworld, and Ra, on the other hand, could be understood as Osiris's posthumous spiritual manifestation (his *ba*). In other words, during the nightly journey of the sun, in the very depths of the Underworld, Ra was resting in Osiris, as well as Osiris was resting in Ra as, for example, the Litany of Ra puts it.[22] A similar double-sided concept is present also in the texts from the tombs of Iufaa and Menekhibnekau. Although the composition explicitly mentions only the sun-god Ra, his body and power, it also refers both to Ra's dominant power and to his corpse located in the Underworld. In this

18 J. Janák, The Akh, in: J. Dieleman/W. Wendrich (eds.), UCLA Encyclopedia of Egyptology, Los Angeles 2013, 1–9. http://digital2.library.ucla.edu/viewItem.do?ark=21198/zz002gc1pn. Accessed on 25.02.2019.

19 J. Assmann, Tod und Jenseits im alten Ägypten, München 2001, 230–234.

20 M. Smith, Following Osiris. Perspectives on the Osirian Afterlife from Four Millennia, Oxford 2017.

21 Assmann, Tod und Jenseits, 504–518; M. Smith, Osiris and the Deceased, in: J. Dieleman/W. Wendrich (eds.), UCLA Encyclopedia of Egyptology, Los Angeles 2008, 1–6. http://escholarship.org/uc/item/29r70244. Accessed on 25.02.2019.

22 Smith, Following Osiris, 271–355 (for explicit quotations from Egyptian texts on Ra resting in Osiris and vice versa, see 302–305).

latter aspect it thus possibly points also to Osiris or at least the Osirian aspect of the sun-god. Moreover, we could see such indirect reference to Osiris in the occurrence of the 14 parts of body, a number of limbs usually connected to Osiris. The main ritual protagonist of the text, who, of course, is the deceased himself, is directly linked with Osiris also by using the phrase Osiris[23] Menekhibnekau or Iufaa, by depicting the deceased in an Osirian form on the sarcophagus and by the very existence of his mummy. Thus, the seemingly direct link between Ra and the deceased may well represent a shortened form of an obvious semantic connection between Ra, Osiris and the deceased, with Osiris being referred to only indirectly in symbolic references.

Acknowledgements

The work was supported by the Charles University, project GA UK No. 22216, by the European Regional Development Fund-Project "Creativity and Adaptability as Conditions of the Success of Europe in an Interrelated World" (No. CZ.02.1.01/0.0/0.0/16_019/0000734) and also by the Charles University Progress project Q11 – Complexity and resilience: Ancient Egyptian civilisation in multidisciplinary and multicultural perspective.

23 For the problem of Osiris N. or Osiris of N., see Smith, Following Osiris, 372–389.

Playing with details:

The hieroglyphic inscriptions of the Susa-statue of Darius I

Anke Ilona Blöbaum

Abstract

The well-known Susa-statue represents Darius I as a so-called Egypto-Persian ruler. Whereas the composition of Egyptian and Achaemenid elements are displayed clearly by the statues iconography, inscriptions are usually embedded in the cultural horizon of their language. Accordingly, the composition of the hieroglyphic inscriptions in general is based mainly on standard Egyptian royal phraseology. However, in detail it represents some peculiar features not attested in Egyptian texts.

An analysis of the main hieroglyphic inscription will show that deviation of the standard in this case might well be a significant part of the inscription's composition: a composition that creates distinct layers of meaning and reflects Egyptian royal ideology in a special adaptation for a foreign ruler.

1 Introduction

The Susa-statue representing Darius I as a so-called Egypto-Persian ruler is well-known and has already been discussed on several occasions.[1] The first edition of the inscriptions was presented by Jean YOYOTTE[2] and Pierre VALLAT,[3] recently supplemented by the work of Melanie WASMUTH.[4]

---

1 The major bibliography can be supplemented by references to J. PERROT (ed.), Le Palais de Darius à Suse. Une résidence royale sur la route de Persépolis à Babylone, Paris 2010; A. I. BLÖBAUM, „Der übersetzte Gott? Transfer von theologischen Konzepten zur Legitimierung von Fremdherrschaft im pharaonischen Ägypten", in: M. LANGE/M. RÖSEL (eds.), Der übersetzte Gott, Leipzig 2015, 15–36; H. STERNBERG EL-HOTABI, Quellentexte zur Geschichte der Ersten und Zweiten Perserzeit in Ägypten, EQÄ 11, Berlin 2017, 88–97; M. WASMUTH, Ägypto-persische Herrscher- und Herrschaftspräsentation in der Achämenidenzeit, Oriens et Occidens 27, Stuttgart 2017, 98–122.

2 J. YOYOTTE, Une statue de Darius découverte à Suse. Les inscriptions hiéroglyphiques. Darius et l'Égypte, in: JA 260, 1972, 253–266; J. YOYOTTE, Les inscriptions hiéroglyphiques de la statue de Darius à Suse, in: CDAFI 4, 1974, 181–183; J. YOYOTTE, La statue égyptienne de Darius, in: PERROT (ed.), Palais de Darius à Suse, 256–299.

3 P. VALLAT, L'inscription cunéiforme trilingue (DSab), in: JA 260, 1972, 247–251; P. VALLAT, Les textes cunéiformes de la statue de Darius, in: CDAFI 4, 1974, 161–170; P. VALLAT, Les principales inscriptions achéménides de Suse. Inscriptions de Darius à Suse: DSab, in: PERROT (ed.), Palais de Darius à Suse, 300–317, quote: 297, figs. 325–326 (photo detail), 312–313.

4 WASMUTH, Ägypto-persische Herrscher- und Herrschaftspräsentation, 101–124.

A brief introduction of the monument in general including an overview of the main layout of the inscribed texts and their interconnections with each other will lead to a focus on the composition of the most elaborate hieroglyphic text on the statue: the eulogy inscribed in the folds of the robe on the statue's left (DSeg2).

2 The Susa-statue of Darius I

The statue was found 1972 by the French Mission at Susa and is now housed in the Teheran National Archaeological Museum.[5] It was discovered near a monumental gateway of the palace complex in Susa.[6] The archaeological context reveals that the sculpture was integrated into the gateway in antiquity and thus, "was considered representative of the imperial decorative program"[7]. However, the origin of the material,[8] the technique of the stone-working and even the inscriptions – the cuneiform as well as the hieroglyphic – point to an Egyptian origin of the statue and most probably to an Atum temple as the original place of erection. Whether this might be in Heliopolis, in Wadi Tumilat or elsewhere remains unsolved,[9] as does how and when the statue was transported to Susa.[10] Furthermore there is archaeological evidence, that the statue might have been reproduced in Susa as part of a pair.[11]

The statue is preserved from the neck down and must have stood originally about three meters tall (Fig. 1).[12] The specific character of this important monument is clearly visible at first glance. While the king looks Persian by costume (Persian court robe, strapless royal Persian shoes), his pose and the decoration of the base is typically Egyptian.[13] According to the Persian costume head and headdress of the king might have been shaped in Persian style as well.[14]

5 Inventory no. 4112.

6 Perrot (ed.), Le Palais de Darius à Suse, 132–133; cf. M. Kevran, Une statue de Darius découverte à Suse. Le contexte archéologique, in: JA 260, 1972, 235–239.

7 H. P. Colburn, Art of the Achaemenid Empire, and Art in the Achaemenid Empire, in: B. A. Brown/M. H. Feldman (eds.), Critical Approaches to Ancient Near Eastern Art, Boston/Berlin 2014, 773–800, quote: 785.

8 J. Trichet/P. Poupet, Étude pétrographique de la roche constituant la statue de Darius découverte à Suse en décembre 1972, in: CDAFI 4, 1974, 57–59; J. Trichet/F. Vallat, L'origine égyptienne de la statue de Darius, in: F. Vallat (ed.), Contributions à l'histoire de l'Iran. Mélanges offerts à Jean Perrot, Paris 1990, 205–208; Yoyotte, La statue égyptienne de Darius, 268–269.

9 For a summary of the discussion, see Wasmuth, Ägypto-persische Herrscher- und Herrschaftspräsentation, 102, 120–121.

10 Most probably the transport took place during the reign of Xerxes I, see Wasmuth, Ägypto-persische Herrscher- und Herrschaftspräsentation, 102–103.

11 S. Razmjou, Assessing the Damage: Notes on the Life and Demise of the Statue of Darius from Susa, in: ArsOr 32, 2002, 81–104, especially 87–89.

12 Maximum preserved height of the figure: 1.95m, including the base: 2.46m (Razmjou, ArsOr 32, 2002, 83).

13 For a comprehensive analysis of the statue's type, iconography and style, see Wasmuth, Ägypto-persische Herrscher- und Herrschaftspräsentation, 105–110; cf. D. Stronach, Une statue de Darius découverte à Suse. Description and Comment, in: JA 260, 1972, 241–246; D. Stronach, La statue de Darius le Grand découverte à Suse, in: CDAFI 4, 1974, 61–72.

14 For a summary of the relevant discussion, see Wasmuth, Ägypto-persische Herrscher- und Herrschaftspräsentation, 118–120.

Fig. 1 Statue of Darius I
(National Museum of Iran, photo: D. Kaviyani)
(https://commons.wikimedia.org/wiki/File:National_Museum_Darafsh_6_(45).JPG#file, accessed on 13.12.2018)

3 The Susa-statue of Darius I: Layout and interconnections of the inscriptions

The statue is inscribed with different texts.[15] Front and back of the base show the Egyptian motive "*zmꜣ tꜣ.wj* – uniting the two lands", a traditional ritual act connected to the coronation of the king and his accession to the throne.[16] The iconography meets Egyptian standards: two fecundity figures are binding a lotus and a papyrus plant together and around the sign *zmꜣ* (Gardiner F36). The scene is framed by three columns of dedication-forms each on the right and left (DSeg4).[17]

(1) *ḏd mdw ḏ(j).n(=j) n=k ꜥnḫ wꜣs nb ḏd.t nb snb nb ꜣw.t-jb nb*
(2) *ḏd mdw ḏ(j).n(=j) n=k tꜣ.w nb ḫꜣs.wt nb dmḏ ẖr ṯb.tj=k*
(3) *ḏd mdw ḏ(j).n(=j) n=k Šmꜥ.w Mḥw m jꜣw n ḥr=k nfr mj Rꜥw ḏ.t*

(1) Words to be spoken: I give you all life and power, all stability, all health (and) all joy.
(2) Words to be spoken: I give you all the lands and all the foreign lands united under your sandals.
(3) Words to be spoken: I give you Upper and Lower Egypt adoring your beautiful face like (that of) Re eternally.

15 Sternberg el-Hotabi, Quellentexte, 94, Abb. 19: The graphic provides a good overview about design and layout of the texts.

16 A. I. Blöbaum, „Denn ich bin ein König, der die Maat liebt". Herrscherlegitimation im spätzeitlichen Ägypten. Eine vergleichende Untersuchung der Phraseologie in den offiziellen Königsinschriften vom Beginn der 25. Dynastie bis zum Ende der makedonischen Herrschaft, AegMon 4, Aachen 2006, 47; for an examination of *zmꜣ-tꜣ.wj*-scenes as part of the figurative programme in Egyptian temples see R. Y. Merzeban, Unusual *smꜣ tꜣwy* Scenes in Egyptian Temples, in: JARCE 44, 2008, 41–71.

17 Sternberg el-Hotabi, Quellentexte, 96; Wasmuth, Ägypto-persische Herrscher- und Herrschaftspräsentation, 121–122; Yoyotte, La statue égyptienne de Darius, 282–283, fig. 304 (photo; front of the base).

Figure 2 presents the columns on the right side of the scene (in direction of the reader) depicted in front of the base. The columns on the left give the same text only mirrored. The texts display the words the two figures address to the king. The phraseology is generic in Egyptian royal contexts. According to the subject of the scene, inscriptions mentioning the union of lands and foreign lands under the sandals or feet of the king are well attested.[18] The gifts to offer, mentioned in the text, relate to the physical well-being of the king, his territorial dominion and the loyalty of the subjects. The back of the base is decorated with the same scene and inscriptions, but while the front is carved in sunken relief, the scene on the back is just incised as a line-drawing.[19] As design, layout and inscriptions follow general Egyptian conventions the location of the scene in front and back of the base is rather exceptional, though some rare examples are attested for Ramses II and Taharqo.[20] The depiction of an icon symbolising Upper and Lower Egypt in front of the base (directly under the feet of Darius I) might emphasise the aspect of the Persian emperor's dominion over Egypt.[21]

Both sides of the base display toponyms representing the people of the empire in a style that combines Egyptian and Persian elements (DSeg5).[22] "[…] the display of the toponyms on the sides of the base follows Egyptian conventions, but instead of bound captives raising out of the crenelated ovals encircling each geographic name, the representatives of these toponyms kneel on top of the wall cartouches and hold their hands upwards in a similar gesture as on the *gātū* bearer reliefs in Persepolis and Naqš-e Rustam. This gesture with upturned open palms is in Egypt used for receiving, offering and supporting."[23]

As a common Egyptian type of sculpture (*Standschreitstatue*) the statue is equipped with a back pillar. Rather atypically, however, it was left blank without any inscription. Thus, with exception of the texts on the base all inscriptions are presented in ideal frontality and at visible height – the inscribed belt as highest point is no more than approximately two meters high. It is evident, that the inscriptions – at least the hieroglyphic ones[24] – were carved to be seen and read by passers-by.

---

18 For different examples see Merzeban, JARCE 44, 2008, 46–47, 50.

19 Yoyotte, La statue égyptienne de Darius, 282.

20 Wasmuth, Ägypto-persische Herrscher- und Herrschaftspräsentation, 121–122: Luxor temple, First courtyard, near gate to the great hypostyle (Ramses II); Museo Egizio Turin N. Cat 1380 (Ramses II); Museum Cairo CG 770 (Taharqo).

21 This interpretation is supported by a similar depiction of Darius I in the temple of Hibis, N. de Garis Davies, The Temple of Hibis in el Khārgeh Oasis III: The Decoration, MMAEE 17, New York 1953, pl. 39; Blöbaum, Der übersetzte Gott?, 30–32.

22 M. Roaf, The Subject Peoples on the Base of the Statue of Darius, in: CDAFI 4, 1974, 73–160; P. Calmeyer, Ägyptischer Stil und reichsachaimenidische Inhalte auf dem Sockel der Dareios-Statue aus Susa/Heliopolis, in: H. Sancisi-Weerdenburg/A. Kuhrt (eds.), Achaemenid History VI. Asia Minor and Egypt: Old Cultures in a New Empire, Leiden, 1991, 285–303; R. B. Gozzoli, The Writing of History in Ancient Egypt during the First Millennium BC (ca. 1070 – 180). Trends and Perspectives, London 2006, 123, fig. 15; Yoyotte, La statue égyptienne de Darius, 286–296; Sternberg el-Hotabi, Quellentexte, 96; Wasmuth, Ägypto-persische Herrscher- und Herrschaftspräsentation, 156–186.

23 M. Wasmuth, Political Memory in the Achaemenid Empire: The Integration of Egyptian Kingship into Persian Royal Display, in: J. M. Silverman/C. Waerzeggers (eds.), Political Memory in and after the Persian Empire, Ancient Near East Monographs 13, Atlanta 2015, 203–237, quote: 211.

24 "The exact way the cuneiform texts are oriented along the pleats of the court robe diverges from standard Achaemenid practice. On the statue of Darius the cuneiform signs are placed so that the readers must turn their heads sideways to read them. These factors further suggest that, although the monument was

3.1 The hieroglyphic inscription on the tips of the belt bow (DSeg1)

Each tip of the belt bow is inscribed with one column of hieroglyphs (Fig. 3).[25] The king's name "Darius" in a cartouche is introduced by the royal titles: *nṯr nfr nb tꜣ.wj* "the perfect god, lord of the Two Lands" on the right and *nzw bjt nb jr(j) jḫ.t* "king of Upper and Lower Egypt, lord of the rituals" on the left, followed by the simplest standard-form of the formula *ꜥnḫ ḏ.t* "May he live forever". Layout, composition and writing of these small columns meet the usual Egyptian standard.[26]

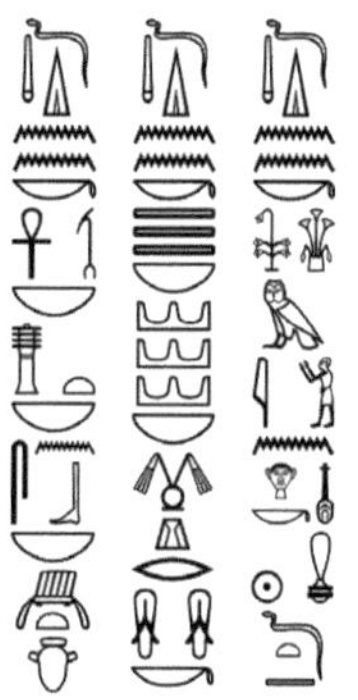

Fig. 2: Dedication-forms on the base (DSeg4)

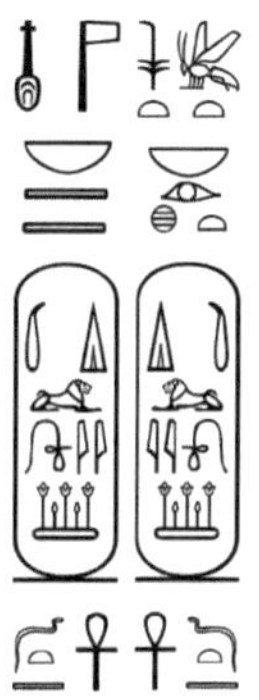

Fig. 3: Cartouches on the tips of the belt bow (DSeg1)

3.2 The cuneiform inscription in the folds of the robe on the right (DSab)

In the folds of the robe on the right a cuneiform inscription is incised vertically forming four columns. The inscription provides three versions of the same text in Old Persian, Elamite and Akkadian.[27] It starts with an invocation of the god Ahuramazda as omnipotent creator of the world and the king. Then the statue itself is described as a monument made in Egypt presenting the Persian dominion over Egypt. The text ends with the Persian royal protocol and a direct speech by the king expressing his hope to be protected by the God Ahuramazda: "A great god is Ahuramazda, who created this earth, who created yonder sky, who created man, who created happiness for man and who made Darius king. This is the statue of stone, which Darius the king ordered to be made in Egypt, so that whoever sees it in time to come will know that the Persian man holds Egypt. I am Darius, the great king, king of kings, king of countries, king on this great earth, son of Hystaspes, an Achaemenid. Darius the king proclaims: May Ahuramazda protect me and all that has been done by me!"[28]

meant to invoke Achaemenid visions of kingship and identity, it was intended to do this in an Egyptian context – not an Iranian one" (Razmjou, ArsOr 32, 2002, 87).

25 Yoyotte, La statue égyptienne de Darius, 262–263, figs. 282–283 (photo, drawing); Razmjou, ArsOr 32, 2002, fig. 23 (photo detail).

26 Blöbaum, Herrscherlegitimation, 55; 67–68; 99–101; 198–202.

27 "Le contenu de l'inscription présente, dans les 3 langues, le même aspect général, et les différences de détail qui apparaissent ne sont dues qu'au génie propre à chacune d'elles" (Vallat, JA 260, 1972, 249); "Ces trois inscriptions (DSab) présentent la traduction d'un seul et même texte." (Vallat, CDAFI 4, 1974, 161); cf. B. Jacobs, Sprachen, die der König spricht. Zum ideologischen Hintergrund der Mehrsprachigkeit der Achämenideninschriften, in: R. Rollinger/G. Schwinghammer/B. Truschnegg/K. Schnegg (eds.), Altertum und Gegenwart. 125 Jahre Alte Geschichte in Innsbruck. Vorträge der Ringvorlesung Innsbruck 2010, Innsbrucker Beiträge zur Kulturwissenschaft NF 4, Innsbruck 2012, 95–130.

28 A. Kuhrt, The Persian Empire: A Corpus of Sources from the Achaemenid Period, London 2010, 478.

The cuneiform text relates to two hieroglyphic texts on the statue. Firstly, the four columns form an element of the visual composition that parallels the hieroglyphic text in the folds of the robe on the other side. Furthermore, the textual content partially finds a counterpart in the hieroglyphic text on top of the base.

3.2 The hieroglyphic text on top of the base (DSeg3)
As mentioned above, the text on the base (Fig. 4 and Tab. 1: DSeg3)[29] corresponds with a part of the cuneiform text, namely the sentence containing details about the production and purpose of the statue. The Egyptian text describes the statue as representation of a king who is legitimated by the gods according to Egyptian theology. Correspondingly, the production and installation of the statue is presented as a sacral donation, using the common Egyptian type of royal donation inscriptions.[30] In contrast, the cuneiform texts denote the statue explicitly as an enactment of Persian dominion ("This is the statue of stone, which Darius the king ordered to be made in Egypt, so that whoever sees it in time to come will know that the Persian man holds Egypt"). The position of Ahuramazda in the cuneiform texts is represented by Atum-Re-Harakhte.[31] It is evident that the text is not composed as a translation of the cuneiform. In fact the hieroglyphic text transfers the main information of the cuneiform into a context that suits Egyptian cultural conventions.[32]

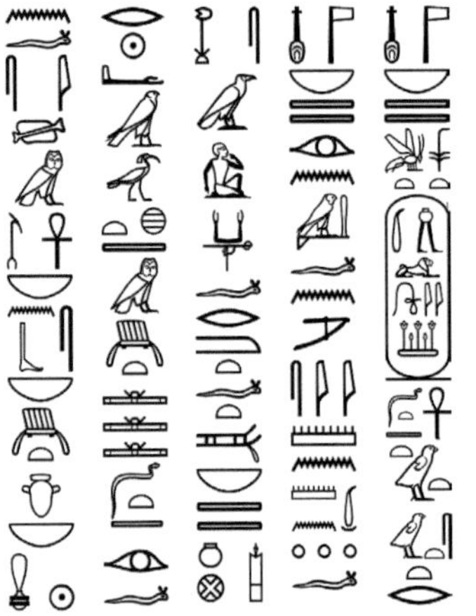

Fig. 4: The inscription on top of the base (DSeg3)

[1]| nṯr nfr nb tꜣ.wj nzw bjt (Ntrjwš)| ꜥnḫ ḏ.t

twt stwt r [2]| nṯr nfr nb tꜣ.wj jr(j).n ḥm=f n-mrw.t smn(.t) mnw=f

[3]| sḫꜣ kꜣ=f r-gs jt(j)=f Jtm nb tꜣ.wj Jwn.wj [4]| Rꜥw-Ḥr.w-ꜣḫ.tj m ꜣw.t ḏ.t

jr(j)=f [5]| n=f jsw m ꜥnḫ wꜣs nb snb nb ꜣw.t-jb nb mj Rꜥw

(1) The perfect god, lord of the Two Lands, king of Upper and Lower Egypt, Darius, may he live forever.

(This is) a statue resembling (2) the perfect god, the lord of the Two Lands, which his majesty has made in order to establish his monument,

(3) (and) to remember his *ka* together with his father Atum, lord of the Two Lands, the Heliopolitan, (4) Re-Harakhte, for the length of eternity.

May he (5) in return grant him all life and strength, all health and all joy as Re

Tab. 1: DSeg3: transliteration and translation

29 Gozzoli, Writing of History, 122–123; Yoyotte, La statue égyptienne de Darius, 279 [3], 281, fig. 300 (photo).

30 S. Grallert, Bauen – Stiften – Weihen. Ägyptische Bau- und Restaurierungsinschriften von den Anfängen bis zur 30. Dynastie, ADAIK 18, Berlin 2001, 34–60.

31 Contradicting Gozzoli, Writing of History, 123; Wasmuth, Ägypto-persische Herrscher- und Herrschaftspräsentation, 118, and Yoyotte, La statue égyptienne de Darius, 281, who understand the sequence of god's names as belonging to two different gods (namely Atum and Re-Harakhte), I read *Jtm nb tꜣ.wj Jwn.wj Rꜥw-Ḥr.w-ꜣḫ.tj* as denomination of one god with reference to an attestation in Papyrus Harris (1,4), cf. P. Grandet, Le Papyrus Harris (BM 9999): Traduction et commentaire, BdE 109, 1–2, Cairo 1994, II, 111 [452]; cf. LGG III, 778–779.

32 Blöbaum, Der übersetzte Gott?, 24–25.

3.3 The hieroglyphic inscription in the folds of the robe on the left (DSeg2)

The hieroglyphic inscription on the left of the statue is arranged visually as the main counterpart to the cuneiform text. It is placed in the vertical folds of the robe. "This is a well-documented Achaemenid practice for royal representations and diverges prominently from the standard Egyptian practice of rendering titulary and prayer formulae on the back pillar."[33] It consists of a eulogy that meets standard Egyptian royal phraseology and theology. The layout of the text follows the space available with four columns (Fig. 5) that have to be read from left to right (from the direction of the reader). Looking at the text in terms of phraseology it reveals a certain composition organised by repetition of the royal titles *nṯr nfr* and *nzw* respectively *nzw bjt*.

In my opinion these titles function as a kind of headline subsuming the subject of the following section of the text with each section focussing on a different subject. However, the composition is neither realised in the layout nor denoted in any other way. It is based on my interpretation of the text relating to syntax, semantics and phraseology. The internal structure of the text – as I understand it – comprises four parts (Fig. 6): two parts (A1–2), each of which entitled by *ntr nfr* "the perfect god"[34] are followed by a third part (B) introduced by *nzw nḫt* "the victorious king"[35] and finally by the king's name and an official protocol (C). Following this structure each part of the text will be discussed in detail below.

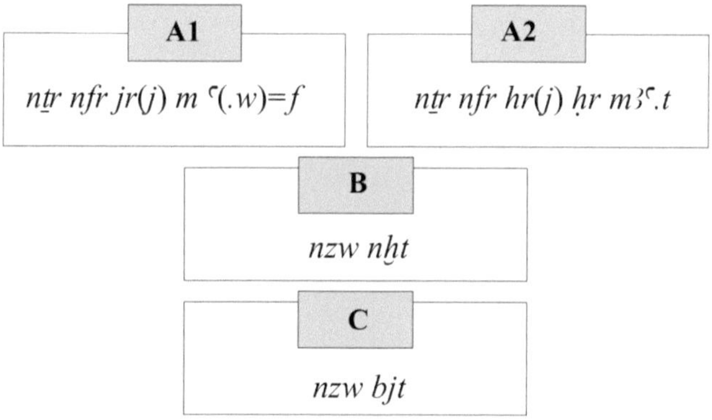

Fig. 5: The eulogy – composition of the text

33 Razmjou, ArsOr 32, 2002, 85.
34 Wb 2, 361.10–362.3; LGG IV, 428–429; Blöbaum, Herrscherlegitimation, 198–199.
35 Wb 2, 315.6; Blöbaum, Herrscherlegitimation, 64–67.

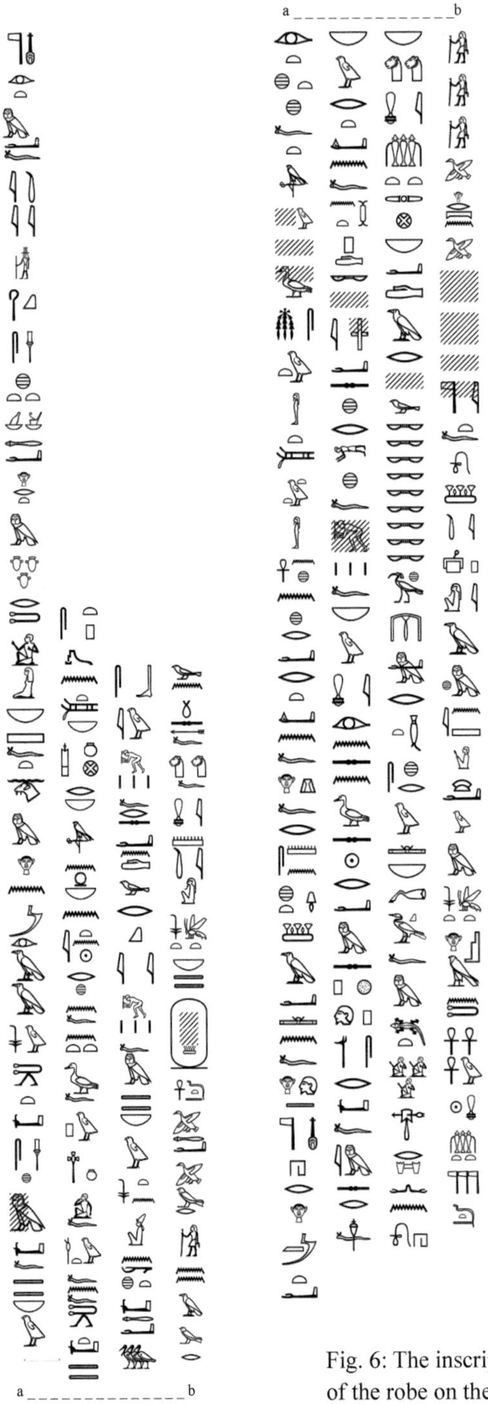

Fig. 6: The inscription on the folds of the robe on the left (DSeg2)

3.4.1 The eulogy: part A1 (Tab. 2)

nṯr nfr jr(j) m ꜥ(.w)=f	The perfect god, who is acting with his own hands,
jt(j).y ḥqꜣ sḫm.tj	sovereign, ruler of the double-crown,
ꜥꜣ ḥr.yt m jb.w rmṯ nb *nb šfy.t m-ḥr-n mꜣꜣ sw*	great of fear in all the hearts of all people, lord of authority over those who see him.
jṯ(j) sḫm=f tꜣ.wj nb.w	whose power seizes the Two Lands (or: all lands),
jr(j) jḫ.t ḫft wḏ nṯr	who is performing the ritual according to the divine order,
↓	
zꜣ […] mst.w Jtm(.w) twt ꜥnḫ Rꜥw *rḏ(j).n=f ḥr ns.t=f r smnḫ šꜣꜥ(.t).n=f ḥr tp tꜣ*	son of […], offspring of Atum, living image of Re, who has placed him on his throne to accomplish what he has begun in the world.

Tab. 2: The eulogy (A1) – transliteration, structure and translation

The first part is introduced by *nṯr nfr jr(j) m ꜥ(.w)=f* "The perfect god, who takes action with his own hand". This phrase functions as a headline presenting the main topic that is developed in this part of the text. Accordingly, the king is the main actor in the entire part with only one exception, namely the last sentence. It is here we find the objective of Darius' action: the god Re places the Persian king on the Egyptian throne. The god takes here the active part.

The text shows a well-designed structure as Table 2 illustrates. The epithets are arranged thematically in an onion-like structure building up references by subject (activity – control/territorial dominion – authority) and vocabulary (*jr(j)* – *sḫm*). Especially the relation of the second and fourth phrase is striking (*jt(j).y:jṯ(j)*; *sḫm.tj:sḫm=f*; *sḫm.tj:tꜣ.wj*). At the same time the text develops a strong sequential dynamic leading to the final phrase.

The description of the king's ability to achieve respect and/or strike fear in people is framed by epithets that show Darius' claim to power focussed on control over Egypt. In this context the focus on *sḫm*-power evolved in this section is remarkable, because *sḫm* "signifies predominately political authority over enemies and regions",[36] and therefore it represents an absolute precondition for reign and dominion.[37] In the headline, his activity and efficacy is expressed in a general way, whereas the corresponding epithet (*jr(j) jḫ.t ḫft wḏ nṯr* "who is performing the ritual according to the divine order") displays ability and intention to act according to the Egyptian normative system. This is linked directly to the next level expressed in the following sentence: his integration into this very system by the Egyptian gods.

At first glance the well-designed structure as well as most of the epithets corresponds to Egyptian conventions and traditions.[38] But looking into details, at least two expressions attract attention.

36 K. Goebs, Crowns in Egyptian Funerary Literature. Royalty, Rebirth, and Destruction, Oxford 2008, 17.

37 H. Roeder, Mit dem Auge sehen. Studien zur Semantik der Herrschaft in den Toten- und Kulttexten, SAGA 16, Heidelberg 1996, 296; cf. Blöbaum, Herrscherlegitimation, 59.

38 Cf. Wasmuth, Ägypto-persische Herrscher- und Herrschaftspräsentation, 112–113.

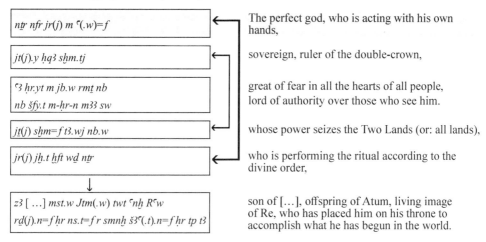

The first one is *ḥq3 sḫm.tj* "ruler of the double crown". The crown (the Two-powerful-ones)[39] as divine donation is well attested in royal inscriptions, as are expressions which describe the king receiving it or appearing with the crown. But the corresponding epithet *nb sḫm.tj* "lord of the double-crown" is mainly used as a divine name in religious contexts,[40] referring to specific aspects of the kingship, i.e. legitimate rule, in the divine sphere.[41] The combination of *ḥq3* and the double-crown, however, is not attested before the Ptolemaic Period, where it is known as divine title of Horus.[42] Of course, it may have been in use prior to the Ptolemaic Period, having simply not survived in any of the extant material, or Darius in fact delivers the first attestation of this version. One could also think of a mistake of the author or the scribe, but the fact is that it differs from the standard known in Late Period royal texts. I do not believe in a simple mistake, because of the highly sophisticated composition the text offers. The signs (hieroglyphic and hieratic) are not confusable so I would claim that for the craftsman as well. Furthermore, there is – in my opinion – a good reason that we do not have earlier attestations of *ḥq3 sḫm.t*. That is because the meaning, although similar to *nb sḫm.tj*, is distinctive in detail. In Late Period texts the term *ḥq3* by default describes a sovereign ruler exercising political control and dominion,[43] whereas *nb* usually refers back to the right of ownership.[44] Although the epithet gives the impression to be almost common it differs in this very detail, because the meaning of *ḥq3* focuses on control and *sḫm.tj* is the object to be controlled. Taking the double-crown as a metaphor for Egypt, Darius is described as an Egyptian king wearing the double-crown in the first place but with the same words he is described as the one who controls Egypt and has achieved this position neither by heritage nor in the line of succession but by his own means of power. Therefore I suggest that *ḥq3* was used intentionally to emphasise Darius' claim to power on the one side and at the same time to focus on his status as a conqueror of Egypt.

Secondly, the royal title *nb jr(j.t) jḫt* "lord of the ritual"[45] is common in Late Period royal phraseology, as well as various versions concerning the proper way of acting as a ritualist.[46] But the addition of *ḫft wḏ nṯr* "according to the divine order" is not attested elsewhere. It seems to be a special adaptation for a foreign ruler who has no natural place in the religious and cultural system.

Furthermore, wherever we expect the expression *t3.w nb.w* "all lands" in the text, it is written *t3.wj nb* or *t3.wj nb.w*.[47] From the Eighteenth Dynasty onwards we have occasional attestations of this writing that becomes common in the Ptolemaic Period.[48] Nevertheless, I would point out, that especially in this text the focus on the Two Lands in the meaning of

39 Wb 4, 250.10–251.10.

40 LGG III, 740b–c; attestations as royal epithet e.g. for Herihor (Karnak, temple of Chons, Architrave: http://aaew2.bbaw.de/tla/index.html, document DZA: 29.521.300 [digitalisiertes Zettelarchiv], accessed on 15.12.2018) and Thutmosis III (Urk. IV, 200C: Semna temple).

41 Goebs, Crowns, 109.

42 Wilson, Ptolemaic Lexikon, 905; LGG V, 523b–c.

43 Roeder, Mit dem Auge sehen, 184–188; Blöbaum, Herrscherlegitimation, 48–52.

44 Blöbaum, Herrscherlegitimation, 53–56.

45 Wb 1, 124.12.

46 Wb 1, 124.12; Blöbaum, Herrscherlegitimation, 99–102.

47 DSeg2: *jṯ(j) sḫm=f t3.wj nb.w* (l. 1, eulogy, part A1); *wḏ(.n)=f n=f jṯ(j) t3.wj nb.w* (l. 2, eulogy, part A2); *wsr=f jm=s r ḫsf sb.jw=f sʿnd rqw=f m t3.wj nb.w* (l. 3, eulogy, part A2).

48 Yoyotte, La statue égyptienne de Darius, 260–261; cf. Blöbaum, Der übersetzte Gott?, 25–26.

"Egypt" might well be intentional. The frequent use of the corresponding title *nb tꜣ.wj* "Lord of the Two Lands" supports this assumption according to my understanding. However, I do not share the opinion of Roberto Gozzoli, who assumes that *tꜣ.wj* in this text might have to be understood as a metaphor for Egypt and Persia.[49]

3.4.2 The eulogy: part A2 (Tab. 3)

nṯr nfr hr(j) ḥr mꜣꜥ.t	The perfect god, who is content in truth
stp.n Jtm nb Jwnw r nb n šnn.t nb(.t) jtn	whom Atum, lord of Heliopolis, had chosen to be master of all that the sun's disc encircles,
rḫ.n=f n.tt zꜣ=f pw nḏ=f	because he had recognised that it is his son who is protecting him.
wḏ(.n)=f n=f jṯ(j) tꜣ.wj nb.w	He has ordered him to seize both of the Two Lands (resp. all lands).
rḏ(j) n=f N.t pḏ.t=s jm(j) ꜥ(.w)=s r sḫr ḫft.jw=f nb	Neith has given him the bow she holds, to throw back all his enemies,
mj jr(j).n=s n zꜣ=s Rꜥw m zp tp.j	acting as she did on behalf of her son Re, on the first occasion,
wsr=f jm=s r ḫsf sb.jw=f sꜥnd rqw=f m tꜣ.wj nb.w	so that he (Darius) may be effective in repelling those who rebel against him, to reduce his opponents in the Two Lands (resp. all lands).

Tab. 3: The eulogy (A2) – transliteration, structure and translation

The second part is introduced by *nṯr nfr hr(j) ḥr mꜣꜥ.t* "the perfect god, who is content in truth". In parallel with the first part (A1), the phrase has the function of a headline introducing the main topic of the following text: the integration of Darius as foreign ruler into the Egyptian normative system. The gods keep the active position.

The composition of this text differs from the first part. The headline entitles a two-piece structure. Again the text in general follows Egyptian conventions. Darius receives world supremacy from Atum and a bow – a symbol of the Persian kingship – from Neith. The comprehensiveness of this part is striking. This could be explained by the fact that with this motif Egyptian and Persian royal ideology is interlaced with each other.[50] Furthermore, with the goddess Neith involved, Darius is connected to the Saite Dynasty as well. The bow is the specific weapon of the goddess Neith.[51] Likewise there is evidence for the motive of the bow given by Neith in a royal Saite inscription of Amasis.[52]

49 Gozzoli, Writing History, 123.

50 Cf. Wasmuth, Ägypto-persische Herrscher- und Herrschaftspräsentation, 113.

51 Cf. a compilation of divine epithets of the goddess Neith concerning her armed with bow and arrows, LGG VIII, 270.

52 "Elephantine stela" of Amasis (Cairo TN 13/6/24/1; on display in the garden of the Nubian Museum in Aswan), l. 10–11: "Seine Majestät stellte sich (11) auf seinen Streitwagen, nachdem er seinen Speer ergriffen hatte wie ein Gott und der Bogen von Silber(?) in seiner Hand war mit der Nennung seines Namens auf Befehl der Neith." K. Jansen-Winkeln, Die Siegesstele des Amasis, in: ZÄS 141, 2014, 132–153, quote: 136. The condition of the text especially in the last part of the sentence is rather bad.

Both parts of this section have a similar structure unfolding the topic from general to particular. The donation of world supremacy by Atum is specified towards seizing the Two Lands, respectively all lands. The particular spelling of the term lends a degree of ambiguity to the text that oscillates between the generic phraseology of seizing all the lands common in royal Egyptian texts and a specific adaptation for Darius as conqueror of Egypt on behalf of the god Atum. We find the same structure in the second part of the section. Darius is armed by Neith in order to throw back his enemies, first in the general sense then, focussed on the Two Lands, respectively all lands with the same ambiguity as described above. In this context the explicit differentiation between *ḫft.jw* "enemy",[53] *sb.jw* "rebel"[54] and *rqw* "opponent"[55] is surely no coincidence. The word *ḫft.j* is known as a generic term in a wider sense,[56] whereas *sb.j* and *rqw* defines mainly political opposition,[57] which might reflect the historical situation during the beginning of Darius' reign.[58]

An alternative subtext of this part of the eulogy would be that Darius receives power and legitimation from Atum, whereas Neith provides him with the means to maintain power and dominion. The effective weapon is the bow, which symbolises both Persian kingship and Egyptian rule.[59]

The reading of the relevant passage mentioning the goddess Neith is relatively certain according to Jansen-Winkeln, although previous editors have offered different interpretations, see the discussion in: ZÄS 141, 2014, 139, 152–153.

53 Wb 3, 276.12–277.5.

54 Wb 4, 87.14–88.7.

55 Wb 2, 456.13–20.

56 J. F. Quack, Demagogen, Aufrührer und Rebellen. Zum Spektrum politischer Feinde in Lebenslehren des Mittleren Reiches, in: H. Felber (ed.), Feinde und Aufrührer. Konzepte von Gegnerschaft in ägyptischen Texten besonders des Mittleren Reiches, AAWL 78.5, Stuttgart/Leipzig 2005, 74–85, especially 79; M. Omar, Aufrührer, Rebellen, Widersacher. Untersuchungen zum Wortfeld „Feind" im pharaonischen Ägypten. Ein lexikalisch-phraseologischer Beitrag, ÄUAT 74, Wiesbaden 2008, 134–137.

57 K. Zibelius-Chen, Politische Opposition im Alten Ägypten, in: SAK 17, 1990, 339–360, especially 345 (*rqw*); Quack, Demagogen, Aufrührer und Rebellen, 82 (*sbj*); Omar, Aufrührer, Rebellen, Widersacher, 100 (*rqw*), 199–200 (*sbj*).

58 For the evidence of political turbulences and rebellion in Egypt, see O. Kaper, Petubastis in the Dakhla Oasis: New Evidence about an Early Rebellion against Persian Rule and Its Suppression in Political Memory, in: J. M. Silverman/C. Waerzeggers (eds.), Political Memory in and after the Persian Empire, Ancient Near East Monographs 13, Atlanta 2015, 125–149; U. Z. Wijnsma, The Worst Revolt of the Bisitun Crisis: A Chronological Reconstruction of the Egyptian Revolt under Petubastis IV, in: JNES 77.2, 2018, 157–173.

59 Persia: C. L. Nimchuk, The "Archers" of Darius: Coinage or Tokens of Royal Esteem?, in: ArsOr 32, 2002, 55–79, especially 63–66; Egypt: O. Keel, Der Bogen als Herrschaftssymbol. Einige unveröffentlichte Skarabäen aus Ägypten und Israel zum Thema „Jagd und Krieg", in: O. Keel/M. Shuval/Ch. Uehlinger (eds.), Studien zu den Stempelsiegeln aus Palästina/Israel. Bd. III: Die Frühe Eisenzeit. Ein Workshop, OBO 100, Göttingen 1990, 27–65, 263–279.

3.4.3 The eulogy: part B (Tab. 4)

Transliteration	Structure	Translation
nzw nḫt ꜥꜣ bꜣ.w	Horus	The victorious king, great of might,
nb pḥ.tj mj Ḫn.tj-ḫm	Horus	lord of strength like the one who resides in Letopolis,
nb ꜥ(.w) dꜣr psḏ.t-pḏ.t		lord of activity, who crushes the nine bows,
ꜣḫ sḫ mꜥr sḫr.w		whose council is effective and whose plans succeed,
nb ḫpš ꜥq=f m ꜥšꜣ.t		master of his arm, when he rushes into battle,
stj r mḏd n whj.n šsr=f	Montu	shooting precisely, his arrow never missing its target,
pḥ.tj=f mj Mnṯ(w)	Montu	he whose strength is like that of Montu.

Tab. 4: The eulogy (B) – transliteration, structure and translation

The third part of the text is introduced by *nzw nḫt ꜥꜣ bꜣ.w* "the victorious king, great of might". This third part meets Egyptian traditions using common royal phraseology. In content it follows the previous part in unfolding the qualities of Darius to maintain power and dominion.

Framed by identification with Horus and Montu the basic characteristics of a victorious Egyptian king are presented. This follows directly on from part A2, where it is described how Darius is supported by the Egyptian gods who offer him the position and the means "that he may be effective in repelling those who rebel against him, to reduce his opponents in the Two Lands". At this point Darius becomes the main actor again. Now he actually is *nzw nḫt* "the victorious king",[60] who has fulfilled this task. The term *nḫt* is primarily connected with military power and leadership competence including the necessary physical and mental abilities to succeed.[61]

The topics addressed in this part are very similar to those in the first part (A1): physical and mental strength in connection with efficacy and activity. Furthermore, the topic concerning the bow is expanded. Now it is connected with the god Montu, who is also known as bowman (*pḏ.tj*).[62] While the rest of the text offers mainly generic epithets and set phrases of Egyptian royal and divine phraseology, the expression concerning competence as bowman represents a more individual character.[63]

The onion-like composition based on topics provides a variation according to section A1. The text offers a variety of textual references to the previous parts while at the same time it continues the sequential dynamic leading forward, in this case to the official royal titulary (part C).

60 Wb 2, 315.6.

61 Blöbaum, Herrscherlegitimation, 85–86.

62 LGG III, 185b; LGG VIII, 248.

63 A similar expression is not attested before the Ptolemaic Period, see Edfou VII, 144, 1–2.

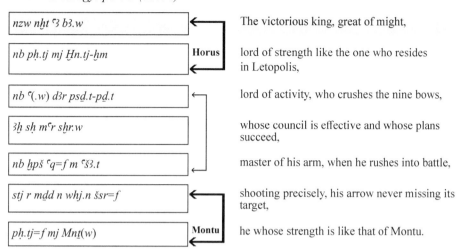

While the first part (A1) emphasises the *sḫm*-power part B focuses on the *bꜣ.w*-power. This marks a shift from a relatively concrete authority rooted in the real-world towards an unspecified numinous force strongly connected to Egyptian theology.[64] It is evident that Darius could not have achieved this force before he had been integrated into the Egyptian normative system and the cosmic order. I would claim that for the identification with Egyptian gods as well.

3.4.4 The eulogy: part C (Tab. 5)

The last part of the eulogy comprises an official protocol that presents a hybrid character interlacing elements of the Egyptian titulary with the Persian royal protocol, well known from other sources.[65]

	nzw bjt nb tꜣ.wj King of Upper and Lower Egypt, Lord of the Two Lands		
Darius	[(*Ntrjw*]*š*)|	*a-da-ma : da-a-ra-ya-va-u-ša*	I am Darius
	ꜥnḫ ḏ.t living forever		
the great one	*pꜣ ꜥꜣ*	*xa-ša-a-ya-θa-i-ya : va-za-ra-ka*	the great king
the great one of the great	*pꜣ wr n nꜣ wr.w*	*xa-ša-a-ya-θa-i-ya : xa-ša-a-ya-θa-i-ya-a-na-a-ma*	king of kings
		xa-ša-a-ya-θa-i-ya : da-ha-ya-u-na-a-ma	king of countries
the chief of the land […]	*pꜣ ḥr.j n pꜣ tꜣ* […]	*xa-ša-a-ya-θa-i-ya : a-ha-ya-a-ya-a : ba-u-ma-i-ya-a : va-za-ra-ka-a-ya-a*	king on this great earth
[son of] the god's father Hystaspes	[*zꜣ n*(*j*)] *jt*(*j*) *nṯr Wštsp*	*vi-i-ša-ta-a-sa-pa-ha-ya-a : pu-u-ça*	son of Hystaspes
an Achaemenid	*Jꜣḫmjnš*	*ha-xa-a-ma-na-i-ša-i-ya*	an Achaemenid
	ḫꜣ(*j*) *m nzw bjt ḥr s.t Ḥr.w n.t ꜥnḫ.w mj Rꜥw ḫn.tj nṯr.w ḏ.t* who has appeared as king of Upper and Lower Egypt on the Horus-throne of the living like Re, first of the gods, forever.		

Tab. 5: The eulogy (C) – transliteration, structure and translation

64 "(…) it may be said that *bꜣw* especially denotes all possible forms and manners by which some transcendental being by nature (such as a god or a dead person) or by role (like the king) can be imagined to make itself to the living my means of an certain event, not just by a characteristic, lasting, embodiment." (J. F. Borghouts, Divine Interventions in Ancient Egypt and its Manifestation [*bꜣw*]), in: R. J. Demarrée/J. J. Janssen, Gleanings from Deir el-Medîna, EU 1, Leiden 1982, 1–70; quote: 2); cf. Goebs, Crowns, 14–17; Blöbaum, Herrscherlegitimation, 89–91.

65 G. Ahn, Religiöse Herrscherlegitimation im Achämenidischen Iran. Die Voraussetzungen und die Struktur ihrer Argumentation, Acta Iranica 31, Leiden 1992, 309.

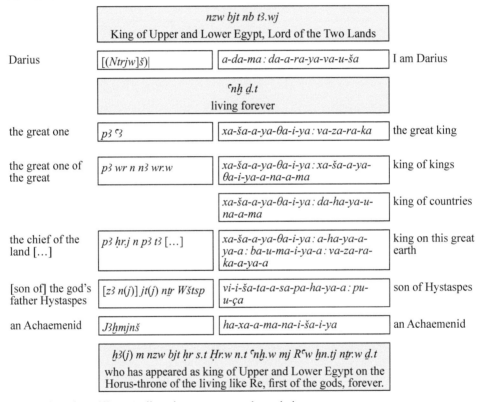

Table 5 gives an impression of the structure. On the right are the elements of the Persian protocol with translation, on the left the hybrid integrated into the Egyptian elements of the eulogy, which are highlighted in grey colour. These elements, the titles *nzw bjt nb tꜣ.wj* followed by the king's name in cartouche, a standard life formula (*ꜥnḫ ḏ.t*) and the closing formula (*ḫꜣ(j) m nzw bjt ḥr s.t Ḥr.w n.t ꜥnḫ.w mj Rꜥw ḫn.tj ntr.w ḏ.t*), provide a framework for a demotic translation of the Persian protocol transposed in hieroglyphs. The figure visualises how the Persian protocol was slightly modified. The title "king of countries" is not included, most probably because the Egyptian title *nb tꜣ.wj* might be judged as equivalent. The father of Darius – without any title in the Persian protocol – is described as *jt(j) nṯr* referring to his non-royal origin.[66] The addition of this title might well be the Egyptian equivalent of the name's indication without any (royal) titles in the cuneiform texts.[67] Interestingly, the translation of the Persian term *xa-ša-a-ya-θa-i-ya* "king" offers different Egyptian terms (*pꜣ ꜥꜣ, pꜣ wr, pꜣ ḥr.j*) well known from royal contexts, but never the word *nzw* that might be (at least in an Egyptological way of understanding) the most accurate translation. This is presumably because the translation was not made for monumental display in the first place, but refers to a demotic version probably originating from an administrative context.[68] However, the hybrid character of this special Egypto-Persian protocol displays the picture of the Persian king in his role as Egyptian pharaoh and therefore, completes the iconographical composition of the statue.

One last detail: An Egyptian standard royal eulogy begins in general with the complete royal protocol even though specific elements could resume in the end or structure throughout the text.[69] In this case – if the Egyptian royal titles on the belt do not stand for that – the eulogy tends towards the official protocol. In terms of context and the sophisticated structure of the text this is significant.

4 Conclusion

The eulogy (DSeg4) does not refer to the cuneiform text (DSab) but presents a kind of "narrative of transformation" of the conqueror Darius into the Egyptian (Egypto-Persian) king Darius (Fig. 7). The hero who takes action and who takes Egypt receives attention, legitimation and support by the Egyptian gods, which leads to a cultural integration of the foreigner into the Egyptian normative system and the cosmic order. Finally he is installed officially and on a legal basis as Persian king and pharaoh subsumed in the last sentence

---

66 „Daß hingegen Hystaspes, der Vater des Dareios, auf der Susa-Statue mit dem Titel ‚Gottesvater' versehen wird, ist nur als Rückgriff auf den alten – in der Spätzeit kaum noch üblichen Gebrauch dieser Bezeichnung als Titel des nichtköniglichen Vaters eines Herrschers erklärbar." (G. Vittmann, Ägypten und die Fremden im ersten vorchristlichen Jahrtausend, Kulturgeschichte der antiken Welt 97, Mainz 2003, 138); cf. Blöbaum, Herrscherlegitimation, 139–140 with n. 53.

67 Cf. Blöbaum, Der übersetzte Gott?, 22–24.

68 Yoyotte, La statue égyptienne de Darius, 254; Gozzoli, Writing of History, 120.

69 C. Maderna-Sieben, Ausgewählte Beispiele ramessidischer Königseulogien, in: R. Gundlach/ U. Rössler-Köhler (eds.), Das Königtum der Ramessidenzeit: Voraussetzungen – Verwirklichung – Vermächtnis. Akten des 3. Symposions zur ägyptischen Königsideologie in Bonn 7.–9. 6. 2001, ÄUAT 36,3. Wiesbaden 2003, 76–98, especially 80; A. Spalinger, New Kingdom Eulogies of Power: A Preliminary Analysis, in: N. Kloth/K. Martin/E. Pardey (eds.), Es werde niedergelegt als Schriftstück. Festschrift für Hartwig Altenmüller zum 65. Geburtstag, BSAK 9, Hamburg 2003, 415–428, especially 416.

"appeared as king of Upper and Lower Egypt on the Horus-throne of the living like Re, first of the gods, forever".

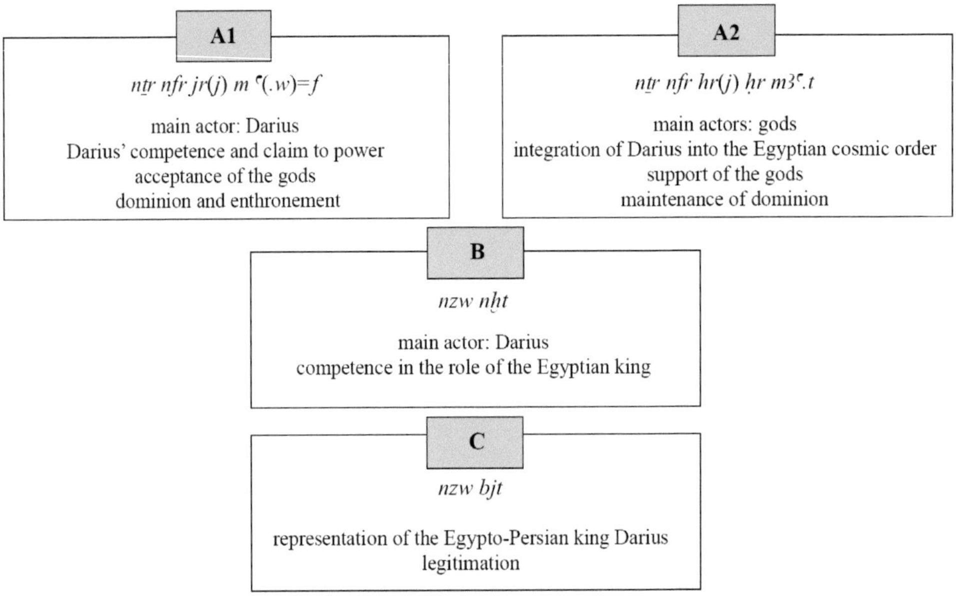

Fig. 7: The eulogy – a narrative of transformation

I conclude that deviation of the standard in this case might well be a significant part of the inscription's composition; a composition that creates distinct layers of meaning and reflects Egyptian royal ideology in a special adaptation for a foreign ruler.[70] Furthermore, almost all peculiarities emphasise Darius' claim to power. Following these deviations the text delivers not only a narrative of legitimation, transformation and integration, but also – even if culturally and theologically transposed into Egyptian speech – a strong focus on the nucleus of information given in the cuneiform: "The Persian man holds Egypt!"

Acknowledgements

For support and essential remarks on this paper, I would like to thank Ellen Rehm and Annik Wüthrich. Furthermore, I am indebted to Sofie Schiødt for kindly revising my English. Any remaining faults are exclusively my own responsibility.

70 A similar example although much more elaborate is the special adaptation of the Egyptian myth of the sun's eye as strategy of legitimation for Pi(anch)y and Taharqo, see A. Lohwasser/M. Becker/A. I. Blöbaum, Relationship between Religion and Politics in First Millennium BC Thebes: A Case Study on the Original Location of the Triumphal Stela of Piankhy, in: E. Pischikova/J. Budka/K. Griffin (eds.), Thebes in the First Millennium BC: Art and Archaeology of the Kushite Period and Beyond, GHP Egyptology 27, London 2018, 394–404; A. Lohwasser, Herrschaft und Heil – Macht und Mythos. Die politische und religiöse Legitimation der nubischen Pharaonen Pi(anch)y und Taharqo, in: M. Becker/A. I. Blöbaum/A. Lohwasser, Inszenierung von Herrschaft und Macht im ägyptischen Tempel: Religion und Politik im Theben des frühen 1. Jahrtausends v. Chr., ÄUAT 95, Münster, forthcoming.

Propaganda associated with the protective function of Ptolemaic rulers

Ewa Laskowska-Kusztal

Abstract

Research on the Ptolemaic sanctuary at Deir el-Bahari and remains of Ptolemaic temples on Elephantine and at Kalabsha resulted in a compilation of images reflecting the readiness shown by foreign rulers to remove dangers which might disturb the harmony of the primordial creation or law and order in the Egyptian state. In both domains, the sense of trust in the protection extended by the king was established by references to his connections with deified mortals who disposed of relevant favours, Imhotep together with Amenhotep son of Hapu, worshipped with the former at Thebes. In the region of the First Cataract, the official theology supported and the worshippers developed cults of protector gods, Arensnuphis, Thoth of Pnubs and, associated with them in this role, Mandulis, as well as the cult of the trinity that promoted the protective role of the ruler – Petempamentes, Petensetis and Petensenis. At the Ptolemaic sanctuary at Deir el-Bahari, visited during the Beautiful Feast of the Valley, rulers protection was associated with the renewal of the act of creation and widely understood cult of ancestors, including the cult of gods termed *S3w.n.sn*.

The religious policy of the Ptolemies included elements which were associated with their intention to convince the inhabitants of Egypt to accept foreign rulers, in particular, the emphasis on their protective functions.

It was a notable enrichment of the definition of the ruler, sanctioned by Egyptian religion, as the one who guarantees the universal order *maat*, on one hand, by his participation in the rituals performed at Egyptian temples, on the other hand, by identification with the divine heir, associated with the *mammisi* ideology, which ensured the perpetuation of the established order by the sequence of generations.

A theological *novum* should be mentioned in the analysis of the protection extended by the Ptolemies over both the universal order and individual well-being. It involved the addition of the royal cult to the Egyptian ideology connected with the ruler, which was inspired by the Greek dynastic cult. During the reign of Ptolemy II it included the ruler and his deceased spouse, and from the reign of Ptolemy III it was expanded to include the royal ancestors.[1] This phenomenon was reflected in the addition of new beneficiaries of the rituals in the

1 J. Quaegebeur, The Egyptian Clergy and the Cult of the Ptolemaic Dynasty, in: AncSoc 20, 1989, 93–116, here: 95–96.

decorations of temples – royal ancestors and the ruling king.[2] The theological concept of this cult, recorded in the scenes added to decoration programmes of Egyptian temples, which focuses on the subject of passing on and sanctioning the divine royal power, is not questioned. Nevertheless, it is essential to distinguish it from individual cults of Ptolemaic queens and from royal cults from the past, inspired by merits of some rulers.[3]

The spread of the royal cult was ensured by the obligation defined in royal decrees, which involved the placement of royal statues in major Egyptian temples. Thus they made it possible for the rulers to participate in the liturgy and, in the form of portable statues, in the rituals traditionally associated with the processional issuing from the temple.[4]

It is difficult to define the perception of this new royal cult by the worshippers or the image of rulers as grantors of favours. It should be considered whether the perception of the divine nature of the ruler, resulting from the divine nature of the royal power, could have been a common phenomenon, or perhaps they were regarded as protectors of the people – intermediaries between gods and people, comparable in their function of intermediaries to Egyptian saints.

The Theban Beautiful Feast of the Valley seems an inspiring element of this discussion, together with the connections of the Ptolemaic sanctuary located at Deir el-Bahari with this festival. The sanctuary in question continued the tradition of Deir el-Bahari temples in the New Kingdom.[5] It is necessary to emphasise the perception of this feast and its rituals by

2 E. Winter, Der Herrscherkult in den ägyptischen Ptolemäertempeln, in: H. Maehler/V. M. Strocka (eds.), Das ptolemäische Ägypten. Akten des internationalen Symposions 27.–29. September 1976 in Berlin, Mainz am Rhein 1976, 147–160; cf. recently R. Preys, Roi vivant et roi ancêtres. Iconographie et ideologie royale sous les Ptolémées, in: C. Zivie-Coche (ed.), Offrandes, rites et rituels dans les temples d'époques ptolémaïque et romaine, CENiM 10, 2015, 149–184; R. Preys, Les scènes du culte royal à Edfou. Pour une étude diachronique des scènes rituelles des temples de l'époque gréco-romaine, in: S. Baumann/H. Kockelmann/E. Jambon (eds.), Der ägyptische Tempel als ritueller Raum. Theologie und Kult in ihrer architektonischen und ideellen Dimension, Akten der internationalen Tagung, Haus der Heidelberger Akademie der Wissenschaften, 9.–12. Juni 2015, Studien zur spätägyptischen Religion 17, Wiesbaden 2017, 389–418.

3 It is certain that the introduction of the Egyptian royal cult and the cult of queens was carried out with full understanding of the difference from deification resulting from their merits and services delivered in their lifetime. This was reflected in the visit paid by Ptolemy II and Arsinoe, who was still alive at that time, to the oracle at Diospolis Parva, an event commemorated by Ptolemy III. This visit raised the deification of a local mortal, who was made into a wife of Neferhotep and identified with Isis, to an official level. It was interpreted as a propaganda event to sanction, by analogy, the cult of Arsinoe II in Egypt, M. Drew-Bear, Arsinoé II Philadelphe: Le passage du trône à l'autel selon des sources égyptiennes, in: L. Gabolde (ed.), Hommages à Jean-Claude Goyon offerts pour son 70e anniversaire, BdE 143, Cairo 2008, 115–121.

4 KO 597; G. Hölbl, A History of the Ptolemaic Empire, London/New York 2001, 88: "The statue cult involves the worship of the divine forces of the king, especially the royal Ka, but not of the king represented as a person…", and 105–111. Cf. also F. Daumas, Les moyens d'expression du grec et de l'égyptien comparés dans les décrets de Canope et de Memphis, CASAE 16, Cairo 1952, 175–176; E. Lanciers, Die ägyptischen Priester des ptolemäischen Königskultes, in: RdE 42, 1991, 117–145, here: 141; Quaegebeur, AncSoc 20, 1989, 102–103.

5 N. Strudwick, Some aspects of the archaeology of the Theban necropolis in the Ptolemaic and Roman periods, in: N. Strudwick/J. H. Taylor (eds.). The Theban Necropolis. Past, Present and Future, London 2003, 167–188, here: 174, 182–183; E. Laskowska-Kusztal, "Le sanctuaire ptolémaïque de Deir el-Bahari". Addendum, in: D. Dzierzbicka/S. Rzepka/A. Wodzińska (eds.), Coffins, Tombs and Beyond…Essays in Honour of Andrzej Niwiński, Warsaw 2019, in press.

generations of worshippers, until the Roman Period, as assistance for eternal life of the mortals buried at the Theban necropolis. The changes which appeared in the rituals of the Beautiful Feast of the Valley after mortuary temples, the main venue for the celebration, ceased to be built at Thebes did not erase the enduring memory concerning the theological message of the festival, which focused on the act of eternal renewal of the existing order, a guarantee of its perpetuation. It was reflected in the location of private tombs along the processional route of the Beautiful Feast of the Valley, chronologically extending to the Ptolemaic-Roman Period.[6] The deceased buried there still remained the beneficiaries of the rituals, with gods and the ruler participating in the procession.[7]

Fig. 1: Temple of Hatshepsut at Deir el-Bahari. Main room of the Ptolemaic sanctuary (photo: W. Jerke)

Research on the late form of the feast and the route of the procession heading for Djeme highlights the fact that under the Ptolemies this route incorporated the sanctuary at Deir el-Bahari, dedicated to Amenhotep son of Hapu, and Imhotep.

The sanctuary at Deir el-Bahari is situated on the third terrace of the temple of Hatshepsut and according to sources, it functioned from the beginning of the reign of the Ptolemies until the Roman Period.[8] The decoration of the main room of the sanctuary was made during the reign of Ptolemy VIII Euergetes II (Fig. 1).

This decoration programme is unique and atypical in comparison with other places of cult. The west wall with the false door and offering formula is connected with the cult of both wise men, who were deified mortals.[9] The north and south walls depict references to their earthly lives, family relations, connections with the world of gods and their charitable activity.[10]

6 Strudwick, Some aspects of the archaeology, 167–188; Laskowska-Kusztal, "Le sanctuaire ptolémaïque". Addendum, in press.

7 Personal participation of the king in the festival could be regarded as sporadic, W. Clarysse, The Ptolemies Visiting the Egyptian Chora, in: L. Mooren (ed.), Politics, Administration and Society in the Hellenistic and Roman World. Proceedings of the International Colloquium, Bertinoro 19–24 July 1997, Stud.Hellen. 36, Leuven 2000, 29–53; A. Cabrol, Les voies processionnelles de Thèbes, OLA 97, Leuven 2001, 744–746.

8 E. Laskowska-Kusztal, Deir el-Bahari III, Le sanctuire ptolémaïque de Deir el-Bahari, Warsaw 1984, 64–69; A. Łajtar, Deir el-Bahari in the Hellenistic and Roman Periods. A Study of an Egyptian Temple Based on Greek Sources, JJP Supplement IV, Warsaw 2006, 36–37, 94–102.

9 Laskowska-Kusztal, Deir el-Bahari III, 27–35.

10 Laskowska-Kusztal, Deir el-Bahari III, 36–54.

The similarity in the location of the wise men and the ruler with regards to the symbolic representations of divine Thebes, whose function was to distribute divine favours, is striking (Figs. 2, 3).

Fig. 2: Ptolemaic sanctuary. North wall (according E. LASKOWSKA-KUSZTAL, Deir el-Bahari III, pls. VI, VII, drawing: E. LASKOWSKA-KUSZTAL)

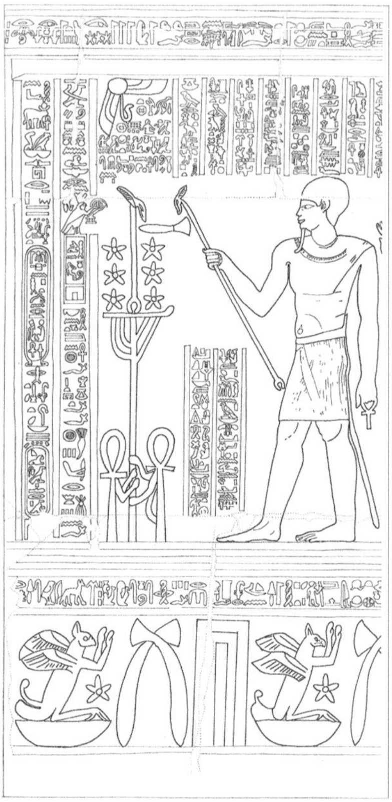

Fig. 3: Ptolemaic sanctuary. South wall (according E. LASKOWSKA-KUSZTAL, Deir el-Bahari III, pls. X, XI, drawing: E. LASKOWSKA-KUSZTAL)

The research on this sanctuary, conducted years later and considering new facts, contributes to the expansion of the existing interpretation. It directs attention to the invocation to Amun from *Ḏsr-st*, situated on the west wall (gable wall), which recalls the mortal nature of the two wise men.[11] It reinforces the theological significance of the group of Djaisu, incorporated in the decoration programme, constituting the causative elements of the primordial creation.[12] Both elements seem to connect the sanctuary with the act of renewal of the original work of creation and theology of Djeme, where the procession of the Beautiful Feast of the Valley headed. The relations with the theology of Djeme remain in harmony with the benevolent

11 LASKOWSKA-KUSZTAL, Deir el-Bahari III, 29–30; LASKOWSKA-KUSZTAL, "Le sanctuaire ptolémaïque". Addendum, in press.

12 LASKOWSKA-KUSZTAL, Deir el-Bahari III, 31, 35; D. MENDEL, Die kosmogonischen Inschiften in der Barkenkapelle des Chonstempels von Karnak, MRE 9, Turnhout 2003, 18–19, 116–120, 156, 178; LASKOWSKA-KUSZTAL, "Le sanctuaire ptolémaïque". Addendum, in press.

and healing activity of the two wise men, always interpreted as the work of revival of the disturbed primordial order.[13]

The composition of the decoration and the mutual location of Amenhotep son of Hapu, Imhotep and the ruler in relation to the beneficiaries of favours imply identification of the king as the wise men's partner in the act of renewal. The king offers sacrifice to the deceased gods, kings and mortals who live in the heavenly city with the stars.[14] The wise men apply for mediation of the same inhabitants of heaven to beg for favours for the ruling king as well as the living and dead inhabitants of Thebes.[15]

Looking for inspiration for the definition of the function of the king, Imhotep's epithet from the west wall, "miraculous revelation of *S3w.n.sn* gods" (*bj3jt nt S3w.n.sn*), should be referred to (Fig. 4). It can also be found associated the same person at the temple at Deir el-Medineh as well as temples of Ptah and Amun at Karnak.[16] Together with this epithet, we enter the complex issue of the so-called *Dieux-gardiens*, discussed in Jean-Claude Goyon's monograph.[17] We face diverse divine personalities described with this term, and this group incorporates divine ancestors, who participate in the act of creation, and gods – guards of the original order.[18] The array of diverse deities associated with this term suggests that it generally covered all categories of deities which provided assistance for the act of creation or participated in it, and their permanent presence ensured the perpetuation of the primordial order.[19] The wide range of personalities and detailed functions of these divine ancestors seems to explain the wide coverage of the term *S3w.n.sn* and the absence of a necessity to associate their protection with a definite object.[20]

Fig. 4: Ptolemaic sanctuary. West wall (according E. Laskowska-Kusztal, Deir el-Bahari III, pl. V, drawing: E. Laskowska-Kusztal)

13 Laskowska-Kusztal, Deir el-Bahari III, 111–112; Laskowska-Kusztal, "Le sanctuaire ptolémaïque". Addendum, in press.

14 Laskowska-Kusztal, Deir el-Bahari III, 55–56.

15 Laskowska-Kusztal, Deir el-Bahari III, 37, 46, 47.

16 Laskowska-Kusztal, Deir el-Bahari III, 33. See also D. Wildung, Imhotep und Amenhotep, Gottwerdung im alten Ägypten, MÄS 36, München/Berlin 1977, 202, 215, 218 and his translation "wunderbare Erscheinung der Götter".

17 J.-Cl. Goyon, Les dieux-gardiens et la genèse des temples d'après les textes égyptiens de l'époque gréco-romaine I, BdE 93, Cairo 1985, 449–496.

18 LGG VI, 126–127: *S3w-n.sn* "Deren Eigenschaft der Schutz ist".

19 E. A. E. Reymond, Worship of the Ancestor Gods at Edfu, in: CdE 38, 1963, 49–70, especially 57–59. Cf. also S. Cauville's commentary illustrating the discussion, S. Cauville, Les inscriptions dédicatoires du temple d'Hathor à Dendera, in: BIFAO 90, 1990, 83–114, here: 100.

20 On the language structure of this term see D. Kurth, Einführung ins Ptolemäische. Eine Grammatik mit Übungsstücken. Teil 2, Hützel 2008, 655–656, note 13; D. Kurth, Wo Götter, Menschen und Tote

In the case of Imhotep, it can also be supposed that it is an allusion to his activity devoted to the restoration of the primordial harmony with regards to the repetition of the act of creation and its protection, which might have been performed by the deities described as *S3w.n.sn*. In the case of the sanctuary at Deir el-Bahari the identity of the *S3w.n.sn* gods mentioned in Imhotep's epithet, was defined by another epithet referring to that saint calling him "excellent god beside the Ogdoad" (*nṯr ỉḳr r-gs Ḫmnjw*) (Fig. 4).[21] Thus it is another allusion to Djeme by reference to the most essential ancestor group in Thebes – the Ogdoad, who took part in the act of the primordial creation and rests at the Theban necropolis.[22] It is crucial for the functioning of the sanctuary as a healing centre and oracle, as well as a place visited by the procession of the Beautiful Feast of the Valley, to define the period of the work of the Ogdoad as the time of *maat*, and to associate it with the legitimisation of the royal power of the god Ra, in whose creation it participated.[23]

The term *S3w.n.sn*, this time understood as a general name for ancestors, is referred to again at the sanctuary at Deir el-Bahari, in the text from the lower frieze situated on the north wall, where they are called companions of the inhabitants of heavenly Thebes (*njwtjw dj šmsw S3w.n.sn*) (Fig. 2).[24] The offering made by the royal couple for these inhabitants, who at the same time are inhabitants of the Theban necropolis, is described in a text from the east wall of the sanctuary.[25] In this case, it could suggested that the mutual connections of both groups result from the fact that the inhabitants of heavenly Thebes and *S3w.n.sn* deities might be incorporated in the group of ancestors, which implies their relations with the original act of creation.

Considering the message connected with the general significance of ancestors for preservation of continuity of the original *status quo*, we should pay attention to the ruler, present at the sanctuary, and connections with gods defined with the term *S3w.n.sn*, deified Ptolemaic ancestors.[26] The ideological message of the royal cult with the presence of the currently ruling king in decoration scenes should also be reminded. It indicates that the legality of the rule, taken over from deified ancestors, which ensured the order in the country, is incorporated in the work of the creator god and the creative powers of the primordial gods.[27]

---

lebten. Eine Studie zum Weltbild der Alten Ägypter, QUIA 3, Hützel 2016, 158–160. I would like to thank Dieter Kurth for referring me to this valuable comment.

21 Laskowska-Kusztal, Deir el-Bahari III, 33–34.

22 Ch. Zivie-Coche, L'Ogdoade à Thèbes à l'époque ptolémaïque et ses antécédents, in: Ch. Thiers (ed.), Documents de Théologies Thébaines Tardives, CENiM 3, Montpellier 2009, 168–225, especially 200, 205.

23 Zivie-Coche, L'Ogdoade à Thèbes, 200, 203.

24 Laskowska-Kusztal, Deir el-Bahari III, 44–45; Goyon, Les dieux-gardiens, 468, 495.

25 Laskowska-Kusztal, Deir el-Bahari III, 55–56.

26 Winter, Der Herrscherkult, 152. It could be supposed that the connection of the royal ancestors with the work of renewal and protection of the primordial creation was also a reason for references to the royal ancestors in texts associated with votive mummies of Sokar-Osiris, which symbolised regeneration and afterlife, prepared for the rituals of the Khoiak festival. M. Minas, Die ptolemäischen Sokar-Osiris-Mumien. Neue Erkenntnisse zum ägyptischen Dynastiekult der Ptolemäer, in: MDAIK 62, 2006, 197–213. It would be an analogy to the function of the Ogdoad, who assisted, together with Thoth and Tatenen, the resurrection of Osiris in the scene from the temple of Opet, Opet I, 118–121; Opet II, pl. 4; Zivie-Coche, L'Ogdoade à Thèbes, 181, 192.

27 Preys, Les scènes du culte royal, 415–416.

Summing up the discussion of the ideological message of the decoration of the sanctuary at Deir el-Bahari, it seems that it reflects the propaganda of the image of the ruler who by offering sacrifice to ancestors buried at the Theban necropolis functions as a partner for Imhotep and Amenhotep son of Hapu, in the restoration and protection of the primordial order. This cooperation could be associated with the Ptolemaic concept of connecting rulers through their own deified ancestors with the group of divine ancestors, *S3w.n.sn,* endowed with a wide range of competences which serve the protection of the original order, which also involves the protection of the perpetuation of the royal power. This particular nature of the royal function, recorded in the decoration programme of the sanctuary, could also be connected with the function of the place as a stopover for the procession of the Beautiful Feast of the Valley on its way to Djeme.

The incorporation of the king and his ancestors with the royal cult, as well as the participation of his statues in the processional festivals, including the Beautiful Feast of the Valley, draws attention to Polyaratos's octracon from the reign of Ptolemy II. This text implies the healing activity of Amenhotep son of Hapu, and of associated gods, who are tentatively connected with *synnaoi theoi* by Adam Łajtar, the author of a monograph devoted to Greek inscriptions left by pilgrims at the sanctuary.[28] This association seems worth attention due to the absence of evidence for the presence of other gods, and even of Imhotep, in the early activity of the oracle at Deir el-Bahari. Taking the early chronology of Polyaratos's ostracon into consideration, it could not have referred to the royal ancestors, termed *synnaoi theoi,* since their cult, which should be combined with the cult of the ruling king, was introduced by the decree of Canopus during the reign of Ptolemy III Euergetes.[29]

We should not reject the suggestion that the text from the ostracon in question was a reference to the sacrifice offered to ancestors, inhabitants of the Theban necropolis – gods, deceased kings and ordinary mortals in the course of the procession of the Beautiful Feast of the Valley. This sacrifice was offered by the *choachytes*, who participated in the procession in the presence of the ruler, represented by his statue.[30] These offerings might have been referred to by the aforementioned text from the east wall of the sanctuary, which mentioned the sacrifice made by the royal couple for the inhabitants of the heavenly city.[31]

To conclude, it should be stated that the sanctuary at Deir-el-Bahari, with its clear connection with the ideology of Djeme, which also included the royal cult,[32] could also be perceived as the propaganda of the participation of the king in the protection of the primordial universal order. The royal participation in this act is shown to the public at the sanctuary at Deir el-Bahari, due to its accessibility and interest of the society in the activity of the place of cult, both among Egyptians and Greeks.

The application of the term *S3w.n.sn* to groups of primordial gods, and groups of guard gods[33], draws attention to the relations of the latter with emanations of the demiurge described

---

28 Łajtar, Deir el-Bahari in the Hellenistic and Roman Periods, 23–26, 396–399.

29 Cf. supra and note 1.

30 F. M. H. Haikal, Two Hieratic Funerary Papyri of Nesmin, BAe XIV, Bruxelles 1970, 15–17; Laskowska-Kusztal, "Le sanctuaire ptolémaïque". Addendum, in press.

31 Laskowska-Kusztal, Deir el-Bahari III, 55–56.

32 On the connection of the royal cult with the rituals of Djeme cf. Preys, Les scènes du culte royal, 408.

33 LGG VI, 126–127.

by Goyon.[34] This element of creation, which constitutes a part of their nature, explains their function of guards who repel evil forces which disturb the primordial order. Such combination of the creative potential with the qualities of guard gods seems to be an important element of the personality of gods with protective functions.

The inclusion of the ruler in the double protection of the universal order, defined the official religious policy and the religious propaganda, which shaped the image of the king in the eyes of the worshippers. From this perspective, *i.e.* due to the perception of the ruler as the protector of the Egyptian order, we can realise the significance of the development of the official cult of Imhotep in the Theban area, association of this cult with the local cult of Amenhotep son of Hapu, and what is most important, the theological concept of correspondence between Imhotep's activity and the function of *S3w.n.sn*. The latter, which connects him with the primordial act of creation, contributes new elements in the perception of the cult of Imhotep in the area of the Cataract.[35] What should be emphasised is the easy and justified implementation of the cult of Imhotep in this area, accounted for by his connections with Memphis and the function of his father, Ptah, as the legislator of the royal power, as well as family relations with creator gods. His filial relations with the Memphite Ptah and Khnum-Tatenen from Elephantine, identified with the primordial ocean – the place of birth for the Nile waters, enriched the range of the benevolent functions of the wise man, which served for the restoration of the primordial order, by including effective assistance in the renewal of the correct Nile flooding.[36] In this context, the hypothesis which related the dedication of a temple on Philae to Imhotep by Ptolemy V as a sign of his gratitude for the birth of a son, together with thanks for the Nile flooding, with which the royal heir was identified, appears to be strongly justified.[37]

The mission of the protection of the primordial order can be analysed from the point of view of the theological situation of *S3w.n.sn*, *i.e.* fusion of the primordial creation and its protection. This draws attention to the identification of Imhotep with the god Tutu, observed in the region of the Cataract and attested, among others, by the proper name Tutu-Imhotep. The source of this identification is indicated in the causative power of both gods with regards to the Nile flooding.[38] This combined function could be expanded by following the manner of interpretation suggested at the sanctuary at Deir el-Bahari – by indicating correspondence between the restoration of the original *status quo* by Imhotep, the son of the creator god Ptah-Tatenen, to the act of creation performed by Neith with her son, the solar god Tutu, whose birth gives rise to the new life.[39] The fact that Tutu is not just an element of creation, but above all its protector[40], makes him the agent combining the idea of restoration of the

34 Goyon, Les dieux-gardiens, XII, 115, 401.

35 Wildung, Imhotep und Amenhotep, 149–184; S. H. Aufrère, Imhotep et Djoser dans la région de la cataracte. De Memphis à Éléphantine, in: BIFAO 104, 2004, 1–20.

36 This aspect of Imhotep's activity, *i.e.* preservation of the primordial order, is associated with his epithet, which calls him the venerable image (*sḫm šps*) of Khnum from Elephantine, which resembles the Theban epithet *bj3jt nt S3w.n.sn* in its ideological significance, Wildung, Imhotep und Amenhotep, 157, 161, 168, 205.

37 Wildung, Imhotep und Amenhotep, 154–156.

38 O. E. Kaper, The Egyptian God Tutu. A study of the Sphinx-God and Master of Demons with a Corpus of Monuments, OLA 119, Leuven 2003, 116–117.

39 Kaper, The Egyptian God Tutu, 66–67.

40 Kaper, The Egyptian God Tutu, 54–58.

primordial order with its protection.

The concept of combining the two aspects of the protection of the universal order was depicted in two cycles of scenes flanking the entrance to the sanctuary of the *mammisi* on Philae.[41] In the scenes situated in the eastern part, Thoth of Pnubs and Imhotep are the beneficiaries of the sacrifice, while in the western part – Arensnuphis and the god Tutu. This fusion of the repetition of the act of creation and its protection can also be found in theological personalities of Arensnuphis and Thoth of Pnubs. As we recognise the warrior nature in Arensnuphis and Thoth of Pnubs[42], we should also consider two other aspects of their personalities, which reflect their participation in the restoration (not only protection) of the primordial order. One of these aspects involves their function of Onuris, *i.e.* the participation of both gods in bringing the Distant Goddess to Egypt.[43] She is identified with the returning Nile flooding and ensures the rebirth of nature and well-being of the country. The other aspect is the share of the two gods in the act of creation, different for each of them. In the case of Arensnuphis, his early identification with Khnum from Elephantine must be remembered.[44] As far as Thoth of Pnubs is concerned, this trait of his personality is inspired by his identification with Thoth from Hermopolis.[45]

As indicated by artefacts from the area of the First Cataract, the cult of these gods, which secured the interests of the country and was promoted by the king, authorised the worshippers to benefit from their protection. The chapel of Mandulis at Kalabsha, bearing cartouches of Ptolemy IX Soter II, which appeared together with the temple of Mandulis erected by this king, was an important illustration of divine protection organised by the state, secured by the repetitive nature of the creation and its protection.[46] While the decoration of the naos of the temple reflects the difficulty with the location of the foreign god with his attributed solar and lunar nature in the Egyptian pantheon, the chapel has a clear propaganda message. In the decoration of its main wall (gable wall), the only one which was finished, Mandulis is depicted accompanied by Arensnuphis and Thoth of Pnubs, deities of the First Cataract, both of whom are present in another two scenes (Fig. 5).[47] The texts found next to Mandulis emphasise his nature of *pantocrator*, the lord of heavens, air, waters of the primordial ocean Nun, deserts, the god who appears in the east of the primordial ocean, and at the same time, they contain the epithet "the lord of power (*nb pḥtj*)", indicating his nature of a warrior deity.

41 Philae II, 68–69.

42 D. Inconnu-Bocquillon, Thot de Pnoubs (la ville) ou Thot du Nébès (l'arbre), in: RdE 39, 1988, 47–62, here: 54; E. Laskowska-Kusztal, Arensnouphis sur une stèle d'Eléphantine, in: ET XIX, 2001, 135–144; LGG VIII, 107 H., 729 H.1., M.2.,730 M.3.,4.

43 D. Inconnu-Bocquillon, Le mythe de la Déesse Lointaine à Philae, BdE 132, Cairo 2001, 158–166, 171, 194–195; 333–334; Inconnu-Bocquillon, RdE 39, 1988, 52–53; LGG VIII, 107 B.3., M.10., P.1., 108 R.9., 730 M.10., P.1., R.9.

44 H. de Meulenaere, Derechef Arensnouphis, in: CdE 52, 1977, 245–251; E. Lanciers, The Cult of Arensnuphis in Thebes in the Graeco-Roman Period, in: SAK 45, 2016, 187–216, here: 207–209.

45 Inconnu-Bocquillon, RdE 39, 1988, 51–52.

46 H. de Meulenaere/M. Dewachter, La chapelle ptolémaïque de Kalabcha, Fascicules 1 et 2, CEDAE, Cairo 1964–1970; E. Laskowska-Kusztal, Relations between the cult centre of Mandulis at Kalabsha and the religious centres on Elephantine and Philae, in: M. Dolińska/H. Beinlich (eds.), 8. Ägyptologische Tempeltagung: Interconnections between Temples, KSG 3,3, Wiesbaden 2010, 111–122, especially 112, 114–115.

47 de Meulenaere/Dewachter, La chapelle ptolémaïque, pl. XXXII.

Particular analogies to these two personalities of Mandulis can be found in the texts referring to personalities of Arensnuphis and Thoth of Pnubs, which seem to inspire the newly formed personality of the foreign god Mandulis. Arensnuphis is represented as the lord of heaven and gods, creator of the earth, directing the waters of Nun, which should be associated with the waters of the Nile flooding in this case.[48] Thoth of Pnubs is also characterised by the double nature, and his warrior personality, described with the epithets "strong, great with power" (*ḳnj ꜥꜣ pḥtj*), should be connected with the personality of Thoth from Hermopolis, with skilled tongue (*spd ns*), a participant in the act of creation.[49]

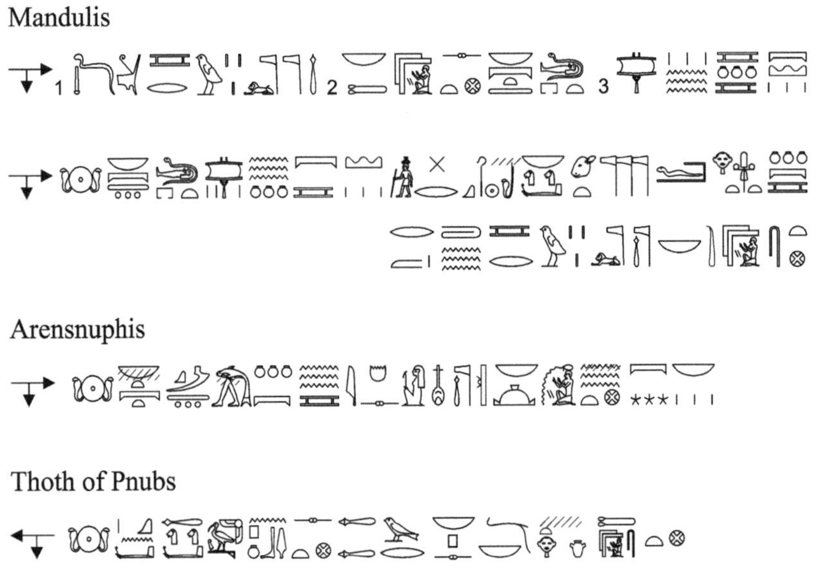

Fig. 5: Ptolemaic sanctuary in Kalabsha. Texts associated with Mandulis, Arensnuphis and Thoth of Pnubs (according H. DE MEULENAERE/M. DEWACHTER, La chapelle ptolémaïque de Kalabcha, Cairo 1964–1970, pl. XXXII)

The fact that the chapel was not dismantled under Augustus and functioned side by side with a new Roman temple might prove that it was a venue of a popular cult, visited by worshippers, who found familiar protective deities there, known from Philae and Elephantine. The significance of the rooted cult of these protector gods is emphasised by the presence of their images in the Roman gate of the sanctuary of the temple of Osiris Nesmeti on Elephantine (Figs. 6, 7). They are placed in symmetric scenes on both sides of the entrance opening, and guard the entrance to the holiest part of the temple.[50] Another important issue

48 LGG VIII, 107 A.1., 7., D.1., E.2.

49 LGG VIII, 719 E.1., 725 R.9.; P. BOYLAN, Thoth the Hermes of Egypt, Chicago 1979, 107–123. It should be noted that under Ptolemy VIII Euergetes II the god Thoth, compiling annals in the scenes of the royal cult from the temple at Edfu, is represented as the primordial divine creator in such scenes for the first time, PREYS, Les scènes du culte royal, 403–404.

50 For more information on the protection of places of cult and access to these places cf. H. KOCKELMANN, Apotropäische Texte und Bilder der Türdekoration in den griechisch-römischen Tempeln Ägyptens. Zum Schutz des Kultbaus und seiner Räume, in: S. BAUMANN/H. KOCKELMANN/E. JAMBON (eds.), Der ägyptische Tempel als ritueller Raum. Theologie und Kult in ihrer architektonischen und ideellen

is the presence of Satet and Anuket in the neighbouring registers, which reminds us of the identification of each of the two goddesses with the Distant Goddess. It seems to suggest that the protective functions performed by Arensnuphis and Thoth should be combined with their function of associates of the Distant Goddess, contributing to the act of renewal of nature.

Fig. 6: Temple of Osiris Nesmeti at Elephantine. Nero gate, south jamb (drawing: E. LASKOWSKA-KUSZTAL)

Fig. 7: Temple of Osiris Nesmeti at Elephantine. Nero gate, north jamb (drawing: E. LASKOWSKA-KUSZTAL)

The terrace of the temple of Khnum on Elephantine accommodates a place of cult of protector gods accessible for the worshippers. Naoses found with stelae located inside, where the worshippers gathered, confirm a popular cult of Arensnuphis and Petempamentes.[51] Gihane ZAKI made an important comment concerning Arensnuphis worshipped on the terrace of the temple of Khnum. She connected the emphasis on the warrior aspect of the god, who

Dimension, Akten der internationalen Tagung, Haus der Heidelberger Akademie der Wissenschaften, 9.–12. Juni 2015, Studien zur spätägyptischen Religion 17, Wiesbaden 2017, 177–196.

51 H. JARITZ, Elephantine III. Die Terrassen vor den Tempeln des Chnum und der Satet, AV 32, Mainz am Rhein 1980, 26–30; E. LASKOWSKA-KUSZTAL, Petempamentes, Petensetis, Petensenis – their Portraits on Elephantine, in: ET XXVII, 2014, 217–231, here: 223.

endowed the king with the power to defeat foreign countries, with the promotion of the saving power of the pharaoh, who protected the country from the invasion from the south.[52]

Eddy Lanciers analysed the popular cult of Arensnuphis worshipped by the *choachytes* living at Djeme. It is a rare case in the religious life of Egypt, which has no confirmation in the official cult developed in the area of Thebes.[53] Neither is it connected with similar mechanisms of human migration as in the case of the cult of Anuket at Deir-el-Medineh.[54] The presence of this cult in Thebes was reflected in the hymn dedicated to the god, which comes from the reign of Tiberius and was found at the temple of Arensnuphis on Philae, who is identified with Amun-Min.[55] The connections of this cult with the priests from Djeme, confronted with his function of the guard of Osiris resting at Abaton on Biggeh, suggest he should be treated as the Theban guardian of Osiris resting at Abaton at Djeme, as well as an officiator of the liturgy performed at Djeme, like Horus.[56] It seems that this line of interpretation of the personality of Theban Arensnuphis could be expanded by inclusion of his identification with Amun-Min, expressed in the hymn from Philae. When the personality of the god Min is considered, one of his hypostases comes to mind – Min the warrior and protector, identified with Horus, the protector of Abaton, and by identification with Horus, was also identified with the god Amenope, the main officiator of the decadal rituals, performed at the holy necropolis at Djeme and perpetuating the renewal of the act of creation.[57] The mention of the god Amenope among the Theban connections of Arensnuphis seems important due to the protection of extended by Amenope over the association of *choachytes*.[58] It is possible that the dominant traits of Min, represented in the iconography of the ithyphallic deity, or the ithyphallic or amorphous form of Amenope, present in the official religion,[59] did not favour the establishment of a local popular cult of these gods. It did not contribute to the formation of the cult of a protector god, worshipped by people on similar terms as the gods from the terrace of the temple of Khnum on Elephantine, which generated the necessity to apply for protection to a god from another region of Egypt, who had already been well-established.[60] Nevertheless, it should be noted that the emphasis on Arensnuphis's connections with Thebes, recorded in the hymn from Philae and drafted by the local priests, thus representing an official cult, might suggest an intervention of the priests from the region of the Cataract in the transfer of the cult of Arensnuphis to West Thebes.

52 G. Zaki, Le Premier Nome de Haute-Égypte du IIIe siècle avant J.-C. au VIIe siècle après J.-C. d'après les sources hiéroglyphiques des temples ptolémaïques et romains, MRE 13, Turnhout 2009, 248–249.

53 Lanciers, SAK 45, 2016, 194–216.

54 D. Valbelle, Satis et Anoukis, SDAIK 8, Mainz am Rhein 1981, 125–126; Lanciers, SAK 45, 2016, 210.

55 G. Daressy, Légende d'Ar-hems-nefer à Philae, in: ASAE 17, 1917, 76–80; Inconnu-Bocquillon, Le mythe de la Déesse Lointaine, 98–99, 167–170.

56 Lanciers, SAK 45, 2016, 211–213.

57 S. H. Aufrère, Le propylône d'Amon-Rê-Montou à Karnak-Nord, MIFAO 117, Cairo 2000, 271–283, 344–350.

58 F. de Cenival, Les associations religieuses en Égypte d'après les documents démotiques, BdE 46, Cairo 1972, 111–112.

59 Aufrère, Le propylône d'Amon-Rê-Montou, figs. 44, 59; M. Doresse, Le dieu voilé dans sa châsse et la fête du début de la décade I., in: RdE 23, 1971, 113–136; M. Doresse, Le dieu voilé dans sa châsse et la fête du début e la décade (suite), in: RdE 25, 1973, 92–135, here: 109–115.

60 Lanciers, SAK 45, 2016, 206–209.

The presence of the cult of Arensnuphis and Petempamentes on the terrace of the temple of Khnum brings to mind the personal commitment of the king to the protection of the primordial order, recorded in the sanctuary at Deir el-Bahari, and connect it with his mission of popularization of warrior gods.

References to these two aspects of the functions of the Ptolemaic ruler can be found in a fragment of a religious structure excavated on Elephantine (Fig. 8). It dates back to the times of Ptolemy VI Philometor, and is decorated, among others, with images of three deities – Petempamentes, Petensetis, and Petensenis, who have been researched for years.[61]

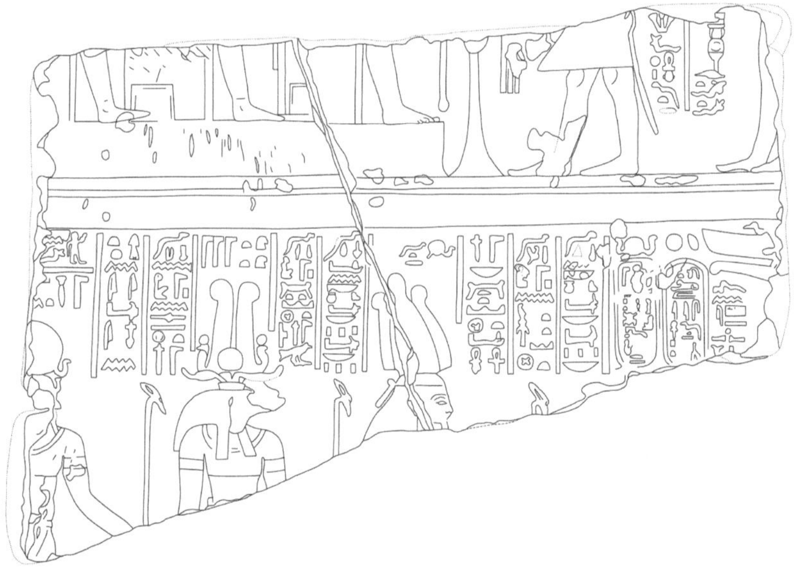

Fig. 8: Fragment of the wall from sanctuary at Elephantine (drawing: E. Laskowska-Kusztal)

The gifts which they offer to the king are power and victory (*ḳnt, nḫt*) which are indispensable for him to perform his actual function of the protector of the country.[62] The essence of the symbolism of the scene does not result from the gifts, which could also be delivered to the king by other gods, but rather from the unique personality of these divine creations. The circumstances of the placement of the names of these gods on the stela from Sehel should also be considered. The stela commemorates the council of a religious community, which gathered on Sehel and was in charge of the royal cult. The cult of the ruler is combined in the text from the stela with adoration of these three gods, who, as it should be supposed on the basis of the fragment of the relief, had their own sanctuary on Elephantine.

The interpretation of the new discovery from Elephantine in the context of the stela from Sehel suggests the protection extended by these local gods over the dynasty of Ptolemies and over the ruling king, who functions as the protector of Egypt. This exceptional coincidence of the function of the king – the protector and the circumstances of the foundation of the stela

61 Laskowska-Kusztal, ET XXVII, 2014, 217–230.
62 Laskowska-Kusztal, ET XXVII, 2014, 220.

draw attention to the fact that already under Ptolemy IV scenes of offering a sword to the ruling king were incorporated in the programme of scenes connected with the Ptolemaic royal cult.[63] We could discuss the hypothesis that the protection by the protector gods, established for the needs of the ruler, was extended to include the worshippers by the foundation of a dedicated sanctuary for the three deities on Elephantine. It could be supposed that they were incorporated into the official cult by inclusion of their images in the decoration programmes of temples as the next step. This cult is confirmed by a fragment of a small portal from the reign of Ptolemy XII Neos Dionysos, which belongs to a religious complex located on Elephantine, to the north of the temple of Satet (the so-called temple Y). In one of the scenes, Petempamentes is the beneficiary of the royal offering, which implies that the symmetrical scene might have featured another of the three gods who constituted the protective shield.[64]

The awareness of the actual protection extended by the king, attested in the fragment from Elephantine, with the images of the divine trinity from Sehel, is also confirmed in an indirect manner by the cult of Bes the warrior, noted from the Ptolemaic Period. This popular cult, attested by the terracotta images of the god with attributes of a soldier of the Lagid army, is interpreted as a consequence of conscription of Egyptians to the Ptolemaic army.[65] It could be perceived as the confirmation of the awareness of the society that the Ptolemaic ruler, the commander of the army, actually protected the country.

Another example for the illustration of the protection extended by the king was reflected in the visiting activity of the king, noted in the Ptolemaic Period. It was often involved dealing with crises or implementation of the national policy by means of religious propaganda.[66] In the light of these diverse aspects of the presence of the Ptolemies in the life of the country, the subject of the perception of the causative powers of the rulers, worshipped in rituals of the royal cult, remains an important element for further research.[67]

63 Preys, Les scènes du culte royal, 400–402, 409–410.

64 E. Laskowska-Kusztal, Elephantine XV. Die Dekorfragmente der ptolemäisch-römischen Tempel von Elephantine, AV 73, Mainz am Rhein 1996, 128–129; Laskowska-Kusztal, ET XXVII, 2014, 220.

65 S. Jędraszek, Egyptian Warriors: Machimoi, in Coroplastic Art – Selected Examples, in: K. Ulanowski (ed.), The Religious Aspects of War in the Ancient Near East, Greece, and Rome, Culture and History of the Ancient Near East 84, Leiden 2016, 272–287.

66 Clarysse,The Ptolemies, *passim.*

67 It is difficult to estimate to what extent the altars dedicated by Greek officials to them, as well as local gods, or gods and royal ancestors, were an expression of faith rather than politics. Regardless of the fact, they actually served for performance of rituals, for instance altars from Elephantine, one of which bears remains of burned offering, another served for libation, H. Maehler, Griechische Inschriften aus Elephantine, in: MDAIK 26, 1970, 169–172; G. Soukiassian, Les autels « à cornes » ou « à acrotères » en Égypte, in: BIFAO 83, 1983, 317–333, here: 332.

'Seeing Double'.

Intercultural dimensions of the royal ideology in Ptolemaic Egypt

Martina Minas-Nerpel

Abstract
When the Ptolemies became rulers of Egypt, they faced the immense task in constructing an identity for their country and their rule, for which they exploited the ancient Egyptian past to create a successful social imaginary. Together with their advisors, both Egyptian and Hellenic, they opened spaces in which theological concepts and political values could be imaginatively (re-)created. The focus of this paper is on both faces of the royal ideology, the Egyptian and the Greek. Specific attention is directed towards Arsinoe II and the cross-cultural exchange that resulted in new modes of self-presentations, both in the textual and visual sources. The emergence of the powerful Ptolemaic queens was the cumulative result of various factors, also of dynamic interactions with Isis and other Egyptian and Greek goddesses. At the same time, these syncretic processes between queens and goddesses also reflected onto the deities and their characteristics, sharing semantic dimensions, with new ones emerging. The discussion therefore includes the question to what extent the Ptolemaic queens and their cults influenced, or even pushed, the successful expansion of the Isis cult across the ancient world – and *vice versa*.

Following Alexander's conquest, the land by the Nile and its new capital Alexandria became the centre of the ancient world, a place where diverse cultures met. When the Ptolemies subsequently became rulers of Egypt, they found themselves not only kings and queens of a Hellenic population but also pharaohs for the Egyptian people. They thus faced the immense task in constructing an identity for their country and their rule, for which they also exploited the ancient Egyptian past to fashion a successful social imaginary. Together with their advisors, both Egyptian and Greek, they created spaces in which theological concepts and political values could be imaginatively (re-)created. The emergence of the powerful Ptolemaic queens was linked with the environment of the Egyptian temples and their dynamic interactions with Egyptian and Greek goddesses, especially Isis. These syncretic processes between the queens and goddesses also reflected onto the deities and their characteristics, sharing and emphasising semantic dimensions, with new ones emerging. The cross-cultural exchange resulted in new modes of self-presentations, especially of Arsinoe II, whose role in the Egyptian and the Hellenic environments is examined, also in regard to her influence on the successful expansion of the Isis cult across the Mediterranean world.

1 Setting the historical and cultural contexts

Egypt played a central role in this widespread transformation of the fourth century BC that was marked by the transitions from Oriental empires to the Hellenistic states. After the first Persian Period (525–404/1 BC), the rulers of the short-lived Twenty-eighth (405/401–399 BC) and Twenty-ninth Dynasties (399–380 BC) were struggling to repel Persian invasions.[1] Nectanebo Nekhtnebef (380–362 BC) and Nectanebo II Nekhthorheb (360–343/2 BC) of the Thirtieth Dynasty were the last native pharaohs who left their legacy to Egypt.[2] Once again, Egypt enjoyed a period of independence before the second period of Achaemenid rule (343/2–332 BC) that was terminated by Alexander's conquest. With his victories, the Persian Empire disintegrated and he took the land by the Nile without resistance.[3] Alexander the Great was possibly crowned as king of Egypt in Memphis and also regarded as the incarnation of Horus and the son of Amun-Re, thus drawing on the ancient Egyptian kingship ideology for his legitimation.[4] His divine descent was further emphasised by the oracle of Ammon at Siwa, a god who was of particular importance because of his far-reaching traditions in Greece.[5]

In addition, it was Alexander's connection with the last native pharaoh of Egypt that was stressed in the Alexander Romance, a fictionalised account of his conquests. It was a popular text that spread across cultural boundaries, being translated over the centuries into Syriac, Arabic, Armenian, and many more languages.[6] According to it, Nectanebo II was Alexander's father, not Philip II of Macedon. As a result, Alexander was both Macedonian-Greek and Egyptian – a powerful, retrospective fiction that also explained Alexander's claim of Egypt. Probably dating as early as the third century BC,[7] it highlights the links of the

1 All dates before Alexander according to J. von Beckerath, Handbuch der ägyptischen Königsnamen, MÄS 49, Mainz am Rhein ²1999. For the historical background see K. Myśliwiec, The Twilight of Ancient Egypt: the First Millennium B.C.E., Ithaca/New York, 2000, 158–176; S. Ruzicka, Trouble in the West: Egypt and the Persian Empire, 525–332 BCE, Oxford 2012, 35–48.

2 For the Thirtieth Dynasty see A. Forgeau, Nectanebo. La dernière dyanstie égyptienne, Paris 2018.

3 See G. Hölbl, A History of the Ptolemaic Empire, London/New York 2001, 9–12, 77–80. M. Chauveau, L'Égypte en transition : des Perses aux Macédoniens, in: P. Briant/F. Joannès (eds.), La transition entre l'empire achéménide et les royaumes héllénistiques (vers 350–300 av. J.-C.). Actes du colloque organisé au Collège de France par la « Chaire d'histoire et civilisation du monde schéménide et de l'empire d'Alexandre » et le « Réseau international d'études et de recherches achéménides » (GDR 2538 CNRS), 22–23 novembre 2004, Paris 2006, 75–404, discusses the transition of Egypt from Persian to Macedonian rulers.

4 For a summary of the evidence, past discussions, and new analysis of Alexander's legitimation strategies as pharaoh, see S. Pfeiffer, Alexander der Große in Ägypten: Überlegungen zur Frage seiner pharaonischen Legitimation, in: V. Grieb/K. Nawotka/A. Wojciechowska (eds.), Alexander the Great and Egypt. History, Art, Tradition, Philippika 74, Wiesbaden 2014, 89–106.

5 S. Schmidt, Ammon, in: H. Beck/P. C. Bol/M. Bückling (eds.), Ägypten Griechenland Rom. Abwehr und Berührung. Städelsches Kunstinstitut und Städtische Galerie, 26. November 2005 – 26. Februar 2006, Tübingen 2005, 192.

6 T. Whitmarsh, Class, in: T. Whitmarsh (ed.), The Cambridge Companion to the Greek and Roman Novel, Cambridge 2008, 83.

7 R. Jasnow, The Greek Alexander Romance and Demotic Egyptian Literature, in: JNES 56.2, 1997, 95–103, here: 101, 103, shows that there is good reason to think that portions of the Alexander Romance derive from an actual written Demotic text about Alexander and Nectanebo. This is also argued by F. Hoffmann, Der Trug des Nektanebos, in: F. Hoffmann/J. Quack (eds.), Anthologie der demotischen Literatur, EQÄ 4, Berlin ²2018, 183–184, 396. Forgeau, Nectanebo, 40, dates, without clear reason, the composition much later, to the end of the second or the beginning of the third century, written by

Egyptian kingship with its ancient traditions. Connections to the Thirtieth Dynasty were also actively cultivated under Alexander and the early Ptolemies, forming a vital part of the wider pattern of interactions and negotiations between the Egyptian elite and the new rulers. In the Memphite area, for example, Nectanebo was venerated by a flourishing statue cult of 'Nectanebo, the Falcon'.[8]

When Alexander died in 323 BC, his Macedonian general Ptolemy son of Lagus took over the country, first as satrap for Philip Arrhidaeus and Alexander IV, then as king.[9] Egypt was transformed once again. The Ptolemies carried to fruition the political aspiration of the Thirtieth Dynasties, the creation of a once more powerful Egyptian empire that dominated the Eastern Mediterranean.[10] With the foundation of Alexandria in 331 BC, Egypt became one of the centres of the ancient world, a place where various cultures met, and the use of these diverse traditions was crucial to form Ptolemaic Egypt. Ptolemy I positioned himself with the attention not only to the Hellenistic world, but also to the Egyptian precedent, faced with the immense task of constructing a distinctive state with a new identity. The ancient Egyptian past and royal ideology were vital for transforming the country and creating a successful social imaginary.

In contrast to the Persians and Alexander, Ptolemy ruled as a resident pharaoh. Already before he even assumed the kingship, Ptolemy was portrayed in royal terms, as demonstrated on the Satrap Stela, dated to 311 BC. It is probably the most significant native Egyptian source for Ptolemy's period as satrap.[11] The monument is dated according the regnal year of the legitimate king, the child Alexander IV, but the satrap exercised real power in Egypt. Ptolemy is described as the *acting* ruler, styled with epithets and a phraseology that refer to him in royal terms. Boyo Ockinga discusses the language used in the Satrap Stela, coming to the following conclusion:[12]

"un autuer de langue greque, mais de culture mixte." For a translation of the Alexander Romance see K. Dowden, Pseudo-Callisthenes: The Alexander Romance, in: B. P. Reardon, Collected Ancient Greek Novels, Berkeley/Los Angeles/London 1989, 650–735 (on Nectanebo as Alexander's father: 656–661). See also K. Nawotka, The Alexander Romance by Ps.-Callisthenes: Historical Commentary. Mnemosyne-Suppl. 399, Leiden 2017, 58–60.

8 Jasnow, The Greek Alexander Romance and demotic Egyptian literature, 101–102, especially note 47; D. J. Thompson, Memphis under the Ptolemies, Princeton [2]2012, 19, 119 (note 116), 132, 197. See also I. S. Moyer, Egypt and the Limits of Hellenism, Cambridge 2011, 87–89.

9 For recent studies on Ptolemy I, see I. Worthington, Ptolemy I. King and Pharaoh of Egypt, Oxford 2016; S. G. Caneva, Ptolemy I: Politics, Religion and the Transition to Hellenistic Egypt, in: T. Howe (ed.), Ptolemy I Soter. A Self-Made Man, Oxford/Philadelphia 2018, 88–127; P. McKechnie/J. A. Cromwell (eds.), Ptolemy I and the Transformation of Egypt, 404–282 BCE, Mnemosyne-Suppl. 415, Leiden/Boston 2018.

10 M. Minas-Nerpel, Pharaoh and Temple Building in the Fourth Century BCE, in: P. McKechnie/J. Cromwell (eds.), Ptolemy I and the Transformation of Egypt, 404–282 BCE, Mnemosyne-Suppl. 415, Leiden/Boston 2018, 120–165.

11 D. Schäfer, Makedonische Pharaonen und hieroglyphische Stelen. Historische Untersuchungen zur Satrapenstele und verwandten Denkmälern, Stud.Hellen. 50, Leuven 2011, 31–203. On the ideology of kingship as reflected on the Satrap Stele, see R. K. Ritner, Khababash and the Satrap Stela – A Grammatical Rejoinder, in: ZÄS 107, 1980, 135–137, here: 136.

12 B. Ockinga, The Satrap Stele of Ptolemy: A Reassessment, in: P. McKechnie/J. Cromwell (eds.), Ptolemy I and the Transformation of Egypt, 404–282 BCE, Mnemosyne-Suppl. 415, Leiden/Boston, 166–198, here: 191.

> … that the echoes of the royal phraseology in Sinuhe's hymn to Sesostris I, Amenemhet's son and successor, were aimed at drawing a parallel between Sesostris and Ptolemy – just as Sesostris as crown prince led the army of Egypt while his father Amenemhet "was in place", so too did Ptolemy, while king Alexander IV was "amongst the Asiatics".

Ptolemy I was strongly interested in the ancient Egyptian past. He was willing to learn from the Egyptian priests and to acknowledge Egyptian traditions. It was the king's duty to care for the gods and their houses. In such fast-moving times with changing foreign rulers, it was the divine office of kingship that mattered for the priests, not so much the individual who happened to be seated on the throne. Horus was the heavenly king and thus the true king of Egypt, and the pharaoh was only his earthly reflection, whose tenure in office was dependent upon his maintenance of *maat*.

The huge and richly decorated Egyptian temples of the Hellenistic Period are the principal surviving monuments of the Ptolemies in the country, so it seems evident that these rulers attached great importance to these enormous structures, even if they probably had very little understanding of the symbolic role of the king or queen depicted in the ritual scenes. Throughout Egypt, the temples, as important economic centres, owned land and produced goods; they needed to exist symbiotically with the pharaoh, a fact that Alexander and the Ptolemies recognised. In Egypt, times of royal strength were usually reflected in the creation of new temples and the development of existing ones. The Ptolemaic Period was very active in temple building, linking closely the pharaoh's dynamics with those of the Egyptian priests. Ptolemaic temple plans are clearly connected to those of the Thirtieth Dynasty. It seems that a master plan was developed, including important elements like the enclosure wall, the axis, the *wabet*, the birth house, and the ambulatory around the sanctuary as well as the sequence of halls, corridors, and rooms. These features were developed under the last native pharaohs or at least are for the first time attested from the Thirtieth Dynasty. The reasons for this continuity might have been to avoid any break from past principles and to connect themselves to legitimate rulers, or, on a more practical level, because most temples of the Old to the New Kingdom had long since disappeared, whereas temples of the Thirtieth Dynasty were still standing when Alexander arrived in Egypt. This pattern also relates to the fact that in the Thirtieth Dynasty older temples were commonly razed to the ground to build new ones, ideally at a larger scale.[13]

Ptolemy I Soter adapted to and transformed the situation inherited from his predecessors, resulting in cross-cultural fertilisation and the introduction of various innovations. The administration, centred in the new capital Alexandria, increasingly functioned in Greek.

---

13 For an overview see MINAS-NERPEL, Pharaoh and Temple Building in the Fourth Century BCE, 120–165, especially 155. See also W. NIEDERBERGER, Der Chnumtempel Nektanebos' II. Architektur und baugeschichtliche Einordnung, AV 96, Mainz am Rhein 1999, 122; N. SPENCER, A Naos of Nekhthorheb from Bubastis. Religious Iconography and Temple Building in the 30th Dynasty, BMRP 156, London 2006, 47–48; N. SPENCER, Sustaining Egyptian culture? Non-royal initiatives in the Late Period temple building, in: L. BAREŠ/F. COPPENS/K. SMOLÁRIKOVÁ (eds.), Egypt in Transition. Social and Religious Development of Egypt in the First Millennium BCE. Proceedings of an International Conference, Prague, September 1–4, 2009, Prague 2010, 441–490, especially 442. See also D. ARNOLD, Temples of the last pharaohs, New York/Oxford 1999, 93–136.

Monetisation was under way and the new Greek settlers formed a 'minority over-class'[14] in the towns and villages of the Egyptian countryside. Ptolemy I, who held Egypt for some forty years, had strengthened the borders of the land by the Nile. His long life, his broad vision and personal characteristics, his sense of history, and his ability to learn from experience allowed him to create a strong power base in Egypt.[15] His son Ptolemy II, together with his sister-wife Arsinoe II, masterfully built on this and used the ancient traditions and Ptolemy I's innovations, built on them and created new ones – with the queen playing a decisive role in these processes.

The Ptolemaic queens were also negotiating for their identity. On one hand, they preserved their Graeco-Macedonian character in Alexandria and on the international stage. On the other, the queen's position in Ptolemaic Egypt is deeply rooted in pharaonic traditions. In ancient Egypt, the pharaoh, as the manifestation of Horus on earth, was the principal symbol of his country, was responsible for maintaining the necessary cultic links between the human and the divine world.[16] The king was complemented by a queen, who was, according to ancient Egyptian understanding, the mortal representative and manifestation of the goddess Hathor, who was the feminine prototype of the creation.[17] The queen was vital for the king's regeneration as representative of the sun-god on earth, which was probably recognised, to a certain extent, at the royal court in Alexandria and must have greatly appealed to the Ptolemies.[18] The queens were included into the Egyptian cults, not only as part of the deified royal couples, but also in their own right, at least in the case of Arsinoe II, with whom, as a *synnaos thea* (co-templar goddess), the ruler cult started in the Egyptian temples.

2 Arsinoe II, queen and goddess in the Egyptian environment

Arsinoe II, the daughter of Ptolemy I Soter, was married to three different kings. At the turn of the third century BC, Ptolemy I arranged her first marriage to Lysimachus, king of Thrace. This union was born of high politics in order to strengthen his alliance with his old comrade, whose daughter Arsinoe I was married to Ptolemy II.[19] After the death of her first husband in 281 BC, Arsinoe II married Ptolemy Ceraunus, her half-brother and the usurper of Lysimachus' throne.[20] After he had her sons by Lysimachus murdered, Arsinoe II fled

---

14 D. J. Thompson, Ptolemy I in Egypt: Continuity and Change, in: P. McKechnie/J. Cromwell (eds.), Ptolemy I and the Transformation of Egypt, 404–282 BCE Mnemosyne-Suppl. 415, Leiden/Boston, 6–26, here: 22.

15 Thompson, Ptolemy I in Egypt, 10, 22.

16 See, for example, J. Baines, Kingship, Definition of Culture, and Legitimation, in: D. O'Connor/D. P. Silverman (eds.), Ancient Egyptian kingship, PÄ 9, Leiden/New York 1995, 3–47. Since the ruler needed his legitimation through the gods, his actions needed to follow divine paradigms: See N. S. Braun, Pharao und Priester – Sakrale Affirmation von Herrschaft durch Kultvollzug. Das Tägliche Kultbildritual im Neuen Reich und der Dritten Zwischenzeit, Philippika 23, Wiesbaden 2013, 281–303.

17 L. Troy, Patterns of Queenship in ancient Egyptian myth and history, Acta Universitatis Upsaliensis: Boreas 14, Uppsala 1986, 53–56.

18 For the context, see M. Minas-Nerpel, Ptolemaic queens as ritualists and recipients of cults: the cases of Arsinoe II and Berenike II, in: AncSoc 49, 2019, 141–183.

19 E. Donelly Carney, Arsinoë of Egypt and Macedon. A Royal Life, Women in Antiquity, Oxford/New York 2013, 31–43.

20 Donelly Carney, Arsinoë of Egypt and Macedon, 54–64.

to Egypt, where she married Ptolemy II, who had divorced his first wife, Arsinoe I. It is unclear whether Arsinoe I might have been conspiring against the king of Egypt or whether she was exiled so that he could marry his sister.[21] Either way, Arsinoe II became the first significant female figure in Ptolemaic history. That her second husband was her half-brother and especially that her third was her full brother, was sensational and changed the position and perception of Ptolemaic queens fundamentally.

Already before Arsinoe II came to Egypt she had been a powerful queen, who controlled entire cities, enjoyed considerable prestige, and possessed a vast amount of wealth.[22] When her brother married her, it was not only to her benefit but also to his, since both siblings could thus consolidate their power and strengthen Ptolemaic rule in Egypt.

Various religious or cultic measures were taken to attract the Greek population and to bind it to Egypt. The first Ptolemy promoted the cult of the Graeco-Egyptian god Sarapis, which became of great importance for the elite and their identification with the country.[23] In 290/289 BC, Ptolemy I had introduced an eponymous cult for Alexander as *ktistes* (founder) in Alexandria.[24] Eighteen years later, in 272/271 BC, Ptolemy II capitalised on that hero cult and took it a step further by associating himself and his sister-wife with this cult, thus seeking divinity for the *Theoi Adelphoi*.[25] In its Hellenistic expression, the Ptolemaic self-presentation was anchored in Alexander's cult. The Ptolemies were also buried first near, and eventually with him in the Sema, the mausoleum, which was built, in its final version, under Ptolemy IV in Alexandria probably dedicated during the Ptolemaia in 215/214 BC.[26] The nearness to the great conqueror implied affinity.

Theoi Adelphoi, the epithet of Ptolemy II and Arsinoe II, referred to the sibling marriage, which was meant to be understood as a *hieros gamos* of Zeus and Hera, celebrated by Theocritus (Idyll xvii) in his encomium of Ptolemy II. For the Egyptian population, this union could relate to Osiris and Isis, so that the *Theoi Adelphoi* absorbed both Greek and Egyptian mythology, and the queen was seen as Isis.[27]

Already during her lifetime Arsinoe became critical to the projection of the image of the Ptolemaic Dynasty, but her importance increased after her death in 270 BC, also by receiving her own eponymous cult in Alexandria, performed by a priestess, the *kanephoros* or

---

21 Donelly Carney, Arsinoë of Egypt and Macedon, 66–70.

22 S. B. Pomeroy, Women in Hellenistic Egypt. From Alexander to Cleopatra, New York 1984, 14. See also Donelly Carney, Arsinoë of Egypt and Macedon, 36–40.

23 S. Pfeiffer, The god Serapis, his cult and the beginnings of the ruler cult in Ptolemaic Egypt, in: P. McKechnie/P. Guillaume (eds.), Ptolemy II Philadelphus and his World, Mnemosyne-Suppl. 300, Leiden 2008, 387–408.

24 M. Minas, Die hieroglyphischen Ahnenreihen der ptolemäischen Könige: ein Vergleich mit den Titeln der eponymen Priester in den demotischen und griechischen Papyri, AegTrev 9, Mainz am Rhein 2000, 87–89 (with references to the evidence).

25 According to Posidippus, AB 63.9, Ptolemy II was now a god and king at once. For a translation see F. Nisetich, The Poems of Posidippus, in: K. Gutzwiller (ed.), The New Posidippus. A Hellenistic Poetry Book, Oxford 2005, 17–64, here: 31; S. Pfeiffer, Herrscher- und Dynastiekulte im Ptolemäerreich: Systematik und Einordnung der Kultformen, MBP 98, München 2008, 31–73.

26 Hölbl, A History of the Ptolemaic Empire, 169.

27 K. Lembke, Interpretatio Aegyptiaca vs. interpretatio Graeca? Der ägyptische Staat und seine Denkmäler in der Ptolemäerzeit, in: Mediterraneo Antico 15, 2012, 199–216, here: 209–211; Donelly Carney, Arsinoë of Egypt and Macedon, 49–64.

'basket-carrier'.[28] In the prescripts of Greek and demotic papyri the *kanephoros* is mentioned directly after the Alexander priest. Although attested only in written sources connected to the Hellenistic ruler cult, the priestess might have been depicted on an Egyptian monument, the Mendes Stela (Fig. 1). This stela is a vital source for Arsinoe's deification and further events that took place under Ptolemy II. The text refers to several royal visits by Ptolemy II or the crown-prince, who dedicated the temple in 264 BC.[29] A new ram was installed between 263 and 259 BC. The monument was probably created to celebrate (one of) these events, and one can assume that rituals were conducted during these occasions.[30] The depiction in the lunette created an imaginary of a visit of the *entire* royal family: behind the king and before the crown-prince the queen is depicted, despite the fact that Arsinoe was long dead. She presents offerings to the gods of Mendes and the new *synnaos thea*, the deified Arsinoe II. The queen is thus represented twice on the Mendes Stela, among the living royals and the gods. If a ritual performance took place to dedicate the temple or rather new parts of it, someone would have to stand in for the deceased queen. A likely candidate for such a substitute could have been Arsinoe's very own priestess, appointed for the eponymous cult in Alexandria, the *kanephoros*, otherwise only attested in written sources connected to the Hellenistic ruler cult. If she was indeed depicted in the lunette of the Mendes Stela as a substitute for the queen, the priestess was linked to both Egyptian and Hellenistic posthumous expressions of the Ptolemaic ruler cult. But it was in the Egyptian context that the cult of this queen really took off,[31] since the text on the Mendes Stela also records the introduction of Arsinoe's cult to all temples of Egypt.[32] Her statues were placed – as those of a co-templar goddess – beside those of the main deities in all temples across Egypt. In line 11 of the Mendes Stela, Arsinoe is praised with the following epithets:[33]

jr nẖb=s m rpꜥ.t wr(.t) ḥsj.w nb(.t) jmꜣ bnr mrw.t ꜥn ẖꜥ.w šsp.t wꜣḏ.tj mḥ sbẖ.t m nfr.w=s mrj(.t) bꜣ wḏꜣ(.t) bꜣ sn.t nswt ḥm.t nswt wr(.t) mr(.t)=f ḥnw.t tꜣ.wj (jrsnꜣy)

28 M. MINAS, Die Kanephoros. Aspekte des Ptolemäischen Dynastiekults, in: H. MELAERTS (ed.), Le culte du souverain dans l'Égypte ptolémaïque au IIIe siècle avant notre ère. Actes du colloque international, Bruxelles 10 mai 1995. Stud.Hellen. 34, Leuven 1998, 43–60; D. M. BAILEY, The Canephore of Arsinoe Philadelphos: What Did She Look Like, in: CdE 74, 1999, 156–160; MINAS, Die hieroglyphischen Ahnenreihen der ptolemäischen Könige, 93–96.

29 D. SCHÄFER, Makedonische Pharaonen und hieroglyphische Stelen, Stud.Hellen. 50, Leuven 2011, 257–60.

30 Egyptian ritual scenes do not necessarily reflect real actions. For a discussion see E. GRAEFE, Die Deutung der sogenannten „Opfergaben" der Ritualszenen ägyptischer Tempel als „Schriftzeichen", in: J. QUAEGEBEUR (ed.), Ritual and Sacrifice in the Ancient Near East: Proceedings of the International Conference organized by the Katholieke Universiteit Leuven from the 17th to the 20th of April 1991, OLA 55, Leuven 1993, 143–156.

31 J. QUAEGEBEUR, The Cult of Cleopatra VII and the Cults of Ptolemaic queens, in: R. S. BIANCHI (ed.), Cleopatra's Egypt. Age of the Ptolemies, New York 1988, 41–54, here: 43.

32 Egyptian Museum Cairo, CG 22181; A. KAMAL, Stèles ptolémaiques et romaines II. Catalogue général des antiquités Égyptiennes du Musée du Caire, nos. 22001–22208, Cairo 1904, pl. LIV–LV; Urk. II, 40,8–10 (death) and 41,11 (cult statues); SCHÄFER, Makedonische Pharaonen und hieroglyphische Stelen, 248–9; 262–3. HÖLBL, A History of the Ptolemaic Empire, 84 and 101–104.

33 Urk. II 39,12–40,4. For a detailed discussion of Arsinoe II's epithets, see MINAS-NERPEL, AncSoc 49, 2019, 151–157.

> Her titulary is established as princess, great of favour, possessor of kindness, sweet of love, beautiful of appearance, who has received the two uraei, who fills the palace with her perfection, beloved of the ram, the whole one (= the perfect one) of the ram, sister of the king, great wife of the king, whom he loves, mistress of the two lands, Arsinoe.

After being designated as *mrj(.t) b3* "beloved of the ram", Arsinoe is called *wḏ3(.t) b3*, "the whole one (= the perfect one) of the ram". [34] The epithet *wḏ3(.t) b3* is very rarely attested in Egyptian texts, usually as a designation of Isis: in the Ptolemaic temple at Aswan, the goddess is praised in a hymn dating to Ptolemy IV Philopator. One of Isis's epithets is identical with Arsinoe's on the Mendes Stela: "beloved of the ram, the perfect one of the ram".[35] In the temple of Kalabsha, dating to the time of Augustus, an exact copy of this Aswan hymn can be found: Isis is called "beloved of the ram, the perfect one of Khnum" *mrj(.t) b3 wḏ3(.t) H̱nm*, with Khnum replacing the Ram of Mendes as the local god in the second part.[36] In the pronaos of the temple of Hathor at Dendera, which dates to the end of the Ptolemaic Period, the epithets *mrj(.t) b3 wḏ3(.t) b3/H̱nm* are repeated twice in a hymn to Isis and its corresponding inscription.[37] Cleopatra VII herself is praised as "the female Horus, daughter of a ruler, adornment of the Ram/Khnum" (*Ḥr.t s3.t ḥq3 ẖkr b3/H̱nm*).[38]

These attestations of the epithet *mrj(.t) b3 wḏ3(.t) b3* in Aswan, Kalabsha, and Dendera are in the same text in different versions, with Kalabsha and Aswan preserving extended ones. Both Arsinoe II and Isis receive the epithets, but one wonders about the appellation's origin: who received the epithet first – goddess or queen – and where? Arsinoe's title is, at least so far, first attested on the Mendes Stela, which was created under Ptolemy II. It is not until his grandson Ptolemy IV that Isis is attested with this title in Aswan. On present evidence, it thus appears as if Arsinoe received this title first. The use for Isis was probably meant to strengthen the goddess's role as a queen[39] by assigning her an epithet of Arsinoe, the dynastically powerful queen *par excellence*, rather than the other way around. It also seems that the epithet originated for Arsinoe in the Delta, with a strong emphasis on the Ram of Mendes. The cultural centre in the Thirtieth Dynasty and the Ptolemaic Period was in the north and the most creative regions were probably in the Delta and the Memphite area. But it was not only in the Delta that Arsinoe received specific attention.

34 LGG II, 649b, s.v. *wḏ3.t b3* "Die Pflegerin (?) des Ba", refers to Isis only, not Arsinoe II.

35 Northern thickness of the lateral (southern) gate to the vestibule: between *wḏ3(.t)* and *b3* there is a lacuna: E. Bresciani/S. Pernigotti, Assuan, Biblioteca di studi antichi 16, Pisa 1978, 80–81: C11.

36 With a clear phonetic writing of Khnum with the *H̱nm*-vase before the ram-headed seated god: H. Gauthier, Le temple de Kalabchah. Permier fascicule: Texte, Les temples immergés de la Nubie, Cairo 1911, 15–16.

37 Frieze inscription on the west wall of the pronaos (Dendara XIV, 146, 8; Dendara XIV = S. Cauville, Le temple de Dendara XIV, Parois intérieures du pronaos, Dendara.net 2007) and in the western part of the soubassement of the southern exterior wall of the naos (Dendara XII 2, 6; Dendara XII = S. Cauville, Le temple de Dendara XII, Les parois extérieures du naos, 2 volumes [texte et planches], Cairo 2007); S. Cauville, Dendara XIV. Traduction. Le pronaos du temple d'Hathor: Parois inteìrieures, OLA 201, Leuven 2011, 199, translates "l'aimée du Bélier, qui prend soin de Khnum".

38 Dendara XII, 1, 5. The head of the seated god is destroyed, but the epithet *ẖkr b3/H̱nm* is repeated on the western side with the same ram-headed seated god as in *wḏ3(.t) b3* (Dendara XII, 10).

39 For Isis and other goddesses as queens, see F. Hoffmann, Königinnen in ägyptischen Quellen der römischen Zeit, in: M. Eldamaty/ F. Hoffmann/ M. Minas-Nerpel (eds.), Ägyptische Königinnen vom Neuen Reich bis in die islamische Zeit: Beiträge zur Konferenz in der Kulturabteilung der Botschaft der Arabischen Republik Ägypten in Berlin am 19.01.2013, Vaterstetten 2015, 139–156, here: 146–147.

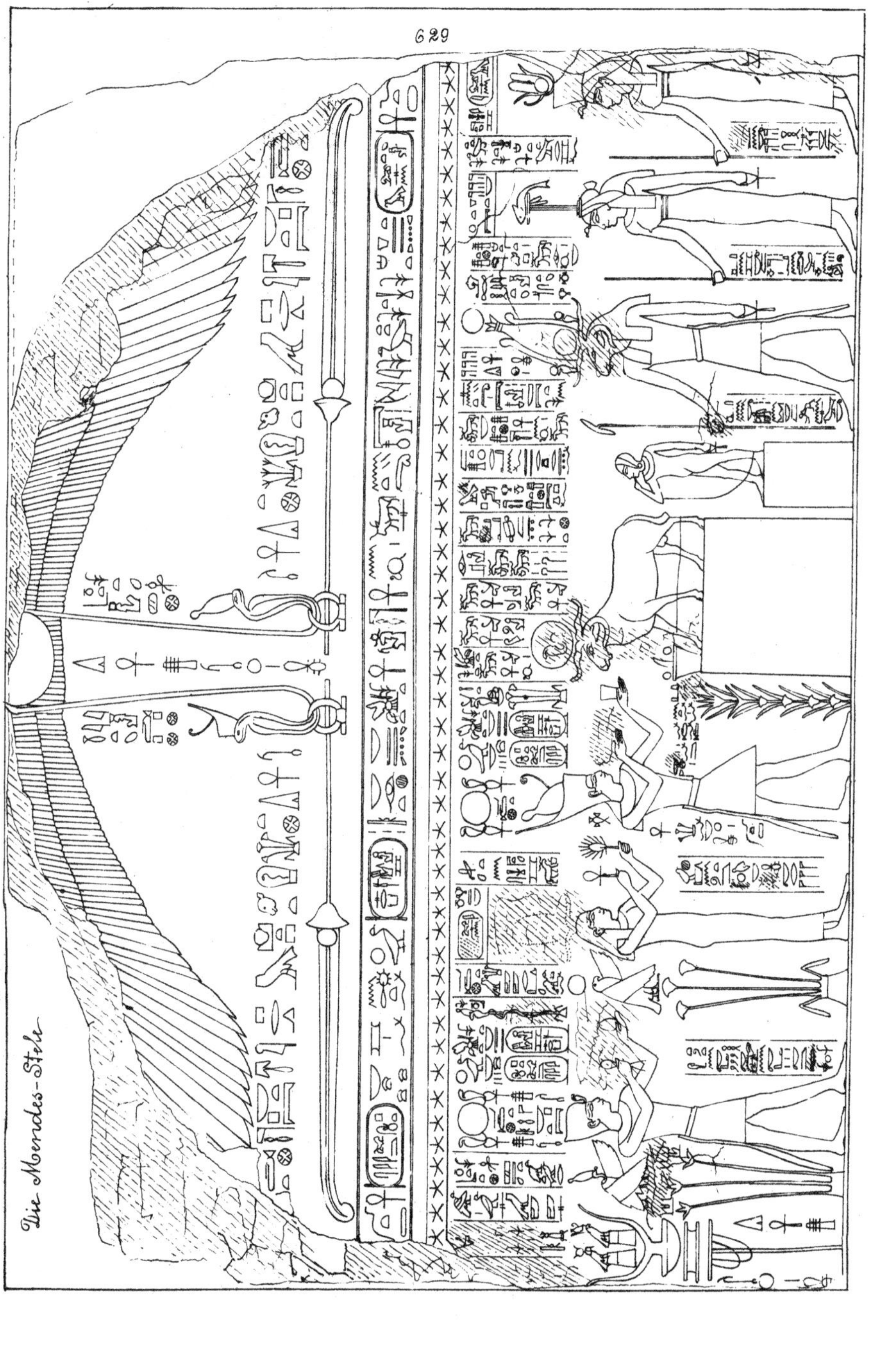

Fig. 1: The lunette of the Mendes Stela: Cairo, Egyptian Museum, CG 22181
(H. Brugsch, Thesaurus Inscriptionum Aegyptiacarum. Altägyptische Inschriften IV: Mythologische Inschriften altägyptischer Denkmäler, Leipzig 1884, 62)

The temple of Isis at Philae was considerably enlarged under Ptolemy II. His sister-wife shared the temple with Isis and participated in her veneration, as demonstrated by the hymns to Isis in her temple at Philae.[40] Here, Arsinoe II was also incorporated in the reliefs of both the sanctuary and the so-called gate of Philadelphus.[41]

How much the Delta traditions might have influenced the theological development of the temple of Isis at Philae is demonstrated by one of the goddess's epithets in the demotic *proskynema* of a Meroitic envoy in Philae. The demotic graffito 416, dating to the mid-third century AD, provides various cult-topographical and historical details. Isis is designated in lines 1–2 as "the beautiful libationer in the place of offering",[42] a designation that is otherwise only attested in a hieroglyphic variant at Behbeit el-Hagar in the Delta (*qbḥ.t nfr.t m s.t n.t wꜣḥ jḫ.t*).[43] Ian Rutherford raises in his discussion of Philae's religious history "that the sanctuary looks south, and is not linked in to the network of Egyptian religion."[44] This interpretation might be justified in some aspects, but it has already been contested by Jeremy Pope, based on his analysis of the above-mentioned Philae graffito 416 AD. With Arsinoe's inclusion in temple of Isis at Philae it can be further demonstrated that Philae was *not* detached from Egyptian religious practices – on the contrary. The inclusion of Arsinoe's cult supports Pope's idea of a "shared cult practice and theological vocabulary which stretched from Behbeit el-Hagar *through* Philae", not only as late as the "final centuries of Demotic literacy", as he puts it, but as early as the massive building and decoration initiative under Ptolemy II.[45] Arsinoe seemed to have functioned as a theological interface.

Isis was not only a goddess, but also a divine concept, which changed from a "ägyptischen Identifikations- zu einem hellenistischen Integrationsmodell".[46] This was one reason to assimilate the Ptolemaic queen with the goddess as a matter of legitimising her. The royal women, first and foremost Arsinoe II, were also a model of integration that was vital in the ideology of Ptolemaic self-fashioning. The concept of Isis proved itself as the "wandelbarste der altägyptischen Götterwelt … und gleichzeitig als das für das Alte Ägypten charakteristischste",[47] to which Arsinoe and her female dynastic successors certainly contributed by conferring certain aspects onto the goddess – an exchange and enrichment

40 See L. V. Žabkar, Hymns to Isis in her temple at Philae, Hanover/London 1988, 12–15, 89–90.

41 Žabkar, Hymns to Isis in her temple at Philae, 3, 12. Arsinoe II is depicted in room I: PM VI 238 (295); room VII: PM VI 241–2 (340); room X: PM VI 243 (354)–(355), (356)–(357); on the gate of Philadelphos: PM VI 214 (69)–(70). See S. Cauville/M. Ibrahim Ali, Philae. Itinéraire du visiteur, Leuven 2013, 90, 232. See also M. Minas-Nerpel, Creativity in Visual Arts, in: K. Vandorpe (ed.), A Companion to Greco-Roman and Late Antique Egypt, Blackwell Companions to the Ancient World, Oxford 2018, 533–550.

42 J. Pope, The Demotic Proskynema of a Meroïte Envoy to Roman Egypt (Philae 416), in: Enchoria 31, 2008/2009, 68–103, here: 75: commentary B.

43 LGG VII, 184b.

44 I. Rutherford, Island of the Extremity: Space, Language and Power in the Pilgrimage Traditions of Philae, in: D. Frankfurter (ed.), Pilgrimage and Holy space in Late Antique Egypt. Religions in the Graeco-Roman World 134, Leiden 1998, 227–256, here: 236.

45 Pope, Enchoria 31, 2008/2009, 103.

46 R. Schulz, Warum Isis? Gedanken zum universellen Charakter einer Göttin im Römischen Reich, in: M. Görg/G. Hölbl (eds.), Ägypten und der östliche Mittelmeerraum im 1. Jahrtausend v. Chr. Akten des interdisziplinären Symposions am Institut für Ägyptologie der Universität München 25.–27. 10. 1996, ÄUAT 44, Wiesbaden 2000, 251–279, here: 266.

47 Schulz, Warum Isis?, 279.

of characteristics that worked in both directions.[48] Although one should not or cannot, in many respects, distinguish clearly between the Egyptian and the Hellenic environment, as demonstrated by Isis' modification, I have chosen both as sub-headings for the discussion of Arsinoe's characteristics, referring to their starting points rather than arguing that both environments can be separated.

3 Arsinoe II, queen and goddess in the Hellenic environment

One of the most extraordinary images of Arsinoe II must have been planned for her temple at Cape Zephyrium east of Alexandria,[49] where she was worshipped as Aphrodite-Zephyritis. The temple was dedicated by Callicrates of Samos, a high-ranking *philos* and the supreme commander of the royal navy from the 270s to the 250s BC, who had a particular interest in promoting this aspect of Arsinoe during her life-time.[50] Peter BING explains that Callicrates also sought to mediate between old Hellas and the new, sometimes unfamiliar, world of Ptolemaic Egypt by bridging the gap between the two, by spreading abroad his rulers' novel cultural policies and by bringing Greek tradition to bear on his Egyptian milieu.[51]

An epigram of the Hellenistic poet Posidippus, generally placed before Arsinoe's death in 270 BC,[52] celebrates this temple, which was probably the most notable dedication to the Cyprian Aphrodite.[53] Originally from Pella in Macedonia, Posidippus lived and worked in Alexandria in the first half of the third century BC, presumably supported by Ptolemy II.[54] In his poems, written in Greek, he addressed and celebrated the Ptolemaic Dynasty, in particular the queens, glorifying them in unprecedented ways. In Posidippus' epigrams 116 and 119, Arsinoe is promoted as a marine goddess, and her sphere of influence is said to have encompassed seafarers and 'chaste daughters of the Greeks'.

48 I wish to thank Svenja Nagel for her comments on Isis. See also her study which was not yet available for consultation for this article: S. NAGEL, Isis im Römischen Reich 1: Die Göttin im griechisch-römischen Ägypten; 2: Adaption(en) des Kultes im Westen, Philippika 109, Wiesbaden 2019.

49 On the location of the temple, see P. M. FRASER, Ptolemaic Alexandria I, Oxford 1972, 239; II, 389 n. 393. See also S. A. STEPHENS, Seeing double. Intercultural Poetics in Ptolemaic Alexandria, Hellenistic Culture and Society 37, Berkeley 2003, 181–182.

50 For Callicrates of Samos as the founder of the new cult and sanctuary dedicated to Arsinoe II, located on Cape Zephyrium, see H. HAUBEN, Callicrates of Samos: a contribution to the study of the Ptolemaic admiralty, Stud.Hellen. 18, Leuven 1970, 41–6, and P. BING, Posidippus and the Admiral: Kallikrates of Samos in the Milan Epigrams, in: Greek, Roman, and Byzantine Studies 43, 2002/3, 243–266. See also H. HAUBEN, Callicrates of Samos and Patroclus of Macedon, champions of Ptolemaic thalassocracy, in: K. BURASELIS/M. STEFANOU/D. J. THOMPSON (eds.), The Ptolemies, the Sea and the Nile. Studies in Waterborne Power, Cambridge 2013, 39–65.

51 BING, Posidippus and the Admiral, 244. See also FRASER, Ptolemaic Alexandria II, 389, n. 393.

52 FRASER, Ptolemaic Alexandria II, 389, n. 393.

53 Aphrodite's patronage on the sea is discussed by D. DEMETRIOU, Τῆς πάσης ναυτιλίης φύλαξ: Aphrodite and the Sea, in: Kernos 23, 2010, 67–89, who also explains (see notes 26–27) that Aphrodite's power over the sea and maritime functions may already be present in Hesiod's account (Theogony, 188–195) of the goddess's birth. In this story, Aphrodite was not born instantaneously from Ouranos' severed genitals that had fallen in the sea; they rather journeyed on the sea-foam for a while before the goddess arose from the sea. She finally arrived in Cyprus, where she set up her abode.

54 D. J. THOMPSON, Posidippus, Poet of the Ptolemies, in: K. GUTZWILLER (ed.), The New Posidippus. A Hellenistic Poetry Book, Oxford 2005, 269–283, here: 272.

> Between the Pharian headland and the mouth of Canopus
> among the waves shining all around me, I have my place –
> this windy spur of Libya rich in lambs, reaching far toward the breath of Italian Zephyrus:
> here Callicrates has raised me up and named me Queen Cypris Arsinoe's temple.
> But come, chaste daughters of the Greeks, to her who will be called Aphrodite Zephyritis,
> and come, too, men who toil in the sea: the admiral made this temple's haven safe from every wave.
> …
> While on the sea and when on land, keep in your prayers
> this shrine of Arsinoe Aphrodite Philadelphus
> whom admiral Callicrates first consecrated here to rule over the headland of Zephyrium.
> She'll grant good sailing or make the sea, for those who call upon her in the storm, smooth as oil.

Posidippus described Cape Zephyrium as being located midway between the shore of Pharos and the Canopic mouth, and the temple located here is said to be standing amidst the surrounding waters. Arsinoe Cypris is portrayed as commanding the Zephyrian shore. Therefore, this temple can be added to the list of Aphrodite's temples located on the coast.[55] No archaeological evidence survives of this temple. According to Pliny, a statue suspended by magnetic fields was to be positioned in its centre, but this project was never completed:[56]

> The architect Timochares had begun to use lodestone for constructing the vaulting in the Temple of Arsinoe at Alexandria, so that the iron statue contained in it might have the appearance of being suspended in mid air; but the project was interrupted by his own death and that of King Ptolemy who has ordered the work to be done in honour of his sister.

We only have literary evidence about the Cape Zephyrium temple, according to which it must have formed a landmark. The nature of the temple's fame at Cape Zephyrium does not reveal itself clearly. Many Classical scholars take it to have been the most important of the Ptolemaic temples to Arsinoe,[57] but Posidippus poetic allusions are practically the only source. Susan STEPHENS therefore questions, to a certain extent, the real bearing and significance of this cult. Was the temple simply the subject for poetic promotion? She points out that in modern discussions, there is a tendency to construct rites and prerogatives for the temple based only on the evidence of the few poems preserved. As STEPHENS states, Posidippus's promotion acted probably as a magnet to draw other events or poems into its orbit.[58] The cult spread

55 For a list of Aphrodite's temples as patroness of the sea in the late Bronze Age and the early Iron Age, see M. ECKERT, Die Aphrodite der Seefahrer und ihre Heiligtümer am Mittelmeer. Archäologische Untersuchungen zu interkulturellen Kontaktzonen am Mittelmeer in der späten Bronzezeit und frühen Eisenzeit, Berlin 2016.

56 Pliny, Naturalis historia 34, 148 (Translation by H. RACKHAM, Pliny. Natural History, Volume IX: Books 33–35, The Loeb Classical Library 394, Cambridge, MA, 1952). For this temple, see also M. PFROMMER, Königinnen vom Nil, Mainz am Rhein 2002, 61–69.

57 For a discussion see S. STEPHENS, Battle of the Books, in: K. GUTZWILLER (ed.), The New Posidippus. A Hellenistic Poetry Book, Oxford 2005, 229–248, here: 245–248. See also S. MÜLLER, Das hellenistische Königspaar in der medialen Repräsentation: Ptolemaios II. und Arsinoe II., Beiträge zur Altertumskunde, Berlin 2009, 215–216, for a short summary and discussion of the different poetic sources.

58 STEPHENS, Battle of the Books, 246–247.

rather swiftly in the Mediterranean, to harbours and cities, which were Ptolemaic possessions or influenced by the Ptolemaic navy.[59]

Aphrodite was known as a patroness of the sea already in the late Bronze Age and the early Iron Age.[60] In Posidippus' poem, Arsinoe-Aphrodite grants smooth sailing (*euploia*). One of Aphrodite's cultic epithets was *Euploia*, attested already from the early fourth century BC.[61] Other cult designations, attested from different periods and places along the Mediterranean coast, point to Aphrodite's dual role as a protector of navigation and harbours,[62] all suitable and important aspects for the Ptolemaic navy, which were conferred onto the deified queen.

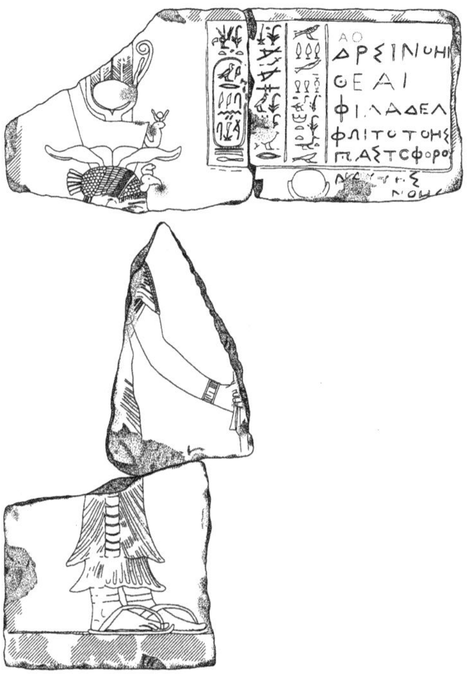

Fig. 2: Stela of Totoes (ALBERSMEIER/MINAS, Ein Weihrelief für die vergöttlichte Arsinoe II, fig. 2; Drawing Ulrike Denis)

But it was not only in the Hellenic environment that Arsinoe was connected with sailors. The bilingual stela of Totoes, a *pastophoros* (priest) and *nautes* (sailor) of Arsinoe II, provides a good example (Fig. 2),[63] even if one should rather imagine a sailor on the river Nile. The monument shows the deified Arsinoe II facing a figure of an Egyptian god, now lost except for his lunar crown, with whom she, as his *synnaos thea*, is worshipped in an Egyptian temple. The queen's elaborate clothing, closely related to the Isis garment, combines Egyptian traditions and Hellenistic innovation.[64] Arsinoe's visual identity is thus a mixture of conventional and new creations, as befits a goddess based in two cultures.

The Ptolemaic queen's maritime connection continued under Ptolemy III, as is attested, for example, by the so-called

59 DONELLY CARNEY, Arsinoë of Egypt and Macedon, 98.

60 See ECKERT, Die Aphrodite der Seefahrer, *passim*.

61 For the evidence see DEMETRIOU, Kernos 23, 2010, note 37. Pausanias, I, 1, 3, recounts the story of Konon who introduced the cult of Aphrodite Euploia to Athens in 394 BC.

62 For the evidence see DEMETRIOU, Kernos 23, 2010, notes 43–44.

63 S. ALBERSMEIER/M. MINAS, Ein Weihrelief für die vergöttlichte Arsinoe II., in: W. CLARYSSE/A. SCHOORS/H. WILLEMS (eds.), Egyptian Religion. The Last Thousand Years. Part I. Studies dedicated to the memory of Jan Quaegebeur, OLA 84, Leuven 1998, 3–29. The stela, originally c. 37cm high, is now in a private collection.

64 S. ALBERSMEIER, Das ›Isisgewand‹ der Ptolemäerinnen, in: P. BOL/G. KAMINSKI/C. MADERNA (eds.), Fremdheit – Eigenheit. Ägypten, Griechenland und Rom, Austausch und Verständnis, in: StädelJb N.F. 19, 2004, 421–432.

Sophilos mosaic from Tell Timai (Thmuis) that shows queen Berenike II in military attire, crowned by a ship's prow.[65] Berenike is presented as a kind of *Agathe Tyche* and a deified ruler who appears to guarantee both prosperity and stability at home and victory at sea.[66]

When Ptolemy III married Berenike, daughter of Magas of Cyrene, this dynastic alliance had considerable political and ideological implications. Egypt and the Cyrenaica were unified once again, and under the couple, Ptolemaic power was at its height and the empire at its greatest extent. While Ptolemy III invaded Syria, Berenike II was left in command of the court in Alexandria. In a poem honouring the queen, Callimachus praised her devotion to the king. She vowed to offer a lock of her hair in exchange for his safe return from the campaign. This lock was dedicated in the sanctuary at Cape Zephyrium, where Arsinoe II was worshipped as Aphrodite. Berenike thus linked herself in cultic terms with her immediate predecessor. Through adoption she also claimed her legitimacy and divine ancestry from the powerful Arsinoe II.[67] Had Ptolemy II tried to explain the consanguinity as a Zeus – Hera respectively Osiris – Isis union, his son Ptolemy III even forced the impression of a feigned sibling marriage and thus stressed the importance of Isis for the queen.

Because the cult of Isis extended in the Hellenistic Period from a Nilotic to a Mediterranean context, she acquired various new aspects, or certain functions were further pronounced, such as *Euploia* or *Pelagia.* In ancient Egypt, Isis was rather linked with the inundation and fluvial navigation, although her connection to the sea was not completely unknown to the ancient Egyptians.[68] As Reinhold Merkelbach summarised it in his seminal work on Isis regina and Zeus Sarapis:[69]

> Solange Isis nur eine Göttin der Ägypter war, fuhr sie nicht zur See. Erst die Griechen zu Alexandria – das auf das Meer blickte und zurück zum Binnenland – machten Isis zur Göttin des Meeres (Pelagia).

It seems obvious that the sphere of influence of the Ptolemaic navy throughout the Mediterranean was expanded by using the figure of the queen, now Aphrodite Euploia, as patroness of the maritime empire. Arsinoe was celebrated as patroness of navigation and nuptial love. As mentioned in Posidippus's poems, the combination of different types of worshippers, who were supposed to come to Arsinoe-Aphrodite's temple – chaste women and men who labour on the sea – is an indication of the interconnectedness of her roles as a

65 Alexandria, Greco-Roman Museum Inv. 21739; 2.70m high. See G. Grimm, Alexandria: die erste Königsstadt der hellenistischen Welt: Bilder aus der Nilmetropole von Alexander dem Großen bis Kleopatra VII., Mainz am Rhein 1998, 79–81 with figs. 81a and c.

66 D. L. Clayman, Berenice II and the Golden Age of Ptolemaic Egypt, Women in Antiquity, Oxford 2014, 136.

67 See W. Huss, Ägypten in hellenistischer Zeit, 332–30 v. Chr., München 2001, 354; B. F. van Oppen de Ruiter, Berenice II Euergetis. Essays in Early Hellenistic Queenship, Basingstoke/New York 2015, 36.

68 D. Müller, Ägypten und die griechischen Isis-Aretalogien. ASAW, Philologisch-Historische Klasse 53,1, Berlin 1961, 41–42, 61–67, linked entries M 15 ("Ich habe die seemännischen Berufe erfunden") and M 39 ("Ich bin die Herrin der Flüsse und der Winde und des Meeres") to Isis's Greek characteristics, but emphasised that this function was based on her bringing the inundation. See also M. Malaise, Le culte d'Isis à Canope au IIIe siècle avant notre ère, in: M.-O. Jentel/G. Deschênes-Wagner (eds.), Tranquillitas. Mélanges en l'honneur de Tran tam Tinh, Québec 1994, 353–370, here: 361–362, n. 58.

69 R. Merkelbach, Isis regina – Zeus Sarapis. Die griechisch-ägyptische Religion nach den Quellen dargestellt, Stuttgart 1995, 66.

patroness of the sea and sex. This portrayal was also celebrated in Hellenistic hymns which are attested on the verso of papyri dating to the second and third century AD.[70]

Arsinoe II was a goddess well suited to maritime export. Laurent Bricault suggests a transfer of the epithet *Euploia* from Aphrodite to Isis via Arsinoe.[71] The evolution of Arsinoe's marine aspects, essentially Greek in origin, was largely promoted by the actions of the admiral Callicrates, when he founded a cult with a sanctuary on Cape Zephyrium According to Hans Hauben, it is possible to suppose that he took an active, not necessarily exclusive, part in re-founding "a network of strategic ports into as many 'Arsinoes', thus helping to spread Arsinoe's cult."[72] On one hand, Arsinoe's power as a divine personality was enhanced by her association with Aphrodite, Isis, and other goddesses. On the other hand, the lasting popularity of Arsinoe as a deified queen and a divinity was particularly important as a facilitator in the broader development of Isis.

Hellenistic poets connected Arsinoe II to Aphrodite's narrative as marine and sea saving goddess. Arsinoe and the later Ptolemaic queens were venerated as Isis, as a female embodiment of Ptolemaic power, and this must have reinforced Isis' power in the minds of her followers and attracted even more to Isis generally.[73] Thus, Isis in her marine aspect was neither entirely Hellenic nor Egyptian, but essentially what her worshippers formed her to be. The development was driven by political and economic implications and especially the shared semantic dimension of polytheistic religion. Because of their interacting networks of powers, both Arsinoe and Isis became attractive as sea goddesses.

But Arsinoe's worship was, according to the surviving sources, not principally concentrated on this specific temple or its aspects. The object category of faience *oinochoai*, truly unique of the Hellenistic world, provides an important counterweight to the poems that associates Arsinoe with Aphrodite, because their iconography is never that of Aphrodite, but of Isis-Demeter or Agathe Tyche. These wine-jugs visualise cross-cultural inspiration. They were limited to a period of about a century from Arsinoe II to Cleopatra I and probably created for use by ordinary citizens at the festival that was established in honour of Arsinoe II, the Arsinoeia,[74] showing in relief the figure of a Ptolemaic queen pouring a libation on an altar, possibly for herself (Fig. 3).[75] Although developed for the Hellenistic cult of the Ptolemaic Dynasty, the fabric – Egyptian faience – is rather foreign to Greek taste, and they show contemporary rites. The large number of dedicatory *oinochoai* with figures of Ptolemaic queens found throughout the Mediterranean testify to the popularity of these women as objects of worship.

---

70 S. Barbantani, Goddess of Love and Mistress of the Sea. Notes on a Hellenistic Hymn to Arsinoe-Aphrodite (*P.Lit.Goodsp.* 2, I–IV), in: AncSoc 35, 2005, 135–165.

71 See L. Bricault, Isis, Dame des flots, AegLeod 7, Liège 2006, 18, 26–9, 33, 101–103, 177–178.

72 Hauben, Callicrates of Samos and Patroclus of Macedon, 52.

73 For the expansion of Isis's and Sarapis's cults, see Merkelbach, Isis regina – Zeus Sarapis, 121–130.

74 D. Burr Thompson, Ptolemaic Oinochoai and Portraits in Faience. Aspects of the Ruler-Cult, Oxford Monographs on Classical Archaeology, Oxford 1973, 71 and 75. When the posthumous festival first took place is not clear, but it must have been after Arsinoe's death in 270 BC and latest in year 18 of Ptolemy II (268/7), when the *kanephoros*, Arsionoe's eponymous priestess, is first attested.

75 Pfeiffer, Herrscher- und Dynastiekulte im Ptolemäerreich, 53–54, summarises that the queens were either the recipients or, alternatively, that they could conduct the offerings themselves. He emphasises that Greek deities could conduct offerings for themselves, which corresponds with the depictions on the *oinochoai*.

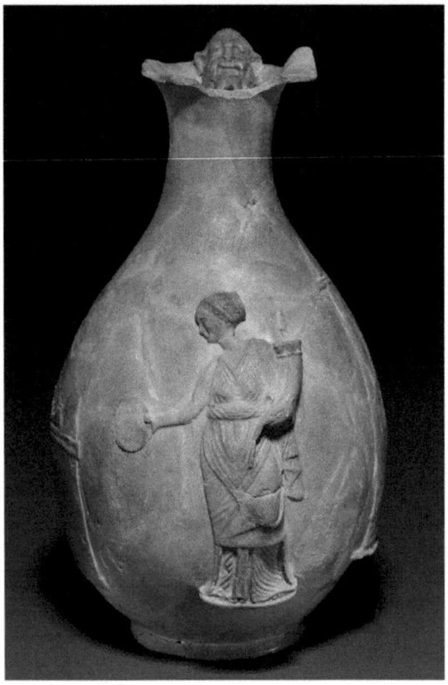

Fig. 3: *Oinochoe*, showing Arsinoe II: British Museum 1873,0820.389 (Image courtesy of the British Museum)

4 Conclusion

There are various reasons why I have chosen 'Seeing double' as a title for this contribution. Firstly, in a rather obvious manner, the heading refers to Arsinoe II as being depicted twice on the Mendes Stela, on both the royal and the divine side. Secondly, it refers to the concept of dualism that is almost omnipresent in Egypt.[76] It pervades all aspects of Egyptian culture, including the masculine and feminine elements, such as the king and queen or Isis and Osiris – an aspect shrewdly exploited for the sibling marriage of Ptolemy II and Arsinoe II. Dualism is expressed geographically as Upper and Lower Egypt or Alexandria and the Chora. Thirdly, it applies culturally, first and foremost, to the Greek and the Egyptian elements. Ludwig KOENEN called it the Janus head of Ptolemaic kingship,[77] which is more than just a metaphor, since it describes the reality of a kingship with new cultural codes, deriving from both the Hellenic and the Egyptian background, and creating new ones – quite different to what had been established previously in Macedonia or Egypt. Last but not least, I have also chosen this title in reference to STEPHENS' book *Seeing Double. Intercultural Poetics in Ptolemaic Alexandria*, published in 2003. She looks at the works of Callimachus and Theocritus and others in their social and political context, including, to a certain level, the Egyptian cultural background.

With few examples, I try to highlight in this article the different strands that need to be analysed in their specific contexts. Different environments borrowed various cultural expressions and transformed them, forming dynamics which are often difficult to understand, or can be seen in different ways, an effect that was probably intended. The creation of the temple of Arsinoe Zephyrites should be understood as part of Callicrates' project to expand the sphere of influence of the Ptolemaic navy throughout the Mediterranean, in part by using the figure of the queen as patroness of the maritime empire. The cult of Arsinoe-Aphrodite Euploia-Zephyritis spread across the Mediterranean, predominantly via harbour cities, with Delos playing a decisive role.[78] Altar plaques of this type were found at various places, including Delos, Paros, Ios, Thera, Miletus, Samos, and other places. The cult was as

76 For the concepts of dualism, see E. OTTO, Dualismus, in: W. HELCK/E. OTTO (eds.), Lexikon der Ägyptologie I, Wiesbaden 1975, 1148–1150. For the concept of antagonism as a "sekundären Dualismus" see J. ASSMANN, Ma'at. Gerechtigkeit und Unsterblichkeit im Alten Ägypten, München 1990, 176–177.

77 L. KOENEN, The Ptolemaic King as a Religious Figure, in: A. W. BULLOCH/ E. S. GRUEN/A. A. LONG/ A. STEWART (eds.), Images and Ideologies. Self-definition in the Hellenistic World, Berkeley 1993, 25–115, here: 25.

78 See, for example, M. BOMMAS, Isis, Osiris, and Serapis, in: C. RIGGS (ed.), The Oxford Handbook of Roman Egypt, Oxford 2012, 419–435, especially 428–429.

widespread throughout the Aegean as it was celebrated in Alexandria.[79] Through the creation of this new cult of Arsinoe II, parts of the Ptolemaic empire were now more closely tied to Alexandria and the Ptolemies.

The admiral's schemes were, most probably, influenced by the Ptolemaic court, as were the poems of Posidippus, Theocritus, or Callimachus. Whether by poetry, cults, festivals, architecture, or other means the Ptolemaic dependants experimented with a variety of symbols and formats to promote their new royal dynasty. The veneration of Arsinoe-Aphrodite was closely linked to that of Arsinoe Philadelphus and the eponymous cults.[80] Both the Hellenistic and the Egyptian expressions of Arsinoe's cult were probably created at or around the same time and all sanctioned by, or an invention of, the royal court in Alexandria, with the cooperation of Egyptian priests. We should thus see the Egyptian and Hellenistic developments of the ruler cult as a cross-inspiration.

As I have shown above and elsewhere,[81] the priority of Arsinoe as "the perfect one of the ram" over Isis could perhaps be compared with the transfer of the epithet *Euploia* from Arsinoe to Isis. It seems that the goddess Isis, especially in her capacity as a Hellenistic integration model, could be readily translated and given new attributes, whether in a formal syncretic and inter-cultural processes, or in the minds of individual worshippers who called on her saving powers. Aphrodite or Arsinoe-Aphrodite may well have been the model for Isis' sea powers. Worshippers could choose to connect Isis to Aphrodite or to any other sea deity. In the Graeco-Roman times, Isis became increasingly a universal goddess, due to her ability to adopt functions of other Egyptian and Greek goddesses, thus extending her ancient Egyptian functions, of which many might not have happened without the Ptolemaic queens.

Acknowledgments
The research for this article was partly conducted at the Getty Villa, Los Angeles, USA; I am very grateful to the Getty Research Institute for the research scholarship in 2016–2017. I wish to thank Julia Budka for inviting me to this stimulating conference and Kenneth Griffin for reading a draft of this contribution.

79 For the evidence see A. Meadows, The Ptolemaic League of Islanders, in: K. Buraselis/M. Stefanou/D. J. Thompson (eds.), The Ptolemies, the Sea and the Nile. Studies in Waterborne Power, Cambridge 2013, 19–38, here: 29–30.

80 See Müller, Das hellenistische Königspaar in der medialen Repräsentation, 266–269.

81 See Minas-Nerpel, AncSoc 49, 2019.

The Ptolemaic Basileus in *proskynesis* before the gods of Egypt.

The ritual *sn-tꜣ* ("Kissing the Earth") in temples of the Ptolemaic Era

Filip Coppens

Abstract

The present paper intends to take a closer look at the *sn-tꜣ* ("Kissing the Earth") ritual, executed by the foreign ruler, and in particular the Ptolemaic Basileus, before the deities of Egypt. Following a general overview of these reliefs and accompanying texts upon the walls of temples from the Ptolemaic and Roman Era, the present paper focuses in particular on the occurrence of the *sn-tꜣ* ritual in the early Ptolemaic Period and its precursors from New Kingdom and Third Intermediate Period times. This is followed by a discussion of plausible reasons for the discontinuity of its portrayal on a temple wall as well as the (changed) nature and characteristics of the scene upon its reappearance on the Horus precinct at Edfu after a long period of absence, in order to gain a better understanding of when and where the Ptolemaic ruler is depicted performing *proskynesis* before the gods of Egypt.

1 Introduction

The first millennium BC represents for many states around the Mediterranean basin an intensification of relations, a gradual introduction of monetary systems, an enhanced organisation of long-distance trade and a remarkable growth in the exchange of ideas and goods, resulting in an archaic globalisation during the Hellenistic age and the integration of regions as far apart as India and Spain.[1] The extent of this early form of globalisation still increased during the early days of the Roman Empire, connecting through trade the entire Roman world with Parthia and even the Han Dynasty in China.

Following in the footsteps of Alexander III and his army, Greeks and Macedonians started to settle into the newly acquired territories along the eastern Mediterranean shores and further inland to the east. Far from being uninhabited regions, wherever they journeyed, indigenous political organisations, religious practices and belief systems, as well as social structures – in other words, traditions going back centuries if not millennia – continuously confronted these new arrivals on the scene. In the end, in each of the newly created Hellenistic kingdoms, it always came down to negotiations and compromises, trying to find a middle ground

---

1 For a general introduction to the period see for instance several recent overviews, such as A. Erskine (ed.), A Companion to the Hellenistic World, Blackwell Companions to the Ancient World, Oxford 2005; G. R. Bugh (ed.), The Cambridge Companion to the Hellenistic World, Cambridge 2006; A. Erskine/L. Llewellyn-Jones (eds.), Creating a Hellenistic World, Swansea 2011; P. Thonemann, The Hellenistic World. Using Coins as Sources, Guides to the Coinage of the Ancient World, Cambridge 2015; P. Thonemann, The Hellenistic Age, Oxford 2016.

acceptable both to the newly arrived ruler elite as well as the existing local powers – not in the least the native priesthoods.

Along the banks of the Nile, the attitude of foreign rulers towards the gods of Egypt and their association with the indigenous priesthood, as for instance expressed by numerous Ptolemaic Era synodal decrees following meetings between representatives of the ruling house and the priesthoods, clearly shows both the ambiguous and ambivalent, but also continuously developing nature of these relationships.[2] Political pragmatism and current events, rather than any religious considerations or beliefs, led for instance to the state funding of some activities on temple domains throughout much of Ptolemaic and early Roman Egypt.[3] On the temple walls the foreign ruler, whether Ptolemaic Basileus or, later on, Roman Emperor, is then continuously depicted performing the role of the traditional Egyptian pharaoh.[4] Among this plethora of scenes, one encounters reliefs depicting these foreign sovereigns performing *proskynesis* before the gods of Egypt, at times even lying flat out on their belly in front of a deity. The present paper intends to take a closer look at the *sn-tꜣ* (or "Kissing the Earth") ritual,[5] executed in particular by the Ptolemaic Basileus.[6] When, where and why do these foreign sovereigns perform the ultimate act of obeisance to the gods of Egypt?

At the outset, it is important to establish that the performance of this ritual act is nothing new or at all typical for the Ptolemaic and Roman Eras. The expression *sn-tꜣ* already occurs in the Pyramid Texts. For example in spell 422 (§755), from the pyramid of Pepy I in South Saqqara, one finds: "Isis speaks to you, Nephthys calls you, the Akhu (*ꜣḫ.w*) come to you in

2 See for instance the discussion in G. Hölbl, A History of the Ptolemaic Empire, London/New York 2001, 105–111, 162–169, 279–285, and most recently D. von Recklinghausen, Die Philensis-Dekrete. Untersuchungen über zwei Synodaldekrete aus der Zeit Ptolemaios' V. und ihre geschichtliche und religiöse Bedeutung I, ÄA 73, Wiesbaden 2018, 181–197.

3 For example D. Arnold, Temples of the Last Pharaohs, London/New York 1999, 147, 309–310; Hölbl, A History of the Ptolemaic Empire, 85–90, 160–162, 257–279; A. Fassone, Last Indigenous Dynasties and the Ptolemaic Period, in: F. Tiradritti (ed.), Pharaonic Renaissance. Archaism and the Sense of History in Ancient Egypt, Budapest 2008, 137–146; or F. Coppens, Designing the Sacred in early Ptolemaic times: A Continuum of Concepts, in: E. Frood/R. Raja (eds.), Redefining the Sacred: Religious Architecture and Text in the Near East and Egypt 1000 BC – AD 300, Contextualising the Sacred I, Turnhout 2014, 107–150, especially 107–109.

4 See for instance the overview of the large variety of ritual acts performed by the Ptolemaic and Roman rulers as depicted on the walls of Egyptian temples in S. Cauville, L'offrande aux dieux dans le temple égyptien, Leuven 2011.

5 Cauville, L'offrande aux dieux, 259–260. For the term: Wb 4, 154; P. Wilson, A Ptolemaic Lexikon: A Lexicographical Study of the Texts in the Temple of Edfu, OLA 78, Leuven 1997, 853–854; Thesaurus Linguae Aegyptiae, TLA lemma-no. 136560. http://aaew.bbaw.de/tla/servlet/GetWcnDetails?u=guest&f=0&l=0&wn=136560&db=0. Accessed on 06.05.2019.

6 The present article will present a general overview of the *sn-tꜣ* ritual depicted in temples of the Ptolemaic and Roman era, but focus in particular on the occurrence of this scene up until the reign of Ptolemaios XII Neos Dionysos at Edfu only. A much more extensive study of this particular rite, including text and scenes from the reign of Cleopatra VII and the Roman Period occurrences, is still ongoing and will be published subsequently in F. Coppens (ed.), Continuity, Discontinuity and Change. Case studies from the New Kingdom to the Ptolemaic and Roman Era, Prague, in preparation. For a brief introduction to the topic of prostration and *proskynese* in Egypt in New Kingdom and Ptolemaic-Roman times in general, see already J. Mynářová/F. Coppens, Prostration before God and Pharaoh, in: L. Bareš/M. Bárta/V. G. Callender/J. Janák/J. Krejčí (eds.), Times, Signs and Pyramids. Studies in Honour of Miroslav Verner on the Occasion of His Seventieth Birthday, Prague 2011, 283–295.

obeisance/bowing down (*m ksw*),[7] while kissing the earth (*sn-tꜣ*) at your feet because of the terror of you (*šꜥ.t=k*)".[8] This particular passage already contains a number of components that later on will become standard elements in the inscriptions accompanying the ruler performing this ritual on temple walls in Ptolemaic and Roman times. This includes next to the obvious expression *sn-tꜣ*, as well as *m ksw* ("in obeisance" or "bowing down"), also the reason for this particular performance: the fear or terror involved. In the Pyramid Texts, this is expressed by the use of the noun *šꜥ.t*,[9] while later on especially the terms *snḏ* and *šfy.t*[10] will become the more common ones.[11]

The act of "kissing the earth" is not only mentioned in texts, but also features on the walls of tombs and temples throughout the entire history of ancient Egypt. One well-known Old Kingdom example derives already from the sun temple of the Fifth Dynasty pharaoh Niuserre at Abu Ghurab: two small fragments depict and mention this particular act of obeisance.[12] New Kingdom Theban tombs, such as that of the Eighteenth Dynasty vizier Ramose (TT 55), likewise portray the tomb owner in obeisance and "kissing the earth" before pharaoh.[13] These acts of obeisance and prostration are more often than not in contemporary tombs associated with foreigners bringing tribute.[14] Similarly, in the festival hall of Osorkon II in the temple at Bubastis, one can still observe on several loose blocks how foreigners (and courtiers) in a variety of gestures (standing, kneeling and lying down) perform obeisance before the ruler (Fig. 1).[15]

---

7 Wb 5, 139–140; Wilson, Ptolemaic Lexikon, 1090; Thesaurus Linguae Aegyptiae, TLA lemma-no. 165450. http://aaew.bbaw.de/tla/servlet/GetWcnDetails?u=guest&f=0&l=0&wn=165450&db=0. Accessed on 06.05.2019.

8 On the west, rear wall of the burial chamber: C. Berger–El-Naggar/J. Leclant/B. Mathieu/I. Pierre-Croisiau, Les textes de la pyramide de Pépy Ier. 1. Description et analyse, MIFAO 118/1, Cairo 2001, 27; I. Pierre-Croisiau, Les textes de la pyramide de Pépy Ier. 2. Fac-similés, MIFAO 118/2, Cairo 2001, plate 1 (nos. 8–9). The spell also occurs in a similar position in the pyramids of Merenre and Pepy II at South Saqqara.

9 Wb 4, 416–417, Wilson, Ptolemaic Lexikon, 993; Thesaurus Linguae Aegyptiae, TLA lemma-no. 152300. http://aaew.bbaw.de/tla/servlet/GetWcnDetails? u=guest&f=0&l=0&wn=152300&db=0. Accessed on 06.05.2019.

10 *snḏ*: Wb 4, 183–184; Wilson, Ptolemaic Lexikon, 878–879; Thesaurus Linguae Aegyptiae, TLA lemma-no. 138740. http://aaew.bbaw.de/tla/servlet/GetWcnDetails? u=guest&f=0&l=0&wn=138740&db=0. Accessed on 06.05.2019; *šfy.t*: Wb 4, 457–459; Wilson, Ptolemaic Lexikon, 1004; Thesaurus Linguae Aegyptiae, TLA lemma-no. 154080. http://aaew.bbaw.de/tla/servlet/GetWcnDetails? u=guest&f=0&l=0&wn=154080&db=0. Accessed on 06.05.2019.

11 For example on the Edfu precinct: Edfou III, 164 (*di=i n=k rsy mḥ.t imn.t iꜣb.t ḥr ẖꜣb rmn n šfy.t=k*), 10; Edfou IV, 227, 4 (*rdi.n=i wi ḥr ẖ.t=i n ꜥꜣ n šfy.t=k*); Edfou V, 141, 1–2 (*rdi.n=i wi ḥr ẖ.t=i n snḏ=k*); Edfou VII, 192, 13 (*ḥpt=i [Gb] (n) ꜥꜣ n šfy.t=k*) and 193, 9 (*/// m ksw n snḏ=k*), and Edfou Mam., 12, 8 (*ptr=i šfy.t n.t šnbty*) and 13, 1 (*di=i n=k snḏ=k r ḥpty šfšf.t=k r-rꜥ stwt itn*).

12 H. Kees, Das Re-Heiligtum des Königs Ne-woser-re (Rathures) III. Die große Festdarstellung, Leipzig 1928, plate 4, scenes 137 and 138. For an overview of numerous other occurrences of this rite in text and image from Old and Middle Kingdom, see B. Dominicus, Gesten und Gebärden in Darstellungen des Alten und Mittleren Reiches, SAGA 10, Heidelberg 1993, especially 32–35.

13 N. De Garis Davies, The Tomb of the Vizier Ramose, MET I, London 1941, plate 34.

14 For example in the tomb of Menkheper-Ra-Seneb (TT 86): N. De Garis Davies, The Tombs of Menkheperrasonb, Amenmose and another (Nos. 86, 112, 42, 226), TTS 5, London 1933, plate 4.

15 E. Naville, The Festival Hall of Osorkon II in the Great Temple of Bubastis (1887–1889), MEEF 10, London 1892, 26–29, plates XIV/1 and XV/7 and 8. See also ibid, 10 and plate II/9 for a similar scene on the opposite wall, or plate XI/6 for a fragmentary other example.

The act of "kissing the earth" was in ancient Egypt not limited to commoners, foreigners, or the nobility, but the king himself also performs this ultimate act of obeisance. On a *talatat* currently exhibited in the Staatliche Museum Ägyptischer Kunst in München, one still notices Akhenaten reaching for the ground in front of an offering to the Aten (München ÄS 5890). Henry G. FISCHER's study of both two- and three-dimensional prostrate figures of the pharaoh indicates that the depiction of this act is encountered rather sporadically in ancient Egypt.[16] According to FISCHER, most known examples of small statuettes of the pharaoh in a prostrated position suggest that these sculptures were either part of a censer or functioned in temple rituals as a substitute for the (absent) pharaoh, while almost all scenes on a temple wall that depict a prostrated ruler show a statue of the ruler and not the king himself.[17]

2 The *sn-tꜣ* ritual in Temples of Ptolemaic and Roman times

At present 24 attestations[18] of the *sn-tꜣ* ritual from Ptolemaic and Roman temples are known to me (overview in Tab. 1).[19] These scenes occur only in temples located in Upper Egypt,

16 H. G. FISCHER, Prostrate Figures of Egyptian Kings, in: UMB 20, 1956, 27–42; H. G. FISCHER, Further Remarks on Prostrate Kings, in: UMB 21, 1960, 35–40. See also P. J. BRAND, The Monuments of Seti I. Epigraphic, Historical and Art Historical Analysis, PÄ 16, Leiden/Boston/Köln 2000, 9–19, especially 18–19 for New Kingdom examples.

17 The depictions of a prostrate Ptolemaios II Philadelphos in Philae (Philae I, plate VII; H. BEINLICH, Die Photos der Preußischen Expedition 1908–1910 nach Nubien 4, Photo 600–799, SRAT 17, Dettelbach 2012, photo 708) or Ptolemaios IX Soter II in Edfu (Edfou Mam., plate 23/3) however depict the king, not his statue (see also further).

18 This number does not include several scenes in which the *sn-tꜣ* performance is also mentioned in the title of the scene, but not as the main ritual act. In these cases, the content of the inscriptions accompanying king and god(s) clearly differ from the texts associated with the royal and divine protagonist(s) in scenes where the *sn-tꜣ* is listed as the main/first ritual activity. See for example Esna VI, 533 or Kom Ombo I, no. 168 (Kom Ombo I = A. GUTBUB, Kôm Ombo I. Les inscriptions du naos [sanctuaires, salle de l'ennéade, salles des offrandes, couloir mystérieux], Cairo 1995, no. 168) (for the older publication: DE MORGAN, Cat. des Mon. 2, no. 769), and compare with the inscriptions from the scenes listed in Table 1 of the present article. The performance of *sn-tꜣ* is also mentioned in the daily temple ritual for Sobek, lord of Tebtynis, as indicated by (fragments of) late hieratic papyri belonging to the library of the Sobek temple and dated to the first to second century AD: G. ROSATI, PSI inv. I 70 e pCarlsberg 307 + PSI inv. I 79 + pBerlino 1443a + pTebt. Tait 25. Rituale giornaliero di Soknebtynis, in: J. OSING/G. ROSATI (eds.), Papiri Geroglifici e ieratici da Tebtynis, Florence 1998, 101–128. For more information on the daily temple ritual in the Sobek temple of Tebtynis, see for instance M. A. STADLER, Zwischen Philologie und Archäologie: Das Tägliche Ritual des Tempels in Soknopaiou Nesos, in: M. CAPASSO/P. DAVOLI (eds.), New Archaeological Researches on the Fayyum. Proceedings of the International Meeting of Egyptology and Papyrology, Lecce, June 8th–10th 2005, Papyrologica Lupiensia 14, Lecce 2007, 283–302 or I. GUERMEUR, À propos d'un nouvel exemplaire du rituel journalier pour Soknebtynis (phieraTeb SCA 2979 et autres variants), in: J.-F. QUACK (ed.), Ägyptische Rituale der griechisch-römischen Zeit, Orientalische Religionen in der Antike 6, Tübingen 2014, 9–23.

19 I would like to thank Anna Dékány (Egyptology, Universität Köln) for bringing the only partially preserved DE MORGAN, Cat. des Mon. 3, no. 569 scene to my attention at the occasion of the 9th Symposium on Royal Ideology. A new edition of this particular scene will form part of the second Kom Ombo volume (*i.e.* La salle médiane avec annexes, la chambre de l'introduction des offrandes, le laboratoire, la chambre de l'inondation, la porte-passage sud-ouest) currently under preparation at the Institut français d'archéologie orientale in Cairo. Likewise, I am very grateful to Kenneth Griffin (The Egypt Centre, Swansea University) for drawing my attention to the Athribis III, 273–274 scene (= Room E 7, 8) (Athribis III = Ch. LEITZ/D. MENDEL, Athribis III. Die östlichen Zugangsräume und

from Athribis in the north to Philae in the south. Far from representing a geographic north-south divide, the spread of its occurrence is rather indicative of the state of preservation and publication of monuments to the north of Athribis.[20] Of more interest is the fact that almost half of the scenes – 10 of 24 to be exact – occur on the Horus precinct of Edfu, in the main temple itself as also in the associated birth house of Harsomtus. The sanctuary with the second most occurrences of this particular scene is – perhaps a bit surprising – the smallish Roman temple of el-Qal'a, located immediately to the north of Coptos, and dedicated to both Isis as well as several desert goddesses.[21]

Scene	Location	Ruler	Crown	Gesture
Karnak	Sanctuary	Alexander III	Bag wig	Arms beside body
Luxor	Sanctuary	Philippos III Arrhidaios	?	?
Philae	Seat o/t First Feast	Ptolemaios II	Bag wig	Lying stretched out
Kom Ombo, de Morgan, Cat. des Mon. 3, no. 569	Salle médiane	Ptolemaios VI	*Destroyed*	Arms beside body (?)
Edfou III, 12–13	Pronaos (screenwall)	Ptolemaios VIII	Blue crown	Arms beside body
Edfou III, 164	Pronaos	Ptolemaios VIII	Blue crown	Arms beside body
Edfou IV, 55–56	Exterior of naos (W)	Ptolemaios VIII	Blue crown	Arms beside body
Edfou IV, 209	Exterior of naos (E)	Ptolemaios VIII	Blue crown	Arms beside body
Edfou IV, 227–228	Exterior of naos (N)	Ptolemaios VIII	Blue crown	Arms beside body
Edfou Mam., 12–13	Sanctuary	Ptolemaios VIII	Blue crown	Arms beside body
Edfou Mam., 42	Chapel D	Ptolemaios IX	Blue crown	Crouching
Edfou Mam., 110	Vestibule G	Ptolemaios IX	Blue crown	Lying stretched out
Edfou VII, 192–193	Enclosure wall	Ptolemaios X	Nemes	Arms beside body
Tôd II, 231	Second vestibule	Ptolemaios X–XII?	Composite	Arms beside body
Edfou V, 140–141	Large open courtyard	Ptolemaios XII	Bag wig	Arms beside body

Seitenkapellen sowie die Treppe zum Dach und die rückwärtigen Räume des Tempels Ptolemaios XII. Band 1: Text, Band 2: Tafeln, Cairo 2017).

20 For example G. Hölbl, Altägypten im römischen Reich. Der römische Pharao und seine Tempel I, Mainz 2000, 47–52 for the state of preservation of the Roman temple remains in the Delta and Middle Egypt. See however Arnold, Temples of the Last Pharaohs, 144 for a different point of view, suggesting as possible reasons the decreased importance of cults in Lower Egypt and the Delta, an overabundance of existing temples in the area following the building activities of the Late Period, or a politically motivated focus on (unruly) Upper Egypt.

21 In general: L. Pantalacci/C. Traunecker, Le temple d'el-Qal'a. Relevés des scenes et des textes I. Sanctuaire central – sanctuaire nord – salle des offrandes n°s 1 à 112, Cairo 1990 (= el-Qal'a I), and L. Pantalacci/C. Traunecker, Le temple d'el-Qal'a II. Relevés des scenes et des textes n°s 113–294, Cairo 1998 (= el-Qal'a II).

Scene	Location	Ruler	Crown	Gesture
Athribis III, 273	Room E 7, 8	Ptolemaios XII (?)	White crown	Arms extended forwards
Dendara V, 5–6	East crypt 1	Cleopatra VII	*Destroyed*	*Destroyed*
Dendara VIII, 22–23	Kiosk on roof	Cleopatra VII	Nemes	Arms extended forwards
Dendara VIII, 28	Kiosk on roof	Cleopatra VII	Nemes	Arms extended forwards
el-Qal'a I, 2	Central Sanctuary	Augustus	Atef (?)	Arms extended forwards
Athribis II, 410–413	Gate to sanctuary C 2	Tiberius	White crown	Arms extended forwards
el-Qal'a II, 129	Exterior of sanctuary	Claudius	Red crown (?)	Arms beside body
el-Qal'a II, 223	*Per-nu*	Claudius	Nemes	Arms extended forwards
el-Qal'a II, 226	*Per-nu*	Claudius	Blue crown	Arms extended forwards

Tab. 1: Chronological overview of the 24 occurrences of the ritual *sn-tȝ* ("Kissing the Earth") in temples of the Ptolemaic and Roman Era

Title (general format)	Period	Occurrences
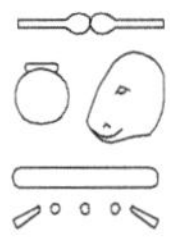 and 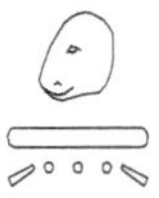	Alexander III – Claudius	5 occurrences Luxor; Edfou IV, 55; Edfou V, 140; el-Qal'a II, 129 and 226
 and 	Ptolemaios VIII – Tiberius	6 occurrences Edfou III, 164; Dendara V, 5; Dendara VIII, 28; Tôd II, 231; Athribis II, 410; Athribis III, 273
	Ptolemaios VIII – Cleopatra VII	6 occurrences Edfou III, 12; Edfou IV, 209; Edfou Mam., 12 and 42; Edfou VII, 192; Dendara VIII, 22
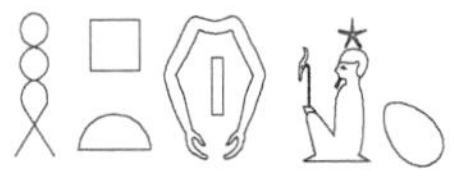	Claudius	1 occurrence el-Qal'a II, 223
Destroyed/no title	Philippos Arrhidaios – Claudius	6 occurrences Karnak; Philae; Edfou IV, 227; Edfou Mam., 110; el-Qal'a I, 2

Tab. 2: General outlook of the title of the ritual *sn-tȝ* ("Kissing the Earth") in temples of the Ptolemaic and Roman Era

The title of the *sn-tꜣ* ritual can be written in a variety of ways and no preference for a particular writing – overall, geographically or chronologically – can be recognised, as can be clearly observed in Table 2. As far as can be established, the use of the combination of the hieroglyphic signs with a person either bending over or lying upon the *tꜣ*-sign occurs – at least in the title of the ritual – only from the reign of Ptolemaios VIII Euergetes II onward. The table also includes a single scene with the title "Embracing Geb" (*ḥpt Gb*) from the temple at el-Qal'a, as it is a clear reference to the spell for "kissing the earth", which regularly opens with "I have kissed the earth; I have embraced Geb" (*sn.n=ỉ tꜣ ḥpt.n=ỉ Gb*). This same passage occurs in the majority of the texts accompanying the depiction of this ritual in temples of the Ptolemaic and Roman Era,[22] but also in its precursors (see further). In the few cases where two scenes depicting the *sn-tꜣ* ritual occur opposite one another in a chapel or chamber, the priestly designers always decided for variety – the title is never written in the same manner in opposing scenes. This is for instance the case in the *per-nu* chapel of the temple of el-Qal'a, decorated during the reign of Emperor Claudius, where the variety is the greatest by placing the *sn-tꜣ* (el-Qal'a II, 226; east wall) opposite the aforementioned phrase *ḥpt-Gb* (el-Qal'a II, 223; west wall). A few more examples to illustrate this pattern: On the interior west wall of the kiosk on the roof of the Dendara temple, dated to the reign of Cleopatra VII, one finds in the titles the two variants of the individual over the sign of the land opposite one another:  (Dendara VIII, 28) versus  (Dendara VIII, 22). In opposite scenes of the ritual on the east and west exterior wall of the naos in Edfu, from the reign of Ptolemaios VIII Euergetes II, again different variants occur: 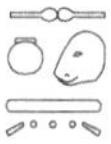 (Edfou IV, 55) and  (Edfou IV, 209).

The general timeframe of the occurrence of this specific ritual act on a temple wall appears to cover the majority of the Ptolemaic and early Roman Era (Tab. 1). The oldest known attestation already dates to the reign of Alexander III and the bark sanctuary of the Luxor temple, while the latest datable manifestations are no less than three scenes from the reign of Emperor Claudius at the el-Qal'a temple (the two aforementioned scenes in the *per-nu* chapel and one on the exterior wall of the Isis sanctuary). In other words, the ritual is – seemingly – attested throughout the entire period of Ptolemaic Egypt and more or less the first century of Roman rule.

Upon taking a closer look, it becomes quickly obvious that its chronological distribution is certainly not equally spread over time. Three of the 24 scenes can clearly be dated to the early Ptolemaic Period (up to the reign of Ptolemaios II Philadelphos; died 246 BC) and show a continuity of a tradition dating back at least to the time of the New Kingdom. After a period of discontinuity in the depiction of this ritual act of obeisance on a temple wall – more or less a century passes without a single trace of this scene on a temple wall, notwithstanding the

22 See for example: Edfou III, 164, 1–2; Edfou IV, 55, 13; Edfou V, 141, 11; Edfou VII, 192, 13; Dendara VIII, 22, 12; and precisely el-Qal'a I, 2. The same passage also occurs in the daily temple ritual for Sobek, lord of Tebtynis, according to late hieratic papyri from the local temple library: ROSATI, Rituale giornaliero di Soknebtynis, Tavole 16 A+B, line 4, 9.

numerous activities on temple sites from the reign of Ptolemaios II Philadelphos onward[23] – this is followed by a sudden explosion of attestations during the reign of Ptolemaios VIII Euergetes II (rule 170/169–164, 145–116 BC) and his immediate successors at Edfu. No less than ten times the ritual appears on either the walls of the temple or the associated birth temple of Harsomtus within the Horus precinct (Tab. 1). Interestingly, the ritual is – with a single exception from the reign of Ptolemaios VI Philometor (180–145 BC) at Kom Ombo[24] – not attested anywhere else during this period and only appears again at the very end of Ptolemaic Egypt, in the temples of Tod (Ptolemaios X Alexander I – Ptolemaios XII Neos Dionysos?)[25] and Athribis (Ptolemaios XII Neos Dionysos?)[26] and finally during the reign of Cleopatra VII (51–30 BC), among others in the kiosk on the roof of Dendara's Hathor temple (Fig. 3).

In the present paper I will focus in particular on the occurrence of the *sn-tꜣ* ritual on temple walls in the early Ptolemaic Period and its precursors from New Kingdom and Third Intermediate Period times (in section 3). This will be followed by a discussion of plausible reasons for the discontinuity of its portrayal on a temple wall as well as the (changed) nature and characteristics of the scene upon its reappearance on the Horus precinct at Edfu after a (long) period of absence (section 4).[27]

23 Not in the least, for instance, in the very core of the Edfu temple (especially the volumes Edfou I and Edfou II), where almost the entire naos was provided with a decorative pattern under the reign Ptolemaios IV Philopator (222–204 BC), including scenes of the daily temple sanctuary ritual in the sanctuary during which the *sn-tꜣ* was undoubtedly performed, but not depicted. See the general overview of the decorative program applied to the interior walls of the sanctuary in M. Alliot, Le culte d'Horus à Edfou au temps des Ptolémées I, BdE 20/1, Cairo 1949, 1–195; S. Cauville, Essai sur la théologie du temple d' Horus à Edfou I, BdE 102/1, Cairo 1987, 1–2; R. David, Temple Ritual at Abydos, London 2016, 166 (see also section 3). In general on the stages of construction and decoration of the Horus temple at Edfu, see: S. Cauville/D. Devauchelle, Le temple d'Edfou: étapes de la construction. Nouvelles données historiques, in: RdE 35, 1984, 31–55, here: 32–35; 44–45; D. Kurth, Treffpunkt der Götter: Inschriften aus dem Tempel des Horus von Edfu, Zürich 1994, 26–27; N. Baum, Le temple d'Edfou. A la découverte du Grand Siège de Rê-Harakhty, Paris 2007, 19–20.

24 The de Morgan, Cat. des Mon. 3, no. 569 scene most likely dates from the latter part of his reign (*i.e.* 152–145 BC) following M. Minas-Nerpel, Die Dekorationstätigkeit von Ptolemaios VI. Philometor und Ptolemaios VIII. Euergetes II. an ägyptischen Tempeln (Teil 2), in: OLP 28, 1997, 87–121, especially 96–97, 110–113.

25 On the first register of the west wall of the temple's second vestibule: Tôd II, 231; Tôd III, 148. The cartouches are left empty, but elsewhere in the second vestibule of the Tôd temple, the reliefs date from the reigns of Ptolemaios X Alexander I (Tôd II, 241; Tôd III, 158) and Ptolemaios XII Neos Dionysos (Tôd II, 235 and 243; Tôd III, 152 and 158 – both reliefs are moreover located on the same west wall as the *sn-tꜣ* scene). The principal gate leading from the first to the second vestibule is likewise dated to the reign of Ptolemaios XII Neos Dionysos (Tôd II, 173–176, Tôd III, 108–109), making him the most likely candidate to be identified with the unnamed Pharaoh depicted performing the ritual of "kissing the earth" in the Tod temple.

26 On the first register of the east wall of Room E 7: Athribis III/1, 273; Athribis III/2, 195. The cartouches are left empty in the entire room (Athribis III/1, 260–284), but the relief on the gate leading from Room C 3 to Room E 7 is dated to Ptolemaios XII Neos Dionysos (Athribis III/1, 249–259).

27 The study of the younger scenes, from the reign of Cleopatra VII onward, is still ongoing and will be published elsewhere – see already note 6 of the present article.

3 The continuation of a tradition: The *sn-tꜣ* ritual in early Ptolemaic times (Alexander III – Ptolemaios II)

A mere three scenes depicting the *sn-tꜣ* ritual on a temple wall can thus far be dated to early Ptolemaic times (Tab. 1). The oldest known attestation already dates to the reign of Alexander III and the bark sanctuary of the Luxor temple.[28] The southernmost scene of the first register on the exterior east wall depicts a standing Alexander III with both arms in front of his body before Amun-Ra-Kamutef while "kissing the earth for his father" (*sn-tꜣ n it=f*). The scene forms part of a sequence of reliefs depicting ritual stages from both the daily temple sanctuary ritual and the offering ritual.[29] The same ritual performance can be observed on the second register of the exterior north wall of the bark sanctuary installed in the core of the Amun temple at Karnak under the reign of Philippos III Arrhidaios.[30] Like the scene from the Luxor bark sanctuary, the Karnak relief also forms part of a much larger decorative program related to the daily temple sanctuary ritual. This is far from surprising when it comes to either bark sanctuary, whether in Luxor or Karnak, as it forms a recurring pattern on the walls of many such structures from the time of the New Kingdom onward.[31]

For the undoubtedly best preserved instances of this particular act of obeisance in the context of the daily temple sanctuary ritual one has to return in time to the Nineteenth Dynasty and the temple of Seti I at Abydos.[32] Remarkably, these are the only occurrences of the "kissing the earth" ritual depicted as part of the daily temple sanctuary ritual from the New Kingdom. In other New Kingdom temples, and especially (bark) sanctuaries, that contain the daily temple sanctuary ritual as part of its decorative program, one finds no single further occurrence of this particular ritual performance.[33] In Abydos, the ritual is depicted in each of the six chapels of the gods, namely of Ptah, Ra-Harakhte, Amun-Ra, Osiris, Isis and Horus (Tab. 3), in the very core of the temple. In the chapels, the scene is in each instance located on the second register of the north wall, near the entrance to the room. In the chapel

28 M. Abd el-Raziq, Die Darstellungen und Texte des Sanktuars Alexander des Großen im Tempel von Luxor, AV 16, Mainz am Rhein 1984, 15 and plate 4/C6.

29 Abd el-Raziq, Darstellungen und Texte, 11; J. Osing, Zum Kultbildritual in Abydos, in: E. Teeter/J. A. Larson (eds.), Gold of Praise. Studies on Ancient Egypt in Honor of Edward F. Wente, SAOC 58, Chicago 1999, 317–334, here: 330–331. On the New Kingdom Offering ritual see now N. Tacke, Das Opferritual des ägyptischen Neuen Reiches, OLA 222, Leuven 2013. For the daily temple sanctuary ritual see further.

30 PM II^2, 99–102; Osing, Zum Kultbildritual in Abydos, 331. The entire decorative program of the bark sanctuary is currently being prepared for publication by a team under the direction of Christophe Thiers and Anaïs Tillier at the Centre franco-égyptien d'étude des temples de Karnak (http://www.cfeetk.cnrs.fr/accueil/programmes-scientifiques/). A selection of these scenes have already been made accessible on the website of the Karnak project (http://sith.huma-num.fr/karnak), but during a final check in January 2019 the scene depicting the *sn-tꜣ* ritual was not yet available for consultation.

31 Osing, Zum Kultbildritual in Abydos, 317–329.

32 A. H. Gardiner/A. M. Calverley, The Temple of King Sethos I at Abydos. Volume I. The Chapels of Osiris, Isis and Horus, London 1933, plates 4 and 13 (chapel of Osiris), 18 (Isis) and 26 (Horus); A. H. Gardiner/A. M. Calverley, Temple of King Sethos I at Abydos, Volume II. The Chapels of Amen-Reʿ, Reʿ-Harakhti, Ptah, and King Sethos, London 1935, plates 4 (Amun), 14 (Ra-Harakhte) and 22 (Ptah). Also David, Temple Ritual, 123–179; for the *sn-tꜣ* ritual in particular: 131, 139, 153, and 162–163.

33 For an overview of numerous New Kingdom depictions of stages from the daily temple sanctuary ritual, see Osing, Zum Kultbildritual in Abydos, 318–329.

of Osiris a second depiction of the *sn-tꜣ* is still depicted on the opposite south wall as well. The pharaoh is usually portrayed in a crouching position with the arms stretched forward in a gesture of praise. He is adorned with either the blue crown or the bag wig with uraeus – two types of crowns that, together with the cap crown, are generally considered to be closely connected and at times interchangeable.[34]

Chapel / Scene	Deity	Location	Crown	Gesture
GARDINER/CALVERLEY, Abydos I, pl. 4	Osiris	N wall, 2nd reg.	Blue crown	Crouching, praising
GARDINER/CALVERLEY, Abydos I, pl. 13	Osiris	S wall, 2nd reg.	Blue crown	Crouching, praising
GARDINER/CALVERLEY, Abydos I, pl. 18	Isis	N wall, 2nd reg.	Bag wig	Crouching, praising
GARDINER/CALVERLEY, Abydos I, pl. 26	Horus	N wall, 2nd reg.	Bag wig	Crouching, praising
GARDINER/CALVERLEY, Abydos II, pl. 4	Amun-Ra	N wall, 2nd reg.	Bag wig	Crouching, praising
GARDINER/CALVERLEY, Abydos II, pl. 14	Ra-Harakhte	N wall, 2nd reg.	Bag wig	Crouching, presenting incense
GARDINER/CALVERLEY, Abydos II, pl. 22	Ptah	N wall, 2nd reg.	Bag wig	Crouching, praising
Luxor	Amun-Ra-Kamutef	E wall, 1st reg.	Bag wig	Standing, arms beside body
Karnak	Amun	N wall, 2nd reg.	?	?
Philae	Isis	N wall, 1st reg.	Bag wig	Lying stretched out

Tab. 3: Overview of the performance of *sn-tꜣ* in the chapels of the gods in the Seti I temple at Abydos (New Kingdom) and in early Ptolemaic times (Alexander III – Ptolemaios II Philadelphos)

The inscriptions accompanying the *sn-tꜣ* scenes in the Abydos chapels show clear parallels with the Twenty-second Dynasty Berlin papyri (pBerlin 3014 and 3055), also known as the daily rituals for Amun and Mut at Karnak (= pAmun I, pAmun II, and pMut).[35] Within the daily temple sanctuary ritual for Amun and Mut one finds no less than six chapters or spells dealing with acts of *proskynesis*. It concerns chapters/spells 12 to 17, with its titles – and

34 E. VASSILIKA, Ptolemaic Philae, OLA 34, Leuven 1989, 92. See also G. STEINDORFF, Die Blaue Königskrone, in: ZÄS 53, 1917, 59–74, especially 70–71; V. DAVIES, The Origin of the Blue Crown, in: JEA 68, 1982, 69–76; K. GOEBS, Untersuchungen zur Funktion und Symbolgehalt des *nms*, in: ZÄS 122, 1995, 154–181; T. HARDWICK, The Iconography of the Blue Crown in the New Kingdom, in: JEA 89, 2003, 117–141.

35 G. MÖLLER, Hieratische Papyrus aus den königlichen Museen zu Berlin. Band 1: Rituale für den Kultus des Amon und für den Kultus der Mut, Leipzig 1901; A. MORET, Le rituel du culte divin journalier en Egypte, Annales du Musée Guimet 40, BdE 14, Paris 1902, 56–67 and 113–115; W. GUGLIELMI/K. BUROH, Die Eingangssprüche des Täglichen Tempelrituals nach Papyrus Berlin 3055 (I, 1 – VI, 3), in: J. VAN DIJK (ed.), Essays on Ancient Egypt in Honour of Herman te Velde, Egyptological Memoirs 1, Groningen 1997, 101–166, here: 125–133; 157–166; DAVID, Temple Ritual, 169–172.

contents – all referring to "kissing the earth" or "placing oneself on the belly", at times with the head bend down, stretching oneself out, or for touching/kissing the earth with one's fingers:

- Spell 12:[36] *r3 n sn-t3*
- Spell 13:[37] *r3 n rdi.t ḥr ẖ.t* or *ky*
- Spell 14:[38] *r3 n rdi.t ḥr ẖ.t m dwn*
- Spell 15:[39] *r3 n sn-t3 iw ḥr m ẖrw*[40]
- Spell 16:[41] *ky*
- Spell 17:[42] *ky*

Large passages from four of these six chapters, namely spells 12, 15, 16 and 17, already feature in the inscriptions accompanying the act of prostration depicted in the Abydene chapels.[43] In contrast, the texts accompanying the scenes of this ritual act of obeisance in the bark sanctuaries at Luxor and Karnak only contain the title of the ritual (*sn-t3* [*n it=f*]), but no other passage from these chapters of the daily temple sanctuary ritual. Next to the title itself and the characteristic portrayal of the ruler in front of the god (Tab. 1, *s.v.* Gestures), the link with the daily temple sanctuary ritual is in the case of the two Theban bark sanctuaries also indicated by the position of this scene within the entire decorative program of the edifice.[44]

The third and final example from early Ptolemaic times is a remarkable scene located in the "Seat of the First Feast" (*s.t-ḥb-tpy*)[45] – an early example of what is more commonly known as the *wabet* in Ptolemaic and Roman temples[46] – in the core of the Isis temple on

36 pAmun I, IV, 7–9; pAmun II, XI, 5–7; pMut IV, 1–4 = Guglielmi/Buroh, Die Eingangssprüche des Täglichen Tempelrituals, 125–127.

37 pAmun I, IV, 9 – V, 2; pAmun II, XI, 8–10 (both *r3 n rdi.t ḥr ẖ.t*); pMut IV, 4–7 (*ky*) = Guglielmi/Buroh, Die Eingangssprüche des Täglichen Tempelrituals, 127.

38 pAmun I, V, 2–6; pAmun II, XI, 10–13; pMut IV, 7 – V, 1 = Guglielmi/Buroh, Die Eingangssprüche des Täglichen Tempelrituals , 127–129.

39 pAmun I, V, 6–8; pAmun II, XII, 1–2; pMut V, 1–3 = Guglielmi/Buroh, Die Eingangssprüche des Täglichen Tempelrituals, 129–130.

40 The chapter also occurs in Abydos, but under a different title, in the chapel of Amun-Ra: "Spell for kissing the earth and placing (oneself) on the belly in order to 'kiss' the ground with his fingers" (*r3 n sn-t3 rdi.t ḥr ẖ.t r sn-t3 m ḏbʿ.w=f*) = Gardiner/Calverley, Abydos II, plate 4.

41 pAmun I, V, 8–9; pAmun II, XII, 2–4; pMut V, 4–6 = Guglielmi/Buroh, Die Eingangssprüche des Täglichen Tempelrituals, 131–132.

42 pAmun I, VI, 1–3; pAmun II, XII, 4–7; pMut V, 6–10 = Guglielmi/Buroh, Die Eingangssprüche des Täglichen Tempelrituals, 132–133.

43 Overview of the inscriptions of all six chapters in: Guglielmi/Buroh Die Eingangssprüche des Täglichen Tempelrituals, 157–166. See also David, Temple Ritual, 177, and 372, n. 29.

44 Osing, Zum Kultbildritual in Abydos, 330–331.

45 F. Coppens, The Open Court in the Temple of Philae. A Complex of *Wabet* and Court in the Making, in: H. Győry (ed.), Aegyptus et Pannonia III. Acta Symposii anno 2004, Budapest 2006, 27–39; F. Coppens, The Wabet. Tradition and Innovation in Temples of the Ptolemaic and Roman Period, Prague 2007, 22–26, 73–145.

46 For the initial identification, see already A. Gutbub, Remarques sur quelques règles observées dans l'architecture, la décoration et les inscriptions des temples de Basse Epoque, in: F. Geus/F. Thill (eds.), Mélanges offerts à Jean Vercoutter, Paris 1985, 123–136, here: 132–133, as well as C. Traunecker, Les ouabet des temples d'el-Qal'a et de Chenhour, in: D. Kurth (ed.), 3. Ägyptologische Tempeltagung.

Philae (Fig. 2).[47] The relief in question is found on the first register of the open chamber's north wall, directly above the doorway leading into the small Chamber of Linen (Room IX) and associated access to a series of crypts both underneath the floor level and in the thickness of the temple's outer wall. In comparison with the two older scenes, located on the exterior of the bark sanctuaries in the core of the Luxor temple and the Amun temple at Karnak, at Philae the scene is not only found in an entirely different location, but the depiction of Ptolemaios II Philadelphos as well as the large amount of text present likewise indicates a modification.

The scene portrays the king spread out on the ground in front of Isis while performing the *sn-tȝ* ritual. The pharaoh – in reality a Greek Basileus – is literally weighed down by a large inscription of ten lines that covers almost the entire available space above the prostrated figure. The reason for depicting the ruler in such an uncommon manner remains open to debate. Could it be as simple as the need for space to be able to include a large amount of text? Alternatively, were the priestly designers of this scene perhaps making a statement, depicting the foreign ruler truly "kissing the ground" in front of the leading lady of the temple? This is, of course, a mere hypothesis. Nonetheless, the manner in which Ptolemaios II Philadelphos is depicted is rather unusual – and when it comes to depictions of this rite in temples of the Ptolemaic and Roman Era, almost unique. Of all the occurrences of the *sn-tȝ* ritual presently known to me from Ptolemaic and Roman temples, only two other scenes depict the ruler in a position other than standing upright.[48] In both cases, the architectural setting of the scene and especially the limited amount of space available appears to have been the main reason for depicting the ruler in an uncommon manner. Both scenes occur in the Harsomtus *mammisi* on the Edfu precinct and date to the reign of Ptolemaios IX Soter II. The first occurrence is located on the interior of a broken door lintel and portrays the pharaoh lying on the ground in front of Hathor.[49] The text associated with this ritual performance is reminiscent of the opening passage of chapter 12 of the daily temple sanctuary ritual – appropriately titled "Spell for kissing the earth" (*rȝ n sn-tȝ*).[50] The only difference between both texts is that in the New Kingdom version it is Geb – the earth – that is embraced, while in the inscription from the Edfu birth temple, it is reduced – most likely by oversight – to a generic deity (*ḥpt.n=i nṯr*). The second scene is located on the north wall of the vestibule preceding the sanctuary.[51] It has the ruler in a crouching position with his arms spread forwards. In both cases, the limited amount of space available – or rather the complete lack of standing room – appears to be the main reason for the manner in which the king is depicted. The latter cannot be said for the scene in the Isis temple at Philae, where the designers had a variety of options available – including the standard depiction in Ptolemaic and Roman times, namely the ruler standing upright with his hands either hanging loosely besides his body or slightly extended forwards. This is exemplified by the portrayal of this act elsewhere in the temples at Edfu,

Systeme und Programme der ägyptischen Tempeldekoration, ÄUAT 33/1, Wiesbaden 1995, 241–282, here: 242–244.

47 Philae I, 22, 11–17 and plate VII; Vassilika, Ptolemaic Philae, database no. 661; Beinlich, Die Photos der Preußischen Expedition 1908–1910 nach Nubien 4, photo 708.

48 See the overview in Table 1 of the various poses or gestures taken by the ruler when performing this particular ritual act.

49 Edfou Mam., 110, 7–8, and especially plate 23/3.

50 pAmun I, IV, 7–9; pAmun II, XI, 5–7; pMut IV, 1–4; Guglielmi/Buroh, Die Eingangssprüche des Täglichen Tempelrituals, 125.

51 Edfou Mam., 42, 7–10; plates 6/1 and 18/2.

Kom Ombo, Dendara (Fig. 3), el-Qal'a, Tod and Athribis (Tab. 1, *s.v.* Gestures). Instead, in Philae, the priestly designers reached a decision to have him depicted while lying stretched out on the ground.

Unlike the depiction of the ritual of "kissing the earth" on the walls of the bark sanctuaries in Luxor and Karnak, which only contain the title of the ritual, the long inscription located above the prostrated pharaoh in the "Seat of the First Feast" at Philae establishes a much more pronounced connection with and continuity of the earlier versions of the daily temple sanctuary ritual as known from the New Kingdom and the Third Intermediate Period. In the present article, I will only go briefly into the inscription that accompanies the act of *proskynesis* in Philae, as I have already studied it in detail elsewhere.[52] The entire text is nothing less than a compilation of four of the six chapters or spells of the daily temple sanctuary ritual as known from the Berlin papyri and the Abydene chapels of the gods. The text opens with a large passage from chapter 12, before continuing with shorter phrases from chapters 13 and 14, to finish with again a longer passage, in this case taken from chapter 17.[53] A number of these phrases will reappear – together with the depiction of the ritual performance of *sn-tꜣ* – a century later, first on the Horus precinct at Edfu and later on in other temples from late Ptolemaic – early Roman times. This concerns among others the following expressions:

- "I kiss the ground, I embrace Geb, and I execute the ritual for/render praise to" the main deity of the temple (*sn=i tꜣ ḥpt=i Gb irr=i ḥsw n* ...).[54]
- "I have placed myself on my belly out of fear of you. I will look up according to your wish" (*rdi.n=i wi ḥr ẖ.t=i n ḥryt=t dgi=i n mrw.t=ṯ*).[55]
- "I have embraced Geb, and Hathor, she makes that I am/shall be great" (*ḥpt.n=i Gb Ḥw.t-ḥr di=s wr=i*).[56]

It is not only the inscription accompanying the prostrated pharaoh that establishes a clear link with earlier versions of the daily temple sanctuary ritual. The entire north wall of the "Seat of the First Feast" at Philae is, in fact, quite remarkable in this perspective. The wall depicts initial stages of the divine dressing ritual as among others known from the daily temple sanctuary ritual.[57] Focusing on the adoration of the deity, the revealing of the face – either by opening the shrines containing the divine statue or by presenting a mirror (in all cases *wn-ḥr*) – and in a final stage the presentation of protective regalia. The inscriptions accompanying all scenes but one on the first and second register of the north wall derive without exception from

52 See especially Coppens, The Wabet, 92–96. Also F. Coppens, Creative Writing in Ptolemy II's Time. Texts from the Temple of Isis at Philae, in: R. J. Dann (ed.), Current Research in Egyptology. Proceedings of the Fifth Annual Symposium, London 2006, 34–42, here: 38–40.

53 First established by Traunecker, Les ouabet des temples d'el-Qal'a et de Chenhour, 243, n. 7.

54 The passage occurs in chapter 12. For some later occurrences of (part) of this passage: Edfou III, 164, 1–2; Edfou IV, 55, 12–13; 227, 3–4; Edfou V, 140, 14–141, 2; Edfou Mam., 110, 7–8; Dendara VIII, 22, 11–12; Athribis III, 410, 6.

55 The passage occurs in chapters 13 and 14. For some later occurrences of (part) of this passage: Edfou III, 12, 2; 164, 2; Edfou IV, 209, 4; Edfou V, 140, 1–2; Edfou VII, 192, 12–14.

56 The passage occurs in chapter 13. For a later occurrence: el-Qal'a I, 2.

57 Overview in David, Temple Ritual, 131, 135–139.

various chapters of the daily temple sanctuary ritual:[58] chapters dealing with similar topics are often combined and edited, to create a seemingly new text, firmly rooted in an ancient tradition. The same holds true for the scenes on the third register, with the only difference that the source material varies (*e.g.* the re-use and adaptation of (part of) PT utterance 600 or BD spell 155).[59]

In conclusion, the overall picture that can be derived from the three early Ptolemaic depictions of the *sn-tꜣ* ritual, in Karnak, Luxor and Philae, clearly indicates that all three fall within the well-established context of the daily temple sanctuary ritual. The continuity of this ritual act of obeisance before the statue of the deity from the New Kingdom onward is illustrated by both text and image and the general position of the scene within the entire decorative program of each individual monument.

4 Continuation and change: The reoccurrence of *sn-tꜣ* ritual in Edfu (Ptolemaios VIII – Ptolemaios XII)

Following the portrayal of a prostrate Ptolemaios II Philadelphos in the Isis temple on Philae, a whole century passes by without a single trace of this particular scene in any other temple, despite the vast array of activities attested upon numerous temple domains for the general period between 250 and 150 BC.[60] The ritual appears for the very first time again on a temple wall in the double temple of Haroeris and Sobek at Kom Ombo during the latter part of the reign of Ptolemaios VI Philometor.[61] The heavily damaged relief is located on the first register in the interior of the eastern gate leading from the so-called "Salle médiane" (also designated as "Salle C")[62] to the small hypostyle hall of the temple ("Salle D"). This is followed by a sudden explosion of attestations during the reign of Ptolemaios VIII Euergetes II and his immediate successors at Edfu. No less than ten times the ritual appears on either the walls of the temple or the birth temple within the Horus precinct (overview in Tab. 1). The gap in time between the occurrence of this ritual in early Ptolemaic times and – with the exception of the single scene in Kom Ombo – the reign of Ptolemaios VIII is remarkable.[63] One cannot dismiss the possibility that this is merely due to the absence of evidence – whether owing to destruction or still awaiting identification – keeping in mind that absence of evidence does not necessarily imply evidence of absence.

58 Passages of the following spells from the daily temple sanctuary ritual feature on the north wall of Philae's "Seat of the First Feast": Spells 10, 11, 12, 13, 14, 17, 24, 25, 27 and 28 (overview in Coppens, The Wabet, 93–107).

59 For an in-depth study of the north wall of the "Seat of the First Feast" in Philae and its connection with earlier traditions, see Coppens, The Wabet, 92–121.

60 See already note 23 in the present article.

61 de Morgan, Cat. des Mon. 3, no. 569 scene most likely dates from the period between 152–145 BC according to Minas-Nerpel, OLP 28, 1997, 96–97, and 110–113. See also already note 19 in the present article regarding its republication.

62 de Morgan, Cat. des Mon. 2, plan between pages 54–55. Compare with A. Gutbub, Kôm Ombo I, xiii, fig. 4.

63 The decorative programme applied to the walls of the Horus temple of Edfu that includes the depictions of the *sn-tꜣ* ritual performed by Ptolemaios VIII Euergetes II (*i.e.* on the exterior of naos and pronaos, and in the sanctuary of the *mammisi*) dates primarily from the period of his reign post 142/140 BC – Minas-Nerpel, OLP 28, 1997, 91–95, 114.

One can speculate whether the development of Ptolemaic Egypt in general – and the overall position and perception of the foreign sovereign in particular – could provide any plausible indication for both the sudden absence as well as reappearance of this very specific act of *proskynesis* by a foreign ruler – the Ptolemaic Basileus – on the walls of traditional Egyptian temples. From a historical perspective, one is faced with two widely different phases in the history of Ptolemaic Egypt. The three early Ptolemaic attestations of the *sn-tꜣ* ritual clearly fall into the formative period of not only the Ptolemaic state, but also of the inscriptional and decorative program to be applied to the newly constructed sanctuaries all over Egypt. The aforementioned north wall of the "Seat of the First Feast" at Philae is one clear example of priestly designers combining, re-editing and re-interpreting older texts and scenes in early Ptolemaic times. It established both a link with the past, but also with the future – at the crossroads of what was and what will be.[64] While most of the other scenes covering this specific wall regularly feature upon temple walls in between the reigns of Ptolemaios II Philadelphos and Ptolemaios VI Philometor/Ptolemaios VIII Euergetes II, this is not the case for the *sn-tꜣ* ritual until the middle of the second century BC. As already stated, this could simply be due to a case of absence of evidence. One should however not lose sight of the fact that from a political and military point of view, Ptolemaic Egypt of the middle of the second century BC is a different nation from that of the middle of the third century BC. Gone is the Ptolemaic *Thalassocracy*, with the Ptolemaic navy supreme in the Eastern Mediterranean region. Vanished into the folds of history is the memory of Ptolemaios IV Philometor's decisive stand at Raphia in 217 BC. Instead, we have now entered a period in the history of Ptolemaic Egypt following devastating internal rebellions in both the north and south, the crucial loss of most foreign territories (excluding Cyprus and the Cyrenaica), the invasion of Egypt by the Seleucids under Antiochos IV Epiphanes and the dramatic intervention of Rome in 168 BC during the so-called "Day of Eleusis".[65]

This begs the question whether it is a coincidence that the ritual of the Ptolemaic Basileus, in the guise of pharaoh, "kissing the earth" in front of the gods of Egypt is absent precisely during the pinnacle in the history of Ptolemaic Egypt? Concomitantly, is it a coincidence that the ritual returns in full force in Egyptian temples post 168 BC at a time when Egypt's international power is curtailed, the nation has suffered a severe loss of prestige, and the image of the ruler as a Basileus becomes less tenable, even credible? Studies of the synodal decrees have already indicated a shift in the balance of power from 238 BC (Canopus Decree; Ptolemaios III Euergetes I) over 217 BC (Decree of Raphia; Ptolemaios IV Philopator) to 196 BC (Decree of Memphis; Ptolemaios V Epiphanes) and beyond, with pharaonic aspects – and the indigenous priesthood – gaining slowly ground over the concept of the ruler as a Greek Basileus.[66] Perhaps the reoccurrence of the *sn-tꜣ* ritual likewise falls within this general context and development. A ruler, having lost part of the trappings associated with the image and the concept of the Basileus (expressed among others by his successful military actions),

64 Coppens, The Wabet, 92–121 for an overview of the reinterpretation and edition of older traditions as well as the occurrence of new texts upon the north wall of the "Seat of the First Feast" in Philae.

65 Hölbl, A History of the Ptolemaic Empire, 125–129 for a general overview of the main historical events of this period as well as numerous references.

66 Hölbl, A History of the Ptolemaic Empire, 105–110, 162–169; R. M. Errington, A History of the Hellenistic World. 323–30 BC, Oxford 2008, 297–298; von Recklinghausen, Die Philensis-Dekrete, especially 190–193.

at a time when the native element and the priesthoods have gained more ground, might again be presented in such a manner. In this perspective, one could still ask the question why this ritual act returns to the fore precisely under Ptolemaios VIII Euergetes II. Looking at the history of his reign, one event stands out that might provide an important indication: the civil war between Ptolemaios VIII Euergetes II and Cleopatra III on the one hand versus Cleopatra II on the other that took place in between 132 and 124 BC. While Cleopatra II had her powerbase in Alexandria and among the Greek and Jewish population, the *chora* – and especially Upper Egypt – remained loyal to Ptolemaios VIII Euergetes II.[67] Is it a coincidence that precisely in this region one witnesses the return of the ritual obeisance of the Ptolemaic ruler before the gods of Egypt – more or less around the time when this area of Egypt, including the local priesthoods, declared for Ptolemaios VIII Euergetes II? Appealing though it may be to draw these conclusions, at the present stage of the research, this has to remain on the level of a hypothesis.

In light of this, it is however interesting to note that Martina MINAS-NERPEL's detailed study of the activities upon Egyptian temple domains under the reigns of Ptolemaios VI Philometor and Ptolemaios VIII Euergetes II has clearly shown a major increase and focus under the rule of the latter sovereign precisely on traditional temples in Upper Egypt.[68] In the conclusion to her study, MINAS-NERPEL also poses the question whether the increase of activities under Ptolemaios VIII Euergetes II on Upper Egyptian temple precincts is due to the sovereign wishing to portray and position himself more as an Egyptian pharaoh than his Ptolemaic predecessors (undoubtedly following the loss of power and prestige on an international level). Alternatively, she suggests that it could also be a clear indication of the increasing power of the indigenous elements in society (not in the least the native priesthoods). A combination of both these aspects appear to be at play here, resulting in major construction and restauration activities on temple domains throughout Upper Egypt, not in the least upon the Horus precinct at Edfu.

The reoccurrence – in a substantial number (Tab. 1; 10 attestations) – of the depiction of the *sn-tꜣ* ritual upon the walls of the temple and birth temple of the Horus precinct at Edfu during the reign of Ptolemaios VIII Euergetes II and his successors shows elements of both continuity (in text and image) and change (in phraseology and general context). The Ptolemaic sovereign performing the ritual act is almost always depicted while standing upright with his arms hanging loosely beside his body,[69] very similar to the portrayal of Alexander III executing the *sn-tꜣ* ritual on the bark sanctuary in the Luxor temple.[70] This general position of the arms only undergoes a change in late Ptolemaic times at Athribis and Dendara (Fig. 3). Under the reigns of Ptolemaios XII Neos Dionysos and Cleopatra VII one

67 I am very grateful to Martina Minas-Nerpel (Egyptology, Universität Trier) for pointing this out to me following the presentation of my paper at the 9th Symposium on Royal Ideology at the Ludwig-Maximilians-Universität München. See also HÖLBL, A History of the Ptolemaic Empire, 257–271.

68 M. MINAS-NERPEL, Die Dekorationstätigkeit von Ptolemaios VI. Philometor und Ptolemaios VIII. Euergetes II. an ägyptischen Tempeln (Teil 1), in: OLP 27, 1996, 51–78; MINAS-NERPEL, OLP 28, 1997, 87–121, especially 116.

69 ABD EL-RAZIQ, Darstellungen und Texte, plate 4/C6.

70 The only exceptions are the two aforementioned depictions of the ritual on the walls of the Edfu *mammisi* from the reign of Ptolemaios IX Soter II: Edfou Mam., plates 6/1, 18/2 and 23/3. In both cases, the very limited amount of space available appears to be the main reason for the manner in which the king is depicted (*i.e.* once crouching and once lying down).

notices, for the first time, the ruler depicted with his arms slightly extended forwards[71] – a pose that will be the dominant position in most Roman Period examples as well (overview in Tab. 1; *s.v.* Gestures, 7 attestations).[72] The blue crown – occasionally worn by the ruler performing *sn-tꜣ* in the Abydene chapels,[73] but not present in early Ptolemaic times[74] – returns to the fore under the reign of Ptolemaios VIII Euergetes II in Edfu – only to disappear again a generation later, with a single reoccurrence during the rule of Emperor Claudius in the el-Qal'a temple (Tab. 1; *s.v.* Crowns, 9 attestations).[75]

The texts accompanying the ruler when depicted performing the *sn-tꜣ* on the Edfu temple walls shows both a continuation with earlier textual versions of the ritual, but also indicate a further development. Even a brief, general glance at the ten scenes at Edfu immediately shows that the amount of space available for the inscriptions makes it impossible to have similarly long passages of text, as was the case in Philae or earlier on in the chapels of the gods at Abydos. What one does find in every single instance is the occurrence of a series of key phrases or small passages that are clearly taken or inspired by the relevant chapters of the daily temple sanctuary ritual. In other words, key words or phrases now occur in combination with new textual material.[76] A few examples to better illustrate this point:

71 Athribis: on the first register of the east wall of Room E 7: Athribis III/1, 273; Athribis III/2, 195 (on dating this scene to the reign of Ptolemaios XII Neos Dionysos, see already note 26 in the present article). Dendara: in two scenes on the interior west wall of the small kiosk on the roof of the Hathor temple: Dendara VIII, plates DCCIV and DCCXI.

72 The only exception is el-Qal'a II, 129 (Claudius), where the ruler is still depicted with the arms hanging loosely beside his body.

73 The pharaoh is depicted with the blue crown only in the Abydene chapel of Osiris: GARDINER/CALVERLEY, Abydos I, plates 4 and 13. See also Table 3.

74 In the early Ptolemaic depictions of the *sn-tꜣ* the pharaoh wears the bag wig (without uraeus), reminiscent of the headgear (bag wig with uraeus) worn predominantly by Seti I in the Abydene chapels when performing the same ritual: GARDINER/CALVERLEY, Abydos I, plates 18 (Isis) and 26 (Horus); GARDINER/CALVERLEY, Abydos II, plates 4 (Amun), 14 (Ra-Harakhte) and 22 (Ptah). See also Table 3.

75 In the *per-nu* chapel: el-Qal'a II, 226.

76 For a similar situation, illustrating both continuity and change of an age old text in Ptolemaic and Roman times, see the remarkable paper of E. GRAEFE, Über die Verarbeitung von Pyramidentexten in den späten Tempeln (Nochmals zu Spruch 600 (§1652a – 1656d: Umhängen des Halskragens), in: U. VERHOEVEN/E. GRAEFE (eds.), Religion und Philosophie im alten Ägypten. Festgabe für Philippe Derchain zu seinem 65. Geburtstag am 24. Juli 1991, OLA 39, Leuven 1991, 129–148. Erhart GRAEFE's study of the scenes from Ptolemaic and Roman temples that combine the opening lines of PT utterance 600 with the offering of the *usekh*-necklace indicates that the utterance had been reduced by early Ptolemaic times to a series of keywords (or *Schlüsselwörter* as he refers to them) that are combined with new textual material. While in all known examples prior to the Ptolemaic Period the text usually appears as a reasonably accurate rendering of the opening lines of the utterance, GRAEFE's study indicated that in Ptolemaic and Roman times this is no longer the case. Unbeknownst to GRAEFE at the time, two fairly accurate copies of the utterance actually exist on the walls of an early Ptolemaic temple. The best preserved is located on the already mentioned north wall in the "Seat of the First Feast" at Philae – coincidentally (or perhaps not) the same wall that also contains the aforementioned scene with a prostrated Ptolemaios II Philadelphos underneath a long inscriptions that copies parts of four chapters of the daily temple sanctuary ritual known from New Kingdom times onward (Fig. 2). The nearby-located sanctuary of the temple contains a shorter version of the same PT utterance 600 (Philae I, 61, 4–6 and plate XXII/I; VASSILIKA, Ptolemaic Philae, database no. 770; H. BEINLICH, Die Photos der Preußischen Expedition 1908–1910 nach Nubien 6, Photo 1000–1199, SRAT 19, Dettelbach 2013, photo 1031). These two inscriptions thus not only represent the oldest known Ptolemaic version

a) The inscription accompanying the depiction of a prostrated Ptolemaios IX Soter II in front of a standing Hathor on the northern broken door lintel leading from the vestibule (G) to the colonnaded forecourt (I)[77] of the Harsomtus *mammisi* at Edfu is a clear continuation of an existing textual tradition, with only the name of the deity modified according to the location of the text (respectively Hathor, Amun-Ra and Isis):

Edfou Mam., 110, 3–4[78]	daily temple sanctuary ritual, spell 12/ Philae I, 22, 11
sn.n=i tꜣ	=> Spell 12/Philae: *sn.n=i tꜣ*
ḥpt.n=i nṯr	=> Spell 12/Philae: *ḥpt.n=i Gb*
rdi.n=i ḥsw n ḥnw.t	=> Spell 12: *rdi=i ḥsw n ꞽImn-Rꜥ nb nsw.t tꜣ.wy*
	=> Philae: *irr=i ḥsw <n> S.t nb.t ꞽIw-rḳ*

b) The more extensive inscription accompanying the scene on the west exterior naos wall of the Horus temple of Edfu[79] from the reign of Ptolemaios X Alexander I (101–88 BC) still has a large number of keywords and phrases that one likewise encounters in the chapters of the daily temple sanctuary ritual as well as in the Philae inscription:[80]

Edfou VII, 192–193[81]	daily temple sanctuary ritual, spells 12–17/ Philae I, 22, 11–17
sn-tꜣ	=> Spell 12: *rꜣ n sn-tꜣ*
ḫf.n=i ḫpr=k	—
ḥpt=i [Gb] (n) ꜥꜣ n šfy.t=k sꜣb-šwt	=> Spell 12: *sn=i tꜣ ḥpt=i Gb*
	=> Spell 13: *ḥpt.n=i Gb*
	=> Philae I, 22, 11: *sn=i tꜣ ḥpt=i Gb*
sdg=i mr.t=k	=> Spell 14: *dgꜣ=i n mr.t=k*
	=> Philae I, 22, 13-14: *dgi=i n mr.t=k*
rdi.n[=i] wi ḥr ẖ.t=i	=> Spell 13 and 14: *rdi.n=i wi ḥr ẖ.t=i n snḏ=k*
	=> Philae I, 22, 13: *rdi.n=i wi ḥr ẖ.t=i n ḥry.t=ṯ*
sn=i tꜣ m ḥr=k nfr	=> Spell 15: *sn=i tꜣ ḥr=i m ḫrw*
di=i iꜣw n kꜣ=k ḥnꜥ psḏ.t ḥm=k	=> Spell 17: *iꜣw n=k iꜣw n ḥꜥ.w=k iꜣw n psḏ.t ꜥꜣ.t imyw-ẖ.t=k*
ḥtp-di-nsw iw=i wꜥb.kwi	=> Spell 17: *ḥtp-di-nsw iw=i wꜥb.kwi*

of PT 600 in a temple context, but also the only accurate copies of the utterance from this era. Perhaps not so surprisingly, the same can be said for the inscription accompanying the pharaoh performing the *sn-tꜣ* in the "Seat of the First Feast".

77 For the plan of the Harsomtus birth temple and the identification of its various chambers: Edfou Mam., plate I.

78 Translation: "I kiss the earth, I embrace the god (Geb), and I render praise/execute the ritual for the lady/mistress (*i.e.* Hathor)".

79 Edfou VII, 192–193. See also F. Labrique, Stylistique et théologie à Edfou. Le rituel de l'offrande de la campagne: étude de la composition, OLA 51, Leuven 1992, 197–201; D. Kurth, Edfou VII. Die Inschriften des Tempels von Edfu. Abteilung I. Übersetzungen, Band 2, Wiesbaden 2004, 349–351.

80 The only phrase of the entire recitation by the king that has no parallel in the earlier versions of the ritual is *ḫf.n=i ḫpr=k*, "I contemplate/perceive your form".

81 Translation: "Kissing the earth: I have contemplated/perceived your form, and I embrace [Geb] (because of) the greatness of the fear of you, oh dappled one of feathers (Horus of Edfu), I see/observe that what you love/desire, after [I] placed myself upon my belly. I kiss the earth before your perfect face, and I give praise to your *Ka* and the Ennead of your majesty. An offering that that king gives as I am purified". See also Labrique, Stylistique et théologie, 197–198 and Kurth, Edfou VII, 349.

c) The only partially preserved inscriptions associated with Emperor Augustus on the first register of the south wall in the sanctuary of the Isis temple at el-Qal'a similarly still contain very comparable key phrases:

el-Qal'a I, 2[82]	daily temple sanctuary ritual, spells 13, 15, 17/ Philae I, 22, 11–17
Title: */// ḥtp.n=i Gb Ḥw.t-ḥr di=s wr=i*	=> Spell 13: *ḥpt.n=i Gb Ḥw.t-ḥr di=s wr=i* => Philae I, 22, 14: *ḥpt.n=i Gb Ḥw.t-ḥr di=s wr=i*
Pharaho: *sn=i n=k tꜣ mi nb-r-ḏr*	=> Spell 17: *sn=i n=k tꜣ mi nb r-ḏr* => Philae I, 22, 17: *sn=i n<=ṯ> tꜣ [mi nb r-]ḏr*
Royal Randzeile: *sn[=i] tꜣ m ḥr=k nfr ///*	=> Spell 15: *sn=i tꜣ ḥr=i m ẖrw* => Edfou VII, 192, 14–15: *sn=i tꜣ m ḥr=k nfr*

The overview of these examples from the Edfu and el-Qal'a temples indicates a clear development from the inscription of the reign of Ptolemaios II Philadelphos in the "Seat of the First Feast" at Philae. Although the latter text is not a copy of a single spell dealing with the *sn-tꜣ* ritual of the daily temple sanctuary ritual, but rather based on a combination of passages from no less than four of these spells, not a single new phrase is added to it in Philae. It is clear that at Edfu and elsewhere, from the reign of Ptolemaios VIII Euergetes II onward, the priestly designers possessed a certain amount of freedom when composing the texts to accompany the pharaoh when "kissing the earth". It is not possible to recognise a standard version of the text, nor is the number of recognisable key phrases the same for every inscription. In several inscriptions, one can observe the use of synonyms as well as the combination of well-known phrases with new textual material. The newly added expressions very often express a set of (physical) activities closely related to the act of "kissing the earth", such as bending or opening the arms (*wn rmn.wy; ḫꜣb/ks ꜥ.wy*). These acts are in fact much more closely related to the manner in which the pharaoh performing the *sn-tꜣ* is actually depicted on a temple wall (Fig. 3). One such text is for instance located on the first register of the western exterior wall of the naos and dates from the reign of Ptolemaios VIII Euergetes II (Edfou IV, 55, 12–15):

sn=i tꜣ n.t wr-nḫ.t	I kiss the earth of the "Great of Might",
mꜣꜣ=i ḳfꜣw.t n.t nḏty-it=f	as I observe the dignity of the Protector of his father
ḥpt=i Gb m-ḫnt ḥw.t-ḳn	I embrace Geb in "The Mansion of Valour"
sn=i sꜣṯw[83] *n.t s.t-wr.t*	I kiss the earth of the "Great Seat"
wn=i rmn.w n ḏrty pr-ꜥ	I open the shoulders (arms)[84] for the Valiant Falcon
ḫꜣb=i ꜥ.wy n sꜣb-šwt	I bend both arms[85] for the Dappled of Feathers.

82 Title: "/// I have embraced Geb, and Hathor, she makes that I am/shall be great"; Pharaoh: "I kiss the earth for you like for the All-Lord"; Royal Randzeile: "[I] kiss the earth before your perfect face ///".

83 The noun for the land *tꜣ*, which usually features in this context, is in this instance replaced by the synonym *sꜣṯw*.

84 For similar expressions by the pharaoh within the *sn-tꜣ* ritual at Edfu: Edfou III, 164, 2–3 (*wn rmn.wy*), and Edfou IV, 227, 7 (*wn=i rmn.wy=i*).

85 For a similar expression by the pharaoh within the *sn-tꜣ* ritual at Edfu: Edfou IV, 209, 3–4 (*ks=i ꜥ.wy=i*). In Edfou III, 164, 10, Horus returns the favour: "I hereby give to you the south, the north, the

A closer look at the specific context in which the *sn-tꜣ* ritual reappears in Edfu during the reign of Ptolemaios VIII Euergetes II and his immediate successors, after an absence of more or less a century, immediately reveals that it no longer features as part of the daily temple sanctuary ritual *per se* as before. Instead, it now occurs in two contexts that are closely associated with one another. First and foremost, the scene appears as part of a larger group of reliefs portraying the king travelling from his palace to the temple to be introduced to the god (the so-called *montée royale*)[86] as a prelude to ritual activity, such as, among others, the performance of the temple foundation ritual. During the *montée royale* the ruler is the beneficiary of the ritual activities performed; the scenes depict the king leaving the palace, being purified, his coronation and finally his introduction to the god/goddess. In the following set of reliefs the pharaoh then brings homage to the god – not in the least by "kissing the earth" (*sn-tꜣ*) before the deity, as well as by "praising" (*dwꜣ*) and "seeing" (*mꜣꜣ*) the god.[87]

This is exemplified by all three scenes of the *sn-tꜣ* ritual depicted on the east, west and north exterior of the naos,[88] as well as in the north-east corner in the interior of the pronaos.[89] All four scenes date to the reign of Ptolemaios VIII Euergetes II (Tab. 1). The same pattern can also be observed in younger occurrences of the ritual at Edfu – whether on the east

west and the east in bending the shoulder because of the awe inspiring fear of you (*di=i n=k rsy mḥ.t imn.t iꜣb.t ḥr ẖꜣb rmn n šfy.t=k*).

86 This group of reliefs has already been studied in detail for the Horus temple at Edfu by LABRIQUE, Stylistique et théologie, 163–195. See also P. BARGUET, Note sur la sortie du roi hors du palais, in: Hommages à François Daumas I, Montpellier 1986, 51–54. The set does not always include all four scenes.

87 LABRIQUE, Stylistique et théologie, 196–220.

88 All scenes are located on the first register. West wall: Edfou IV, 55–56; Edfou X, plate LXXXV; East wall: Edfou IV, 209; Edfou X, plate XCI. The decorative pattern applied to the opposing east and west exterior wall of the naos has exactly the same sequence: the four scenes of the *montée royale* are followed by the king seeing the god, kissing the earth, and praising the god (Edfou IV, 49–57, and 202–211; Edfou X, LXXXIV–LXXXV, XC–XCI). This set of reliefs is followed by two scenes of an apotropaic nature: the king slaying/spearing a crocodile (*itḥ msḥ/šnt*) and a hippopotamus (*smꜣ/sni db*), before starting with purification rites for Horus. On the destruction of the crocodile, see P. WILSON, Slaughtering the Crocodile at Edfu and Dendera, in: S. QUIRKE (ed.), The Temple in Ancient Egypt: New Discoveries and Recent Research, London 1997, 179–203. North wall: Edfou IV, 227–228; Edfou X, plate LXXXIX. The set on the north wall is reduced to a scene depicting the pharaoh leaving the palace and then "kissing the earth". This is followed by the ruler praising (*dwꜣ*) Hathor and handing the temple over to Horus (east section) or seeing (*mꜣꜣ*) Horus (opposite the *sn-tꜣ*), praising (*dwꜣ*) Hathor and once more handing over the temple to its lord (north wall, opposite west section; Edfou IV, 68–74; Edfou X, plate LXXXVIII). See also Dendara VIII, 22–23, and plate DCCIV (also Fig. 3 of the present article) as well as Athribis III/1, 270–271 (E 7, 5) and 273–274 (E 7, 8) and Athribis III/2, 193 and 195, for other examples of the close connection between "seeing/praising the god" (*mꜣꜣ/dwꜣ nṯr*) and "kissing the earth" (*sn-tꜣ*). A similar situation most likely occurred on the first register of the gate leading from the Hall of the Ennead (Room C 2; *wsḫt psḏt*) to the first sanctuary room (D 1) in the Athribis temple, but the title of the scene opposite the *sn-tꜣ* relief was never written (Athribis II/2, 402–404, and 410–413; Athribis II/3, 35 and 40) (Athribis II = Ch. LEITZ, D. MENDEL, Y. EL-MASRY, Athribis II. Der Tempel Ptolemaios XII. Die Inschriften und Reliefs der Opfersäle, des Umgangs und der Sanktuarräume. Band 1: Die Opfersäle und der Umgang, Band 2: Die Sanktuarräume, Band 3: Tafeln, Cairo 2010).

89 First register of the east wall of the pronaos: Edfou III, 164, and Edfou IX, plate LXIII – part of the king leaving the palace to perform the temple foundation ritual. See also the associated scenes in Edfou IX, plates LXI, LXII and LXIV.

exterior wall of the temple enclosure (Ptolemaios X Alexander I)[90] or on the south wall (east section) of the open court, at the side of the temple pylon (Ptolemaios XII Neos Dionysos).[91]

The appearance of the *sn-tꜣ* ritual as part of a group of scenes in the general framework of the king travelling to the temple and paying homage to the god from the reign of Ptolemaios VIII Euergetes II onward is most likely also closely linked with the second context in which the "kissing the earth" relief recurrently features. The *sn-tꜣ* scene occurs on the Edfu precinct also near entrances or along the axis leading from the entrance to the core of sacred structures – whether the Horus temple itself or the Harsomtus birth temple. Examples of this type are for instance the three scenes in the *mammisi*; all located along the axis from the entrance to the sanctuary.[92] The ritual appears in a similar position also on the screen-wall of the pronaos.[93] In both these contexts the *sn-tꜣ* ritual is evidently linked with the king entering the temple, while the scene no longer features as a part of the daily temple sanctuary ritual, as we know it from New Kingdom times at least down to the reign of Ptolemaios II Philadelphos.

A final topic that I would still like to touch upon concerns the return on investment. What does the (foreign) sovereign actually gain when performing the ultimate act of obeisance to the gods of Egypt? The Berlin papyri (pAmun I, pAmun II, pMut) do not mention this, while in the chapels of the gods at Abydos, the reciprocal gifts are – when at all present and/or not destroyed – reduced to (general) terms as *ꜥnḫ*, *wꜣs*, *ḏd* and *snb*.[94] At Luxor, it is the strength of the two lords (*pḥty n nb.wy*) that Alexander III acquires forever and a day.[95] Remarkably, this particular gift is not repeated in any of the later inscriptions accompanying the ritual act of *proskynese*. Instead, the inscriptions accompanying that notable scene from the "Seat of the First Feast" at Philae appear to have set the tone for generations to come. In exchange for the Ptolemaic Basileus truly "kissing the earth", lying spread out on the ground in front of Isis, the goddess rewards the ruler as follows: "I hereby give you all foreign lands under both your sandals" (*di.n<=i> n=k ḫꜣs.wt nb ḫr ṯb.ty=k*)[96] and "I hereby give you all [foreign lands?] in obeisance/bowing down" (*di.n<=i> n=k [ḫꜣs.wt?]*[97] *m ksw*). The topic of the foreign

90 Edfou VII, 192–193. The four scenes of the *montée royale* are followed by the king kissing the earth, praising the god (*dwꜣ nṯr*) and presenting Maat (*ḥnk mꜣꜥ.t*) (Edfou VII, 189–196; Labrique, Stylistique et théologie, plates 11–16).

91 Edfou V, 140–141; Edfou X, plate CXVII. The four scenes of the *montée royale* are followed by the king kissing the earth, praising the god (*dwꜣ nṯr*) and slaying the enemies (*smꜣ sby.w*) (Edfou V, 136–144, Edfou X, plates CXVII–CXVIII).

92 Edfou Mam., 12, plate XII: on the first register of the south jamb of the gate leading from the sanctuary to the preceding hall of offerings (opposite scene: *nḏ-ḥr*; date: Ptolemaios VIII Euergetes II); Edfou Mam., 42, plate VI/1 and XVIII/2: on the north wall of the vestibule preceding the sanctuary; Edfou Mam., 110, plate XXIII/3: on the northern interior of a broken door lintel leading from the columned courtyard to the vestibule (both latter scenes date from the reign of Ptolemaios IX Soter II).

93 Edfou III, 12–13, Edfou IX, plate LI: on the westernmost screen-wall of the pronaos (opposite, easternmost scene: *dwꜣ nṯr*; date: Ptolemaios VIII Euergetes II).

94 Gardiner/Calverley, Abydos I, plates 4 (*ꜥnḫ, ḏd, wꜣs*), and 26 (*ꜥnḫ, wꜣs*); Gardiner/Calverley, Abydos II, plate 4 (*ꜥnḫ, wꜣs, ꜣw.t-ib, snb*).

95 Abd el-Raziq, Darstellungen und Texte, 11: "I hereby give you the strength/power of both lords forever and ever" (*di.n=i n=k pḥty n nb.wy ḏ.t sp-sn*).

96 For similar examples from the core of the Isis temple: Philae I, 23, 9; 37, 2; 57, 8 and 11.

97 The term *ḫꜣs.wt* was most likely engraved here. On the first pylon of the temple (Philae I, 83), we find for instance: *di.n<=i> n=k ḫꜣs.wt rsy.w m ksw*. See also further for similar expressions associated with the performance of the *sn-tꜣ* ritual in Edfu.

lands under the king's sandals and in obeisance to the ruler is a subject matter that will be repeated time and again, but also further expanded upon in Edfu. In all instances, in Edfu it is always Horus Behedety who rewards the foreign ruler with control over the all lands and its inhabitants. Thematically one can distinguish the following categories among the gifts:

a) The Two Lands in obeisance or bowing down, once even under the king's sandals:
- Edfou III, 12–13: *tꜣ.wy m ksw ////* and *ḏi=i n=k tꜣ.wy* [*m k*]*sw //// ḥr ṯbtyw=k*
- Edfou IV, 227–228: *tꜣ.wy ẖꜣb n bꜣ.w=k*
- Edfou VII, 193: [*tꜣ.wy*] *m ksw n snḏ=k*

b) In two cases, this is still specified as the *Pat* and *Rekhyt* people bend the head:
- Edfou III, 164: (*tꜣ.w nb.w m ksw*) *pꜥ.t rḫyt m wꜣḥ-tp*
- Edfou IV, 55: *pꜥ.t rḫyt m wꜣḥ-tp*

c) The foreign lands and their inhabitants likewise appear in obeisance, either under their produce or labour, or in servitude:
- Edfou IV, 55: *ḫntyw(-š) mntyw m ksw* and *ḳmꜣtyw m nḏyw*
- Edfou IV, 209: *wḥꜣtyw ẖr in.w=sn*
- Edfou IV, 227–228: *tꜣ.w fnḫw ẖr bꜣk.w=sn*
- Edfou VII, 193: *ḫꜣs.wt ẖꜣb n bꜣ.w=k*

d) The cardinal points and their inhabitants are also found bowing down and praising:
- Edfou III, 164: *rsy mḥ.t imn.t iꜣb.t ḥr ẖꜣb rmn n šfy.t=k*
- Edfou IV, 209: *rsytyw mḥtyw ẖꜣm* and *imntyw iꜣbtyw m ksw*
- Edfou V, 141: *rsy mḥ.t m iꜣw imn.t iꜣb.t m ksw*

e) Finally, the entire world and all upon it are in obeisance, kissing the earth and in prayer:
- Edfou III, 164: *tꜣ.w nb.w m ksw*
- Edfou IV, 55: *tpyw-tꜣ ḥr sn n=k tꜣ*
- Edfou IV, 227–228: *ḫtmn sn-tꜣ m-sꜣ wr=k tꜣ.w nb.w ḥr nḥ mꜣꜣ=k*
- Edfou VII, 193: *bw nb m wꜣḥ-tp*

Overall, control over the world and all its inhabitants can certainly be considered a most worthy gift in return for "kissing the earth" in front of the gods of Egypt.[98] In an ironic twist of fate, however, precisely at this moment in time that a royal act of *proskynesis* places the entire world in obeisance before the Ptolemaic ruler, Ptolemaic Egypt had already lost most of its overseas territories with the exception of Cyprus and Cyrenaica.[99]

98 The same topics still return elsewhere as divine rewards: Tôd II, 231, 7 – Montu-Ra: *tꜣ.wy m ksw n ḥr=k ḏ.t*; el-Qal'a I, 2 – Geb: *ḫꜣs.wt nb.w r nḏyw*; Nut: *tꜣ.wy m ksw ḫꜣs.wt m wꜣḥ-tp*; Neith: *pḏt ẖꜣb n ḥr=k*; el-Qal'a II, 129 – The Great Goddess: *ḥr.w nb.w ḫꜣs.wt m wꜣḥ-tp*; Ta-Iret-Per-Atum: *tꜣ.w nb.w m ksw*.

99 One should not forget that in the years to come, it would be precisely the Ptolemaic rulers, by means of their wills and testaments, that in the first half of the first century BC would provide the Roman republic with the means to annex the last two foreign territories still under Ptolemaic control. a) Cyrenaica – 98 BC: last will of Ptolemaios Apion, illegitimate son of Ptolemaios VIII Euergetes II and king of Cyrenaica (Titus Livius, *Periochae* LXX/5: "Ptolemaeus, Cyrenarum rex, cui cognomen Apionis fuit, mortuus heredem populum R. reliquit et eius regni civitates senatus liberas esse iussit."), 75/74 BC:

5 Concluding remarks: Continuity, discontinuity and change within the portrayal of a ritual act in Ptolemaic Egypt

The still ongoing research already clearly indicates a development within the nature of, and the depiction and inscriptions related to the *sn-tꜣ* ritual throughout the Ptolemaic era. In early Ptolemaic times (Alexander III – Ptolemaios II Philadelphos) the *sn-tꜣ* ritual executed by the Ptolemaic ruler was still part of the portrayal of the ritual acts performed on a daily basis in the temple sanctuary upon the statue of its main deity. Text and image show clear connections with earlier attestations of said performance whether in the Abydos chapels or the Berlin papyri. Following the reign of Ptolemaios II Philadelphos, the ritual only comes to the fore again, more or less a century later, during the reign of Ptolemaios VIII Euergetes II. At that time, six new attestations occur on the walls of the Horus temple, with four more scenes engraved upon the walls of temple and birth temple at Edfu, under the rule of his immediate successors (Ptolemaios IX Soter II – Ptolemaios XII Neos Dionysos). The reason for the absence of the depiction of the *sn-tꜣ* ritual on temple walls for several generations or the reason for its sudden reappearance still remains open to debate – whether a mere matter of absence of evidence or a deliberate design by the priests planning the decorative program for the temples as a consequence of the changing political situation. It is clear, however, that when the ritual returns onto the temple walls, it no longer forms part of the daily temple sanctuary ritual, but now relates to the king entering the sacred structure. This is expressed on the one hand by positioning the scene near the entrance to or along the axis leading into sacred structures. Alternatively, the scene features as part of a larger group depicting the journey of the king from palace to temple (the so-called *montée royale*) as a prelude to a variety of ritual activities. While no longer featuring as a part of the daily temple sanctuary ritual, the inscriptions accompanying these scenes still show their connection to it through the continued use of keywords and key phrases taken from the ritual. This is a phenomenon not limited to the Ptolemaic Period, but continues as well in early Roman times – as is attested for example in the scenes from the el-Qal'a temple. An initial survey of the *sn-tꜣ* scenes from the reign of Cleopatra VII onward leads me to believe that the context in which the ritual appears in late Ptolemaic and early Roman times has undergone yet another development; an aspect of the research that is still in progress.

Acknowledgements

This paper was written within the framework of the Czech Science Foundation – Grant GA ČR 19-07268S: "Continuity, Discontinuity and Change. Adaptation Strategies of Individuals and Communities in Egypt at Times of Internal and External Transformations".

Cyrenaica becomes a Roman province. b) Cyprus – 88 BC: last will of Ptolemaios X Alexander I, 58–56 BC: annexation of Cyprus as part of the Roman province of Cilicia. E. Badian, The Testament of Ptolemy Alexander, in: Rheinisches Museum für Philologie 10, 1967, 178–192. See also Hölbl, A History of the Ptolemaic Empire, 210–211, 225–226; Errington, A History of the Hellenistic World, 301–303.

Fig. 1: Performance of the ritual *sn-tꜣ* ("kissing the earth") on a loose block from the festival hall of Osorkon II in Bubastis.
The photo corresponds to NAVILLE, Festival Hall of Osorkon II, plate XIV/1
(Photo courtesy of Jan Koek; Stichting Mehen)

Fig. 2: Performance of the ritual *sn-tꜣ* ("kissing the earth") by Ptolemaios II Philadelphos on the north wall of the "Seat of the First Feast" (*s.t-ḥb-tpy*) in the Isis temple on the island of Philae.
The photo corresponds to Philae I, plate VII, and BEINLICH, Die Photos der Preußischen Expedition 1908–1910 nach Nubien 4, photo 708 (Photo by the author)

Fig. 3: "Seeing the god" (*m33 nṯr*) and "kissing the earth" (*sn-t3*) on the interior west wall of the kiosk on the roof of the Hathor temple at Dendara. The photo corresponds to Dendara VIII, plate DCCIV (Photo by the author)

"Symposium zur ägyptischen Königsideologie" 1 – 9

(The Previous Publications)

1. Symposium zur ägyptischen Königsideologie

Selbstverständnis und Realität : Akten des Symposiums zur Ägyptischen Königsideologie in Mainz 15. – 17.6.1995 / hrsg. von Rolf Gundlach und Christine Raedler. –
Wiesbaden: Harrassowitz, **1997.**
(Ägypten und Altes Testament ; 36,1 : Beiträge zur altägyptischen Königsideologie ; 1)

2. Symposium zur ägyptischen Königsideologie

Das frühe ägyptische Königtum : Akten des 2. Symposiums zur Ägyptischen Königsideologie in Wien, 24. – 26.9.1997 / hrsg. von Rolf Gundlach und Wilfried Seipel. –
Wiesbaden: Harrassowitz, **1999**.
(Ägypten und Altes Testament ; 36,2 : Beiträge zur altägyptischen Königsideologie ; 2)

3. Symposium zur ägyptischen Königsideologie

Das Königtum der Ramessidenzeit : Voraussetzungen – Verwirklichung – Vermächtnis. Akten des 3. Symposiums zur Ägyptischen Königsideologie in Bonn 7. – 9.6.2001 / hrsg. von Rolf Gundlach und Ursula Rößler-Köhler. –
Wiesbaden: Harrassowitz, **2003**.
(Ägypten und Altes Testament ; 36,3 : Beiträge zur altägyptischen Königsideologie ; 3)

4. Symposium zur ägyptischen Königsideologie

Egyptian Royal Residences : 4. Symposium zur Ägyptischen Königsideologie ; London, June 1st – 5th 2004 / ed. by Rolf Gundlach and John H. Taylor. –
Wiesbaden: Harrassowitz, **2009**.
(Königtum, Staat und Gesellschaft früher Hochkulturen ; 4,1 : Beiträge zur altägyptischen Königsideologie)

5. Symposium zur ägyptischen Königsideologie

Palace and temple : architecture – decoration – ritual ; Cambridge, July, 16th – 17th, 2007; 5. Symposium zur Ägyptischen Königsideologie/5th Symposium on Egypytian Royal Ideology / ed. by Rolf Gundlach and Kate Spence. –
Wiesbaden: Harrassowitz, **2011**.
(Königtum, Staat und Gesellschaft früher Hochkulturen ; 4,2 : Beiträge zu altägyptischen Königsideologie)

6. Symposium zur ägyptischen Königsideologie

„Die Männer hinter dem König" : 6. Symposium zur ägyptischen Königsideologie / 6th Symposium on Egyptian Royal Ideology ; Iphofen, 16. – 18. Juli 2010 / hrsg. von Horst Beinlich. –
Wiesbaden: Harrassowitz, **2012**.
(Königtum, Staat und Gesellschaft früher Hochkulturen ; 4,3 : Beiträge zu altägyptischen Königsideologie)

7. Symposium zur ägyptischen Königsideologie

Royal versus divine authority : acquisition, legitimization and renewal of power;
7. Symposium zur ägyptischen Königsideologie / 7th Symposium on Egyptian Royal Ideology; Prague, June 26–28, 2013; / ed. by Filip Coppens, Jiří Janák and Hana Vymazalová. –
Wiesbaden: Harrassowitz, **2015**.
(Königtum, Staat und Gesellschaft früher Hochkulturen ; 4,4: Beiträge zur altägyptischen Königsideologie)

8. Symposium zur ägyptischen Königsideologie

Constructing Autority : Prestige, Reputation and the Perception of Power in Egyptian Kingship; 8. Symposium zur ägyptischen Königsideologie / 8th Symposium on Egyptian Royal Ideology; Budapest, May 12–14, 2016; / ed. by Tamás Bács and Horst Beinlich. –
Wiesbaden: Harrassowitz, **2017**.
(Königtum, Staat und Gesellschaft früher Hochkulturen ; 4,5: Beiträge zur altägyptischen Königsideologie)

9. Symposium zur ägyptischen Königsideologie

Egyptian royal ideology and kingship under periods of foreign rulers – case studies from the first millennium BC; 9. Symposium zur ägyptischen Königsideologie / 9th Symposium on Egyptian Royal Ideology; Munich, May 31 – June 2, 2018; / ed. by Julia Budka. –
Wiesbaden: Harrassowitz, **2019**.
(Königtum, Staat und Gesellschaft früher Hochkulturen ; 4,6: Beiträge zur altägyptischen Königsideologie)

Index

H

I

J

K

L

M

N

O

P

R

S

T

U

V

Addresses of authors

Dana Bělohoubková and Jiří Janák
Charles University
Faculty of Arts
Czech Institute of Egyptology
nám. Jana Palacha 2
116 38 Prague 1 – Czech Republic
belohoubd@gmail.com
jiri.janak@ff.cuni.cz

Anke Ilona Blöbaum
Sächsische Akademie der Wissenschaften Leipzig
Strukturen und Transformationen des Wortschatzes der ägyptischen Sprache
c/o Ägyptologisches Institut der Universität Leipzig
Goethestraße 2
04109 Leipzig/
Westfälische Wilhelms-Universität Münster
Institut für Ägyptologie und Koptologie
Schlaunstr. 2
48143 Münster – Germany
blobaum@uni-muenster.de

Julia Budka
Ludwig-Maximilians-Universität München
Institut für Ägyptologie und Koptologie
Katharina-von-Bora-Str. 10
80333 München – Germany
Julia.Budka@lmu.de

Filip Coppens
Charles University
Faculty of Arts
Czech Institute of Egyptology
nám. Jana Palacha 2
116 38 Prague 1 – Czech Republic
Filip.Coppens@ff.cuni.cz

Shih-Wei Hsu
Nankai University
College of History
Nr. 38, Tongyan Road
Haihe Educational Park, Jinnan District
300350 Tianjin – P. R. China
swhsu2012@gmail.com

Olaf E. Kaper
Leiden University
Faculteit der Geesteswetenschappen
Leiden Institute for Area Studies
SMES Egyptologie
Matthias de Vrieshof 4
2311 BZ Leiden – Netherlands
o.e.kaper@hum.leidenuniv.nl

Carola Koch
Julius-Maximilians-Universität Würzburg
Institut für Altertumswissenschaften
Lehrstuhl für Ägyptologie
Residenzplatz 2/Tor A
97070 Würzburg – Germany
Carola.Koch@uni-wuerzburg.de

Ewa Laskowska-Kusztal
Polish Academy of Sciences
Department of Ancient Egyptian and Near East Cultures
Institute of Mediterranean and Oriental Cultures
72, Nowy Świat st.
00-330 Warsaw – Poland
emlaskow@gmail.com

Angelika Lohwasser
Westfälische Wilhelms-Universität Münster
Institut für Ägyptologie und Koptologie
Schlaunstr. 2
48143 Münster – Germany
a.lohwasser@uni-muenster.de

Martina Minas-Nerpel
Universität Trier
FB III: Ägyptologie
54286 Trier – Germany
minas@uni-trier.de

Essam Nagy
Ludwig-Maximilians-Universität München
Institut für Ägyptologie und Koptologie
Katharina-von-Bora-Str. 10
80333 München – Germany
essamnagy678@hotmail.com

Alexander Schütze
Ludwig-Maximilians-Universität München
Institut für Ägyptologie und Koptologie
Katharina-von-Bora-Str. 10
80333 München – Germany
Alexander.Schuetze@lmu.de

Anthony Spalinger
University of Auckland
Department of Classics and Ancient History
Private Bag 92019
Auckland Mail Centre
Auckland 1142 – New Zealand
a.spalinger@auckland.ac.nz